T0285047

Deconstructing Postmodernist Nietzscheanism

Historical Materialism Book Series

The Historical Materialism Book Series is a major publishing initiative of the radical left. The capitalist crisis of the twenty-first century has been met by a resurgence of interest in critical Marxist theory. At the same time, the publishing institutions committed to Marxism have contracted markedly since the high point of the 1970s. The Historical Materialism Book Series is dedicated to addressing this situation by making available important works of Marxist theory. The aim of the series is to publish important theoretical contributions as the basis for vigorous intellectual debate and exchange on the left.

The peer-reviewed series publishes original monographs, translated texts, and reprints of classics across the bounds of academic disciplinary agendas and across the divisions of the left. The series is particularly concerned to encourage the internationalization of Marxist debate and aims to translate significant studies from beyond the English-speaking world.

For a full list of titles in the Historical Materialism Book Series available in paperback from Haymarket Books, visit: www.haymarketbooks.org/ series_collections/1-historical-materialism.

Deconstructing Postmodernist Nietzscheanism

Deleuze and Foucault

Jan Rehmann

Translated by
Kolja Swingle and Larry Swingle

Haymarket Books
Chicago, IL

First published in 2022 by Brill Academic Publishers, The Netherlands
© 2022 Koninklijke Brill NV, Leiden, The Netherlands

Published in paperback in 2023 by
Haymarket Books
P.O. Box 180165
Chicago, IL 60618
773-583-7884
www.haymarketbooks.org

ISBN: 978-1-64259-917-6

Distributed to the trade in the US through Consortium Book Sales and
Distribution (www.cbsd.com) and internationally through Ingram
Publisher Services International (www.ingramcontent.com).

This book was published with the generous support of Lannan
Foundation, Wallace Action Fund, and the Marguerite Casey Foundation.

Special discounts are available for bulk purchases by organizations and
institutions. Please call 773-583-7884 or email info@haymarketbooks.org
for more information.

Cover art and design by David Mabb. Cover art is a detail of *Luibov
Popova, Untitled Textile Design on William Morris Wallpaper for Historical
Materialism*, edition of 100, screen print on wallpaper 2010.

Printed in the United States.

Library of Congress Cataloging-in-Publication data is available.

Contents

Introduction

I

Marco Tullio Giordana's 1980 film *Maledetti Vi Amerò* shows a young man named Ricardo, who, torn between leftist terrorism and yuppie culture, spells out a new variant of post-leftist political correctness just before his suicide:

> Eroticism is left, pornography is right. Even penetration is right, whereas foreplay is left. Heterosexuality is right, but homosexuality has deep merit as transgression and is therefore left. Hashish is left, but amphetamines, coke and heroin are right. Nietzsche has been re-evaluated and is now left, but Marx is right.

Then he sticks the pistol into his mouth. This 're-evaluation' of Nietzsche, which scrambled the film hero's brain before he finally destroyed it and himself, is the subject of the following investigation. The film scene records one moment of a complex ideological process in which a highly elaborated paradigm of Nietzsche interpretation arrives in the incoherent 'common sense' (Gramsci) of the post-68 generation and connects with the disappointments of failed or silted up political initiatives. Two of the most influential representatives of this reassessment of Nietzsche are Gilles Deleuze and Michel Foucault. In 1962 Deleuze presented in *Nietzsche et la philosophie* an interpretation which deeply shaped several generations of poststructuralist or postmodernist intellectuals; Foucault always considered himself to be a Nietzschean, both in his 'archaeological' and in his 'genealogical' phase, and claimed to continue and concretise the Nietzschean critique of the subject, of humanism and of morality, using the historical material of modernity.

In 1973, in his essay on 'nomadic thinking', Deleuze sums up his thoughts toward a revaluation of Nietzsche as follows: Marx and Freud represented the emergence of modern bureaucratic culture; their project is that of a recoding: of the state with Marx, of the family with Freud. In contrast, Nietzsche represents the advent of the counter-culture. He transforms thinking into a nomadic force, into a 'war machine' against the rational, administrative machinery whose philosophers speak in the name of pure reason. Thus Deleuze's Nietzsche addresses himself directly to the revolutionaries of today: we need this kind of 'war machine', which will not produce a state apparatus again.[1]

---

1   Deleuze 1995, pp. 142, 149.

Where else should the readers in the seventies have located the nomadic war machines than on the horizon of the Italian Red Brigades or the West German Red Army Faction? Of course the association should also not be understood all too literally. There are no real projectiles, only Nietzsche's aphorisms, which are supposed to constitute the 'battering rams' of this war machine, and its destructive power is directed above all against the literary form of the 'maxim'.[2] Furthermore, the 'nomads', too, do not really need to move; they only withdraw themselves from the code of the stationary by taking 'trips of intensity'.[3] So here, too, nothing is eaten as hot as it is cooked. War and war machines are loud metaphors, which are supposed to paint an esoteric philosophical discourse with the revolutionary flair of guerrilla war.

Of course, the reassessed Nietzsche did not usually lead to suicide in the student protest environment but, on the contrary, provided a solution, however imaginary, for how to keep on living: to withdraw oneself from the dead-end of radical leftist forms of praxis without having to abandon one's self-image as a radical. The price is a contradictory aestheticisation of the political, which can take a turn either to the left or to the right.

> The left turn: smash truth, cognition and morality, ... and live luxuriantly in the free, groundless play of your creative powers. The right turn ...: forget about theoretical analysis, cling to the sensuous particular, view society as a self-grounding organism, all of whose parts miraculously interpenetrate without conflict and require no rational justification, ... think with the blood and the body.[4]

The ambivalence has been noticed by various authors and either condemned or appreciated, depending on their own perspectives. Among authors who, coming from Marxism, have become open to poststructuralist approaches, the polymorphism and the dispersion of the subject have been welcomed as liberation from determinism and class reductionism.[5] In contrast, Habermas assigns the leftist-Nietzschean line stretching from Georges Bataille to Foucault and then Derrida to the 'young-conservatives' and thus alludes to the 'conservative revolutionaries' in the Weimar Republic around Martin Heidegger, Ernst

---

2 See the comparison in Deleuze and Guattari's *A Thousand Plateaus*, in which the maxim is referred to as an 'organic State act' (Deleuze and Guattari 1987, p. 439; Deleuze and Guattari 1980, p. 467).
3 Deleuze 1995, p. 149.
4 Eagleton 1990, pp. 368 et sq.
5 E.g. Laclau and Mouffe 1985, pp. 2, 69 et sqq., 97 et sqq.; Barrett 1991, pp. 131 et sq., 134.

Jünger and Carl Schmitt. 'On the basis of modernistic attitudes they justify an irreconcilable antimodernism'.[6] Manfred Frank postulates a 'tendency to "dangerous thinking"'[7] per se, which poses no danger to real domination and at the same time can be exploited from left to right.[7] Descombes has observed a peculiar ambiguity in the philosophical discourses of poststructuralist anti-Hegelianism, which makes itself evident, for example, in that the Hegelian master-servant dialectic is articulated by the same authors, at times in a Marxist manner as an exploitation relationship, and at times in a Nietzschean, in the sense that the modern bourgeois represents a contemptible nature because he is only a freed slave who has internalised his master.[8] Ferry and Renaut generalise this observation into the accusation of a 'double game', in which on the one hand power appears in the language of a Marxist social critique of exploitation, repression and exclusion as 'pseudo-rationality', and on the other, is criticised in the name of an 'irrational' in the framework of a Nietzsche-Heideggerian paradigm from the viewpoint of what is excluded from 'reason' (e.g. insanity).[9]

It is advisable not to clear up the ambiguities of the phenomenon too quickly. In the culture in which these discourses 'arrive', radical impulses are not simply relinquished; instead they shift from the transformative to the subversive – 'a way of keeping warm at the level of discourse a political culture which had been flushed off the streets'.[10] The sensitisation for differences and opposites in gender relations and race relations contributed to a sustained transformation of social movements. Also, at the point where anti-ideological scepticism has merged with spontaneous ideologies of the market, neoconservative intellectuals such as Daniel Bell, Amitai Etzioni and Peter Koslowski perceive a corrosion of bourgeois values and in particular of the work ethic.[11] According to Eagleton, in its functional interaction with capitalism, postmodernism is both iconoclastic as well as incorporated, because capitalism itself is split: an anarchistic market logic, which continually dissolves the higher values anti-ideologically, is accompanied by a systemic requirement for compensatory ideologies. Uncritical in relation to the fragmenting functional modes of the capitalistic market, postmodernism is at the same time subversive in that it questions the system where it is dependent on absolute values, metaphys-

6   Habermas 1987, p. 155.
7   Frank 1989, pp. 343 et sq.
8   Descombes 1980, p. 158.
9   Ferry and Renaut 1990, pp. 75 et sq., 77, 79.
10   Eagleton 1996, pp. 4, 17, 24 et sq.
11   Cf. for this Huyssen 1993, pp. 28 et sqq.; Harvey 1990, p. 113; Zima 2012, pp. 38 et sqq.

ical foundations and self-identical subjects.[12] Fredric Jameson describes it as a 'force field in which very different kinds of cultural impulses ... must make their way', of course with a 'cultural dominant', which he specifies as the increasing integration of aesthetic production into 'late capitalistic' commodity production.[13]

Referencing Gramsci's hegemony theory, one could call the process a 'passive revolution', which here exhibits the feature of being directly applied to the cultures of 'gauchism'. Gramsci proceeded from two revolutions which were not only 'active' but also (at first) successful: namely the Jacobin revolution in France, against which the nation states in Germany and Italy developed as reactions, and the Bolshevik revolution in Russia, to which the West reacted with new 'Fordist' forms of regulation and integration, which proved in the long run to be historically victorious.[14] Despite the historical distance, the basic idea is still instructive, namely that we are dealing with a 'passive' social transformation, which occurs in the 'absence of a popular initiative'. Leadership is held by the dominant bloc, which reacts against a 'sporadic, elementary and non-organic rebelliousness' and '[accepts] a certain part of the demands expressed from below'.[15] Thus the term 'passive revolution' reveals a 'morphology of advanced capitalism ... as if the relations of capitalist production were possessed of ... a certain plasticity, which allows them to "restructure" in periods of crisis'.[16]

II

Unexpectedly we have landed in the postmodernism debate and must ask ourselves the question whether and in what sense it is at all justified to speak of a postmodernist Nietzscheanism. The claim that Nietzsche reception played a central role in the development of poststructuralism and postmodernism is undisputed in the literature.[17] The term 'postmodern' is used in adjectival form

12 Eagleton 1996, pp. 132 et sq.; Eagleton 1990, pp. 373 et sq.
13 Jameson 1984, pp. 56 et sq.
14 Cf. on the continental-European reaction to the French revolution e.g. Gramsci 1992, p. 229; Gramsci 1975, Q. 1, § 150; Gramsci 1971, p. 117; Gramsci 1975, Q. 10.11, § 61. To newer parliamentary and 'syndical' integration forms e.g. Gramsci 2007, p. 257; Gramsci 1975, Q. 8, § 36; Gramsci 1971, pp. 219 et sqq; Gramsci 1975, Q. 13, § 27; Gramsci 1971, p. 106; Gramsci 1975, Q. 15, § 59.
15 Gramsci 1995, p. 373; Gramsci 1975, Q. 10.11, § 41.XIV.
16 Buci-Glucksmann 1979, p. 209.
17 For Habermas, Nietzsche is the 'pivot point' of postmodernism (Habermas 1990, p. 83);

for the first time in 1917, in the periphery of the George circle, based on the Nietzschean concept of the 'Übermensch' [Overman]: 'the postmodern man' is, according to Rudolf Pannwitz,[18] the 'athletically hardened', 'nationalistically conscious', 'militarily educated' and 'religiously excited' man, who opposes the 'futile and ridiculous' cultural efforts of modern Europe.[19] On the other hand, Foucault spurned being subsumed under postmodernism: he does not know what it deals with, how modernity is constituted, from what it repels itself, and which problem-type is common to the postmodernists or poststructuralists.[20]

The initial inspection of the terrain already leads us into a 'minefield of contradicting terms'.[21] Alone the distinction between 'postmodernism' and 'poststructuralism' is controversial. Boyne and Rattansi want to use the first only for aesthetic concepts, which are directed against modernistic art forms, but admit that this distinction does not correspond to the usual uses of the term.[22] For Huyssen poststructuralism is a 'theory of modernism in the stage of its exhaustion' and in this respect belongs more to the continuation of modernity than to its postmodern surmounting.[23] Ermarth thinks it is possible to differentiate the two designations by the temporal reference of what they critique: whereas the poststructuralists (here Derrida and Irigaray) want to critique the entirety of western thought, the postmodernists refer critically to modern Enlightenment and humanism, so that postmodernism is grasped as a historical concept, 'indicating something that comes after modernity'.[24] Of course, here it can be asked what remains of poststructuralism then, if the constitutive reference to

according to Frank neostructuralism is separated from linguistic structuralism 'through a reconsideration of Nietzsche's overcoming of metaphysics' (Frank 1989, p. 22). 'The Nietzschean Left was a postmodernism *avant la lettre*' (Resch 1989, p. 514). It could legitimately be argued that philosophical postmodernity is born with Nietzsche's work (Vattimo 1994, p. 164). Zima lets postmodernism begin with Nietzsche, because he considered the possibility that dialectical 'ambivalence as unity of incompataiable values ... leads to *Indifference*, defined as interchangeability of the values' (Zima 2012, p. 15). 'Poststructuralism must be defined as the *overwhelmingly positive, assimilative embrace of Nietzsche*. And it is as such that it persists today' (Waite 1996, p. 108). For Münker and Roesler the poststructuralistic approach in France consists primarily in 'perpetuating the Nietzschean perspective on our modern culture' (Münker and Roesler 2000, p. XII).

18   Pannwitz 1917, p. 64.
19   Cf. Meier 1989, p. 1142; Welsch 1991, pp. 12 et sq; Aschheim 1992, pp. 22 et sq., 75 et sqq.; Zima 2012, pp. 8 et sq.
20   Foucault 1998a, pp. 447 et sq., 2001b, Nr. 330, pp. 1265 et sq.
21   Harvey 1990, p. VIII.
22   Boyne and Rattansi 1990, pp. 10 et sq.
23   Huyssen 1993, pp. 33, 39 et sq.
24   Ermarth 1998, pp. 587, 589.

structuralism disappears from the definition. And the definition of postmodernism provides no indication at all as to the criteria which allow us to declare 'modernism' to be at an end. Moreover, the association of postmodernism with an epoch 'after' modernism has been questioned, for instance by Umberto Eco, who argues that, similar to mannerism, it can appear in various epochs.[25] Larrain attempts a political distinction by using poststructuralism for authors such as Derrida, Foucault, Hindess, Hirst, Laclau and Mouffe, 'who do not dissolve social reality into fragmentary images and signs and who still think it possible ... to be politically constituted by progressive discourses which resist power or aim at socialism', whereas postmodernism is supposed to be identified in the examples of the positions of Lyotard and Baudrillard, 'who no longer hope that meaningful change can be attempted and tend to dissolve reality into simulacra'.[26] However, the continuing argument shows that the central topics of poststructuralism – dismissal of the ideology concept, 'discourse' as the central authority of social life, refusal of a linear concept of history, critique of the autonomous 'subject' and its universalistic 'truth' – re-appear in those authors designated as postmodernist, and it remains unclear why the modifications they have undertaken should be the basis for a new paradigm change.[27]

I would like to propose a conceptual distinction which could liberate us from the obligation to fit the authors and currents into an artificial either-or arrangement leading only to uninteresting and inconclusive classification controversies: based on the meaning of the word, 'poststructuralism' should designate a *theoretical* formation which developed particularly in France as the claimed succession to and surmounting of structuralism. It is not a concept contrary to postmodernism, but one of its theoretical currents, or, as Manfred Frank has put it, 'thought under the conditions of the postmodern era'.[28] Whatever postmodernism means precisely, as reaction, successor, or surmounting of modernism, it is in any case more widely conceived than a specific theoretical direction that attempts to set itself off critically against French structuralism. The term postmodernism was already established in US-American literary criticism in the 1950s, became in the sixties the key word of an avant-garde critique of 'aesthetic modernism' and in the early seventies morphed into 'a kind of comprehensive term for newer developments particularly in architecture, but also in dance, in theatre, in painting, in film and in music'.[29] Only then, or more

---

25   Eco 1989, p. 66.
26   Larrain 1994, p. 91.
27   Larrain 1994, pp. 104 et sq., 106 et sqq.
28   Frank 1989, p. 19.
29   Huyssen 1993, pp. 13, 17 et sq., 23 et sqq.

accurately, following Lyotard's *La Condition Postmoderne* of 1979, did the term become a distinctive identifying reference in philosophical discourses. Thus it is advisable to refer with 'postmodernism' generally to a modern-critical expression which runs through aesthetics, culture and modes of life, captures various philosophical tendencies and also includes the theoretical shift from structuralism to poststructuralism. So there is nothing wrong with calling Deleuze and Foucault *poststructuralists* if one wants to emphasise their claim to leave structuralism (eg. of the Saussurean or Lévi-Straussean variety) behind; but there is also nothing wrong with treating them as representatives of *postmodernism* if one is interested in how they distance themselves from the anthropological 'utopias', or so-called 'great theories', of modernism (such as eg. humanism, psychoanalysis and Marxism), which Lyotard has subsumed under the term 'metanarratives' [métarécits].

However, with this kind of terminological agreement we still have in no way gained a useful analytical concept of postmodernism. This becomes evident through the fact that the definitions which attempt to express the scope of the concept usually pay for this with a degree of generality that reduces the explanatory value toward zero. Thus the *Historische Wörterbuch der Philosophie* defines postmodernism as a word 'labelling, propagating or criticizing phenomena ... which, without being premodern, cannot be subsumed seamlessly under the term modernism because they do not meet the essential ideals and paradigms of the same'.[30] According to this definition, everything depends on the specification of the 'nature' of the modern epoch, which is to be left behind through the proclamation of a new epoch. The concept of postmodernism implicitly requires the procedure of constituting 'the' modernity as a uniform bloc, which could then be dismissed *en bloc*. Of course, this is a strangely essentialist conceptualisation, one which actually would have to be ruled out by the methodological self-understanding of postmodernism.

It is no coincidence that most critics of postmodernism start off with its construction of a uniform modernism. Habermas's objection can be summed up as stating that the postmodern departure from 'modernity as a whole' presumes a transcendental position and suppresses the counter-discourses inherent in modernity itself, which attempted to enlighten the Enlightenment about its own narrow-mindedness.[31] Instead of retaining the emancipatory contents of reason and defending them against the one-sided rationality of bourgeois society, postmodernism pursues a Nietzschean critique of modernity which

---

30   Meier 1989, p. 1142.
31   Habermas 1990, pp. 4 et sq., 302.

dispenses with the dialectic of enlightenment.[32] Frank situates the counter-discourses of modernity, which have been made unrecognisable by postmodernism, primarily in the romantic self-criticism of idealism, which has already stated that the view with which we explore our world has not been produced by us, but has been 'implanted' in us, 'in-oculated': that is, it has been pre-structured through discourse formations.[33] The 'decentring of the subject', announced as a post-modern achievement, has its place in 'modern' philosophy history itself, since the most varied philosophers from Spinoza to Fichte and Schelling, to Feuerbach, Marx and Freud all agree to let the subject be grounded 'in something that itself is not conscious'.[34] Ulrich Beck objects that postmodernism identifies modernity falsely with the modernity of industrial society and is therefore unable to conceive of 'several modernities': at the first sign of a crisis of industrial society's paradigm the postmodernists desert the field instead of taking up the constructive task of drafting a post-industrial model of 'reflexive modernization'.[35]

Another critique has been formulated by Michael Hardt and Antonio Negri in their book *Empire*. According to them, postmodernism and post-colonialism blend opposite meanings of the 'modern', that is, on the one hand a renaissance humanism from Duns Scotus to Spinoza, which is characterised by the discovery of immanence and the stress on singularity and difference, and on the other hand a philosophical 'Thermidor of the Renaissance revolution'.[36] This second line from Descartes through Kant to Hegel would, through the 'transcendental apparatus' of a schematism of reason, pin down and control the utopian forces set free in the Renaissance.[37] This 'Thermidor' would finally arrive at the concept of modern sovereignty and develop a 'sovereignty machine' which transforms the 'multitude' of humans into an ordered totality.[38] Thus, at bottom postmodernism would pose a challenge 'neither to the Enlightenment nor to modernity in toto ... but specifically to the tradition of modern sovereignty', and here again above all to dialectics as the 'central logic of

---

32   Habermas 1990, pp. 55 et sq., 85 et sq., 94.
33   Frank 1989, pp. 90 et sq., 92 et sq. Frank describes the modern self-criticism of idealism using the example of Fichte's reinterpretation of Hegel's absolute self-awareness to a 'power into which an eye is implanted', and Schleiermacher's 'feeling of absolute dependence' (Frank 1989, pp. 89 et sq).
34   Frank 1989, pp. 190, 192 et sq.
35   Beck 1997, p. 22, cf. 14.
36   Hardt and Negri 2000, p. 140.
37   Hardt and Negri 2000, pp. 78 et sq.
38   Hardt and Negri 2000, p. 87.

modern domination, exclusion and command'.[39] This self-misunderstanding makes postmodernism incapable of determining its own historical place and leads to a loss of critical potency: on one hand the postmodernists are 'still waging battle against the shadows of old enemies', namely against the modern forms of sovereignty, which in the meantime have been eliminated by 'Empire' itself and replaced by cross-border dispositifs of difference,[40] on the other hand they are incapable of the political-ethical construction of a countervailing power which could help the fragmented multitude to a new coherence.[41] Taking recourse to the renaissance humanist triad, 'to be-to know-to be able' [esse-nosse-posse], and here especially to Spinoza's concept of the capacity to act [potentia agendi], Hardt/Negri design the subject-becoming of the 'multitude': *Posse*, in this Spinozian sense, refers to 'the power of the multitude and its telos, an embodied power of knowledge and being, always open to the possible'.[42]

Despite all their differences, the objections demonstrate the extent to which the concept of postmodernity depends on the presupposed construction of a homogenised modernity which masks its manifold contradictions and flattens them out beyond recognition. When Lyotard describes modernity as a type of legitimation which proceeds through meta discourses such as the dialectic of the spirit, the hermeneutics of meaning, the emancipation of reasoning or the working subject, and defines postmodernism as the loss of faith [incrédulité] in meta-narratives of this kind,[43] he himself is telling a grand narrative which even surpasses the ones it aims to send off: 'the greatest possible meta narrative, the narrative after the narratives, which is so precocious that it has always known everything to be ignorance'.[44] According to Osborne, 'The narrative of the death of metanarrative is itself grander than most of the narratives it would consign to oblivion'.[45]

The methodological self-contradiction raises doubt as to whether 'postmodernism' is at all viable as an analytic concept. Any attempt to define its specific intellectual character tends to culminate in absurdity: if it is to designate a

---

39   Hardt and Negri 2000, p. 140.
40   'The structures and logics of power in the contemporary world are entirely immune to the "liberatory" weapons of the postmodernist politics of difference'. (Hardt and Negri 2000, p. 142). This corresponds much more with 'the current ideology of corporate capital and the world market' (Hardt and Negri 2000, p. 150).
41   Hardt and Negri 2000, pp. 142, 408.
42   Hardt and Negri 2000, p. 408.
43   Lyotard 1984, p. XXIII.
44   Haug 1993, p. 11.
45   Osborne 1995, p. 157.

radical questioning of humanism and the Enlightenment, then apparently one must also reckon the Enlightenment critique of the conservative Pope John Paul II as postmodern, says Harvey;[46] Eagleton quips that if its specifics lie in the criticism of universalistic truths then one can call Pontius Pilate the 'first postmodernist'.[47] That is not quite as absurd as it sounds, for in *The Antichrist* Nietzsche points to Pilate as the only figure in the New Testament who, because of his devastating critique of truth, one is 'obliged to respect'.[48] Hardt and Negri also treat Islamic fundamentalism as a phenomenon of postmodernism: it follows Islamic modernity and stands in opposition to it because this modernity is hyper-encoded as subjection under western hegemony. The difference consists above all in the fact 'that postmodernist discourses appeal primarily to the winners of the processes of globalization and fundamentalist discourses to the losers'.[49] And finally, according to Heiner Müller, if we regard Lenin as the representative of socialist modernity, this means that Stalinism is our postmodernism: 'the substitution of the word, the writing, the paper for reality. Our simulacra are the (fictitious) documents, with which history is simulated'.[50]

Even if some of this borders on mockery, it is nevertheless intelligent mockery. It points to a postmodern discourse strategy which follows the imperatives of effective self-marketing, instead of meeting the standards of reflection necessary for forming theoretical concepts. The fact that the methodological problem lies deeper is shown by the inconclusive debates around the scope of the concept of 'enlightenment': Is it describing the eighteenth century, which considered itself to be the 'siècle des lumières'? Or does it mean the impulse to break out of immaturity and irrational domination in general, as set forth in the antique concept of enlightenment? The ambiguity indicates 'that "intellectual-historical" epochal concepts have in themselves an uncertain basis, the multilayered and antagonistic process of history'.[51] This suggests that postmodern-

---

46   Harvey 1990, p. 41.

47   Eagleton 1996, p. 41.

48   Nietzsche 1968b, p. 174; Nietzsche 1999a, Vol. 6, p. 225. 'What is truth?', replied Pontius Pilate in the trial of Jesus, who had declared he came into the world in order to witness for the truth (Joh 18, 37 et sq). And Nietzsche comments: 'To take a Jewish affair *seriously* – he cannot persuade himself to do that. One Jew more or less – what does it matter? ... The noble scorn of a Roman before whom an impudent misuse of the word, "Wahrheit" was carried on has enriched the New Testament with the only expression which *posesses value*, – which is its criticism, its *annihilation* even: What is truth!' (Nietzsche 1968b, p. 174; Nietzsche 1999a, Vol. 5, p. 225; see also Nietzsche 1999a, Vol. 11, p. 100).

49   Hardt and Negri 2000, pp. 148 et sqq.

50   Müller and Weimann 1991, pp. 182 et sq.

51   Haug 1984, p. 719.

ism be understood not primarily as an intellectual-historical phenomenon, but rather as something to be reconstructed social-theoretically from the transformations in the modes of production and reproduction.

In this sense Fredric Jameson has proposed using 'postmodern' to designate a 'superstructure' which in the transition from Fordism to post-Fordism has brought forth a new 'structure of feeling'.[52] According to him, the crucial task is to examine new praxis and feeling structures in relation to the production and organisational forms of global capitalism and to understand this connection not as reflex, but as the production of subjects who can function in the new socio-economic relations.[53] An attempt of this kind is undertaken by David Harvey, for example, when he arranges postmodernity in a sequence of successive 'time-space compressions', which are generated by the pressure of capital accumulation.[54] A fragmenting of linear conceptions of time came about for the first time through the great over-accumulation crisis in the mid-nineteenth century. It resulted in the development of 'modernism' in the visual arts and in literature, the crisis awareness of which was heightened by the experiences of the First World War and the Russian revolution.[55] The over-accumulation crisis from the late 1960s until approximately 1973 led to a new acceleration of the turnaround times in production, circulation and consumption. This in turn produced new space-time compressions, which presented a condition for the development of postmodernity.[56]

Since capitalistic development produces these kinds of compressions again and again in the space-time fabric, it is extraordinarily difficult to differentiate the intellectual-historical periods sharply from each other. Harvey suggests understanding the terms modernism and postmodernism as 'static reifications' of dynamic opposites: both terms are to be dissolved 'into a complex of oppositions expressive of the cultural contradictions of capitalism'.[57] 'The sharp categorical distinction between modernism and postmodernism disappears, to be replaced by an examination of the flux of internal relations within capitalism as a whole'.[58]

Looking at the 'mode of production' of postmodernist theory, we can see that it is, to a large degree, the result of a complex genealogy that proceeds

---

52   Jameson 1991, p. XIV.
53   Jameson 1991, p. XV.
54   Harvey 1990, pp. 306 et sq.
55   Harvey 1990, pp. 260 et sqq.
56   Harvey 1990, pp. 147, 189, 285, 326 et sqq.
57   Harvey 1990, p. 339.
58   Harvey 1990, p. 342.

from France to the US and then back again to Europe and, following the academic channels of US hegemony, appears on a global scale. As François Cusset
has demonstrated, 'French theory' is, by and large, a product fabricated in the
academia of the United States by way of a de-contextualising appropriation.
As soon as it became predominant in the American Humanities and Literature departments, it lost its influence in France.[59] Nevertheless, according to
Jameson, 'postmodern' has become customary to the extent 'that, for good or
ill, we cannot not use it'.[60] If we follow this argument, we should not misun-
derstand the term as an analytical concept, but use it provisionally and fluidly
for the description of ideological and cultural shifts, over whose general features the literature is, however, amazingly united, despite all the contradictions
when it comes to evaluation: an understanding of time, with which modernistic waiting for the fundamentally new is replaced by an orientation toward
events and breaks; a celebration of immediacy and availability oriented toward
commodity aesthetics; a fragmenting, which, following Lacan's definition of
schizophrenia, can be described as the tearing of coherent chains of signifiers;
a lack of aesthetic depth, which Jameson illustrated with the confrontation of
van Gogh's farmer's shoes and Andy Warhol's 'Diamond Dust Shoes';[61] a loss of
historicity, which is compensated for by tendencies to spatialisation, the preference for 'eclectic facades, pastiches and quotation art';[62] an 'era of indifference',
i.e. of 'exchangeable individuals, relations, values and ideologies'.[63]

Many of these descriptions can be integrated into Eagleton's interpretation,
according to which postmodernity collects the material logic of late capitalism
and turns it aggressively against its spiritual foundations.[64] However, it is to
be considered that the social transformations underlying postmodernism produce an 'explosion of conflicting tendencies', which also contain compensatory
needs for 'deeper questions' and eternal truths.[65] After all, the postmodern USA
is still a country of the most intolerant fundamentalisms. It is to be expected
that 'postmodernism' will be replaced by more precise terms, as soon as the
outlines of 'post-Fordism' and 'high tech capitalism'[66] become more clear.

---

59   Cusset 2003, p. 22.
60   Jameson 1991, p. XXII.
61   Jameson 1991, pp. 5 et sqq.; Jameson 1984, pp. 59 et sqq.
62   Huyssen 1993, p. 13.
63   Zima 2012, p. 16.
64   'Postmodernism, in short, scoops up something of the material logic of advanced capital-
      ism and turns it aggressively against its spiritual foundations' (Eagleton 1996, p. 133).
65   Cf. Harvey 1990, pp. 292, 302 et sq.
66   Cf. Haug 2003.

I will not attempt to investigate these connections further, but instead, using the examples of Deleuze and Foucault, limit myself to the reshapings and incorporations of the Nietzsche image, which have taken place in the context of the postmodern paradigm shift.

III

I will deal with the recoding of Nietzsche into the 'new' plural-differential Nietzsche in Chapter 1. In reality it is not new, but the result of a paradigm shift in Nietzsche interpretation which took place quite some time ago. Deleuze's Nietzsche book, on which I concentrate first, appeared in France as early as 1962. If one includes Georges Bataille, who strongly affected both Deleuze's and Foucault's understanding of Nietzsche, one would even go back to the thirties and forties. Müller-Lauter, who is generally considered to be the founder of a 'pluralistic' interpretation of the 'Will to Power' in Germany, published his Nietzsche book in 1971, and the recapitulatory essay in 1974. The age of this 'new' Nietzsche stands in strange contradiction to the fact that an influential 'Nietzsche-industry' has been announcing him as a brand new discovery for more than half a century. In a Nietzsche reader published by David B. Allison, which might still be the most widely read textbook on the topic in the English-speaking world, the texts by Klossowski, Foucault, Deleuze and Derrida among others are still marketed in the seventh edition of 1995 as 'The New Nietzsche' (in 1977 the same reader was still called 'The Will to Power').[67] It is the success of an orthodoxy which has developed a tremendous inertia through the permanent evocation of the new. In France, which had been exposed to the poststructuralist Nietzsche image longest, the attraction seems to be exhausted to a great extent; in Germany and the English-speaking world the novelty value lasts longer, not least because of the time lag brought about through translating from the French, which lets the literature appear more current than it is.[68]

The focus will be on the observation of how Deleuze *reads* Nietzsche, first in his *Nietzsche et la philosophie* (1962), then in *Différence et répétition* (1968) and in the volumes *Anti-Oedipe* (1972) and *Mille Plateaux* (1980), written together with the Lacan disciple Felix Guattari. Strangely enough, this is an enquiry that is hardly pursued in the extensive literature on Nietzsche's significance for post-structuralism and postmodernism: in general, credulity prevails, by which it

---

67   Allison 1995.
68   See for example the Nietzsche reader of Sedgwick (1995), the literature survey by Appel 1999, pp. 1–15 and Ottmann 1999, pp. 462 et sq.

is tacitly assumed that Deleuze will have correctly read his Nietzsche. For the
most part Nietzsche quotations have the function of illustrating the interpretation and not of examining it critically. This is true not only of the lovers of a
postmodernist Nietzscheanism, but also of prominent critics of the same. 'It
is fitting ['mit Recht'] that Nietzsche, mediated by Gilles Deleuze, has become
influential in structuralist France as a theoretician of power', claims Habermas,
for example.[69] How does he know that 'it is fitting' (or rather 'justified', 'mit
Recht') that this happened if he does not take the trouble to compare Nietzsche's and Deleuze's concepts of power with philological diligence? Habermas, who is probably the most well-known critic of postmodernism, assumes
without closer inspection that Nietzsche really is the anarchist rebel 'against
everything normative', as Deleuze describes him.[70] In fact, this interpretation
is part of the Habermasian intention to subsume Nietzsche, together with postmodernism and the critical theory of Horkheimer and Adorno, under the heading of an anti-modern 'ideology critique'.[71] It suppresses the master-standpoint
from which the late Nietzsche articulated his critique of norms and ideology,
thereby missing both the scope and the problem of postmodern recoding.

In contrast to Habermas, I will focus on the Deleuzian construction of a 'new'
Nietzsche, and this with the perspective of deconstructing it. As soon as one
confronts the 'plural' interpretation with the texts to which it claims to refer,
one encounters a procedure designed to make the specific 'perspectivism' of
the late Nietzschean phase invisible. In the midst of an anti-Hegelian interpretation of Nietzsche one can observe the remarkable procedure of Deleuze deriving the concept of 'difference', which is to replace that of the dialectical contradiction, from Nietzsche's aristocratic 'pathos of distance'. That which in the
Genealogy of Morals describes an explicit 'social' [ständisch] divide between
the higher-ranking and the lower is transformed into a 'differential element',
which is intended to distinguish the life-affirming active forces from the passive and negating ones. Paradoxically, this kind of levelling not only prevents any
serious criticism of Nietzsche, but also defeats the possibility of being aware
of the ideology-critical potentials of his blunt discourse of unfettered domination. My argument is by no means directed against the openness to being
inspired by the perceptiveness of Nietzsche's intuitions, but against the con-
formism of using him as symbolic capital without revealing his 'obsession with
hierarchy'.[72]

---

69   Habermas 1990, p. 127.
70   Habermas 1990, pp. 123, 125.
71   Cf. Habermas 1990, pp. 97, 107, 120 et sq., 126, 353 et sq.; Note 8.
72   For the distinction between the valuable 'intuitions' of Nietzsche and his 'obsession hier-
      archique' see Boyer 1997, pp. 4, 6.

In the centre of Deleuze's interpretation is the equation of Nietzsche's 'will to power' and the Spinozean concept of power [potentia agendi] as a cooperative capacity to act. A philological reconstruction of the respective concepts of power and will shows that here, under the cover of linguistic equivocations, opposite meanings are lumped together. In contradiction to the postmodern rejection of historical 'linearities', Deleuze himself constructs a linear relationship between Spinoza and Nietzsche that suppresses the sharp anti-Spinozean turn of the late Nietzsche. As a consequence, following the failed revolts of the 68s, Nietzsche can appear in Spinozean disguise as a nomadic rebel, while his concept of power is transposed into that of desire. However, what had been repressed in the postmodernist reception of Nietzsche returns again and can be heard in the most radical discourses as an elitist attitude and a subterranean 'elective affinity' to neoliberal flexibilisation.

IV

In the following chapters the emphasis shifts to Foucault, whose idea of Nietzsche is strongly affected by Deleuze: 'Nietzsche was a revelation for me' (1982); 'we needed his figures ... of the overman [Übermensch] and the eternal return in order to awaken from the sleep of dialectic and anthropology' (1963); an invitation to question the category of the subject and to tear it from itself (1978); his announcement of the end of man 'has taken a prophetic value for us' (1966); his 'presence is increasingly important' (1975); 'Nietzsche and Heidegger, that was the philosophical shock', but finally the former became prevalent (1984).[73]

Foucault, from the beginning to the end of his writing, professed so consistently and frequently to being a Nietzschean that his 'fundamental Nietzscheanism'[74] is not disputed in the literature. However, what is disputed is wherein Foucault's Nietzscheanism lies, and what effects it has on the theoretical and methodological configuration of his investigations. The problem can be brought to a point with the following question: what does it mean theoretically that, in the midst of a supposedly radical critique of power and the subject,

---

73   According to the order of the Foucault quotations – 1982: Foucault 2001b, Nr. 362, p. 1599;
        1963: Foucault 1998a, p. 76, Foucault 2001a, Nr. 13, p. 267; 1978: Foucault 2000, pp. 240, 247–
        49, Foucault 2001b, Nr. 281, pp. 862, 867–9; 1966: Foucault 1998a, p. 266, Foucault 2001a,
        Nr. 34, p. 531; 1975: Foucault 1980, p. 53, Foucault 2001a, Nr. 156, p. 1621; 1984: Foucault 1996,
        p. 471, Foucault 2001b, Nr. 354, p. 1522.
74   Foucault 1996, p. 471, Foucault 2001b, Nr. 354, p. 1522.

one is again and again referred to a philosopher whose anti-metaphysical thinking, primarily in his late phase, is connected with the most radical enthusiasm
for hierarchical power and domination and whose proto-fascist and fascist
effect is an unquestioned *fact*, i.e. independently of the various debates around
his 'true' motivation or the 'abuse' and 'misunderstanding' of his role in the
Nazistate?

To specify this as a relevant problem for theoretical reflection does not
mean declaring Nietzsche a direct 'precursor' of Italian or German fascism. As
Domenico Losurdo has shown, a linear intellectual-historical connection, such
as was made primarily by Georg Lukács through the assignment of Nietzsche
to the philosophical 'irrationalism from Schelling to Hitler', disambiguates the
ambivalences in Nietzsche's philosophy and jumps over the historical distances
between the late nineteenth century and the period of fascism's formation after
the First World War.[75] The relationship between Nietzsche and the Nazistate is
to be understood neither in terms of the history of ideas as a preordained development of the Nietzschean thought world, nor in instrumental terms as 'abuse'
by the Nazis, nor yet as a conspiracy of the sister.[76] As Martha Zapata Galinda
has shown, at the beginning of the Weimar Republic a 'fascistisation' of Nietzsche reception set in, which can only be adequately grasped if one examines
it as independent ideological 'interventions into concrete political and social
situations'.[77] Also, the relations of philosophy in the Nazistate were such that
the Nietzscheans did not have a monopolistic position by any means, but were
challenged both by competing schools of philosophy and by the national conservative and clerical intellectuals, who were themselves striving for privileged
positions among the ruling Nazi organizations.[78] But the fact remains that no
philosopher was celebrated as enthusiastically by the ss-elite, and could be
used so directly for the justification of the destruction of 'lives unworthy of
being lived', as could Nietzsche.[79] Especially the antimetaphysics as well as
the criticism of universalistic ideologies and claims to truth, which present
an important connecting point for postmodernism, received in their fascist
reworking the meaning which blew away the normative thresholds inhibiting

75   Losurdo 2020, pp. 613 et sqq., 732 et sqq.
76   Cf. e.g. Aschheim 1992, pp. 315 et sqq., Zapata Galinda 1995, pp. 34 et sq.; Losurdo 2020,
      pp. 711 et sqq.
77   Zapata Galinda 1995, p. 14.
78   Zapata Galinda 1995, pp. 113 et sq., 118 et sqq.
79   For example, with reference to Nietzsche's literary estate note from October 1888, in which
      he calls it a 'requirement of human love' to 'cut out' the degenerate parts (Nietzsche 1999a,
      Vol. 13, pp. 599 et sq.). See. e.g. for this Klee 1983, pp. 16 et sq., Zapata Galinda 1995, pp. 126
      et sq., 167 et sq., Aschheim 1992, pp. 243, 245, Losurdo 2020, pp. 582–602.

war and genocide. Derrida, who argues against a linear connection between Nietzsche and Nazism and understood the latter as 'reactive inversion', points out that there is nothing contingent 'about the fact that the only political regimen to have effectively brandished his name as a major and official banner was Nazi'.[80]

What we derive from this is the question of how the tension between the Nietzschean fascination with domination and the project of a radical critique of power is identified and worked through by Foucault and the Foucault literature, or on the other hand, with which procedures it is denied and repressed. Is there a basic theoretical 'dispositive' based on Nietzsche that runs counter to Foucault's claim to be critiquing power and undermines it? Posing this question encounters difficulties immediately: Nietzsche as an enthusiast of domination or as a 'protofaschist' philosopher does not emerge with Foucault, so that it seems there is no tension at all between his use of Nietzsche and his project of a critique of power. When he speaks of Nietzsche's moral critique, his rejection of the 'lesser ones' and their 'resentment', his overcoming of the 'little people' by the 'overman', etc., this does not seem to have anythingto do with the standpoint of an uncompromising rule of the elite. Add to this that the postmodernist understanding of reading dismissed the idea of semantics inherent in the text in favour of its flexible usages. Thus Foucault explains in an interview in 1975 that the question of the 'faithfulness' to a text is completely uninteresting for him: his only acknowledgment in relation to Nietzschean thinking is that 'it is used, distorted, abused and made to scream [de l'utiliser, de la déformer, de la faire grincer, crier]'.[81]

As a result, the possibility of a philological critique is eliminated from the beginning. The profession of eclecticism protects Foucault against the question about the principle of selection that is applied in his reading of Nietzsche and what has been excluded by it. *Which* Nietzsche Foucault uses can then only be accepted and recounted descriptively. This is actually the procedure which became accepted in the literature to a great extent. But from the standpoint of a historical-critical reconstruction, the usage of a text is not to be separated from the specific selection that precedes it. The 'new' Nietzscheanism propagated by Foucault also has its 'archaeology' and its discursive 'rules of formation', in the language of Foucault. In order to decipher them, we must focus on how Foucault *reads* Nietzsche, and on which readings of Nietzsche he depends.

---

80   Derrida 1985, p. 31.
81   Foucault 2001a, Nr. 156, p. 1621.

V

Chapter 2 concentrates on the early Foucault of the 1960s, and here in particular on the *Order of Things* (1966), which, with the assistance of Nietzsche's 'Last
Man', declares the humanist and utopian theories of the 'anthropological era'
to be obsolete. When Nietzsche rejects the human 'species' because it alleges
an equality which stands in the way of breeding the super-powerful, this radical anti-egalitarianism is transformed by Foucault into an anti-anthropology
which is supposed to overcome the concepts of alienation (Marx) and the
unconscious (Freud). It will have to be inquired why Foucault, Klossowski and
Deleuze fall back on Nietzsche exactly here, where he sets about founding his
own religion with the doctrine of the eternal recurrence, and why right here
they forgo any critique of religion. Due to the absence of any critical analysis
of the 'overman', Foucault misses the alienated dynamic by which the 'free-
spirited' hedonist necessarily morphs into a figure of unlimited domination.
Foucault belongs to a line of reception in which both the master race and the
new-religious dimensions of Nietzschean philosophy are blocked out.

Chapter 3 deals primarily with the period between 1969 and 1972, which
coincides with the time of Foucault's radical left-wing commitment. I will trace
how Foucault rejected an early concept of ideology from Althusser by dissolving it first into the category of 'knowledge', and then, by way of the Nietzschean
connection between truth and the will to power, lets it merge into the category
of power. This procedure leads not, as most commentators claim, to a stronger
consideration of the varieties of power, but on the contrary to a reductionist
relapse behind the differentiation level of the ideology-theoretical approaches
of that time. On one hand, the 'determinate negation' of ideology critique is
replaced by a 'fictionalism' which loses any discriminatory power, while, on
the other, Foucault introduces a concept of power which is located 'behind'
the social relations of production and domination. At this point, the claim
to extend the analysis of power beyond the Marxist 'appropriation' paradigm
flips over into an essentialism which hides any concrete social practices and
struggles. A philological examination of the essay *Nietzsche, Genealogy, History*
(1971) comes to the conclusion that the contrast between 'Herkunft' (descent)
and 'Ursprung' (origin), claimed by Foucault, doesn't exist with Nietzsche. Foucault overlooks the fact that the textual material is pervaded by another contradiction, one between Nietzsche's middle, 'ideology-critical' phase and the
renewed verticalisation of his late phase.

In Chapter 4, I will turn to Foucault's *Discipline and Punish* of 1975, of which
he said that it takes up the topic of Nietzsche's *Genealogy of Morals* again. Following this trail, I will examine how the neo-Nietzschean configuration affects

his own historiography. A textual comparison with the classic study *Punishment and Social Structure* by Rusche and Kirchheimer (1939) leads to an ambivalent result: on one hand, Foucault extends the social-historical approach in the direction of an analysis of spatial and temporal dispositives of subjection and subject constitution, and on the other hand, his ideal-typical arrangement of the historical material falls behind the differentiation level of Rusche and Kirchheimer. Where they have carefully differentiated between various prison periods and functions, Foucault constructs a continuous proliferation of the prison-dispositive up to the 'disciplinary society', without worrying about the differences between primarily economic and primarily pedagogical penal systems, or between democratic prison reforms and the systematic immiseration of prisoners in the Nazistate.

This is primarily owing to the fact that Foucault has assumed the viewpoint of Nietzsche's *Genealogy of Morals*, that of perceiving the development of punishment in the simple juxtaposition of direct physical violence (torture) and the muted and more subtle influence of power on the subject. This is complemented by a neo-Nietzschean power concept which oscillates in a contradictory manner between the rhetoric of manifold 'micro physics' and the essentialist concept of an all-penetrating 'phagocytic essence' (Poulantzas). Foucault opposes one-sidedly and sweepingly any social-pedagogisation of the penal system. Furthermore, he disregards the position of the prison in the 'coercion armour' of society, as well as in the social politics of bourgeois society. This narrowness makes it impossible to comprehend the penal systems in connection with the respective modes of regulation of capitalism and is unsuited for the analysis of current developments, such as the connection between disciplinary neoliberalism and the 'Prison Industrial Complex'.

VI

The main part of the book (Chapter 1 to 4) was submitted in June 2003 as a postdoctoral thesis (Habilitationsschrift) in the faculty of Philosophy and Humanities at the Free University of Berlin and subsequently published by Argument-Verlag in 2004.[82] After that, I continued and deepened my studies on Nietzsche, on the one hand with regard to Nietzsche's transformation of protestant anti-Judaism, in particular with the example of Julius Wellhausen,[83]

---

82   Cf. Rehmann 2004a.
83   Cf. Rehmann 2004b.

on the other hand in the context of editing the German edition of Domenico Losurdo's monumental oeuvre *Nietzsche, il ribelle aristocratico. Biografia intellettuale e bilancio critic.*[84] As Harrison Fluss summarises in his introduction to the English edition, Losurdo's book 'ends the domestication process that has mummified Nietzsche for so long' and rediscovers him as a political philosopher to be taken in earnest 'without being absorbed uncritically'.[85] In 2009 my book was translated into Italian (by Stefano Azzarà) and published by Odradek with an appendix on Foucault's concept of 'governmentality'.[86]

The present English book is an updated and extended new edition. In Chapter 2, I have integrated an excursus on Nietzsche's reworking of Protestant Anti-Judaism (in particular with the example of Julius Wellhausen), not least because the textual analysis provides valuable insight into the controversies surrounding Nietzsche's anti-Semitism (or anti-anti-Semitism) – a subject that is completely avoided by Deleuze and Foucault. And above all, the book now contains an additional Chapter 5 titled 'Forays into the late Foucault'. This chapter focuses on the one hand on the much debated convergence between Foucault and the ideological framework of neoliberalism, and, on the other hand, on the later development of his concept of power stretching from 'biopower' through the different varieties of 'governmentality' to the widening of his power concept towards techniques of the self, which are, however, designed in an individualistic way. This is due partly to the fact that his studies on Greek-Roman 'self care' and its substitution by the Christian 'confessions of the flesh' move within Nietzsche's grand narrative counterposing an ancient aristocratic ethics and a Jewish-Christian 'transvaluation'. According to Murray Bookchin, Foucault's turn to practices of self-care was part of a 'lifestyle anarchism' which replaced political engagement with gestures of a 'personal insurrection'.[87] Indeed, the transformation of Foucault's power concept was accompanied by a sharp turn against socialism and in particular, in the context of his review of André Glucksmann's book *The Master Thinkers* (1977), against Marx himself, whom he portrayed as being the 'truth' of Stalinism. My analysis will deal with the seeming paradox that the potentially productive opening of Foucault's power concept towards the strategies of self-conduct was inspired and overdetermined by his encounter with neoliberal theories, in particular with Gary Becker's concept of 'human capital'. In Chapter 6, a former version

---

84   Losurdo 2002, 2009; see my review article of Losurdo's book (Rehmann 2007).
85   Fluss, in Losurdo 2020, pp. 12 et sq.
86   Cf. Rehmann 2009, pp. 215–24.
87   Bookchin 1995.

of which was also published in the book *Foucault and Neoliberalism*,[88] I try to reconstruct how the Foucauldian 'governmentality studies' reproduce neoliberalism's ideology instead of deconstructing its hegemony.

Throughout the book, I contour the neo-Nietzschean theory constructions observed with Deleuze and Foucault by relating them to the various traditions of 'critical theory'. In this designation 'critical' is not capitalised, that is, it is used in a broader sense which extends far beyond the 'Frankfurt School'. Since Marx, Engels and the subsequent Marxist theoreticians are usually dealt with in postmodernist presentations in their official 'Marxist-Leninist' interpretation, i.e. vulgarised as economists, determinists and objectivists, it seemed to me necessary to focus on those approaches that conceive of Marxism as a radical critique of multiple dominations and as a self-reflective 'philosophy of praxis' (Gramsci). Diverse approaches have been included, extending from Adorno and Horkheimer through Jürgen Habermas and Axel Honneth up to the Althusser school (including Dominique Lecourt and Michel Pêcheux) and Stuart Hall, from Ernst Bloch's *Principle of Hope* to Günther Anders's critique of Heidegger, from Walter Benjamin to Sartre, from Max Weber to Manfred Frank's 'hermeneutic' criticism, from Ernst Tugendhat's moral philosophy to Barrington Moore's theory of justice. The comparison with the approaches of Pierre Bourdieu and Nicos Poulantzas has also proved productive, because they overlap with Foucault's conception of power while at the same time turning their analysis into a different direction.

My own approach is shaped, among other things, by the many years of cooperation in the *Projekt Ideologietheorie* (*PIT*) and by my subsequent research on various ideology-theories,[89] which might help explain why I see Deleuze's and Foucault's dismissal of the concept of ideology in the name of desire, of discourse and power, as a case in point of a fashionable 'superannuation' of Marxism that turned out to be harmful for the anchorage of critical theories in academia in general. This touches upon a fundamental difference: Whereas Marxist ideology-theories investigate the production of speeches and texts in connection with their respective ideological apparatuses and fields, postmodernist theories tend to isolate them from the practical and institutional contexts in which they are embedded. The result is a disembodied linguistic idealism.[90] The undeniable fact that language is found

---

88   Rehmann 2016a, pp. 134–58; cf. Rehmann 2013, chapt. 11.

89   For example, Rehmann 2013 and 2015a.

90   David McNally uses this term in his critique of Derrida's disembodied notion of language, which in his opinion reproduces the fetishistic rule of abstract value over use value, abstract labour over concrete labour (McNally 2001, pp. 56 et sqq., 66 et sqq.).

everywhere as a component of social practices and relations is pushed to the point that language seems to be *all* there is. The consequence of this one-sidedness is that postmodernism's valuable deconstructive project of a de-*natural*isation of fixed meanings and identities regularly morphs into a two-fold de-*material*isation: a de-*material*isation of human practices and relations, which reduces the social to the symbolic, and a de-*material*isation of the body and thus a disembodiment of human subjects, who appear as effects of discourses and of chains of signifiers.[91]

VII

Finally, here is reference to some limitations in the ambition and scope of the present work. It is not an attempt to reveal the totality of the diverse phenomena of a 'postmodern Nietzscheanism'. This becomes clear already in that it does not deal with the differently constituted neo-Nietzschean borrowings by Derrida, but is restricted to the interrelated Nietzschean constructions of Deleuze and Foucault. The fact that in their treatment the accent is unmistakably on critique is, of course, not in contradiction to the wish to be inspired by the productive sides of their approaches; on the contrary it makes possible their judicious evaluation. The same applies to Nietzsche. It cannot be the concern of this work to conduct an overall evaluation of his philosophy. For example, the early Nietzsche is not analysed in a systematic way.[92] To the extent that my reading of Nietzsche is concentrated on those areas and aspects which are repressed or distorted to a point beyond recognition by postmodernist Nietzsche interpretation, it must also be selective. It does attempt to evaluate the strengths of Nietzsche's intuitions and suggestions, yet in so doing concentrates on working out the anti-democratic and domination-affirming standpoint logic in which they are embedded. Most of the selected texts come from the 'middle' (ideology-critical) and the 'late' periods, and the investigation is interested here primarily in the impetus to verticalisation occurring in the transition from one to the other. When critiquing universalistic postulates of morality and truth, it is insufficient to appeal to Nietzsche's insight into the 'perspectivism' of seeing without being concerned about wherein the social perspectivism of his own seeing consists. Postmodern Nietzsche interpretation established itself as an integral part of what Domenico Losurdo con-

---

91   Cf. Rehmann 2018, pp. 220 et sqq.
92   Cf. on the early Nietzsche, Varela 2010.

vincingly criticised as a 'hermeneutic of innocence', which dissolves the most brutal avowals of elite rule and exterminism of the weak in melodious metaphors and allegories.[93] We are in need of a new deconstruction, which connects philological preciseness with a deciphering critique of domination and ideology.

VIII

For valuable criticism and suggestions I thank among others Gunter Gebauer, Winfield Goodwin, Wolfgang Fritz Haug, Sauli Havu, Peter Jehle, Brigitte Kahl, Tilman Reitz and Christoph Türcke. I would particularly like to thank the translators Kolja and Larry Swingle, who, in addition to their diligent translation and the enormous bibliographical search connected to it, helped me a lot with updating the book and with adapting it to the Anglo-Saxon context. It was a pleasure working with them.

Jan Rehmann, New York, March 2022

---

93   Cf. Losurdo 2020, pp. 609 et sq., 612, 614 et sq., 738 et sqq., 743 et sqq., 814 et sqq., 991 et sqq., 1009 et sq.

Deleuze and the Construction of a Plural-Differential Image of Nietzsche

1   Plural Differences Instead of Dialectical Contradictions

Deleuze's book *Nietzsche and Philosophy* is a settling of accounts with dialectics. He concludes that there is no possibility of a compromise between Nietzsche and Hegel because Nietzsche's entire philosophy was concerned with exposing the three principles of dialectic: namely the power of the negative as a theoretical principle (expressed in opposition and contradiction); the value of suffering and sadness as a practical principle (splitting, tearing apart); and positivity as both the theoretical and practical product of negativity. All of this goes back to a false image of difference, i.e. to a negation of that which differs [de ce qui diffère].[1]

In contrast, according to Nietzsche the will simply wants 'to affirm its own difference' and enjoy doing so.[2] *Difference* is also the term with which Deleuze's book begins, namely that of values. Kant did not accomplish a true critique because he did not know to pose their problem in terms of the 'values', or more exactly, in the underlying evaluations and value-*setting* criteria. Nietzsche does this. By raising the problem of their *creation*, he undertakes a reintroduction of the Kantian critique on new foundations and with new concepts.[3] He does this by introducing 'the high and the low, the noble and the base'. These categories designate no values in themselves, but 'represent the differential element, from which the value of the values themselves derive'.[4] They are what make a creative and active critique possible.[5]

Where 'difference' is established as a basic category, plurality is not far behind. The 'force' that represents the subject of the Deleuzean arrangement is 'plural'.[6] Nietzsche's philosophy is not understood as long as its 'essential plur-

---

1   Deleuze 2013, pp. 184 et sq.; Deleuze 1962, pp. 223 et sq.
2   Deleuze 2013, pp. 8 et sq.; Deleuze 1962, p. 10.
3   Deleuze 2013, pp. 1, 48; Deuleuze 1962, pp. 1, 59.
4   Deleuze 2013, pp. 1 et sq.; Deleuze 1962, p. 2.
5   Deleuze 2013, p. 3; Deleuze 1962, p. 3.
6   Deleuze 2013, pp. 6 et sq. 'L'être de la force est le pluriel; il serait proprement absurde de penser la force au singulier.' (Deleuze 1962, p. 7).

alism' is not considered, and this is nothing less than the 'only guarantor of freedom in the concrete spirit' and ultimately the fiercest and sole opponent of dialectic.[7]

Here we see Deleuze with a lot of pathos setting up an opposition in which philosophical and political frontlines overlap and mutually strengthen each other. Not just since the *Nouveaux Philosophes* of the 80s, but already for the prior-to-68s-Deleuze, 'difference' and 'plurality' stand against the 'totalitarianism' of dialectic. 'We are listening to Radio Free Nietzsche', one could quip with Geoff Waite, who directs this mockery against Georges Bataille's announcement shortly after 1945, that Nietzsche is now the only liberal alternative to Marxism.[8] Beyond that, in Deleuze's anti-dialectical stance a general paradigm change in philosophy announces itself, one in which a metaphysics of identity is declared to be the general denominator of the prevailing 'western' history of philosophy and replaced by concepts of preceding and underlying differentiation. Common among the different efforts is the strategy of countering the traditional line of identity philosophy, so to speak on the same ontological level, with the concept of a 'primary' autonomous play of differences. In this sense, for example, Derrida's concept of *différance* denotes an 'original' activity of difference, or more exactly, a movement of play which 'produces' the differences as effects, and indeed in such a way that they cannot be subordinated to an identity concept any longer.[9] In the attempt at an original founding of the difference one could recur to Heidegger among others, who had called the difference between *Sein* [Being] and *Seiendem* [beings] the 'ontological difference' and later emphatically articulated this as 'the distinction of all distinctions' and as 'the beginning of all distinguishing'.[10]

The poststructuralist rejection of identity philosophy is typically portrayed as a challenge to the model of Plato, in which differences represent only secondary deviations from self-identical original ideas. Here, the objects themselves function as mere copies of an original image. There are many couches and tables, said Plato in the *Politeia*, 'but as for ideas for these furnishings, there

---

7   Deleuze 2013, pp. 4, 8; Deleuze 1962, pp. 4 et sq., 9.
8   Waite 1996, p. 186.
9   In his lecture, 'La différance' before the *Société Française de philosophie* on January 1968 Derrida specifies the term as the 'activity of the originary' difference – 'l'activité de la différence, originaire', or as 'that movement of play, which "produces" these differences, these effects of the difference, by that which is not simply activity – le mouvement de jeu qui, "produit", par ce qui n'est pas simplement une activité, ces différences, ces effets de différence' (Derrida 1986, pp. 14, 17; Derrida 1972, pp. 12, 15).
10   Heidegger 1999, p. 105; Heidegger 1998, p. 151; cf. also for this Muck (1972), Probst (1972), Knebel (2001).

are presumably two, one of couch, one of table'. If the *Idea* or the *Eidos* has been made by a God, its conversion to material products takes place via a craftsman class, while the illustration of the products is carried out by painters and other imitators.[11] This progression from divine 'image maker' to 'artefact maker' and finally to the artistic 'imitator' reflects an increasing distance from the truth, so that poetry, sculpture and painting are counted in the *Sophistes* as the production of illusory images.[12]

Poststructuralist criticism is applied primarily at two points of this construction: on one hand it inverts the subordination of the differences under an originating idea, on the other hand it questions the Platonic distinction between adequate image and illusion (*eidolon*, or in the translation of Lucretius: *rerum simulacrum*) by declaring the simulacra to be the location of the constitutive play of differences. 'Deleuze's inversion consists in granting to the simulacra its own model, the model of difference in itself ..., a world without prior identity and without internal resemblance, a world full of monsters of energy, demonic visitations, and dark precursors'.[13] Baudrillard will take up this thread when he characterises representation as a 'theology of truth and secrecy', and opposes it to simulation.[14] 'Whereas representation attempts to absorb simulation by interpreting it as as a false representation, simulation envelops the whole edifice of representation itself as a simulacrum.'[15]

The front against Hegel is more complicated because here the concept of identity is connected from the beginning with the concept of an 'autonomous negation',[16] which has the ability to apply to itself in a self-referential manner (negation of the negation), and in this way bring forth an affirmation. This 'power of the negative as a theoretical principle' is attacked by Deleuze, in particular because it would lead to the subordination of difference and diversity under the 'development of the opposite or contradiction'.[17] His critique, which here dispenses with any bibliographic reference, probably aims at Hegel's reflection-logical development from identity to difference to opposite and contradiction. Self identity is already defined as negativity, i.e. as abstrac-

---

11   Plato, Republic x, 596b et sqq.
12   Plato, Sophistes 236a–b; see among other things for this Haug (1994, pp. 7 et sqq.); Franz (1995, pp. 228 et sqq.). Nietzsche criticises the exclusion of the ingenious artist from the Platonic state as 'rigid consequence ... of the Socratic judgement of the arts' (Nietzsche 1999a, Vol. 7, p. 349).
13   Ansell Pearson 1999, p. 17.
14   Baudrillard 2010, pp. 5 et sqq.
15   Baudrillard 2010, p. 6.
16   Henrich 1976, p. 215.
17   Deleuze 2013, pp. 148, 184; Deleuze 1962, pp. 181, 223.

tion from all difference,[18] and contains a diversity, which, if it is not to be 'external', is based on a contradiction (as the unity of identity and diversity).[19] Difference as such 'is already implicitly contradiction', and the contradiction 'is only the developed nothing which is contained in the identity'.[20] The *Vorstellung* [picture-thinking] forgets the 'negative unity' and is content with the indifferent diversity of the definitions, but the '*thoughtful* reason sharpens, as it were, the blunt difference of diverse terms, the mere manifold of representation, to *essential* distinction, to *opposition*'.[21] Here Hegel formulates the specific subordination of the differences under the dialectical contradiction: 'Only when driven to the extreme of contradiction are the many of that manifold quickened and alive to each other: they hold the negativity in them which is the inner pulse of self-movement and life'.[22]

To the extent that dialectic is identified with this Hegelian ontology, Deleuze can object with some justice that it ignores 'the far more subtle and subterranean differential mechanisms'.[23] Tilman Reitz argues that this objection, taken for itself, could open the possibility of bringing into view various differences, frictions and conflicts which then unite in oppositions, and this could help comprehend 'the situativeness of opposites in changing relations of difference'.[24] Adorno had pointed out in *Negative Dialectics* that the contradiction is not 'what Hegel's absolute idealism was bound to transfigure it into: it is not of the essence in a Heraclitean sense. It indicates the untruth of identity'.[25] In this sense, the method of dialectical sublation [Aufhebung] of contradictions can be defined as their freeing from polar solidification and their retranslation into differences.[26] To be sure, such a liquefaction does not mean to defuse the opposition and remove it from the world by re-baptising it as mere difference. This happened e.g. in Croce's 'dialectic of distinctions', which Gramsci criticised as a 'degenerate and mutilated form of Hegelianism', driven by a blind fear of Jacobin movements – a diluted version, according to which

---

18   Hegel 2010, pp. 355 et sq.; Hegel 1986b, pp. 38 et sq.

19   Hegel 2010, p, 367, Hegel 1986b, p. 55.

20   Hegel 2010, pp. 373 et sq., 381 et sq.; Hegel 1986b, pp. 65, 74 et sq.

21   Hegel 2010, pp. 383 et sq.; Hegel 1986b, pp. 77 et sq.

22   Hegel 2010, p. 384; Hegel 1986b, p. 78.

23   Deleuze 2013, p. 149.

24   Reitz 2001, pp. 34 et sq.

25   Adorno 1973, p. 5.

26   Something similar is suggested by Baecker with the term of negation: he specifies it as a 'technique for making distinctions among already made differentiations' and as procedure for their 'marking'. For this one must 'return them to the practice of distinction which makes them visible'. (Baecker 1996, pp. 98, 101 et sq.).

the thesis is not to be destroyed by the antithesis, but just 'preserved' by it, finding its way into the synthesis.[27] Instead of a flattening out of this kind, dialectics requires a serious 'opposition-work' [Gegensatz-Arbeit], i.e. practical working through and 'talking through' – this is the Greek sense of the word dialectic – of rigidified opposites and contradictions of social life and personal existence.

Precisely at this point at which postmodern critique of metaphysics could become operative, Deleuze sidesteps the challenge. He rejects working on oppositions in the name of difference, which is for him the 'only principle of genesis or production ... which itself produces opposition as mere appearance'.[28] However, to declare the development of oppositions to be 'mere appearance' overleaps speculatively the fact that in social reality many of the varied differences are actually merged into antagonisms and thus consolidated. To the extent that Deleuze merely inverts the Platonic dichotomy of original-image, truth-appearance, he remains within the logic of the essentialism which he pretends to challenge. The attacked metaphysics of negation and contradiction is replaced by a metaphysics of difference, by which all the constellations which contain more and other than indifferent multiplicities are rendered unreal.

This makes the Deleuzean critique of dialectic weaker than it first appears in the pathos-filled announcement of its overcoming. The all-out attack is based on two basic methodical decisions: namely on one hand to regard dialectic not as a contradictory theory form, a method disputed in its meaning and execution, but to identify it with the speculative form that Hegel gave it, primarily in his logic; and on the other hand, to counter the speculative principle of negation, opposition and contradiction with the no less speculative difference 'principle'.

The reductionism of this definition of dialectics becomes evident when one looks at the many differences it levels out in the name of 'difference'. In no way must speaking of oppositions mean adopting the Hegelian conceptual play of negation and contradiction. Because contrary to 'diremption' [Entzweiung] the concept of opposition does not refer back to a prior unity, and contrary to 'contradiction' [Widerspruch] it refers primarily to real relations [Realverhältnisse]

---

27   Gramsci 1995, pp. 341–3; Gramsci 1975, Q. 10.I, §6; cf. 1995, pp. 399–401; Gramsci 1975, Q. 10.II, §41.X. Croce had suggested to supplement the Hegelian oppositions dialectic with a 'dialectic of distinctions', according to which 'a distinct concept is presupposed by and lives in its other, which follows it in the sequence of ideas.' (Croce 1969, p. 9).

28   Deleuze 2013, p. 149; Deleuze 1962, p. 181.

and is 'not formed from the standpoint of an overall systemic connection'.[29] A prominent example is the concept of a 'real opposition without contradiction' that Kant developed in his *Attempt to Introduce the Concept of Negative Magnitudes into Philosophy* (1763): he differentiated there between a type of opposition which is logically formed by contradiction, and one which is 'real, that is to say, without contradiction': characterised by 'real opposition' [Realrepugnanz].[30] This means that the forces themselves are 'something truly positive', that are only 'opposed to the positive magnitude'.[31] Seen this way, the concept of opposition has nothing at all to do with the 'power of the negative as theoretical principle' as Deleuze assumes. 'Real opposites are not, as in contradiction, negatives in themselves', argues, for example, Colletti: 'The negation which each exerts on the other consists only in the fact that they mutually annul their effects. ... [In a] relation of contrariety (*Gegenverhältnis*), the extremes are both positive, even when one of them is indicated as the negative contrary of the other'.[32]

In this sense one can speak of a dialectical line counter to Hegel's speculation – a 'counter-line', which can sometimes also be found in Hegel's writings themselves, namely to the extent to which he develops his formulations of contradiction from the historical material. This line emerges again and again where it is not a concern to legitimise the regulated functioning of an overall system (philosophical or political), but where the primary concern is deciphering the inner strife of the world as opposed to metaphysical unitary constructions. Thus Feuerbach intends to lead the dialectic back from Hegel's construct of an absolute knowledge into the dialogical again, with which the real oppositions of the human species-being can be talked through: 'The true dialectic' is not 'a monologue of a solitary thinker with himself; it is a dialogue between I and thou', is how it is stated in the *Principles of the Philosophy of the Future*.[33] Marx, who certifies that Feuerbach 'annihilated the dialectics of concepts, the war of the gods that was known to the philosophers alone',[34] describes his own dialectical method as 'the direct opposite' of the Hegelian. According to Marx's approach, dialectic's 'rational form' as opposed to Hegel's 'mystified form' is a method which 'regards every historically developed social form as the fluid state of its motion, and therefore grasps its transient aspect as well; and because

---

29   Reitz 2001, pp. 14 et sqq.; cf. pp. 22 et sq.
30   Kant 1992a, p. 211; Kant 1968a, p. 783.
31   Kant 1992a, p. 209, Kant 1968a, p. 781.
32   Colletti 1975, p. 7.
33   Ludwig Feuerbach 1966, § 62, p. 72.
34   Marx and Engels 1845a, p. 93; Marx and Engels 1957–, Vol. 2, p. 98.

it does not let itself be impressed by anything, being in its very essence critical and revolutionary'.[35]

With Marx, dialectic 'is translated into history, whereby everything preconstructed is to be left behind', and this radical this-worldliness 'makes the relationship to the initiator, Hegel, problematic', argues Haug.[36] However, in the follow-up there comes a re-ontologisation by Engels, who defined his philosophy of nature as a 'science of universal inter-connection' with fixed 'main laws'.[37] This kind of expansion contradicts the note by Marx, even in Marxism hardly evaluated, that it is a matter of a dialectics 'whose limits have to be defined', and 'which does not abolish real difference'.[38] The passage refers to the difference between real object and cognition object, which the Hegelian dialectic lets coincide in the development of the spirit.[39] But beyond that, an operational meaning of dialectic is suggested here by Marx, with which the 'real differences' are not subordinated to a preconstructed logic of contradiction, but are themselves the starting point for an analysis of opposition and contradiction.

Therefore, to the extent that poststructuralism's anti-metaphysical claim is serious, it could find ample intersections with Marx's praxis-philosophical approach. Deleuze fails to see that a fissure goes through dialectics itself, one which is connected ultimately with oppositional positions in the power fields of social domination: as Adorno remarks in *Minima Moralia*,[40] dialectics has on one hand 'subsequently developed, as against philosophia perennis, into a perennial method of criticism, a refuge for all the thoughts of the oppressed, even those unthought by them', on the other hand, 'as a means of proving oneself right, it was also from the first an instrument of domination, a formal technique of apologetics'. Bertolt Brecht described the dialectical method of critique in the *Meti* as the ability 'to recognise and make use of processes in things. It

---

35   Marx 1867, pp. 19 et sq.; cf. Marx 1976, pp. 102 et sq. (translation modified); Marx and Engels 1957–, Vol. 23, pp. 27 et sq.

36   Haug 1995, p. 662.

37   E.g. Engels 1878, p. 313; Marx and Engels 1957–, Vol. 20, p. 307.

38   Marx 1857a, p. 46; Marx and Engels 1957–, Vol. 13, 640. A second reference is the remark in the *Urtext* that the dialectical form of representation is only correct, 'if it knows its limits' (Marx and Engels 1975–, Vol. 11.1.1, p. 43, Marx 1953, p. 945). On the philological evaluation of the Marxian passages on the 'Limits of Dialectic', cf. Haug (2001c).

39   Marx 1857a, pp. 37 et sq.; Marx and Engels 1957–, Vol. 13, pp. 631 et sq. In the *Phenomenology of Spirit* the dialectical presentation is 'this course that generates itself, going forth from, and returning to, itself', which 'constitutes what formerly the proof was supposed to accomplish' (Hegel, 1977 [1807], pp. 39 et sq.; Hegel 1986a, p. 61).

40   Adorno 1974, No. 152, p. 244.

teaches how to ask questions that make action possible'.[41] For Walter Benjamin being a dialectician is 'having the wind of history in one's sails. The sails are the concepts. ... What is decisive, is knowing the art of setting them'.[42] Of course, here 'history' is not conceived teleologically in the sense of progress happening through prior determination. In his homogenised construction of dialectics Deleuze not only said farewell to the critical and subversive applications of the dialectical art of detection, but also undercut its analytic potentials by his metaphysics of non-opposing differences.

2   Deleuze's Combination of Hume's Empiricism and Bergson's Vitalism

This is due, among other things, to the fact that even before his Nietzsche book Deleuze had already gained the anti-dialectical use of the 'difference' from his own peculiar combination of empiricist and vitalist approaches. An early indication of this can be found in his book about David Hume, *Empirisme et subjectivité*, from 1953. Deleuze sees Hume's merit in his having grasped the given far from any kind of transcendental speculation, as a 'flux du sensible, une collection d'impressions et d'images, un ensemble de perceptions'.[43] He explains the anti-transcendental thrust of empiricism by Hume's assumption of a 'progressive sequence of distinct perceptions', or more exactly a moving succession of perceptions, *to the extent* that they are distinct – 'en tant qu'elles sont distinctes'.[44] Based on this emphasis, Deleuze now concludes: What assigns constitutive status to experience in empiricism, is the 'principle of the difference'.[45]

The accentuation of a difference principle of this kind cannot be confirmed by Hume's argumentation in the *Treatise*. Certainly, for Hume the perceptions are not transcendentally unified, and are to this extent differentiated and multiform. But the 'simple impressions' on which he establishes his theory of knowledge are characterised by the fact that they permit neither distinction nor separation, and what interests Hume here in particular is how they are connected by the relationship of 'similarity' into complex impressions.[46] Aside from

41   Bertolt Brecht 2016, p. 85.
42   Benjamin 1999, p. 473.
43   Deleuze 1953, p. 92.
44   Deleuze 1953, p. 93.
45   Ibid.
46   Hume 1978 [1739], I.I.I. Impressions are associated 'only by resemblance' (ibid., II.I.4).

similarity, the linkage of ideas has still other modes of linkage (e.g. contiguity, causation), but Hume deliberately does not reckon difference among them, because he regards it 'rather as a negation of relation, than as anything real or positive'.[47] In any case, there is no talk of a 'principle of difference' with Hume. The quotation from which Deleuze attempted to deduce such a 'principle' says nothing more than that separable objects are also distinguishable, and as distinguishable are also different.[48]

There are many indications that the Deleuzean search for a 'principle' attempts to inherit Hume's empiricism right where it has its weakest points: where Hume is *not* able to develop his central concept of 'habit' from social life, and therefore declares it to be a principle of nature, Deleuze emphasises approvingly that Hume is interested not in genesis but only in principles.[49] Hume is uncritically praised where he naturalises *habit*, which is of course due to the fact that he lacks the conceptual instruments for a social-analytic explanation, e.g. a sociological *habitus*-concept in the sense of Bourdieu. It is questionable whether dialectics (also the Hegelian) can be seriously challenged from the point of view of this kind of dogmatic and anti-genetic setting of 'principles'.

Deleuze adopted the critique of negation in the name of affirmation primarily from the vitalism of Bergson, with which he concerned himself in 1956 in two essays.[50] In his *Évolution créative* of 1907, to which Deleuze primarily refers, Bergson attempted to prove that the 'nothingness' which concerns so many philosophies is, from the point of view of the positive movement of life, only a 'pseudo idea' and 'a mere word', the negation nothing but an affirmation of second degree.[51] As soon as one approaches 'being' by way of 'nothingness' it is conceived statically (order fills the emptiness of the disorder, etc.), but as soon as one seeks to grasp it directly, and as 'duration' – and this cannot be done through dialectic, but only through 'intuition' – it shows itself as the movement of life, driven by an original *élan vital*.[52] Not to have seen

47   Hume 1978 [1739], I.I.5.
48   Deleuze 1991a, pp. 87 et sq.; Deleuze 1953, p. 93. 'Whatever objects are separable are also distinguishable, and whatever objects are distinguishable are also different.' (Hume 1978 [1739], I.I.7).
49   Deleuze 1991a, pp. 108 et sq.; Deleuze 1953, p. 122. 'Habit is nothing but one of the principles of nature, and derives all its force from that origin' (Hume 1978 [1739], I.III.16).
50   Deleuze 1956a, pp. 292–299 and Deleuze 1956b, pp. 77–113.
51   Bergson 1998, pp. 276 et sqq., 283, 288.
52   Bergson 1998, pp. 87 et sqq., 298. For the relationship between dialectic and intuition and/or between intellect and intuition see e.g. Bergson 1966, pp. 239 et sq., 267 et sq. Ultimately, philosophy has the task to take intelligence back into the intuition [réabsorber l'intelligence dans l'intuition] (Bergson 1966, p. 271).

the meaning of this positive vital impetus in evolution is the main reproach directed at Darwinism.[53]

'Bergson contains much that remains important for an appreciation of Deleuze's thinking', in the opinion of Ansell Pearson, who traces back to the influence of Bergson the later considerations in *Anti-Oedipus* and in *A Thousand Plateaus* with respect to the organs as barriers to life.[54] Unfortunately, he is so fascinated by this connection that it doesn't occur to him to critically evaluate its claim to overcome dialectic. Bergson conceives of 'life' as a kind of vital anti-matter, a river of consciousness, or 'super-consciousness', which in the transition from the animal realm to the human leaves the prison of matter. 'Life' is an ascending tide, which opposes the descending movement of matter.[55] And when Bergson shares his intuitions about the fundamental meaning of this idealistic life current, it is not done nearly as differentially as one would assume from Deleuze's account. Where Deleuze sees in Bergson the 'vital difference' and the 'difference in the living' at work, Bergson emphasises the ability of his life impulse to create the unity of the organised world [l' unité du monde organisé, unité féconde].[56] The tremendous wave of life spreads out from 'a centre' [se propage à partir d'un centre], and when it appears as if it would divide itself into different individualities, then this is only because of the matter which it carries along with it, and into whose gaps it inserts itself – all these differences are simply the result of consciousness adjusting itself to matter.[57] Life itself is an 'impulsion unique, inverse du mouvement de la matière, et, en elle-même, indivisible', humankind is presented as an 'immense army' which gallops beside, before and behind each one of us, and overruns all resistances.[58]

As Horkheimer observes, Bergson's philosophy 'reduces the whole world to a single eternal essence'.[59] 'Thinking here seeks to be as fluid as life, even more fluid. ... For the Bergson of the élan vital there exist no things, only calculable causes, not even purposes: ... its course [is] constant change, constant novelty of beginning', summarises Bloch in *Heritage of our Times*.[60] In *The Principle of Hope* the critique is stated more precisely: that which Bergson presents as a *novum* 'is impressionistic, and liberal-anarchistic, not anticipatory. ... Where

---

53 Bergson 1998, p. 106.
54 Pearson 1999, pp. 40 et sqq.
55 Bergson 1966, pp. 261, 264, 266 et sq. 'Un flot qui monte, et que contrarie le mouvement descendant de matière' (Bergson 1966, p. 269).
56 Bergson 1998, p. 106; Bergson 1966, p. 106.; cf. Deleuze 1956b, p. 92; Deleuze 1968a, p. 102.
57 Bergson 1966, pp. 266, 270.
58 Bergson 1966, p. 271.
59 Horkheimer 2005, p. 12; Horkheimer 1988, p. 233.
60 Bloch 1991, pp. 319 et sq.

everything ought to be constantly new, everything remains just as it was'.[61] Instead of criticising dialectical teleology for its 'pre-arranged' goal, he eliminates 'any and every trace of the onward, the Where To and any openly pursuable goal whatsoever'.[62] Helpful for a critique of vitalist anti-dialectic is above all Bloch's observation that movement of this kind, conceived as a 'principle', tips over into immobility, congeals 'into that equally dead antithesis to repetition which reduces the New to a merely endless, contentless zigzag'.[63] The process remains empty, the Futurum ends in a 'l'art pour l'art of vitality', the stream of consciousness contains almost nothing more of an actual stream, but becomes 'stationary in itself': 'Élan vital and nothing more is and remains itself a Fixum of contemplation'.[64] Also Adorno observes that, raised to an absolute, 'pure becoming, the pure act' tips over into the same timelessness which Bergson criticises in metaphysics since Plato and Aristotle: 'The dialectical salt was washed away in an undifferentiated tide of life, ... The hate of the rigid general concept established a cult of irrational immediacy, of sovereign freedom in the midst of unfreedom'.[65]

Bergson's vitalism gives us an indication of some paradoxes in the Deleuzean critique of dialectic. Just as Bergson's movement principle solidified to immobility, here, too, a connection of qualitative changes cannot be thought using the instruments of a culture of difference without opposition. 'What remains is a multiplicity of formally equivalent particularist interests, of which actually those which are economic and state-power related assert themselves most strongly'.[66] Whereas dialectical critique leaves behind philosophical speculation and directs its view toward the actual oppositions in society, postmodern critique of dialectic takes the path back into philosophical speculation; whereas dialectical critique encounters real differences, the Deleuzian critique of dialectic is content with conjuring up a 'difference principle' while erasing the real differences in what is critiqued. In the name of a most radical critique of metaphysics nothing is more passionately pursued than work on a new metaphysics – a 'philosophy of origins in the garb of deconstruction'.[67] It is this tension between rhetoric and actual procedure which will meet us again and again.

61   Bloch 1986, p. 140.
62   Bloch 1986, pp. 140 et sq.
63   Bloch 1986, p. 140.
64   Bloch 1986, pp. 201 et sq. and 291.
65   Adorno 1973, pp. 8 et sq.
66   Reitz 2001, p. 15.
67   Roth 2000, p. 134.

3   Nietzsche as Anti-Dialectician?

Almost all the features that we connect with postmodernism and neostructuralism today, from the dismissal of mediation to the decentring of the subject, 'go back to Deleuze's resurrection of Nietzsche against Hegel', notes Cornel West.[68] It is appropriate to take a closer look at this wide-reaching anti-
Hegelian resurrection of Nietzsche. The fact that in the different phases of his
work Nietzsche criticised both dialectics generally, as well as the philosophy of
Hegel in particular, is undisputed, but the question is whether this was carried
out for the reason and in the way Deleuze ascribes to him.

The early Nietzsche of 1870 had characterised Socrates' and Plato's aspira-
tion to overcome political conflict and the art of rhetorical controversy (Eristik)
through a dialectical-consensual finding of the truth as the 'optimism of dialectics', and criticised it as an identity-philosophical 'metaphysics of logic'.[69] If
he rejects dialectical philosophy as 'imperativist and aggressive', then this is not
because of its 'negativity', but because of its idealistic truth-optimism.[70] What
caused Nietzsche to become the opponent of Hegelian historical teleology is,
initially, by no means an 'affirmation' of life, but instead Schopenhauerian pessimism, which he considers to be superior to Hegel's 'incurable optimism'.[71] The
disassociation from Hegel's 'trite' or 'cow-like' optimism is a line of thought
which runs through all of Nietzsche's phases from this point onwards.[72] As
Nietzsche puts it, retrospectively, in his last published writing, *Nietzsche contra
Wagner*, he saw pessimism as the 'symptom of a greater strength of thought, of
a more triumphant fullness of life, than had found expression in the philosophy
of Hume, Kant, and Hegel'.[73]

But in fact, Nietzsche's criticism of dialectical 'optimism' is crossed with a
critique of dialectical 'negation', which is interpreted as plebeian questioning
of aristocratic domination. When with Socrates the Greek taste changes 'in
favour of dialectics', this means that 'with dialectics the rabble gets on top' –
and this 'can be only a last-ditch weapon, in the hands of those who have
no other weapons left'.[74] To the extent that dialectic is attacked as a sign of

68   West 1999, p. 283.
69   Nietzsche 1999a, Vol. 7, p. 134.
70   Nietzsche 1999a, Vol. 7, p. 388.
71   Nietzsche 2003a, pp. 36 et sq.; Nietzsche 1999a, Vol. 1, pp. 191 et sq.
72   Cf. e.g. Nietzsche 1999b, pp. 164 et sq.; Nietzsche 1999a, Vol. 7, p. 595; Nietzsche 1999a, Vol. 8,
        p. 57, Nietzsche 1999a, Vol. 13, p. 536.
73   Nietzsche 1982, p. 669; Nietzsche 1999a, Vol. 6, pp. 424 et sq.
74   Nietzsche 1968a, pp. 41 et sq.; Nietzsche 1999a, Vol. 6, pp. 69 et sq.

plebeian 'revenge' and 'resentment of the rabble',[75] it is at the same time a component of the 'reversal of values' which was introduced by the 'Jews' and further propagated by the Christians:[76] 'The Jew is dialectician: and Socrates was also one', is written in a second version of the passage from the *Twilight of the Idols*.[77] As Domenico Losurdo has observed, Nietzsche works here on the direct fusion of the two ideological figures, the Jewish-Christian tradition and the Socratic-Platonic philosophy, which are in his view ultimately responsible for the intellectual culture of the subversive democratic cycle resulting from the French Revolution.[78] In this confrontation with the 'democratic age' what is dangerous above all is the alliance between a 'plebeian' spirit of subversion and revolt and an historical optimism produced by dialectic.

Nietzsche's confrontation with Hegel does not completely coincide with his general critique of dialectics, but is subjected to complicated fluctuations. Naturally, Nietzsche's critique of optimism must also be directed against Hegel's teleology.[79] Hegel is the one who taught the generations, which he 'made thoroughly sour', to admire the 'power of history' and the success which Nietzsche describes as the 'idolatry of the factual'.[80] What here in the confrontation with Hegel-epigonism is articulated as exposing intellectual mediocrity, receives a somewhat different colouring in other contexts. In the sharp turn of the late Nietzsche against 'the English', Kant, Hegel, Schopenhauer, and Goethe stand together as representatives of German depth against the 'English mechanical stultification of the world' by Hobbes, Hume and Locke: in England what is lacking is 'real power of intellect, real depth of intellectual perception, in short, philosophy'.[81] Hegel's philosophy is repeatedly appealed to as the embodiment of the 'German' spirit, of the 'contradictory-nature of the German soul', etc., whereby the meanings vary between positive appreciation and ironical dissociation.[82] The evaluation is again different when it concerns the

---

75   Nietzsche 1968a, p. 42; Nietzsche 1999a, Vol. 6, p. 70.

76   Cf. e.g. Nietzsche 1997, pp. 63 et sq.; Nietzsche 2013a, p. 22; Nietzsche 1999a, Vol. 5, pp. 116 et sq., 267.

77   Nietzsche 1999a, Vol. 14, p. 414. Somewhat similar is Plato, the philosopher 'who had already picked up Jewish habits (– in Egypt?)' (Nietzsche 1999a, Vol. 12, p. 580), 'the instinctual anti-Hellene and Semite' (Nietzsche 1999a, Vol. 13, p. 114), 'who perhaps went to school with the Jews' (264). 'When Socrates and Plato took sides with the party of virtue and justice they were *Jews*'. (Nietzsche 1999a, Vol. 13, p. 331).

78   Losurdo 2020, pp. 466 et sq., 564 et sq.

79   Nietzsche 1999b, pp. 225 et sq.; Nietzsche 1999a, Vol. 7, pp. 660 et sq.

80   Nietzsche 2003a, pp. 143 et sq.; Nietzsche 1999a, Vol. 1, p. 309.

81   Nietzsche 1997, p. 117; Nietzsche 1999a, Vol. 5, p. 195.

82   'We Germans are Hegelians, even though there had never been a Hegel, inasmuch as we … instinctively attribute to becoming, to evolution, a profounder significance … than to that

comparison with Kant. Whereas Kant erects an otherworldly realm of moral values, Hegel demonstrates 'a provable development, visible becoming of the moral realm'.[83] Even if Nietzsche rejects both moral philosophies because 'we' no longer believe in morality,[84] he notes attentively the Hegelian orientation toward the state as an historical achievement: Hegel's success against romantic sensitivity is owing to his belief in 'the greater reason on the side of the victorious ones', as well as his 'justification of the real "State" (in place of "humanity" etc.)'.[85] In contrast to this, Kant with his 'moral Fanaticism' is still completely eighteenth century, 'without any view for the reality of his time, ... fantast of the concept of duty'.[86] In turn, Hegel's orientation to the state is perceived with ambivalence, since on one hand the state makes possible the preservation of 'so many losers', and on the other hand also can protect a few geniuses 'in whom humanity will culminate'.[87]

The diversity of these and other passages suggests that there is a multilevel dialectic in Nietzsche's relationship to Hegel which should not be forced into a rigid opposition. If Hegel is an antipode to Nietzsche, then this is also and not least in the sense of a rival to be overcome, someone whom he admires and at the same time envies, and whom he attempts to combat with his own weapons. As Nietzsche's *Ecce Homo* claims in hindsight, *The Birth of Tragedy* was actually not influenced by Schopenhauer, but smells 'offensively Hegelian':[88] 'An "idea" – the antithesis of the Dionysian and the Apollonian – translated into the realm of metaphysics; history itself as the development of this "idea"; in tragedy this antithesis is sublimated into a unity'.[89] Then, in the transition to his middle, 'ideology critical' phase, Nietzsche attempts to get rid of this kind of idealism, as a 'higher swindle', by resorting to the natural sciences.[90] But it is the late Nietzsche who applies the term 'grandiose initiative' to Hegel's philosophical overcoming of the moral god by means of pantheism, 'in which evil, error and suffering are not felt to be arguments against divinity'.[91] Contrary

which "is"' (Nietzsche 2017, p. 144; Nietzsche 1999a, Vol. 3, p. 599; translation modified). Cf. Nietzsche 1984, pp. 120 et sq.; Nietzsche 1999a, Vol. 3, pp. 166 et sq. and Nietzsche 1999a, Vol. 7, p. 109.

83   Nietzsche 1999a, Vol. 12, p. 162.
84   Nietzsche 1999a, Vol. 12, p. 163.
85   Nietzsche 1999a, Vol. 12, p. 442.
86   Nietzsche 1999a, Vol. 12, p. 443.
87   Nietzsche 1999b, p. 226; Nietzsche 1999a, Vol. 7, p. 661.
88   Nietzsche 2000, p. 726; Nietzsche 1999a, Vol. 6, p. 310.
89   Nietzsche 2000, p. 727; Nietzsche 1999a, Vol. 6, p. 310.
90   Cf. Nietzsche 2000, pp. 739 et sqq.; Nietzsche 1999a, Vol. 6, pp. 322 et sqq.
91   Nietzsche 2000b pp. 79; 83 et sq.; Nietzsche 1999a, Vol. 12, pp. 113, 126.

to Deleuze's anti-dialectical interpretation, Nietzsche here appreciates a Hegel who replaces the dichotomies of a moral philosophy with a dialectical concept of oppositions which are mutually conditioning and penetrating. Of course, Nietzsche's attacks on Hegel's 'theology', his 'Gothic heaven storming', 'pantheistic steams', 'Swabian trust in God', etc. are numerous,[92] but these polemics do not deter him from transferring components of his dialectical method of thinking to his own historical conception. Deleuze's anti-dialectical interpretation of Nietzsche misses the fact that he was certainly interested 'to use all forms of dialectical incorporation when it suits his pleasure'.[93]

That Nietzsche thinks much more 'dialectically' than Deleuze wants to admit can be demonstrated with an example in the third part of the *Genealogy of Morals* in which the 'self-contradiction' of the ascetic denial of life is analysed.[94] Paradoxically, the ascetic ideal arises from its opposite, argues Nietzsche, namely from 'the prophylactic self-preservative instincts' of life; in the ascetic denial of life and with its assistance, life struggles against death. It is a 'stratagem for the preservation of life'.[95] To that extent the ascetic priest, 'this apparent enemy of life, this denier ... is among the vital conserving and affirming forces of life. ... His "no", which he utters to life, brings to light as if by magic an abundance of gentler affirmations; even when he wounds himself, this master of destruction, of self-destruction, it is subsequently the wound itself that compels him to live'.[96]

This intriguing tension of an oppositional dynamics is obviously something quite different from the thinking in 'plural' differences that Deleuze perceives. And as with Hegel, the opposites which are set in motion push towards a 'self sublation': first the ascetic priest serves the philosophers as 'appearance' or 'grub' form, without which they would not be at all possible,[97] but between content and form a conflict unfolds which bursts the latter open. According to the *Gay Science*, what has triumphed over the Christian god is 'Christian morality itself, the concept of veracity, taken ever more strictly, the confessional subtlety of the Christian conscience, translated and sublimated to the scientific conscience'.[98] The *Genealogy of Morals*, in which this passage is taken up, drives

---

92   For example, Nietzsche 1999a, Vol. ll, pp. 151 et sq., 253, 262, 605; Nietzsche 1999a, Vol. 13, p. 536.
93   Waite 1996, p. 108.
94   Nietzsche 2013a, p. 104; Nietzsche 1999a, Vol. 5, p. 363.
95   Nietzsche 2013a, p. 106; Nietzsche 1999a, Vol. 5, p. 366.
96   Nietzsche 2013a, pp. 107 et sq.; Nietzsche 1999a, Vol. 5, pp. 366 et sq.
97   Nietzsche 2013a, p. 102; Nietzsche 1999a, Vol. 5, pp. 360 et sq.
98   Nietzsche 2017b, p. 144; Nietzsche 1999a, Vol. 3, p. 600. In the *Dawn*, Nietzsche proclaims that morality is terminated and indeed 'Out of morality! ... Fulfilling itself in us is, in case

the thought further: if Christianity as dogma went under as a result of its own morality, now morality must also go under to the extent that truthfulness asks the question, what does the will to truth actually mean?[99] It is not without irony that this thought, from which Foucault will derive his neo-Nietzschean concept of power (see below Chapter 3.4 and 5), is justified with a dialectical 'law of life': 'All great things perish by their own accord, by a deliberate act of self-destruction; this is the law of life, the law of necessary "self-conquest" in the essence of life'.[100]

The construction according to which the 'will to power' overcomes its opposite of asceticism and morality has been interpreted as a naturalistic variant of the Hegelian 'cunning of reason'.[101] The call for the 'revaluation of all values', with which Nietzsche ends the *Anti-Christ*,[102] answers to the first 'Jewish' and then primarily Pauline 'revaluation of all antique values' in a way which one can easily bring into the form of a negation of the negation.[103] In fact, in lieu of Deleuze's anti-dialectical interpretation, we can observe the opposite, namely that Nietzsche's texts unfold their intellectual and aesthetic attraction precisely to the extent that they make use of artful dialectic figures of thought. It is here that we also find interesting overlaps between Nietzsche and Marx regarding the dialectical 'liquefaction' of solidified ways of thinking and acting, although with different procedures and from opposite standpoints.

In contrast, Deleuze summarises his reading of Nietzsche in the following contrast:

> Nietzsche's 'yes' is opposed to the dialectical 'no'; the affirmation of dialectical negation; the difference to dialectical contradiction; joy, enjoyment, to dialectical labour; lightness, dance, to dialectical heaviness; beauteous irresponsibility [belle irresponsabilité] to dialectical responsibilities. The empirical feeling of difference, in short hierarchy, is the

---

you want a formula, the self-sublation of morality' (Nietzsche 2011, pp. 5 et sq.; Nietzsche 1999a, Vol. 3, p. 16).

99   Nietzsche 2013a, p. 143; Nietzsche 1999a, Vol. 5, p. 410.

100   Ibid.; Nietzsche 1999a, Vol. 5, p. 410.

101   E.g. Schweppenhäuser 1988, p. 81.

102   Nietzsche 1968b, p. 199; Nietzsche 1999a, Vol. 6, p. 253.

103   Cf. for the 'Jewish' revaluation among other things (Nietzsche 2013a, pp. 33 et sq.; Nietzsche 1999a, Vol. 5, p. 267; Nietzsche 1968b, pp. 146, 170; Nietzsche 1999a, Vol. 6, pp. 192, 220); the Christian 'God on the cross' – never before had there been such 'boldness in inversion, nor anything at once so dreadful, questioning, and questionable as this formula: it promised a transvaluation of all ancient values' (Nietzsche 1997, p. 34; Nietzsche 1999a, Vol. 5, p. 67).

essential motor of the concept, deeper and more effective than all thought about contradiction.[104]

We can regard this as an early document of a postmodern 'Lorianism'[105] which advertises itself as a hedonistic spectacle and makes fun of the dialectical strenuousness of the concept. The extent to which it misses the mark to represent dialectic as an enterprise of gloom is already evident in Brecht's literary project, where theatre is used for the sake of 'making pleasure' out of dialectic: the wit of contradictoriness produces 'entertainment from the aliveness of people, things and processes', enhances the 'art of living as well as its joyfulness'.[106] In contrast, Deleuze's anti-dialectic produces simple, pre-dialectical dichotomies, which also flatten the thoughts of Nietzsche into a caricature.[107] Not only the letters and the biographies, but also the published texts and posthumous writings provide plentiful evidence of how desperately Nietzsche's fatalistic 'yes' was wrested from illness and pessimism. According to *Ecce Homo*, Nietzsche owes his 'Amor fati' to 'great pain', 'that long, slow pain, in which we are burned with green wood, as it were'.[108] A dogmatic anti-dialectic reading must overlook the fact that Nietzsche's affirmation is infused with its opposite. When Deleuze unites the dichotomies affirmative/negative and active/reactive with the dichotomy pleasure/labour, he apparently adopts the Nietzschean master lineage of an antique slave owner society, in which work is considered beneath human dignity and philosophy is based on the leisure of contemplation. For Nietzsche's utopian aristocrats 'there must be those who sew togas for these men so that they don't walk around like beggars', and without them, 'the Dionysian dithyrambs would fall silent immediately', notes Horkheimer.[109]

And how are we to understand that Deleuze identifies the 'empirical feeling of difference', which we would so gladly understand in the sense of a sensitive perception of the other both in their otherness and as an equal, with that of an 'order of rank' [hiérarchie]? It seems that, if we wish to understand how Deleuze derives his 'difference' from the Nietzschean body of work, we must return to the text.

104   Deleuze 2013, p. 9; Deleuze 1962, p. 10.
105   Gramsci had termed as 'Lorianism' (derived from Achille Loria) the playful irresponsibility of the intellectuals (e.g. Gramsci 1975, Q. 9, § 28); cf. also for this Reitz 1997.
106   Brecht 1967, Vol. 16, p. 70.
107   Rogozinski pointed out the contradiction between the Deleuzean dismissal of opposites in the name of difference and his own construction of dichotomising opposites: 'The dramatising of the movement of thought by the appeal to bipolar contrasts seems ... to be a constant in the work of Deleuze' (Rogozinski 1996, p. 84).
108   Nietzsche 1982, p. 680; Nietzsche 1999a, Vol. 6, p. 436.
109   Horkheimer 1978, p. 32, Horkheimer 1974, p. 248.

4   The Birth of the Postmodern 'Difference' out of the 'Pathos of
       Distance'

A reference point can be found right at the beginning. According to Deleuze,
Nietzsche sets the 'pathos of difference or distance' in place of a transcendental foundation of value in the sense of Kantian universality or the 'simple
causal derivation' of utilitarianism.[110] The terms are used again immediately
thereafter for the definition of genealogy: 'difference or distance in the origin'.[111] Far more than 'difference', 'distance' is a well-known Nietzschean term,
used in the *Genealogy of Morals* (I, Aph. 2) to indicate the social gap between
the 'noble' and the 'low'.[112] Deleuze actually quotes the sentence from this text
which claims that it was from the 'pathos of distance' that 'they' first seized the
right to create values.[113] However, it does not become clear from the quoted text
fragment who is actually meant with 'they'.

       In Nietzsche's text those specified in the preceding sentence are the 'noble,
the powerful, those of high degree, the high-minded'. With the 'pathos of nobility and distance' Nietzsche means the 'feeling' of a 'higher race [Art] ... in comparison to a subservient "race" [Art], to a "below"'.[114] The specifics of the Nietzschean argumentation lie in the fact that the contrasted terms high-low, noble-
vulgar, good-bad are to be understood not in the 'moral' sense, but designate a
social, 'class' opposition: 'Then I found', he writes in Aph 4, 'that everywhere
"aristocrat", "noble" in *the* social sense [im ständischen Sinne, i.e. literally in the
social sense of an 'estate'] is the root idea out of which "good" in the sense of
"with aristocratic soul", "noble" in the sense of "with a noble soul", "with a privileged soul" have necessarily developed'.[115] The etymological observations list
in succession the Greek Dorian aristocracy of Theognis, about which Nietzsche
had written his final paper as a high school student in 1864,[116] the Roman 'warri-
ors' and the Arian race of conquerors and rulers.[117] At the core of the aristocratic

---

110   Deleuze 2013, p. 2; Deleuze 1962, p. 2.
111   Deleuze 2013, p. 2; Deleuze 1962, p. 3.
112   Nietzsche 2013a, p. 15; Nietzsche 1999a, Vol. 5, p. 259.
113   quoted from Deleuze 2013, p. 2; cf. Deleuze 1962, p. 2.
114   Nietzsche 2013a, p. 15; Nietzsche 1999a, Vol. 5, p. 259.
115   Nietzsche 2013a, p. 17; Nietzsche 1999a, Vol. 5, p. 261.
116   For Nietzsche's evaluation of the Theognis text in the sense of an original 'Aryan' caste sys-
      tem in Greece, see the *Historisch-Kritische Gesamtausgabe der Werke und Briefe Nietzsches*
      (Nietzsche 1933–42, vol. 3, pp. 16 et sq., as well as the German summary in pp. 69–75). Cf.
      also for this v. Reibnitz 1992, pp. 12 et sq., Cancik 1995, pp. 9 et sqq. and for the Nietzschean
      construction of a proto-Greek 'higher caste' generally, see Cancik-Lindemaier and Cancik
      1999, pp. 90 et sqq.
117   Nietzsche 2013a, p. 18 et sq.; Nietzsche 1999a, Vol. 5, pp. 263 et sq.

races 'the beast of prey, the magnificent, marauding blond beast lusting after victory and spoils is impossible not to recognize'.[118] Also the contrast between 'clean' and 'unclean', which a priestly aristocracy will then sharpen and internalise, should initially be understood as essentially 'non-symbolic': 'clean' is 'only a man who washes himself', eats no unhealthy meals, who 'does not sleep with the unclean women of the lower classes, who has a strong aversion to blood'[119] – obviously not a 'human', but 'only a man', and a 'noble' one at that.

That is Nietzschean blunt language in the strong and extremely contestable sense. The potentials of Nietzsche's approach exist more in the claim than in the execution, that is, in the intention of stepping out of the abstract generality of the philosophical value-heaven, not to conceive the history of morality 'into the blue', but to seek in the 'grey', 'documentary evidence', 'capable of definite proof', 'that which has actually existed',[120] i.e. in the social antagonisms of antiquity and their master or slave moralities. Losurdo sees here a peculiar ideology-critical capacity that connects him to his great antagonist Marx, namely to decipher every domain of history, morals, religion, science and art as a class struggle – with the difference, however, of considering it ahistorically as an eternal struggle between masters and slaves.[121] For whatever intentions: Nietzsche enters thereby the terrain of a social-historical, not to say historical-materialistic subject matter, for the treatment of which he obviously neither has, nor desires to have, the analytic equipment. His argumentation in *On the Genealogy of Morals I* can be summarised under this aspect in the following statements: 1) First the opposition of 'good' and 'bad', then of 'good' and 'evil', has its source in the social oppositions between aristocratic rulers and plebeian ruled; 2) here the aristocratic ruling order is to be regarded as the original, and is not, for example, as Max Weber will explain later in *Economy and Society*, to be reconstructed from pre-state societies with still fluid power relations lacking fixed 'administrative staff';[122] 3) the methodical starting point of 'a real history' of morality is therefore the social distinctions of the ruling aristocracy, to which the dominated then react with their 'revalued' slave and resentment morality.

118   Nietzsche 2013a, p. 29; Nietzsche 1999a, Vol. 5, p. 275.
119   Nietzsche 2013a, p. 20; Nietzsche 1999a, Vol. 5, p. 265.
120   Nietzsche 2013a, p. 9; Nietzsche 1999a, Vol. 5, p. 254.
121   Losurdo 2020, pp. 830 et sqq.
122   Weber 1978, p. 231, cf. Weber 1980, p. 133.

As soon as one follows Nietzsche onto the field of a 'real' moral genealogy, the imaginary elements of his construction also become clear. Based on his studies of classical and pre-classical Greece, Nietzsche asserts an aristocratic rule as the origin of human history. Almost at the same time, the late Engels developed in *Ludwig Feuerbach and the End of Classical German Philosophy* (1888) his concept of the state as the first 'ideological power over man' and of law as the second ideological power, followed by philosophy and religion as the 'higher ideologies'.[123] In this ideology-theoretical framework, the dominant morality of a society is to be explained from the relations of force between the developing classes, which require a socially transcendent power of the state 'above' society for the regulation of their oppositions, together with the appropriate religious and moral compromise formations.[124] Instead, Nietzsche develops the heroic fiction of an aristocracy that stands for itself, one which 'creates' the dominant values out of its noble pathos of distance.

But no more than it can 'create' economic values, upon which it feeds, can it 'create' the ideological values out of nothing. Various ethnological investigations have demonstrated the great importance of an ethics of 'reciprocity' in pre-state societies, which by means of marriage rules, potlatch regulations of gift and counter gift, and various egalitarian sanctions have hindered the stable accumulation of wealth and power over long periods of time.[125] It belongs to the most general patterns of class and state emergence that such reciprocity-ethics are to a large extent destroyed as real institutions, and at the same time transposed in an imaginary way into the new relations of domination. According to Meillassoux, reciprocity norms, which in domestic modes of production correspond to primarily egalitarian forms of circulation, are maintained in aristocratic class societies on the level of an 'ideology of reciprocity', which is used to justify relations of exploitation.[126] As Barrington Moore observes, 'In general, rulers and dominant groups talk in terms of reciprocity ..., to stress *their* contribution to the social units they head, and to praise the virtues and necessities of harmonious social relationships contained therein'.[127] To the extent

---

123   Engels 1886, p. 392 et sq.; Marx and Engels 1957-, Vol. 21, p. 302.
124   Cf. Engels 1892, p. 269; Marx and Engels 1957-, Vol. 21, p. 165; cf. Rehmann 2013, pp. 58 et sqq., 241 et sqq.
125   Cf. for the ethical function of the potlatch see the classic investigation by Marcel Mauss 1966, pp. 2 et sq., to the effective prevention of wealth and power accumulation e.g. Clastres 1989, pp. 22 et sqq., 209 et sq.; Meillassoux 1981, pp. 61 et sq.; Mann 1986, pp. 6 et sqq., 53; Sigrist 1994, pp. 169 et sqq., 186 et sqq.; Böhm 1993, pp. 230 et sq.; Haude and Wagner 1998, pp. 372 et sqq.
126   Meillassoux 1981, p. 66.
127   Moore 1978, p. 508.

that these rules of reciprocity are claimed at the same time by the dominated in order to question the legitimacy of the domination, they function as a kind of 'universal code', whose interpretation in ideological struggles is disputed: their observance defines what is perceived as 'just', and their violation determines what is considered as unjust.[128] According to the 'Project Ideology Theory' (PIT), the dialectic of the ideological (and to that extent also of morality) lies in a 'compromise formation' in which antagonistic forces are condensed in the framework of the structure of domination. Ideologies with a popular impact are 'subject to antagonistic reclamation', i.e. are interpreted and claimed in opposite ways. They are nourished from 'horizontal' energies and must in addition – however displaced – relate to an overreaching community.[129]

Nietzsche's genealogy of morality misses both sides of this contradictory connection. On one hand, the effectiveness of a horizontal ethics of mutuality rooted in the cooperation of social labour is unthinkable in his mythology of aristocratic origin. According to Ernst Tugendhat, the emergence and maintenance of ethics is based on relations of societal co-operation,[130] which, however, is inconceivable in Nietzsche's moral genealogy. In the alternative between a slave and an aristocratic morality where should e.g. Hesiod's *Works and Days* be accommodated, which contrasts the bounty devouring drones and lazy spendthrifts of the aristocracy with a self-confident (thus not 'slave-like') rural work ethic?[131] On the other hand, Nietzsche does not see that the compromise formation between opposite classes and groups is a necessary condition for the functioning of an ideological socialisation from above. He rejects any such compromises because he suspects them of containing the perspectivism of the 'weak', and thus of providing a protected shelter for the lower ranks. Paradoxically, for precisely this reason, Nietzsche's radically 'domination-affirming critique of ideology' provides no realistic guidance for the reproduction of hegemony-supported domination but is suited primarily for elitist internal ideologies.[132] Due to the systemic need for ideological compensation, Nietz-

---

128 Moore 1978, pp. 26, 506 et sqq.
129 Cf. for the concept 'compromise formation', taken over from Freud, Haug 1987, pp. 71 et sq. and Rehmann 2013, pp. 254 et sqq.
130 Cf. Tugendhat 1997, p. 224.
131 Cf. Hesiod 1998. Nietzsche concentrates his remarks on Hesiod primarily on the position of competition (e.g. Nietzsche 2017a, p. 179; Nietzsche 2011, pp. 31 et sq.; Nietzsche 1999a, Vol. 1, pp. 785 et sq.; Nietzsche 2011, pp. 31 et sq.; Nietzsche 1999a, Vol. 3, pp. 45 et sq.) and the meaning of hope (Elpis) in the Pandora legend (e.g. Nietzsche 1994, p. 58; Nietzsche 1999a, Vol. 2, p. 82; Nietzsche 2011, p. 32; Nietzsche 1999a, Vol. 3, p. 46), without being interested in the Hesiodian work ethic.
132 Haug 1993, p. 18.

sche's suggestion that metaphysics be given up could not be accepted by the bourgeoisie after all, notes Eagleton.[133] For the same reason, Nietzsche is not to be seen as an immediate forerunner of German Nazism, as portrayed, for example, by Georg Lukács, because his radical aristocratic elitism remains at odds with the fascist project of an 'authoritarian populism', which tries to integrate the popular classes into an organic *Volksgemeinschaft*, defined by its opposition to other peoples and races.[134]

We can now estimate the extent of what has been abandoned in Deleuze's difference-translation: both the social-historical material of ancient relations of domination, which Nietzsche claimed to decipher, as well as the inadequacy of his treatment. The recoding begins with the fact that in his Nietzsche quote Deleuze omits the noble powerful ones as subjects, which makes it possible for him to present their distance-pathos vis-à-vis the commoners as 'difference'. It continues with a small shift by which the previously omitted aristocratic 'noble' is introduced through the back door, but now as 'nobility' or 'nobleness': 'Genealogy means nobility [noblesse] and baseness ... in the origin'.[135] They are what first make possible an 'active', 'positive', 'creative' wielding of the 'differential element'.[136]

But what do 'noble' and 'base' mean? The answers are to be found farther on, at the end of the second chapter: noble is presented as 'energy ... which is capable of transforming itself'.[137] 'What Nietzsche calls noble, high, and master is sometimes active force, sometimes affirmative will. What he calls base, vile and slave is sometimes reactive force, sometimes negative will'.[138] The latter characterises not the less strong, but 'that which, whatever its strength, is separated from what it can do';[139] the former designates simply the affinity of the active forces for the affirmation of the 'internal characteristic of what is affirmed ..., what is put into action ..., what is enjoyed'.[140] Finally, also the term 'hierarchy' means nothing more than the superiority of the active in relation to the reactive forces, or the triumph of the latter over the former.[141]

---

133   Eagleton 1990, p. 375.
134   Cf. the detailed analysis of Domenico Losurdo 2020, pp. 726 et sqq., 769 et sqq.; cf. Rehmann 2007.
135   Deleuze 2013, p. 2; Deleuze 1962, p. 3.
136   Deleuze 2013, p. 3; Deleuze 1962, p. 3.
137   Deleuze 2013, p. 39; Deleuez 1962, p. 48.
138   Deleuze 2013, p. 51, cf. p. 53; Deleuze 1962, p. 62, cf. p. 65.
139   Deleuze 2013, p. 56; Deleuze 1962, p. 69.
140   Deleuze 2013 pp. 80, 112; Deleuze 1962, pp. 98, 137.
141   Deleuze 2013, pp. 55 et sq.; Deleuze 1962, p. 68.

When one looks from here back to the beginning, the almost impercept-
ible omissions and shifts become evident as a basic operation for erasing
what Nietzsche was concerned with in the *Genealogy of Morals*. Already on
the first pages of his interpretation, Deleuze has dissimulated the domination
and gender relations, which Nietzsche interpreted as the origin of morality.
As soon as 'nobleness' has taken the place of class-based nobility a hermeneutic displacement is initiated, into which the Nietzschean master discourse
is allowed to feed in again smoothly, but now solely as metaphor.[142] While
the material strength of the Nietzschean genealogy is abandoned, its ideological nature becomes even more obscure: if with Nietzsche the imaginary consisted primarily in the fact that he disguised the aristocratic rulers as the 'active
ones', although he himself knew exactly that they live from the domination
and exploitation of the active ones who do the work for them, for Deleuze in
the origin there is only 'active' and 'reactive', 'affirming' and 'negating' forces,[143]
which are called allegorically 'noble' and 'base'. Against the widespread habit
of labelling Deleuze a 'radical' thinker, this is neither a radical nor at all a
critical procedure, but moves in the traditional paradigm of a highly speculative re-philosophising, by means of which outsiders such as, e.g. Feuerbach,
Kierkegaard, Marx, Benjamin, Bloch, and also Nietzsche, are smoothed out and
brought back into the dissimulating discourse of institutional philosophy.[144]

The translation of the noble pathos of distance into 'difference' and 'plurality' proved to be extraordinarily successful. It was taken up by the most diverse
Nietzsche interpretations and determines the image of Nietzsche up to the
present day. Thus it fell especially to the category of 'difference' to assume the
function of making the various discourses of postmodernism compatible with
the ideologies of neoliberalism. It should be a cause for concern that ironically this connection is achieved by a term which – in any case in its Deleuzean
version – was read out from Nietzsche's explicitly anti-democratic project
of aristocratic domination. Also in *Différence et répétition*, published in 1968,
Nietzsche is presented as the one who first made it possible for that term to

---

142 Matthew Sharpe characterises Deleuze's method as an 'ontological catachresis', by which
       ostensibly political terms in Nietzsche are predicated of non-political or sub-political real-
       ities – 'changing the subject, and not alerting readers to the change' (Sharpe 2021, pp. 4,
       9).
143 Deleuze 2013, p. 51 et sq.; Deleuze 1962, p. 63.
144 The categories philosophical/aphilosophical function as a 'binary arrangement', the set-
       ting of which decides the inclusion and exclusion of discourses related to the institution
       philosophy. 'Thereby what is counted as a "philosophical" discourse, is often a specifically
       dissimulating one and as "aphilosophical" discourse, one that is designating' (Haug 1993,
       p. 185).

possess its own concept.[145] Despite all metaphorical thinning out, the category is caught up again and again by its repressed elitist pathos of distance. Of course, 'difference' means many things in various contexts, but as a polemical counter concept to dialectic and its work on oppositions, it functions not least as a euphemism for social distinction.

5   The Debate about the 'Will to Power': Metaphysical or Plural?

There is probably no Nietzsche topos on which the discoverers and rediscoverers of the plural Nietzsche have worked harder than his 'Will to Power'. Here the resistance of Nietzsche's writings seemed to be strongest, since the well-known use of the term seemed to point in exactly the opposite direction, towards a metaphysics of power. Hadn't Nietzsche characterised the will to power as the 'essence' of the world?[146] 'The world seen from within, the world defined and designated according to its "intelligible character" – it would simply be Will to Power and nothing else'.[147] It is an 'integral part of all that happens', all purposes, goals and appreciations are only its 'modes of expression and metamorphoses', and we follow its 'commandment because we *are* that commandment'.[148]

Supported by these and similar passages in the text, Heidegger in his Nietzsche lectures had interpreted the will to power as 'essential will' [Wesenswille] and as the 'basic character of beings [des Seienden] as such'.[149] The shift consists among other things in the fact that Heidegger also ascertains in Nietzsche's concept of power aspects of 'subjectivism', through which the modern '*mise-en-scène*' of man is unwillingly abetted.[150] In contrast to this he wants to purify the will to power of the admixtures of any subjective voluntarism, and with the assistance of a 'more original inquiry'[151] recast it into an ontology of 'Being'.[152] In connection with the claimed 'pivoting' from 'beings' [Seiendes] to 'Being' [Sein], Nietzsche's philosophy is described as 'the consummation [Vollendung] of Western metaphysics', which is being both resumed and overcome by Hei-

---

145   Deleuze 1994, pp. 40 et sq.; Deleuze 1968b, pp. 59 et sq.
146   Nietzsche 1997, p. 56; Nietzsche 1999a, Vol. 5, p. 107.
147   Nietzsche 1997, p. 28; Nietzsche 1999a, Vol. 5, p. 55.
148   Nietzsche 2003b, p. 217; Nietzsche 1999a, Vol. 13, pp. 44 et sq.
149   Heidegger 1991a, v. I, pp. 60 et sq.; Heidegger 1991b, v. III, p. 193.
150   Heidegger 1991b, v. III, pp. 4, 155 et sq.
151   Heidegger 1991a, v. II, p. 206.
152   Cf. e.g. Nietzsche 1991a, vol. I, pp. 3 et sq., 18, 21, 25, vol. II, pp. 199, 206.

48 CHAPTER 1

degger's 'fundamental ontology'.[153] In the following part we will be occupied in more detail with this twist in Heidegger's critique of metaphysics, which makes of Being an otherworldly metaphysics (see below Chapter 2.3).

Jaspers comes to the critical finding that Nietzsche's radical critique of metaphysics has nevertheless diverged into the thought-form of metaphysics, whereby the 'opener' in the end appears 'to close' again, because he makes the will to power into an absolute, essential being.[154] According to him, the contradictions 'become incapacitating, for there is a dead finality about them that prevents them from giving rise to anything new'.[155] It was above all this demonstration of the self-contradiction in Nietzsche's thinking which offered German post-war philosophy the possibility of being able to philosophically criticise Nietzsche immanently, without having to speak directly about the involvement of his philosophy in the ideologies of pre-fascism and fascism.

This narrow, politically defused possibility for philosophical critique then came under fire from the Nietzsche-pluralisers. The stakes are high. Should they succeed in substituting the 'old' paradigm by a new reading, according to which Nietzsche was not concerned with a metaphysics of power, but with 'will-to-power-pluralism', as Müller-Lauter claims,[156] then the objection of a self-contradiction is void and the immanent Nietzsche critique of the philosophers delegitimised. If we follow the train of thought of Müller-Lauter, the proof is astonishingly simple: wherever he detects the will to power in the grammatical plural form (e.g. the 'wills' to power), or even in connection with the plural forms of those terms (worlds, forces, subjects, etc.), he believes himself to have furnished the proof that Nietzsche always had 'in view factical pluralities of will to power',[157] a 'plurality of forces in conflict with each other',[158] plural 'power *quanta*'.[159] When Nietzsche grants each people its own will to power, for example,[160] when he characterises this power-will as a 'succession

153 Heidegger describes his 'pivoting' opposite the still all-too-'anthropomorphic' Nietzsche as follows: 'The pivoting is: beings-Being; the fulcrum of the pivoting is: the truth of Being. The pivoting is not a turnabout; it is a turning into the other ground, as abyss' (Heidegger 1991b, v. III, p. 155). On Nietzsche's 'consummation' of metaphysics, cf. Heidegger 1991b, v. III, pp. 6 et sqq., 8, 187 et sqq.
154 Jaspers 1997, pp. 309, 318.
155 Jaspers 1997, p. 330.
156 Müller-Lauter 1992, p. 54.
157 Müller-Lauter 1992, p. 45.
158 Müller-Lauter 1992, p. 41.
159 Müller-Lauter 1992, pp. 48, 51.
160 Nietzsche 2006, p. 42; Nietzsche 1999a, Vol. 4, p. 74.

of ... processes of subjugation, more or less independent ... from each other',[161] Müller-Lauter reads nothing other than 'plural', as if the theoretical status of a concept could be read from the grammatical form in which the word is articulated.

Müller-Lauter can find support for the paradigm change he seeks from Deleuze's plural force and power concept, among others.[162] Deleuze in turn refers back to Nietzsche's definition of the will to power as the 'internal will' [vouloir *interne*] of the concept of force.[163] The quotation is inaccurate because in the appropriate text of Nietzsche's unpublished works what is spoken of is not an 'internal will', but the 'internal world' [innere Welt], through which the force is supplemented.[164] Be that as it may, Deleuze also sets off together with Nietzsche in search for a movens of the 'forces' through which these can be explained *from the inside*. The will to power is 'the genealogical element of force', whereby 'genealogical' consists of two parts: it is 'differential', in that it drives the quantity difference of the forces, and 'genetic', to the extent that it produces the 'quality' of each force.[165] With the concept of the *quantity* difference Deleuze intends to designate the difference between dominating and dominated forces [dominantes-dominées]; the *qualities*, also called 'primordial' [qualités originelles], refer to whether the corresponding force is 'active' or 'reactive'.[166]

In short: the will to power is the both quantitative and qualitative 'determining principle' of the relations between the forces[167] – a strange expression, since the concept of determination should actually be replaced by that of differentiation. 'It is as if life were merged into the very movement of differentiation', writes Deleuze in his introduction to Bergson.[168] Also in Deleuze's reading there is nothing that is not determined by the will to power. Wherever 'forces' affect each other, act, react, dominate, are dominated, they are propelled by it. Have we not landed again with Schopenhauer's concept of a metaphysical essence of will that is fundamental to activities, so to speak lying 'behind' them as a 'thing-

---

161   Nietzsche 2013a, p. 63; Nietzsche 1999a, Vol. 5, p. 314.
162   Müller-Lauter 1992, pp. 42, 96 et sq.
163   Deleuze 2013, p. 47; Deleuze 1962, p. 56.
164   Nietzsche 2003b, p. 26; Nietzsche 1999a, Vol. 11, p. 563.
165   Deleuze 2013, p. 49; Deleuze 1962, p. 56.
166   Deleuze 2013, p. 49; Deleuze 1962, p. 60 et sq.
167   Deleuze 2013, p. 49; Deleuze 1962, p. 60.
168   Deleuze 1991b, p. 94. 'Tout se passe comme si la vie se confondait avec le mouvement même de la différenciation', Deleuze 1968a, p. 96. This takes the place of the Darwinian 'determinations' (102). In the same context the term of the possible is replaced by that of the virtual (100 et sq.).

in-itself'?[169] No, answers Deleuze – and with him the mainstream of Nietzsche studies[170] – because, contrary to Schopenhauer, Nietzsche's will to power, as a 'plastic' principle, can never be separated from the concrete forces and thus represents a 'superior empiricism' which 'reconciles empiricism with principles'.[171] We see here how Deleuze tries to approach Hume's makeshift solution of the nature 'principle' with Nietzsche's assistance. The breaking point with Schopenhauer refers exactly to the question of 'whether the will is unitary or multiple' [une ou multiple] – 'everything else flows from this'.[172]

Deleuze's argument is obviously based on the view that a philosophical postulate of essence is then no longer 'metaphysical' if a) one defines this essence as a mobile and diverse principle and b) does not search for it 'behind' the forces, but defines it as an 'internal principle'.[173] But also Schopenhauer had regarded his will as 'the innermost essence, the kernel, of every particular thing and also of the whole'.[174] Who tells us then that the will to power claimed by Deleuze as the interior drive of force is not also a metaphysical world lying behind, which is projected into the phenomena? Apparently, in order not to appear as a metaphysician himself, Deleuze gets into the difficulty of how even to distinguish the power from the force from which he may not 'separate' it. The answer is linked to the presumed 'inside' of force: 'Force is what can, will to power is what wills.'[175] However, with this definition Deleuze has dissolved what was to be explained, namely a specific will to power, into simple willing as such. The argumentation is put in such a manner that everywhere Deleuze sees someone 'will' something he can extrapolate to the fundamental effect of an omnipresent will to power. This tautology is for Deleuze sufficient basis to formulate anew his differentiation of quality, now on the level of will: '*active* and *reactive* designate the original qualities of force, but *affirmative* and *negative* designate the primordial qualities of the will to power'.[176] This distinction is needed in order to establish affirmation as 'power of becoming active' [puis-

---

169   Cf. Schopenhauer 1969, *The World as Will and Representation*, Second Book, §§ 21–23, e.g.: 'The *will* as thing-in-itself is quite different from its phenomenon, and is entirely free from all the forms of the phenomenon into which it first passes when it appears' (Schopenhauer 1969, Vol. 1, Second Book, § 23, p. 112).
170   E.g. see the corresponding argumentation in Abel (1998, pp. 59–71).
171   Deleuze 2013, p. 46; Deleuze 1962, p. 57.
172   Deleuze 2013, p. 7; Deleuze 1962, p. 8.
173   Deleuze 2013, p. 47; Deleuze 1962, p. 57.
174   Cf. Schopenhauer 1969, Second Book, § 21, p. 110.
175   Deleuze 2013, p. 47; Deleuze 1962, p. 57.
176   Deleuze 2013, p. 50; Deleuze 1962, p. 60.

sance du devenir actif], and thus as its precondition.[177] Deleuze thinks that with this he has reached a stage of philosophical recognition of the essence, with which affirming and negating are not only 'immanent' to (empirical) active and reactive forces, but also 'transcendent': 'Affirmation takes us into the glorious world of Dionysus, ... negation hurls us down into the disquieting depths from which reactive forces emerge'.[178]

The conceptual apparatus spits out what Deleuze has put into it beforehand. The ghostly world of the 'active' and 'reactive' forces, which represented the starting point of his Nietzsche interpretation, is there again, however 'deepened' and 'elevated' by the will to power, which reveals itself in the basic attitude of affirmation or negation. Having started out with the intention of clearing up the interpretation of a metaphysical will to power, Deleuze has come around to introduce it again as the metaphysical 'transcendence' of force. Of course it is no longer the Hegelian world spirit which drives history, but the 'affirmation', from which everything else, the noble as well as the base, the ruling as well as the ruled, is derived. 'Affirmation remains as the sole quality of the will to power', reads the last sentence of Deleuze's Nietzsche book.[179]

It is time to get off this carousel of feinted de-metaphysisation and actual re-metaphysisation and return to Nietzsche himself.

6   Nietzsche's Combination of Decentring and Hierarchisation

In fact, Nietzsche has several passages concerning the decentrality of the subject and its will-activity which could support the thesis of pluralisation. One of the strongest references is aphorism 19 of *Beyond Good and Evil*, in which Nietzsche rejects the metaphysical unity of the Schopenhauerian concept of will. Willing is something very complicated, objects Nietzsche: some feelings are directed toward the state from which one wants to get away, others toward that to which one wants to go. In addition comes thinking, as a 'commanding thought' with a specific affect, namely an 'emotion of supremacy in respect to him who must obey: "I am free, he must obey"'. 'A man who wills commands something within himself which renders obedience'.[180] The complic-

---

177   Deleuze 2013, p. 50; Deleuze 1962, p. 61. Deleuze's Nietzsche interpretation concentrates 'on the conflict between the active and reactive forces, that on a deeper level is doubled by the duel between affirmation and denial' (Rogozinski 1996, p. 84).

178   Deleuze 2013, p. 50; Deleuze 1962, p. 61.

179   Deleuze 2013, p. 187; Deleuze 1962, p. 226.

180   Nietzsche 1997, p. 13; Nietzsche 1999a, Vol. 5, p. 32.

ation of the will consists not least in the fact that in willing we are the one commanding and at the same time the one obeying, overriding this duality by means of the synthetic term 'I'.[181] Precisely this identification of the commanding one with the (obeying) executing one produces the will's state of pleasure, which is described as 'Freedom of the Will'.[182] 'Our body is but a social structure [Gesellschaftsbau] composed of many souls', he continues, and the willing/commanding one appropriates all these under-souls: in this way 'what happens here is what happens in every well-constructed and happy commonwealth, namely, that the governing class identifies itself with the success of the commonwealth'.[183]

Indeed, Nietzsche seems to anticipate here some of the later deconstruction of traditional concepts of the subject, from Freud's 'topical' model of the instances id, ego, super-ego, where the 'ego' adopts an extremely precarious central position, up to that which Althusser, with the help of Lacanian psychoanalysis, will call the subject-effect, which is produced through the mirror imagination of a unified 'I'.[184] The Ego is not a uniform being, writes Nietzsche in a posthumously published note from the autumn of 1880, but 'a majority of person-like forces, from out of which this one and soon that one stands in the foreground .... The subject jumps around ... We treat ourselves as a majority and carry in these "social relationships" all the social habits that we have toward humans, animals, things'.[185] And one year later: 'Actually we are a multiplicity *which imagines itself to be a unity*. The intellect as the means of deception with its coercive forms "substance", "equality", "duration" – it has first banished multiplicity from sense'.[186] As Manfred Frank sums up, Nietzsche's subject is 'an organ of misapprehension in that it considers itself to be the ruler of the dark life, whereas it is actually ruled by it'.[187]

However, there is much more to evaluate here than the simple decentring of the subject and the forces and powers which constitute it. The 'plural' interpretation stops half-way and inquires neither what Nietzsche's soul as 'social structure' [Gesellschaftsbau] and the ensemble of 'social relationships' is about, nor

---

181   Nietzsche 1997, pp. 13 et sq.; Nietzsche 1999a, Vol. 5, pp. 32 et sq.
182   Nietzsche 1997, p. 13; Nietzsche 1999a, Vol. 5, p. 33.
183   Nietzsche 1997, p. 14; Nietzsche 1999a, Vol. 5, p. 33.
184   Cf. Freud's comparison of the Ego with the rider, who has to rein the superior power of the horse, now however not with own forces, but with those borrowed from the Id (Freud 1953–74, Vol. 19, p. 25). For Althusser's concept of the subject, cf. Althusser 1996b and 2014, as well as the critical evaluation in Rehmann 2013, pp. 165 et sqq.
185   Nietzsche 1999a, Vol. 9, pp. 211 et sq.
186   Nietzsche 1999a, Vol. 9, p. 582.
187   Frank 1989, p. 202.

how Nietzsche imagines the unification of the disparate soul forces. The two questions are tightly connected.

As is evident in the material quoted from *Beyond Good and Evil*, Aph. 19, the description of the body as a 'social structure of many souls' is the prelude to an analogy between the willing and the governing class of a 'happy commonwealth', which appropriates its successes and identifies itself with them.[188] What interests Nietzsche about this comparison is the functioning of a 'formation of rule [Herrschafts-Gebilde] which *means* "one", but *is* not "one"', or one whose unity is a unity 'only as *organization and connected activity*'.[189] The question is, how does one conceive of a type of domination which is not simply given as uniform, but whose unity must be produced anew again and again. Nietzsche describes the multiplicity of the subject as 'a kind of *aristocracy* of "cells", in which mastery [Herrschaft] resides', and where the aristocrats are used to rule and to command as equals.[190] The 'plural' is conceived after the paradigm of the aristocrat class here, which must have learned to govern together despite their conflicting interests. It is not about 'multiplicity' as such, instead it actually concerns a 'governing multitude and aristocracy'.[191]

The order of domination also affects the manner in which Nietzsche imagines the unification of the subject. The postmodern interpretation is so fascinated by Nietzsche's cavorting subject that it ignores the strict command structure which ropes it in again: 'willing' takes place as commanding in some and obeying in the other instances, and it is only due to a synthetic illusion that this polar arrangement is perceived as a coherent free will.[192] The plural composition of the Nietzschean subject is permanently permeated by a binary logic. It is as if a Descartian dualism were to reproduce two substances such that the spirit instructs the body which movements it has to carry out. Even if Nietzsche did not grant the spirit such a position, he still affirms the dualistic dispositive.

In Spinoza's anti-dualistic ethics of the affects, willing could not be conceived as this kind of command-obedience relationship, if only for the fact that an affect cannot be limited here by a different kind of authority, but only by another stronger affect.[193] Hume will concur and treat the will here primarily in its dependence on passions, as well as on pleasure and pain experiences –

---

188   Nietzsche 1997 p. 14; Nietzsche 1999a, Vol. 5, p. 33.

189   Nietzsche 2003b, 2[87], p. 76; Nietzsche 1999a, Vol. 12, p. 104.

190   Nietzsche 2003b, 40[42], p. 46; Nietzsche 1999a, Vol. 11, p. 650.

191   Nietzsche 2003b, 37[4], p. 30; Nietzsche 1999a, Vol. 11, p. 578.

192   Nietzsche 1997, pp. 32 et sq.; Nietzsche 1999a, Vol. 5, pp. 32 et sq.

193   Spinoza 1996, IV, prop. 7.

as simple 'internal impression' of body movements and perceptions it would not be suitable as a command authority anyway.[194] With Freud the will is conceived as an I-function and as such is largely determined by the feeling range between pleasure and unpleasure.[195] Bloch counterposes the military-Spartan concept of the will (later continued by Loyola), 'which practices in obedience the beginnings of command', with the concept of Paracelsus, which determines the will by a 'working image' [wirkendes Bild], which comes from the heart.[196]

These approaches direct the attention toward the embedding of willing in experiences and needs, which has been lost in Nietzsche's reductionist framework of command and obedience. Klaus Holzkamp, the founder of German *Critical Psychology*, has pointed out an ambiguity of the will which can be empirically differentiated often only with difficulty: it can appear as a component of motivated acting and designates there the ability to temporarily renounce the immediate satisfaction of a need for the sake of achieving a longer-term need. However, without the person affected having to be aware of the difference, the same human ability to will under conditions of external or internal compulsion can become an 'aspect of psychic function which is split off from motivation' and thus causes people to act contrary to their vital interests.[197] Only under the precondition of such a splitting is it meaningful to define the act of the will according to the pattern of command and obedience. In Nietzsche's view the will is from the beginning torn out from any connection with a motivated capacity to act, which in turn cannot even be perceived in the context of the command structure of his concept of will. This invisibility is a symptom of the compulsive separation between will and motivated capacity to act, of which Holzkamp speaks. It is an alienated functional mode of the will to which Nietzsche gives philosophical expression.

Just as willing is reduced to the sequence of commanding-obeying, so is power conceived of as an 'overwhelming, taking mastery' over the less powerful,[198] suppressing, raping and exploiting.[199] The meaning of the syntagm 'will to power' consists in naturalising the power to rule and rape by transferring it into the 'essence of life'. The will to power inherits the achievement of the

---

194   'By the will, I mean nothing but *the internal impression we feel and are conscious of, when we knowingly give rise to any new motion of our body, or new perception of our mind*' (Hume 1978 [1739], *Treatise* II, III, 1). For the dependence of the will on desire and pain, cf. I.III, 10; II, III, 3.
195   Freud 1963 [1915], pp. 86 and 98; cf. Freud 1969–75, p. 166.
196   Bloch 1986, pp. 675 et sq. and pp. 683 et sq.
197   Holzkamp 1985, pp. 323 et sq.
198   Nietzsche 2013a, pp. 63 et sq.; Nietzsche 1999a, Vol. 5, pp. 313 et sq.
199   Nietzsche 1997, p. 126; Nietzsche 1999a, Vol. 5, p. 208; Nietzsche 1999a, Vol. 13, p. 258.

Kantian subject, namely to bring 'order into sensual chaos', notes Manfred Frank: 'To the degree that the subject of modern philosophy is rejected as a mere "thing of fantasy", the subject of the will to power inherits the function that the transcendental subject vacated'.[200] Equipped with this transcendental authority, the function of the will to power lies in a large-scale construct of equivalences: between social domination and subject-interior, 'spirit' and body, humans and protoplasm, whose divisions Nietzsche defines in the categories of slavery and castes,[201] and between organic and inorganic nature in general. On whatever level: it is solely 'the sovereign office [herrschaftliche Rolle] of the highest functionaries ..., among which the life-will appears as an active and formative principle'.[202] All of that which is active, creative and form-giving is represented as the result of domination, which in turn is disguised as the affirmation of life.

It is amazing that postmodern theories which set out to assert the dispersed and scattered against the 'terror' of the truth, reason, of the general and repres- entation, should overlook in silence Nietzsche's philosophical super-elevation of non-rational command and direct despotism. Yet he himself very clearly explained why he wished to base organic and inorganic life on a tyrannical power of domination: the 'democratic instincts of the modern soul' invoke the laws of nature in order to legitimise their 'vulgar antagonism to everything priv- ileged and autocratic'. With the same art of interpretation, however, one could deduce from the same nature 'just the tyrannically inconsiderate and relentless enforcement of the claims of power', so that even the word tyranny will appear too mild for the will to power.[203] Whatever variant of natural law Nietzsche is aiming at (ranging from mechanistic materialism through popular Darwinism to Eugen Dühring), he turns against a widespread popular linking of nature with democracy, which Gramsci characterised with the statement that 'we are all born naked'.[204] And he fights against this connection – in contrast, e.g. to his neo-Hegelian and neo-Kantian colleagues – not on the level of a hermen- eutics of the spirit (Dilthey), or of neo-Kantianism's eternal value relationships (Windelband/Rickert), but on the terrain of nature itself.[205]

---

200   Frank 1989, p. 203.
201   Cf. Nietzsche 1999a, Vol. 9, pp. 490 et sqq., Nietzsche 1999a, Vol. 12, pp. 92, 424; Nietzsche 1999a, Vol. 13, pp. 360 et sq.
202   Nietzsche 2013a, pp. 64 et sq.; Nietzsche 1999a, Vol. 5, p. 316.
203   Nietzsche 1997, p. 16; Nietzsche 1999a, Vol. 5, p. 37; see Nietzsche 2013a, pp. 64 et sq.; Niet- zsche 1999a, Vol. 5, p. 316.
204   Gramsci 1971, p. 363; Gramsci 1975, Q. 10.II, § 35, p. 1280.
205   For the different hermeneutic or value-philosophical positions of this time against the connection of democracy and 'naturalism', see Rehmann 2015a, pp. 199 et sqq.

The question of whether Nietzsche's will to power is 'metaphysical' or 'plural' cannot be answered meaningfully, since as Eagleton notes, it appears in both shapes: it is 'once the inward shape of all there is, yet nothing but local, strategic variations of force. As such, it can provide an absolute principle of … ontological foundation while being nothing of the sort, as fleeting and quicksilver as the Fichtean process of becoming'.[206] Something else is relevant in our connection: Nietzsche's conflation of the active power to act and the power of domination is what is jointly repressed by the 'metaphysical' as well as the 'plural' Nietzsche schools. Who understands the will to power as a 'drive to seize power' or as 'sheer lust for violence' corrupts metaphysics, according to Heidegger, who sees the will to power as the 'basic character of beings as such'.[207] Also in Deleuze's reading, terms such as fight, war and rivalry are foreign to Nietzschean thinking, for they only represent the means 'by which the slave reverses hierarchy'.[208] Even if this were philologically correct, which it certainly is not,[209] it would not be a real objection, because in times of stability rule does not necessarily have to articulate its power in categories of struggle and war. According to Deleuze, will to power does not mean by any means that the will wants power, but that 'power is the one that wills in the will'.[210] It remains obscure, which willing should then remain left over for the will itself. Finally, one does not even know anymore whether anything at all may still be wanted, because the will to power, which is presented as 'essentially creating and giving', 'does not aspire, it does not seek, it does not desire, above all it does not desire power. It gives …, as the "bestowing virtue"'.[211] These characteristics are taken directly from the third part of *Zarathustra* (1884), but also mutilated here again, because there these do not simply praise the will to power, but imperiousness [Herrschsucht] as 'bestowing virtue'.[212] Shortly beforehand (1883) Nietzsche had clearly warned of such a 'gift': 'this is about more than giving: it's about creating, about raping! … Our "gifts" are dangerous!'[213] It is as if Nietzsche's obsession for aristocratic domination had changed itself under

---

206   Eagleton 1990, p. 248.
207   Heidegger 1991b, v. III, pp. 193 et sqq.
208   Deleuze 2013, p. 77; Deleuze 1962, p. 93.
209   E.g. Nietzsche criticises that in Spinoza's concept of reason the fight is missing (Nietzsche 1999a, Vol. 9, pp. 490, 517).
210   Deleuze 2013, p. 79; Deleuze 1962, p. 96.
211   Deleuze 2013, p. 80, cf. p. 186; Deleuze 1962, p. 97, cf. p. 225.
212   Nietzsche 2006, p. 151; Nietzsche 1999a, Vol. 4, p. 238.
213   Nietzsche 1999a, Vol. 10, p. 512.

Deleuze's supple hands into a post-Christian concept of grace, which on the basis of an inner world affirmation pours its affirmative light over the whole of life.

Deleuze has accepted Nietzsche's dangerous gift and passes it on. If one searches for the philosophical reasons for this procedure then at strategic points of his argumentation one bumps into the claim that the will to power goes back to Spinoza. The thesis already has weight, since, with several books concerning Spinoza, Deleuze is considered an expert.[214]

7   Flattening out the Late Nietzsche's Departure from Spinoza

Deleuze's transformation of the Nietzschean concept of power into one of life-affirming activity is only possible because he secretly exchanged it with Spinoza's concept of *potentia agendi*. We will watch him perform this exchange step by step. Since the relationship among forces is determined by the fact that one force is affected by another, Deleuze argues one could conclude 'that the will to power is manifested as the capacity for being affected'.[215] Obviously one can make this claim only if one has previously reduced the Nietzschean will to power to the interior of force in general. However, what Deleuze describes as the ability of the body 'to be affected in a great many ways ... and of affecting external bodies in a great many ways', is actually an important characteristic of the human capacity to act (*potentia agendi*) with Spinoza.[216] Of course, Deleuze still has to show, based on the text, that Nietzsche's will to power is also characterised by such a sensibility. Instead he continues; here it can only with difficulty be denied that Nietzsche found inspiration in Spinoza, who had defined the force of every body through its affectability, which could be both passive and active.[217] What a surprise! Deleuze himself just pushed the capacity of being-affected into the Nietzschean will to power. Next step: 'Just the same with Nietzsche', and this shows up in the passages in which Nietzsche defines power as 'primitive affective form', from which all other affects emerged. Therefore the will manifests itself as 'differential sensibility' of force.[218] But why should Nietzsche's claim that his will to power underlies all affects as 'prim-

---

214   Deleuze 1968c, 1970, 1981.
215   Deleuze 2013, pp. 57 et sq.; Deleuze 1962, p. 70.
216   Spinoza 1996, Ethics IV, P38, p. 137.
217   Deleuze 2013, p. 58; Deleuze 1962, p. 70.
218   Deleuze 2013, p. 58; Deleuze 1962, pp. 70 et sq.

itive affect form'[219] be equivalent to a qualitative determination of the will to power as affectability and sensibility?

With this transfer of the will to power to the *potentia agendi*, the way is free for Deleuze to transform the contradictory relationship of Nietzsche to Spinoza, varying between fascination and repulsion, into a simple and seamless line of continuity. This 'line' forms a core both of his Spinoza books as well as the later works with Guattari. The assumption of a continuity between Spinoza's and Nietzsche's concepts of power is then reaffirmed in Michael Hardt's study on Deleuze.[220] It is therefore hardly a surprise to see it emerge again in Hardt and Negri's *Empire*, which describes Nietzsche's concept of power in terms of an 'expansive power', so that its difference to Spinoza is reduced to an 'omnilateral expansiveness of the power to act'.[221] This interpretation contradicts, however, Negri's own finding that Spinoza's concept of power is characterised by expansiveness and is thereby to be mediated with Marx's concept of productive forces.[222] A 2013 conference on 'Spinoza and Nietzsche in Dialogue' at the University of London was marked by the commonly shared opinion that there is a 'remarkable affinity' between Spinoza's and Nietzsche's concepts of power, and that the ethical position of Nietzsche's will to power is the same as Spinoza's potentia.[223]

In a majority of the Nietzsche studies, approximately the following view prevails: Nietzsche adopted Spinoza's concept of power and in two ways developed it further philosophically: on one hand by separating it from the outdated connection with a reason aligned to the knowledge of God, on the other by not identifying it with a simple static impulse for self-preservation.[224] However, this far-reaching consent in the secondary literature contradicts the fact that also Spinoza did not by any means conceive of power as static, but was interested in an extension of the *potentia agendi*.[225] And Nietzsche knows this as well, because in his Spinoza-excerpt he quotes Spinoza as saying that 'we do what we do in order to preserve and to increase our power'.[226] But this knowledge does not prevent him from criticising in *The Gay Science* the self-preservation prin-

219   Nietzsche 1999a, Vol. 13, p. 300; see Nietzsche 1997, pp. 27 et sq.; Nietzsche 1999a, Vol. 5, pp. 54 et sq.

220   Hardt 1993, pp. 34 et sqq.

221   Hardt and Negri 2000, pp. 358 et sq.

222   Negri 1991, pp. 137 et sqq., 220 et sq., 228 et sq.

223   Cf. Grosse Wiesmann 2013; Rutherford 2013.

224   See Deleuze 2013, pp. 193 et sq., note 18; Wurzer 1975, pp. 171 et sq., 200 et sqq., Abel 1998, pp. 52 et sq.

225   E.g. Spinoza 1996 III, Def 3, p. 70; and P 11, pp. 76 et sq.

226   Cf. Nietzsche 1999a, Vol. 12, p. 261.

ciple of the 'consumptive Spinoza' from the point of view of his own concept of power enlargement as an expression of 'people in distress', caused by their descent from the popular classes.[227] He thereby sets his readers on a wrong track, and a large part of Nietzsche scholarship has lost its way in this maze.

In order to break open this consensus we must also take a closer look here. That Nietzsche had let himself be inspired by Spinoza's criticism of teleology, of morality and 'sad feelings', already emerges from the well-known postcard to Overbeck in 1881, in which he characterises Spinoza as his 'predecessor': because 'he denies free will – ; purpose–; a moral world order–; the nonegotistical–; evil'.[228] As Wurzer's detailed investigation shows,[229] Nietzsche's positive reception of Spinoza coincides rather exactly with his 'middle' period, which stretched from his break with Wagner around 1876 to the end of 1882, when he started preparing *Thus Spoke Zarathustra* (published in 1883). It is usually portrayed as the 'enlightened' period, characterised by Nietzsche's attempt to rid himself of what he described in *Ecce Homo* as 'the opiate Wagner',[230] a peculiar combination of romantic idealism, German nationalism and anti-Semitism. During his middle period, Nietzsche collaborated intensely with his Jewish friend Paul Rée, a moral philosopher who was in turn influenced by Spinoza. It was also Rée who introduced Nietzsche to the French moral critics de Montaigne, de La Rochefoucauld, de Vauvenarges, de La Bruyère, and Stendhal. It seems that Nietzsche's friendship with the Jewish intellectual helped to throw his earlier anti-Semitism into crisis, at least partially and temporarily.[231] Indeed, in *Human, All Too Human*, Nietzsche combined his naturalist materialism with praise of the Jewish people for having provided humanity not only with Christ, as the noblest man, but also with Spinoza, as the 'purest sage'.[232] The anti-Semitic trope of the nomadic and rootless cosmopolitanism of the Jewish people is revaluated as a positive model for Nietzsche's vision of multinational and multiracial Europe.[233] During this period, he also appeals

---

227 Nietzsche 2017b, pp. 136 et sq.; Nietzsche 1999a, Vol. 3, p. 585.
228 Nietzsche 1975-, Vol. III, l, p. 111.
229 Wurzer 1975, pp. 40–71.
230 Nietzsche 1989, pp. 286, 288; Nietzsche 1999a, Vol. 6, pp. 322, 325.
231 Cf. Losurdo 2020, p. 261.
232 Nietzsche 1994, p. 229; Nietzsche 1999a, Vol. 2, p. 310.
233 Nietzsche 1994, pp. 228–30; Nietzsche 1999a, Vol. 2, pp. 309–11. However, the picture remains contradictory. At the same time, the middle Nietzsche maintained the anti-Semitic stereotype of the "Börsenjude" (stock-exchange Jew) as the "most repugnant invention of the whole human race" (Nietzsche 1994, p. 229; Nietzsche 1999a, Vol. 2, p. 310). Cf. the analysis in Losurdo 2020, pp. 243–9.

to a 'drive for preservation',[234] thus to a concept which he will attribute later, from the point of view of his will to power, to Spinoza's physical weakness and 'consumption'.[235] It is no coincidence that Wagner and other contemporaries blamed Rée's 'destructive' influence for Nietzsche's separation from the ideals of his early period. The Wagnerian 'milieu' of Nietzsche's early period responded to his ideology critique by mobilizing anti-Semitic stereotypes.[236]

Most of the commonalities lie in the critique of idealism, its illusions of freedom and its teleology, but clearly not in the will to power. On the contrary. In order to understand this we need to have a closer look at the transition to his late period. This period, starting about the end of 1882, is characterised by a radicalisation of his antidemocratic aristocratism. Also, the anti-Semitism of his early Wagnerian period re-emerges, but it is now more consistently integrated into a radical classism against all subaltern classes.[237] This transition is a highly overdetermined process that comprises manifold social, political, and also biographical aspects. Toward the end of 1882, Nietzsche's friendship with Paul Rée turned into hostility and contempt because both fell in love with Lou Andreas-Salomé. This crisis of unhappy love coincided with the composition of the *Zarathustra*, by means of which Nietzsche had 'elevated himself "vertically" from this low point to [his] altitude', as he writes in a letter to Overbeck.[238] This new and precarious 'altitude' will accompany Nietzsche during his late period, until his breakdown in 1889.

In November 1882, again at the time of his break with Salomé and Rée, Nietzsche introduced for the first time his concept of a 'will to power',[239] which from then on replaced the concept of 'self-preservation.' As soon as Nietzsche sets himself to arranging his material anew around this universal principle, he turns not only against Paul Rée and the 'English' moral genealogists, but, from spring 1883 onward, also ever more sharply against Spinoza, whose *conatus* of self-

234 Nietzsche 1994, p. 75; Nietzsche 1999a, Vol. 2, p. 95.
235 Nietzsche 2017b, p. 137; Nietzsche 1999a, Vol. 3, p. 585.
236 See Pfeiffer (1970, pp. 252, 286, 310). Cosima Wagner (quoted in Treiber 1999, p. 515) notes in her diary of 1 November 1876: 'Dr. Rée pays us a visit in the evening, but his cold and blunt character does not appeal to us. On closer examination we find out that he must be an Isrealite'.
237 According to Losurdo, the position of the late Nietzsche is to be analysed in the framework of a 'transversal racialisation' (razzizzazione trasversale) directed immediately against the popular classes and the poor (2020, pp. 760–3, 782–5,804–7).
238 Nietzsche 1975-, Vol. III., 1, p. 324. 'If I don't find this alchemist trick to transform these feces into gold, I am lost', Nietzsche writes in a letter of 25 December 1882 (Nietzsche 1975–, Vol. III., 1, p. 312).
239 Nietzsche 1999a, Vol. 10, p. 187.

preservation he attacks as a plebeian 'foundation of English utilitarianism'.[240]
Instead of erasing the tension or flattening it to a mere difference, one must
try to grasp the vehemence with which Nietzsche must repel himself from the
'consumptive Spinoza' and his allegedly ever paler conceptual 'rattle', until he
finally consigns him to the opposing camp of the 'refined vindictive poison
mixers'.[241] The fact that what he reproaches Spinoza for – that he is a person
'in states of distress' –[242] applies precisely to himself gives an eerie imaginary
character to the dissociation. In the autumn of 1884 he writes a mocking poem
in which he exposes Spinoza's religion critique as 'Jewish' hate:

> Yet secretly beneath this love [of God], devouring
> a fire of revenge was shimmering:
> The Jewish God devoured by Jewish hatred ...
> Hermit! Have I recognized you?[243]

What is to be reflected on is, therefore, a turning point in the relationship
between Nietzsche and Spinoza which, when understood as dialectic, would by
no means rule out further borrowings from Spinoza in Nietzsche's late phase.
But despite all the emphasis on the fragmentary and nonlinear, the postmodern Spinoza-Nietzsche-filiations do not permit any contradictions and breaks.
Common to the various 'linear' interpretations is the assumption that Nietzsche and Spinoza mean in principle the same thing when they speak of power.
Thereby it is overlooked that power is an extremely ambiguous term, whose
meaning can be reconstructed only from the respective usages and discursive
combinations.

---

240   Nietzsche 1999a, Vol. 11, p. 224.
241   Compare Nietzsche 2017 p. 136 et sq., 156 et sq.; Nietzsche 1999a, Vol. 3, pp. 585, 624; Nietz-
      sche 1997, p. 20; Nietzsche 1999a, Vol. 5, p. 43; Nietzsche 1968a, p. 91 et sq.; Nietzsche 1999a,
      Vol. 6, p. 126; Nietzsche 1968b, p. 139 et sq.; Nietzsche 1999a, Vol. 6, p. 84; Nietzsche 1999a,
      Vol. 10, p. 340, Nietzsche 1999a, Vol. 11, p. 226, Nietzsche 1999a, Vol. 13, pp. 504, 537.
242   Nietzsche 2017b, p. 137; Nietzsche 1999a, Vol. 3, p. 585.
243   Nietzsche 1999a, Vol. 11, p. 319.

62

CHAPTER 1

8 The Confusion of Spinoza's Power to Act with Nietzsche's Power of Domination

The terminological coincidence is already problematic and goes back to a questionable translation. It is very likely that Nietzsche had never read Spinoza's writings themselves. He had only a secondhand knowledge, in particular through Kuno Fischer's *History of Newer Philosophy*, in which the *potentia agendi* is usually given simply with 'power' [Macht].[244] In the newer German edition of the *Ethics*, supported by Jakob Stern's translation, the term is usually given as 'Tätigkeitsvermögen' (capability of activity), in the *Historical-Critical Dictionary of Marxism* (HKWM) it is defined as 'Handlungsfähigkeit' (capacity to act), and thus associated with the homonymic concept 'agency' of the Critical Psychology school founded by Klaus Holzkamp – a subject-theoretical key concept that is designed to connect individual and social reproduction in a nonreductionist manner.[245]

In fact, the etymological origin of the term 'power' or *'Macht'* (in Gothic *mahts* and *magan*) refers to the primary meaning of *to be capable* which is still evident in the German verb *vermögen* (to be able). The fact that from this word 'vermögen', the middle-high German verb 'mögen' in the sense of gladly wanting [gern wollen] and liking [gern haben] can be derived, is an indication of how close the competence for action and the affect of a joyful 'turning-to' were felt to be; there is another branching to 'possibility' [Möglichkeit]. These semantic linkages are not a special German case, but are to be found similarly in the Romance-languages: thus, e.g. in the French both *pouvoir* and *puissance* go back to the verb *pouvoir* (to be capable), and the same is true for the Spanish verb 'poder'. In both language families Macht/power is connoted with Möglichkeit/possibility, so that the Zedler *Universal-Lexikon* of 1739 could define power as the capacity 'to make the possible real'.[246] When Michael Hardt and Antonio Negri describe the 'power of the multitude' in terms of its 'becoming subject', they refer to the Latin verb *posse*: 'power as a verb, as activity', part of the Renaissance triad esse-nosse-posse, being-knowing-having power, expressing 'what a body and what a mind can do'.[247]

---

244 E.g. Fischer 1880, pp. 490, 500, 507. See the detailed philological studies of Brobjer (2004) and Sommer (2012).
245 Cf. Reeling Brower 2001 and Markard 2001. Regarding the basic concept of 'agency' in Critical Psychology, see Holzkamp 2013.
246 Quoted in Röttgers 1980, p. 585.
247 Hardt and Negri 2000, pp. 407 et sq.

The etymological findings can be connected with Max Weber's observationthat power is 'sociologically amorphous'.[248] Tied to a complex of capacities, it might express both reciprocal relationships and unequal ones (such as in a pedagogical constellation), competencies monopolised by elites as well as cooperative capacities to act from below. Whereas power is in principle open to democratisation, the concept of domination is formed around the ancient figure of the dominus ('master'), which embodies the intersection of patriarchal and class rule, both usually overdetermined by racism. It cannot, therefore, be conceived without its constitutive meanings of hierarchy and verticality. Whereas power is to be found on opposite sides of class, gender, and race divides, domination is an 'institutionalized, structurally anchored asymmetric power relation of superiority and subordination',[249] bolstered by an 'administrative staff' ready to exercise the 'necessary compulsion' [Verwaltungsstab zur Erzwingung].[250]

What power as capacity to act is actually capable of depends, of course, to a large degree on the respective position in the social system with its distributions of power. This means that the primary meaning of 'being able to' can easily slide into a specific capacity qua power of domination, and this in a flowing transition without the word having to change. The entire history of philosophical concepts of power is pervaded by this inherent ambiguity, which can itself be deciphered as a field of struggles for hegemony. It circles like an ellipse around the two poles of a general capacity to act and a narrower meaning, with which the *dynamis* or *potentia* of the action-capacity is chalked up to, and monopolised by, the side of the ruling power. This narrowing already begins with the Sophists's teachings on power, as it is conveyed in Thucydides's *Melian Dialogue* and in Plato's *Republic* and *Gorgias*. Nietzsche, too, puts his will to power expressly into this line of the 'Sophist culture', which opposed the 'morality-and-ideal swindle of the Socratic schools, which was then breaking out everywhere', with the strict 'realism' of the old 'Hellenic instinct'.[251]

In the case of Spinoza a completely different picture emerges. Noticeable is, first, that he knows a second power concept, that of the *potestas*, which he employs most of the time in the sense of a power of subordinationfrom above, and thus as a concept counter to the potentia.[252] In chapter 16 of the

---

248 Weber 1978, p. 53; Weber 1980, p. 28.

249 Goldschmidt 2004, p. 83.

250 Weber 1978, pp. 53 et sq.; Weber 1980, p. 29.

251 Nietzsche 1968, pp. 118 et sqq., Nietzsche 1999a, Vol. 6, pp. 156 et sqq.

252 The relationship between *potentia* and *potestas* with Spinoza is disputed in the literature. Whereas Negri speaks of a constant and 'absolute antagonism' (Negri 1991, p. 229), this is

Theological-political Treatise on the foundations of the state, *potestas* is used in the meaning of higher state power [superiores potestates], while the *potentia* designates the power competence which individuals transfer to such a higher government power. Spinoza considers a power transfer of this kind necessary and endorses a strong *potestas* of the state, not least in order to be protected from the *potestates* of the Jewish and Christian religious communities, which were denouncing and persecuting him.[253] Nonetheless, he keeps the *potestates* of the state and the *potentiae* of the many conceptually at a distance. For the necessary transfer of power, democracy is the 'most natural' system of government because nobody transfers his right to someone else in such a way 'that they are not thereafter consulted, but rather to the majority of the whole society of which they are a part. In this way all remain equal'.[254] This leads him to the idea 'that ... the whole of society (if this is possible) should hold power together, collegially, so that they are all subject to themselves and nobody must serve their equal'.[255]

In the context of the 'absolutist' seventeenth century Spinoza's *potentia* articulates a significant democratic counterweight.[256] In contrast to Hobbes's *Leviathan*, with Spinoza the transfer of power is subject to revocation at any time, and the *potentia* of the many remains decisive for the state's power to rule. In fact, the *potentia* is never fully surrendered to the *potestas* of the state. 'No one will ever be able to transfer his power [potentia] ... to another person in such a way that he ceases to be a human being; and there will never be a sovereign power [potestas] that can dispose of everything just as it pleases'.[257] People have never 'given up their right and transferred their power to another in such a way that the very persons who received their right and power did not fear them'.[258] The ultimate purpose of the state is 'not to dominate or control people by fear or subject them to the authority of another. On the contrary ... freedom'.[259]

Matheron argues that there is no proper power transfer because sovereignty remains defined not by the potestas of the sovereign, but by the potentia of

---

        challenged by Terpstra (1990, pp. 4, 80 et sqq., 396 et sqq.) and Saar (2013, pp. 175 et sq.). For an evaluation of the debate, cf. Rehmann 2014, pp. 219 et sq.; Rehmann 2019b, pp. 244 et sqq.

253   Cf. Spinoza *Tractatus*, 2007, pp. 199 et sq., 202, 238, 247.
254   Spinoza 2016, p. 202.
255   Spinoza 2016, p. 73.
256   For an analysis of the political and religious context, see e.g. Balibar 1998, pp. 16–24.
257   Spinoza 2016, p. 208.
258   Ibid., (translation modified).
259   Spinoza 2016, p. 252.

the multitude.[260] According to Balibar, Spinoza's state of nature is not abolished by a homogeneous state law; the conceptual arrangement maintains a dialectical openness to the opposition between the established summae potestates and the *multitude*: the potestas can only put its power into practice effectively if the people, who constituted it, consider it as a law that corresponds to their will.[261] In this vein, Spinoza even takes up the much discussed term of an 'absolute' power of the state and redefines it – against the grain – in terms of society's 'internal stability': it is about a process of internal transformation of the *potentia multitudinis*, through which power that was passive becomes active.[262] Obviously, Spinoza struggles with a key problem of hegemony that was later elaborated by Marxist theories: the *potestas* of the state – its characteristics as political society (società politica), as Gramsci would call it – depends in the long run on the consensus of the people and thus remains bound to their *potentia agendi* (in whatever illusory and displaced manner). It is obvious that Spinoza has no elaborate theory of how such a mass consensus can be fabricated by ideological apparatuses from above.

In any case, Spinoza emphasises a competence of the *Multitudo*, which Nietzsche wants to be rid of with his concept of a direct and uncompromising power of domination. In this respect there is no 'line' from Spinoza to Nietzsche, but more accurately a connection from Nietzsche to Hobbes's concept of a 'natural' appropriation and power to dominate, 'perpetual and restless desire of Power, after Power, that ceaseth only in death'.[263] Nietzsche had already drawn such a connection in 1873 in his critique of David Strauß: if Strauß had the 'undaunted sensibility' of a Hobbes, he would have been able 'to deduce from bellum omnium contra omnes and the privileges of the strong the moral prescriptions for life'.[264]

In Spinoza's *Ethics* the *potentia* emerges first at the centre of his concept of God, where it is conceived not in terms of transcendent religion as power *over* human and nonhuman beings, but rather in the sense that God does and thinks an infinitude of things in an infinite way: the 'power [potentia] of God is nothing but the active essence of God [Dei actuosa essentia]',[265] a 'substance consisting of infinite attributes',[266] 'existing from the necessity of

260   Matheron 1997, pp. 214 et sq.
261   Balibar 1997a, pp. 174 et sqq.
262   Balibar 1998, pp. 120 et sq.
263   Hobbes 1961/62, Vol. 3, pp. 85 et sq.
264   Nietzsche 2003a, p. 39; Nietzsche 2017a, p. 173; Nietzsche 1999a, Vol. 1, pp. 194, 772.
265   Ethics II, Prop 3, Dem and Schol.
266   Spinoza 1996, I, Def 6.

its own nature alone', and determined to action by itself alone.[267] It is the active essence of *potentia* that mediates and holds together Spinoza's equation:
God = substance = nature (natura naturans). God is conceived as a universal potentiality of production that operates within each individual reality. As
Matheron observes, Spinoza's God coincides with the 'internal self-productivity
of every individual reality'.[268] This self-productive totality is the starting point
for Negri's project to mediate the *potentia* of Spinoza with the Marxian concept
of the productive forces and to interpret Spinozean philosophy as 'metaphysics
of production'.[269] The notion of God as a depersonalised, subject-less productive force is also the foundation of a critique of transcendent religion, which in
its anthropocentrism ascribes human affects to God.[270] Seduced by this anthro-
pocentric teleology, humans 'assert that the gods ordained everything for the
use of man' and thus degrade the gods to an instrument of their own 'blind
cupidity and insatiable avarice'.[271] Althusser, who uses Spinoza's philosophy
to de-Hegelianize Marxism, links Spinoza's concept of an imminent God to
his philosophical critique of teleology: 'Spinoza, because he "begins with God",
never gets involved with any Goal'; not only did he refuse such a Goal but he also
explained it 'as a necessary and therefore well-founded illusion', which leads
Althusser to the conclusion that Spinoza formulated the "first theory of ideology ever thought out".[272]

When one examines the passages on the *potentia agendi* one will find that
this human capacity to act is nowhere treated as the power of rule over others. Like everything, it is determined by the desire (conatus) to persevere in
its being.[273] It differs from the divine *potentia* primarily in that it is infinitely surpassed and limited by the *potentia* of external causes.[274] Therefore,
humans must adapt to nature out of necessity and are subject to suffering [pas-
sionibus].[275] By suffering/enduring (passio/pati) Spinoza means a happening
which we ourselves do not cause 'adequately', but to which we are subjected; it
stands in contrast to acting [agere], for which we ourselves are exclusively the

---

267 Spinoza 1996, I, Def 7.
268 Matheron 1969, pp. 21, 23.
269 Negri 1991, pp. 218, 228 et sq.
270 Spinoza 1996, I, Prop 8, Schol 2.
271 Spinoza 1996, I, Appendix.
272 Althusser 1976, p. 135. Althusser specifies three characteristics of Spinoza's ideology-
      theory: '(1) Its imaginary "reality"; (2) its internal inversion; (3) its "center": the illusion
      of the subject' (ibid.); for a critical evaluation, see Rehmann 2013, pp. 160–5.
273 Spinoza 1996, III P6, p. 75.
274 Spinoza 1996, IV P3, p. 118.
275 Spinoza 1996, IV P4 Cor, p. 119.

'adequate cause'.[276] Spinoza's *potentia agendi* refers to this emphatic concept of a self-caused, self-determined, yet also de facto always limited action, which then forms the pivot point from which in parts III and IV of the *Ethics* both the affects and the ethical virtues and vices are defined and ordered anew.

Spinoza's *Ethics* is a moral critique to the extent that it challenges the validity of transcendentally founded values by developing a 'geometry' of the feelings and virtues,[277] which are measured according to their action-promoting or -restraining characteristics. Here in particular, Deleuze claims to be able to detect a significant commonality with Nietzsche.[278] But the concept of 'power' from which Spinoza criticises morality is conceived of as a cooperative capability. Contrary to Nietzsche's elitist cult of heroic loneliness, Spinoza is interested in what Balibar calls a processual 'transindividuality' oriented toward relations of synergy with others.[279] Society is useful and necessary, in order to obtain many other advantages.

> For unless human beings were willing to give each other mutual assistance, each one's own personal skill and time would be inadequate to sustain and preserve him as much as would otherwise be possible. For people are not equally able to do everything. ... He would have neither the capacity nor the time ... [if he had to] ... plough, sow, reap, grind ... for himself ...'.[280] 'So let the satirists laugh as much as they like at human affairs, let the theologians curse them, let melancholics praise as much as they can a life that is uncultivated and wild, let them disdain men ... Men still find from experience that by helping one another they can provide themselves much more easily with the things they require, and that only by joining forces can they avoid the dangers which threaten on all sides.'[281]

Spinoza's agency is anchored in this cooperative union. As he puts it in the appendix of Part 4, if man lives among individuals who agree with his nature, 'his power of acting [potentia agendi] will thereby be aided and encouraged'.[282] The *potentia* is the capacity which lets humans agree with one another, whereas incapacity [impotentia] and passive suffering separate them and make them

---

276   Spinoza 1996, III Def 1 and. 2, pp. 69 et sq.
277   Spinoza 1996, III Pref, pp. 68 et sq.
278   Deleuze 1970, pp. 34 et sq.
279   Balibar 1997b.
280   Spinoza 2016, p. 72.
281   Spinoza 1996 IV P35 S, p. 133.
282   Spinoza 1996, caput 7, pp. 156, 158.

contrary to each other.[283] The virtue derived from this capacity to act is based on generalisability, that is, the good which one wants for oneself is also desired for the remaining human beings.[284]

In Spinoza's 'geometry' of the affects everything depends on the proof that the affects of acting, primarily those of strength of mind [animositas] and generosity [generositas], are stronger than those of being subjected. A key role in the transformation of passive into active affects is played by *reason*, which is able to free itself from the deceptions of sense impressions, as well as to regard several things at the same time and in their necessary connection; this for Spinoza coincides with thinking 'sub aeternitatis specie'.[285] As this kind of knowledge of connection, it can also meet the problem that the needs are usually short-sighted, and the enjoyment of the moment is more powerful than the knowledge of the future.[286]

At times Spinoza characterised the position of reason with regard to the affects as domination [imperium] or overcoming;[287] this nourished Nietzsche's interpretation that he wanted 'to destroy' the affects by analysis and vivisection.[288] But Spinoza's concrete explanations show clearly that the relationship between reason and the affects is conceived of as being far more flexible and 'democratic' than could ever be conceived of in Nietzsche's command structure of the will to power. First, knowledge as such, i.e. as far as it is 'true', can limit no affect at all, but only if it is an affect itself, a stronger one.[289] It must, as Nietzsche in his Spinoza excerpt also noted, 'be an affect in order to be motive'.[290] Secondly, the 'imperium' over the affects is explained as an enlightenment of the affects about themselves, connected with the optimistic expectation that a passive affect will become active as soon as it is adequately recognised.[291] Instead of suppressing the impulses Spinoza thinks rather to strengthen the self-caused parts of instinctual life as against the ones suffered. Ultimately it is not a matter of 'overcoming' the affects, but of 'ordering and connecting' them [ordinandi & concatenandi] in a reasonable way, balancing the excessive dominances of individual desires, creating a uniformity of the affectability, as he

283 Spinoza 1996, IV P32–34, pp. 130–32.
284 Spinoza 1996, IV P37 p. 134 et sq.
285 Spinoza 1996, II P29 S, p. 52; II P44, Cor II, p. 60.
286 Spinoza 1996, IV P15–17, p. 123 et sq.
287 E.g. Spinoza 1996, V pref, p. 160 et sq.
288 Nietzsche 1997, p. 64; Nietzsche 1999a, Vol. 5, p. 118; cf. Nietzsche 1999a, Vol. 11, p. 226, Nietzsche 1999a, Vol. 13, p. 269.
289 Spinoza 1996, IV P7, p. 120 and P14 and Dem, p. 123.
290 Nietzsche 1999a, Vol. 9, p. 517.
291 Spinoza 1996, V P3–4, pp. 163 et sqq.

sees it realised, e.g. in serenity or hilarity [hilaritas].[292] Hilarity in turn brings it about that 'all the parts of the body are equally affected, that is to say, the body's power of action is increased'.[293] Spinoza's reason is one which is able to 'surf' on the affects, instead of commanding them in a Nietzschean manner; it is an 'intuitive knowledge',[294] not the dictates of a master.

If one neglects to reconstruct the operational meaning of the Spinozean *potentia agendi* from its connections with cooperative production and reciprocal relationships, one will also not be able to understand what is really done with its appropriation by Nietzsche. Whereas the perspective of Spinoza's concept of power lies in achieving an 'accumulation of power in each part of an aggregate' through the connection with others for common activities,[295] the late Nietzsche's approach is based on its exact opposite: on an esoteric concept of power which is built around the disempowerment of the many. Nietzsche's terminological borrowings from Spinoza are components of a hostile takeover, through which the elements that have been broken off are built into a contrary arrangement. The contrast is disguised by Nietzsche's usage of Kuno Fischer's generic translation of *potentia agendi* with 'power' [Macht]. When Spinoza lets virtue fall together with agency [potentia],[296] Nietzsche notes in his Spinoza excerpt: 'Virtue and power are identical. ... What is good, is what promotes our power: evil the contrary'.[297] Let us see what happens when Nietzsche transitions from his excerpt to the text of the *Antichrist*: 'What is good? Everything which increases the feeling of power, the will to power, increases power itself in humans', and bad is 'that which originates from weakness'. Therefore: 'The weak and ill-constituted shall perish: first principle of our philanthropy. And one shall help them to do so'.[298] In fact, his appeal to the weak and failed to commit suicide in order to show a remainder of virility, as well as the eugenic fantasy that they should be 'assisted', belong to the ongoing obsessions of the late Nietzsche, for whom the creation of the future man requires on the one hand his systematic breeding and on the other hand the 'annihilation of millions of failures'.[299] Nietzsche thus overwhelmed Spinoza's capacity to act and incorporated it into his power of domination, the elaboration of which he pursues consistently up to the perishing of the 'weak'.

---

292   Spinoza 1996, V P10, p. 166; P14, p, 168; III P42 Dem, pp. 92 et sq.
293   Spinoza 1996, IV, P 42 Dem, pp. 138 et sq.
294   Spinoza 1996, II P40 SII, p. 57.
295   Röttgers 1980, pp. 597 et sq.
296   E.g. Spinoza 1996, IV Def 8, p. 117.
297   Nietzsche 1999a, Vol. 12, p. 261.
298   Nietzsche 1968, p. 128; Nietzsche 1999a, Vol. 6, p. 170; cf. Nietzsche 1999a, Vol. 13, p. 192.
299   Cf. Nietzsche 1999a, Vol. 11, p. 98.

What is suppressed in the postmodernist construction of a homogeneous Spinoza-Nietzsche line is nothing less than the 'difference' between social cooperation and projected mass extermination. To erase this glaring opposition is, of course, utterly irresponsible, intellectually and ethically. To list the things they have in common in the moral critique and to systematically 'overlook' the contradictory perspectives on power from which they are made, reproduces Nietzsche's revaluation of Spinoza's philosophy to its opposite and continues it.[300] Unfortunately, this applies to Negri as well. In his *Spinoza for Our Time*, he cannot but realise that Nietzsche's critique of Spinoza is 'extremely harsh and combative',[301] but he does not even try to explain this hostility. This is due to the prejudgment, inherited from Deleuze, that 'there is nothing in Nietzsche that thrusts toward reaction'.[302]

The widespread refusal to take cognizance of Nietzsche's open stance of radical aristocratism provides the precondition for his triumphal success in poststructuralism and postmodernism – in the disguise of a refurbished Spinoza. Here a new and more radical deconstruction is necessary, one which breaks open the linear constructions of postmodernism and liberates Spinoza from Nietzschean alienation. Spinoza was not a proto-Nietzschean, argues Geoff Waite, because he wanted to destroy the self-destructive readiness of the masses for voluntary subordination as 'superstition', whereas Nietzsche was concerned with exploiting it. 'Hence a philosophically coherent and politically emancipatory project must forge its way *back* to Spinoza *past* the Nietzschean self and only then ... *into* the future'.[303]

The confusion between Nietzsche and Spinoza, the former having absorbed and overwhelmed the latter, now forms the basis for the shift of the image of Nietzsche to the 'left', under the influenceof the movement of the '68ers and its failures.

---

300   At the same time as Deleuze transforms Nietzsche into a kind of rejuvenated Spinoza, he submits Spinoza to a Nietzschean interpretation, inspired by life philosophy (Oittinen 1994, p. 65). As Karl Reitter has shown, he replaces Spinoza's free community with Nietzsche's 'strong individual' and thus gives his philosophy an 'a-social turn' (2011, p. 350). Landon Frim and Harrison Fluss demonstrate that Deleuze's interpretation of Spinoza's 'necessitarianism', 'immanence' and 'univocity' takes out the mediating structures between infinite modes (natural laws) and 'horizontal' transient causation between finite modes and thus destroys the dialectical relationships of his system (2018, pp. 203 et sqq., 208 et sqq.).

301   Negri 2013, pp. 72 et sq., 80.

302   Negri 2013, p. 67.

303   Waite 1996, p. 14.

9 Will to Power as Desire Production

At one place Deleuze comes to speak of Nietzsche's role in the fascistisation of bourgeois civil society. What do we do with the texts which have a fascist or anti-Semitic resonance?, he asks in 1973 in *Pensée Nomade*. Even if Jean Wahl, Bataille and Klossowski had made it clear how much Nietzsche was misunderstood and distorted by the Nazis, it was not worth it to Deleuze to deny that he was and is attractive for many young fascists. For him, Nietzsche's text is an 'exterior field', on which fascist, bourgeois and revolutionary forces cross, and what matters is to find the external revolutionary force which runs through and transects the text.[304] This is said rather easily, as if the text had no inner logic at all that could impose definite limits to the various ways of interpretation. But it is not the abstract problem, of whether or not in principle a 'revolutionary' appropriation of Nietzsche is possible, that is to be discussed here, but more concretely the issue of how Deleuze understands the problem and intends to approach it.

The question about the 'external' revolutionary force is easier to understand as soon as one refers to Deleuze himself: he found this 'external' force in the movement of '68, in the process of which he turned Nietzsche into a kind of 'nomadic' liberation fighter. The shift runs inter alia through the connection of the Nietzschean concept of power with the Freudo-Marxist debates in France. Already in his Nietzsche book of 1962, Deleuze indicates his interest in the project to criticise Freudian psychoanalysis and overcome its fixation on the 'reactive' aspects of the inner life with the assistance of Nietzsche's will to power – here still with reference to Otto Rank and C.G. Jung.[305] With *Anti-Oedipus* (1972) and *Mille Plateaux* (1980), written together with Felix Guattari, the focus is on Wilhelm Reich, and here primarily on his late 'bio-genetic' orgone-theory.[306] However, Deleuze does not actually work on a Freudo-Marxist synthesis, which he rejects as 'sterile parallelism',[307] but 'subsumes Marx and Freud within a Nietzschean framework'.[308] In the course of this subjugation, Nietzsche's will to power is transformed into the concept of a 'desire production', which in turn is to provide the basis for the Marxian concept of social production. 'Here the will to power is written as productive desiring', writes

---

304 Deleuze 1995, pp. 145 et sq.
305 Cf. Deleuze 2013, pp. 230 et sq. note 6 and 11.
306 E.g. Deleuze and Guattari 2009, pp. 290 et sq.; Deleuze and Guattari 1972, pp. 345 et sq.
307 Deleuze and Guattari 2009, p. 61; Deleuze and Guattari 1972, p. 75.
308 Bogue 1989, p. 83.

Lange.[309] According to Alan D. Schrift, the procedure can be understood as a 'functionalistic translation': 'Nietzsche's biologism becomes Deleuze's machinism; Nietzsche's "everything is will to power" becomes Deleuze's "everything is desire".[310]

The Deleuzean critique of Freudian psychoanalysis can be presented only in rough outline here. Regarded generally, it is part of the various efforts of this time to 'socialise' the basic psychoanalytic concepts, whether by a reinterpretation of the unconscious in categories of 'language' and the 'symbolic order' (Lacan), or by mediating it with Marx's fundamental category of the 'productive forces'. At the centre of *Anti-Oedipus* stands the ambition to extract the unconscious from the oedipal triangle Papa-Mama-I, to destroy its oedipalisation through a 'de-oedipalisation', which transfers it from the 'exploded triangle' of Oedipus into the 'open social field' again.[311] In reality, Klaus Theweleit summarises, the child directs desire immediately onto 'the reality outside of the family', toward the social field, and is thrown back to the family by the frustrations arising here: 'And so the story doesn't go: because he couldn't take possession of the mother, he subjected the Earth to himself (Freud). It goes: because he wasn't allowed to use the Earth and produce, he went back to his mother'.[312]

The liberation of desire from oedipal familiarism is accomplished by two methodical operations: on one hand desire is released from the solidifications of the Ego-formation, as well as from the condition of lack [manque-à-être] connected with it, and identified with a free flow of anonymous manifoldnesses of the kind of 'a schizophrenic out for a walk';[313] on the other hand, Deleuze and Guattari let schizoid-multiform desiring go directly together with 'social production', thereby declaring it part of the 'infrastructure' of society: 'the desire ... always belongs to the infrastructure, not to ideology: [it] is in production as social production, just as production is in desire as desiring-production'.[314]

---

309   Lange 1989, p. 63.
310   Schrift 1995, pp. 259 et sq. When Ansell Pearsons writes that Deleuze's and Guattari's libidinal streams of desire would 'come close to' the Nietzschean will to power (Ansell Pearson 1999, p. 172), he assumes a similarity which makes the construction character of the postmodern interpretation invisible.
311   Deleuze and Guattari 2009, pp. 96, 112; Deleuze and Guattari 1972, pp. 114, 133.
312   Theweleit 1987, p. 213.
313   Deleuze and Guattari 2009, pp. 2 and 22 et sqq.; Deleuze and Guattari, 1972, pp. 7 and 29 et sqq.
314   Deleuze and Guattari 2009, p. 348; Deleuze and Guattari 1972, pp. 416 et sq.; cf. 2009, pp. 63 et sq.; Deleuze and Guattari 1972, p. 75.

Accordingly, the 'production process' of desiring is consistently described as a 'workshop', 'industry', 'desire machine' or 'factory', among other things.[315]

It is doubtful that the claim to a 'truly materialist psychiatry' can be borne out through such metaphorical equations.[316] This is shown by the fact that Deleuze and Guattari do not seek actual mediations between social conditions of work and desiring productions, but simply collapse the latter into the former: 'The truth of the matter is that *social production is purely and simply desiring-production itself under determinate conditions*'.[317] In the language of a radical 'materialism' of the libido, the real economic and social conditions of people's lives are made radically unreal. As Loick observes, in the hypostatisation of a deterritorialised, 'nomadic' desiring, for example, its historical character is ignored.[318] The criticism of the late period Foucault is aimed (implicitly) not least at Deleuze and Guattari: their treatment of desiring as a constant meant 'that desire and the subject of desire were withdrawn from the historical field'.[319] Frank criticises the talk of savage desire and its unbroken, negation-free positivity as 'a mere phantasm from a precritical age'.[320] According to Jean Baudrillard, modern Rousseauism 'has taken the form of the indeterminacy of drive, of the wandering of desire and of nomadism [a pris la forme de l'indétermination de la pulsion, de l'errance du désir et du nomadisme]', but, all of this has existed nowhere except 'in the imaginary of the dominant order'.[321] The evocation of flowing per se (whether of blood, sperm or money) and the idealisation of decoded, deterritorialised flows into 'revolutionary investment of desire' indicate that Deleuze and Guattari, using Freudo-Marxist rhetoric, have revived the vitalistic concept of a neo-Bergsonian *élan vital*.[322] What comes out is a generalised 'dionysian' libido, which permeates world affairs monistically as an ur-unity of life sustainment, sex and will to power.

315   Deleuze and Guattari 2009, 3 et sq., 24, 36 et sq.; Deleuze and Guattari 1972, p. 7 et sqq., 31, 43 et sqq; on the Deleuzian concept of the 'machine', cf. Schmidgen 1997.

316   Deleuze and Guattari 2009, p. 22; Deleuze and Guattari 1972, p. 29.

317   Deleuze and Guattari 2009, p. 29; Deleuze and Guattari 1972, p. 36.

318   Loick 2000, p. 103.

319   Foucault 1990, p. 4.

320   Frank 1989, p. 334.

321   Baudrillard 2010, p. 140; note 3.

322   E.g. Deleuze and Guattari 2009, p. 378; Deleuze and Guattari 1972, p. 454.

10   Primitive Inscriptions and State-Imperial Overcodings

Following Nietzsche's questioning of the priests, Deleuze and Guattari criticise the psychoanalyst as a 'new kind of priest', a 'director of bad conscience', who takes up the 'age old task of the ascetic ideal'.[323] The strategy is basically to integrate the 'structuralistic' approaches to the emergence of domination and 'culture' (above all of P. Clastres, Lévi-Strauss and G. Dumézil) into the theoretical framework of Nietzsche's *Genealogy of Morals*. This and not Marcel Mauss's *The Gift* is 'the great book of modern ethnology', primarily because in its second part it analyses primitive economics not on the level of exchange or interest 'à l'anglaise', but on the level of the debtor-creditor relationship.[324] The dismissal of Mauss is strangely displaced, because Mauss had in no way projected a bourgeois exchange of commodities 'à l'anglaise' into the early period, as Deleuze suggests he did, but instead investigated how segmentary societies regulate themselves by means of the obligatory reciprocity of gift and countergift, which, culminating in festively wasteful potlatches, are directed against the accumulations of wealth and thus against the development of class rule. So, obviously it is not about an anti-bourgeois use of Nietzsche, but about the attempt with his assistance to cancel out one of the most prominent conceptualisations of pre-state and domination-free, although by no means powerless, regulatory systems.[325]

In their place Deleuze and Guattari paint the picture of a 'primitive social machine',[326] which is determined by a creditor-debtor relationship. What Nietzsche described as a pre-historical 'enjoyment of making to suffer', burning into the skin of the debtor, the cutting of the debt from his body,[327] is now mediated with the Lacanian category of 'inscription', an 'inscription sauvage', which marks the body with the 'writing' of a 'terrible alphabet'.[328] Only in the interaction between 'speaking voice', marked body and enjoying eye does one burn a collective memory into the forgetful human animal, consisting of words and signs instead of things and effects; only here does it learn to speak and become capable of alliances.[329] Becoming human is for Deleuze and Guattari,

---

323   Deleuze and Guattari 2009, p. 332; Deleuze and Guattari 1972, p. 397.
324   Deleuze and Guattari 2009, p. 190; Deleuze and Guattari 1972, p. 224.
325   E.g. Mauss (1966, pp. 27, 31, 35, 38 et sq.); for the concept of 'power' in pre-state societies and its analytic distinction from the concept of domination, e.g. see Haude and Wagner (1998).
326   Deleuze and Guattari 2009, p. 145; Deleuze and Guattari 1972, p. 170.
327   Nietzsche 2013a, pp. 46 et sq., 51; Nietzsche 1999a, Vol. 5, pp. 295 et sq., 300.
328   Deleuze and Guattari 2009, pp. 144 et sq., 186, 191; Deleuze and Guattari 1972, p. 169 et sq., 218, 225.
329   Deleuze and Guattari 2009, pp. 144 et sq., 190; Deleuze and Guattari 1972, pp. 169 et sq., 225.

as already for Nietzsche, only conceivable within this creditor-debtor relation-ship and its bloody inscriptions; socialisation and language can only be ima-gined as the product of direct violence.

Deleuze and Guattari differentiate between this primitive social machine and the despotic-imperial 'machine' of the state. Thereby they base themselves on Nietzsche, who in the *Genealogy of Morals* describes the development of the state as a lightning-like act of violence, in which a master race of bellicose con-querors (a 'herd of blond beasts of prey') overwhelms a perhaps numerically superior, yet 'wild and uncultivated population', and oppresses them with ter-rible tyranny.[330] Only 'under the pressure of their hammer strokes', continues Nietzsche, is the instinct for freedom forced back inside and transformed into a 'bad conscience', which is then submitted to a process of moralising and made durable, first with the debtor, but then also with the creditor, who becomes afflicted with a curse.[331]

Deleuze and Guattari now transfer this to the despotic state of 'asiatic pro-duction', which lets the village communities exist and at the same time exploits them.[332] The primitive inscriptions are inserted into the state-imperial inscrip-tions and 'over-coded' [surcodé] by these; the hitherto uncoded flow of desiring is diverted onto domination, and works from now on destructively, e.g. as a 'death instinct'; an imperial signifier is established in the shape of the des-pot and his increasingly monotheistic god, which monopolises the previously decentralised and 'rhizomatic' forms of movement; debt, which in the pre-state society still existed in the shape of 'mobile, open and finite debt blocks' [blocs de dette mobiles, ouverts et finis], is transformed into infinite debt. It is to Nietzsche's credit that he pointed out how the despotic state has made every perspective of liberation impossible through the machinery that 'renders the debt infinite' [infinitivation].[333]

Out of Nietzsche's *Genealogy of Morals* Deleuze and Guattari have read a fun-damental opposition between a primitive and an imperial 'inscription', which they on the one hand apply to the 'Marxist' opposition between 'Asiatic modes of production' and segmentary village communities, and on the other hand combine with their 'schizo-analytic' opposition between multiple decentred desire productions and their despotic overcoding. A first effect of this theory-mix is that we see Nietzsche suddenly standing on the side of a decentred

330   Nietzsche 2013a, p. 72; Nietzsche 1999a, Vol. 5, p. 324.
331   Nietzsche 2013a, pp. 77 et sq.; Nietzsche 1999a, Vol. 5, p. 331.
332   Deleuze and Guattari 2009, pp. 195 et sq.; Deleuze and Guattari 1972, pp. 231 et sq.
333   Deleuze and Guattari 2009, pp. 192, 195 et sq., 197; Deleuze and Guattari 1972, pp. 227, 232, 236.

pre-statehood and arguing against a totalitarian state despotism. Of course, this pre-statehood is determined by an original creditor-debtor relationship, in which the enjoyment side of the rhizomatic desiring streams might have to be found more on the side of the enjoying creditor eye than on that of the tormented body of the debtor.

Deleuze and Guattari mask this projection of an all-pervasive domination in pre-state societies by opposing Nietzsche's primitive creditor-debtor relationship with a bourgeois backward projection of commodity exchange and interest 'à l'anglaise'. However, if we follow Nietzsche, it looks as though the one is not to be had without the other: the 'oldest and most basic personal relationship' is for him that 'between buyer and seller, between creditor and debtor: here it was that individuals first met, here measured themselves against one another'.[334] What preoccupied the 'primal' thoughts of man was 'establishing prices, assessing values, determining equivalents, trading', so that humans can be defined as 'the being who values and measures values'.[335] Instead of being 'anti-bourgeois', Nietzsche projects here a combination of *homo oeconomicus* and person flayer into primeval times. In so doing he pushes his domination myth to a point that reveals the procedure of his backward projection again: the 'personal rights', consisting of purchase and sales, are supposed to be older than all social beginnings. The characteristic 'to compare power with power, to measure, to compute' receives the status of a pre-social apriori, and only from there is it transferred onto 'the most elementary of the social complexes'.[336]

It is obvious that the image of Nietzsche as a critic of the state is also misleading. What Deleuze and Guattari present as opposition between segmentary society and 'Asiatic' state, Nietzsche himself designated as opposition between an 'independent nobility' and a state 'despotism' that overwhelms it.[337] This is the same contrast which had occupied the Graecist since his school exit thesis of 1864 *On Theognis of Megara*, namely that between a pre-classical, aristocratic caste society of 'Dorians' and the 'ideal state' of the attic democracy and classical philosophy.[338] As the investigations of Cancik and v.

---

334   Nietzsche 2013a, p. 56; Nietzsche 1999a, Vol. 5, pp. 305 et sq.
335   Ibid.
336   Nietzsche 2013a, p. 56, Nietzsche 1999a, Vol. 5, p. 306.
337   Nietzsche 2013a, p. 76; Nietzsche 1999a, Vol. 5, pp. 329 et sq.
338   Losurdo interprets the positions taken for slavery in Nietzsche's Theognis work against the political background of the simultaneous war of secession in the USA (Losurdo 2020, pp. 389 et sqq.). For the Nietzschean opposition of pre-classical and classical antiquity see *The Greek State*, a text written against the background of the Paris Commune (Nietzsche 2017a, pp. 167 et sqq.; Nietzsche 1999a, Vol. 1, pp. 764 et sqq), as well as the notes in Nietzsche 1999a, Vol. 8, pp. 53, 58, 96, 101.

Reibnitz show, the construction of a Dorian aristocratic ur-Greece belongs to a romantic-reactionary line of German philhellenism.[339] Whenever Nietzsche turns against the 'state', this is only because it impairs the 'freedom' of aristocratic rule by formations of social compromise. At the same time, he has a positive interest in the state as long as it does not appear as an 'ideal state', but as a 'fierce' conqueror and oppressor state which forces a 'chemical' separation of the classes.[340] Also, in the *Genealogy of Morals* Nietzsche has no objection to the 'hammer-strokes' of the tyrannical state: of bad conscience one must not think little, he insists, because it is engendered by the will to power and as 'activistic bad conscience' brings into existence for the first time the ideal and imaginative capacities of beauty and affirmation.[341] Deleuze and Guattari have overlooked the fact that Nietzsche clearly differentiates this 'activistic' bad conscience from the bad conscience of 'resentment', which is only produced by the moralising revaluation of the plebeians and their 'Jewish' priests.[342]

11   Faire de la pensée une machine de guerre

In a next step Deleuze and Guattari rescind the idea of a temporal sequence from (aristocratic) pre-state to state, which Nietzsche had suggested,[343] and instead introduce the category of the ur-state [German *Urstaat* in the original] as 'eternal model' and 'horizon of all history': 'Under every Black and every Jew there is an Egyptian'.[344] In this connection they turn against Pierre Clastres,

---

339   Shaped among other things by Curtius, F. Creuzer, K.O. Müller and J.J. Bachofen, this line is directed primarily against Winckelmann's 'liberal' orientation toward classical Greece (cf. v. Reibnitz 1992, pp. 62 et sq., 98 et sq., 106; Cancik 1995, pp. 125 et sq.). For Nietzsche's criticism of the 'humanistic' image of Greece cf. e.g. Nietzsche 1999a, Vol. 8, p. 58.
340   Nietzsche 2017, p. 171; Nietzsche 1999a, Vol. 1, p. 769; see also Nietzsche 1999a, Vol. 8, pp. 91–5.
341   Nietzsche 2013a, pp. 72 et sq.; see 71, 74; Nietzsche 1999a, Vol. 5, pp. 325 et sq.; see Nietzsche 1999a, Vol. 5, pp. 323, 327.
342   See *Genealogy of Morals* I, Aph. 7 (Nietzsche 2017a, p. 17; Nietzsche 1999a, Vol. 5, pp. 266 et sq.) and implicitly relating to it the beginning of *Genealogy of Morals* II, Aph. 21 (Nietzsche 2017a, p. 64 et sq.; Nietzsche 1999a, Vol. 5, p. 330).
343   E.g. Nietzsche's idiom of the 'break' and 'leap' of the emergence of the state (Nietzsche 2017a, 60) as well as of the 'earlier criterion' of the creditor-debtor relationship (Nietzsche 2017a, pp. 62 et sq.; Nietzsche 1999a, Vol. 5, pp. 324, 327).
344   Deleuze and Guattari 2009, p. 217. 'L'Urstaat originel, éternel modèle ...; c'est la formation de base, elle horizone toute l'histoire. ... Sous chaque Noir et chaque Juif, un Égyptien, un Mycénien sous les Grecs, un Etrusque sous les Romains.' (Deleuze and Guattari 1972, p. 257).

who still proceeded 'evolutionistically' from a succession of pre-state societies and statehood, and replace it with the concept of a synchronous coexistence of the despotic state in the centre, and nomadic-warrior secessions at the periphery: the opposition takes place only simultaneously, 'in a perpetual field of interaction'.[345]

On the basis of this continuous interplay of central government authority and peripheral secession, a last shift takes place in the image of Nietzsche: he becomes a bellicose nomadic rebel. Nietzsche's description of the founders of the state, who fatefully and 'suddenly as lightening' are there,[346] is now supposed to refer to a 'war machine', which suddenly 'from without' breaks into the dualism between the magic-despotic and priestly-judicial bodies of the state.[347] In contrast to Nietzsche, now the state no longer attacks a roaming population 'from without', but 'without' now means outside of the state. Now there is no more holding back for Deleuze and Guattari: from the assumption that the 'war machine' cannot simply be reduced to the state apparatus, they come to the conclusion that the next step is to define it as the 'pure form of exteriority' [pure forme d'extériorité].[348] Thus it is established that the 'war machine' holds the segmentary society together and is directed against the sovereignty of the state. War, with whose assistance the conquerors created their state according to Nietzsche, has now morphed into the most secure mechanism against the development of the power organs of the state.[349] Invented by the 'nomads', the war machine is decentral, multiple, mesh-like, 'rhizomatic'.[350] Their intellectual is Nietzsche, because with his aphorisms he makes thinking into a war machine: 'faire de la pensée une machine de guerre'.[351]

Romance of the guerrilla war, Pol-Pot terror or fascist death squads? Plausible here is Manfred Frank's notion of an 'inclination to "dangerous thinking"' per se, which poses no threat to real domination, and at the same time can be exploited by left as well as right.[352] For their aestheticisation of Parisian 'gauchism' Deleuze and Guattari have actually sought out exactly the most irrational components of its war and violence rhetoric, imported from the 'third world' (or rather projected onto it), which also have a firm place in the 'revolu-

345   Deleuze and Guattari 2018, p. 420; Deleuze and Guattari 1980, p. 446.
346   Nietzsche 2013a, p. 72; Nietzsche 1999a, Vol. 5, 325.
347   Deleuze and Guattari 2018, p. 412; Deleuze and Guattari 1980, p. 437.
348   Deleuze and Guattari 2018, p. 412; Deleuze and Guattari 1980, p. 438.
349   Deleuze and Guattari 2018, pp. 416 et sq.; Deleuze and Guattari 1980, p. 442.
350   Deleuze and Guattari 2018, pp. 417, 432, 443; Deleuze and Guattari 1980, pp. 443, 459 et sq., 471 et sq.
351   Deleuze and Guattari 2018, p. 439; Deleuze and Guattari 1980, p. 467.
352   Frank 1989, pp. 343 et sq.

tionary' rhetoric of right-wing populist and fascist movements. How quickly and smoothly the transition from far left to far right could take place can be observed in the example of the elevation of 'revolutionary' violence by the Bergson disciple Sorel,[353] who changed over from the proletarian general strike to the support of Mussolini in the shortest time. It would, of course, be inappropriate to suggest that Deleuze and Guattari were disposed to such a change of sides, and Deleuze remained faithful to his leftist commitment when he separated from Foucault because of the latter's support of the *Nouveaux Philosophes* (see below Chapter 5.5). But with the philosophical exaltation of the 'war machine', a discourse field is constructed in which leftist radicalism and the new right can overlap easily.

Here we encounter the paradoxical existence of a 'leftist Nietzscheanism', which Waite attributes to the extraordinary ability of Nietzsche to pull the 'wool' over the eyes, bodies and if necessary corpses of the subaltern.[354] However, a picture like this still says nothing to us about the attractions of such a blinding. Nietzsche has – not least under the influence of Spinoza – found a powerful language for the articulation of active and formative attitudes. He aligns these capacities to act at the same time with unfettered domination, so that the latter could appear in the disguise of a free and active affirmation of life. The 'leftist Nietzscheanism' of postmodernity borrows above all the 'Spinozean' articulations of a 'moralism-free' approach to life which Nietzsche absorbed (and reversed). Since this postmodernist Nietzscheanism is not able to differentiate them analytically from Nietzsche's master standpoint, it carries along undetected the opposite standpoint, that of naturalised domination, in the language of the most radical liberation.

To that extent 'leftist Nietzscheanism' can be understood as the attempt to introduce into oppositional and alternative movements a contradictory combination of fatalistic affirmations of domination and illusory and particularistic 'vanishing lines' of liberation: at the same time that Deleuze and Guattari spread the slogan of letting desiring and production coincide, they degrade what Marx and Engels described as the 'production of life' in the double sense of one's own in labour and of reproduction,[355] the desires for competence involved in it, its 'memories', its co-operation ethics – with the effect that they reduce all of this to an inscription effect of torture: their 'linguistics' consists not least, with reference to Spengler, in attributing all speaking to the basic unit of the command [mot d'ordre], in which a small death sentence is to

353   Cf. Sorel 2018 [1908].
354   Waite 1996, p. 337.
355   Marx and Engels 1845b, p. 43.

be found: 'dans tout mot d'ordre ..., il y a une petite sentence de mort'.[356] Moreover, while they pretend to turn against bourgeois backward projection into primeval times, aided by Nietzsche's creditor-debtor relationship and the 'Urstaat', they set about burying again the possibilities for thinking about pre-state societies not yet dominated by class rule, patriarchy and state rule. And finally, their dichotomy of desiring and its overcoding, which is at the same time the pole between 'schizoid-revolutionary' and 'reactionary-fascistising', is based on the elitist opposition between 'individual' and 'herd' which they have taken over from Nietzsche:[357] according to the *'laws of large numbers'*,[358] from the level of the organism up to that of the society, the 'individual' stands against the 'mass', the 'molecular' against the 'molar', 'micro physics' against the 'macro physics' of large groups.[359] According to Ishay Landa, Nietzsche's enormous influence on popular culture has created an elective affinity between an 'outright elitism' on the right, and a 'critical elitism' on the left.[360] Left-Nietzscheanism's elitism 'rules out a wholehearted popular commitment [...], weakens the left's ability to convincingly challenge reactionary politics, take a resolute stand against outright elitism'.[361] It seems that an ethics inspired by Nietzsche's philosophy can never get rid of its inherent 'pathos of distance', an attitude which manifests itself even in its most 'leftist' forms as a celebration of social distinctions against ordinary, 'unenlightened' people.

As Deleuze and Guattari themselves emphasise, the process of 'deterritorialising' and 'decoding' is conducted by capitalism itself, even if, in their opinion, inconsistently. This development should be advanced until the earth becomes so artificial that deterritorialising, from itself and from 'necessity', creates a new earth.[362] Does the revolutionary attitude consist of behaving in relation to the earth as if we had a second one in the trunk (or on the Internet)? What is announced as a liberation perspective reads like a neoliberal flexiblisation programme, which aims to clean up the last 'territories' of nature, of soci-

---

356 Deleuze and Guattari 2018, p. 89; Deleuze and Guattari 1980, p. 96.
357 'Formations statistiques ou grégarités', 'forme de grégarité', 'ensemble grégaire' (Deleuze and Guattari 1972, pp. 332, 409, 439; cf. Deleuze and Guattari 2009, pp. 280, 342, 367).
358 Deleuze and Guattari 2009, p. 287; Deleuze and Guattari 1972, p. 342.
359 E.g. Deleuze and Guattari 2009, pp. 279 et sq., 342, 365 et sq.; Deleuze and Guattari 1972, pp. 332 et sq., 409 et sq., 439 et sq.
360 Landa 2007, pp. 79–85.
361 Landa 2018, p. 417.
362 'Nous nous écrions: Encore plus de perversion! Encore plus d'artifice! Jusqu'à ce que la terre devienne tellement artificielle que le mouvement de déterritorialisation crée nécessairement par lui-même une nouvelle terre.' (Deleuze and Guattari 1972, p. 384; cf. Deleuze and Guattari 2009, p. 321).

ety and subjectivity. Along the recommended vanishing lines of desiring, the 'decentred' subjects can easily be driven apart and isolated by the digitalised commodity aesthetic and the illusion industry. Nietzsche's gifts have become no less dangerous.

CHAPTER 2

The Death of Man and the Eternal Recurrence

1   Survey of the Terrain: Uncritical Replication, Normative Critique, Leftist Helplessness

The freedom demanded by Foucault to 'use, distort, abuse, let scream' Nietzsche's philosophy without the bond of 'fidelity' to the text,[1] usually goes unchallenged in the literature: typically, supporters and critics of Foucault agree with each other to take Nietzsche prima facie as he is presented. Naturally, this is easiest for those who want to understand Nietzsche as the postmodern pioneer of a 'new art of living'.

The prototype of this line of interpretation is the collection of articles by Deleuze published in 1986 under the title *Foucault*, which Fink-Eitel seeks to credit for having placed 'Foucault philosophically there, where he belongs, in between Nietzsche and Heidegger'.[2] Deleuze sees the encounter between Foucault on one hand, and Nietzsche and Heidegger on the other, primarily in the shared criticism of the 'subject' and the conception of man as a 'fold of Being'.[3] However, since Foucault is ultimately not so much interested in Heidegger's ontology but rather in Nietzsche's 'will to power', it is really about a 'histoire nietzschéenne plutôt que heideggerienne'.[4] This story is re-narrated empathetically in a hermetic-esoteric diction and without the slightest analytical distance: Foucault's omnipresent concept of power – 'un profond nietzschéisme';[5] the announcement taken over from Nietzsche of the imminent 'death of man' and his overcoming by the 'overman' – parable of a new combination of the inner forces of man with new external forces, especially of silicon and genetics.[6] The presentation assumes approval, explains nothing, and questions nothing.[7]

Since it was Deleuze himself who decisively influenced Foucault's Nietzsche image with his 1962 book *Nietzsche et la philosophie*, a circular movement

---

1   Foucault 1997a, pp. 297 et sq., Foucault 2001a, Nr. 156, p. 1621.
2   Fink-Eitel 1990, p. 381.
3   Deleuze 2000, pp. 110 et sqq., 128 et sqq., Deleuze 1986, pp. 117 et sqq, 136 et sqq.
4   Deleuze 1986, pp. 137, 120 et sqq.; Deleuze 2000, pp. 129, 159.
5   Deleuze 1986, p. 78; Deleuze 2000, p. 71.
6   Deleuze 2000, p. 131, cf. pp. 87 et sqq., Deleuze 1986, p. 140, cf. pp. 93 et sqq.
7   'Deleuze does not argue, Deleuze states. Deleuze does not represent, Deleuze decrees.' (Roth 2000, p. 136).

is closing here. Foucault takes up the Nietzsche-image from Deleuze, which the latter then certifies in return. Together they take on the publication of the complete critical edition of Nietzsche's works in 1966 in France. Indeed, the construction of postmodernist Nietzscheanism is carried out to a large extent in interplay between Deleuze and Foucault, who produce amplifying effects by means of exuberant reviews, prefaces, interviews, etc. The most popular and at the same time most untenable example of this highly successful advertising strategy is Foucault's proclamation in 1970 that 'perhaps one day, this century will be known as Deleuzian'.[8]

The bulk of the literature on Foucault is still under the spell of a postmodernist Nietzscheanism. For Wilhelm Schmid, for instance, Nietzsche is simply the one who 'answered the search for meaning with the new foundation of ethics as an art of living'.[9] Accordingly, he wants above all to show how the concept of an 'aesthetics of existence', developed by the late Foucault in 1984 in Volumes 2 and 3 of his *History of Sexuality*, 'can be linked to Nietzsche's thinking'.[10] Schmid's book compiles a wealth of material in which Foucault directly or indirectly referred to Nietzsche and Heidegger (or could have referred to them), but it does so without any critical distance. Regarding Nietzsche's concept of power, Schmid appreciates the 'ethical' dimension of a 'self-constitution of the individual',[11] without noticing the concept's perspective of radical domination. 'Nietzsche was essentially an ethical thinker. He discovers the subject of self practice, the self shaping of the individual'.[12] Therefore, to be a 'Nietzschean' means to advocate a 'post-teleological model of ethics', diametrically opposed to ethics of the type of the categorical imperative, and with 'personal choice' at its centre.[13] This plays down the fact that both Nietzsche and the late Foucault read the model of this 'post-teleological' ethics out of the male-elite of the Greek slave-holding society.

Paradoxically, the tendency toward indiscriminately adopting a postmodernist image of Nietzsche can be found even in Habermas, perhaps the best-known critic of postmodernism. In 1980 in his speech at the award of the Adorno Prize, Habermas detected a 'young conservative' line from Bataille to Foucault to Derrida and related it to the resurrection of Nietzsche in the 70s.[14]

---

8   Foucault 1970, p. 343.
9   Schmid 1991, p. 219.
10   Schmid 1991, p. 159.
11   Schmid 1991, p. 196.
12   Schmid 1991, p. 186.
13   Schmid 1991, pp. 307, 384.
14   Habermas 1987, p. 155.

His polemical classification promises more than the theoretical argument can deliver, because Habermas's Nietzsche is not much more than a (too) radical questioner of modernity. He simply 'showed how one totalises critique'; through his 'totalizing self-outperformance' of ideology-critique, he became a role model for a critique of modernity from right to left, calling into question the 'achievements of Occidental rationalism' diagnosed by Weber.[15] Not unlike the postmodern Nietzscheans, Habermas also once again erased the master from Nietzsche's 'anarchism of the masters' (Bernstein), though this time in order to be able to direct all the pathos of indignation against a 'radical' ideology-critique. This restricted point of view is due to a great extent to his endeavour to situate Horkheimer and Adorno in proximity to Nietzsche and his 'totalising' critique of modernity. What connects Nietzsche with the postmodernists, with Horkheimer/Adorno, Benjamin up to Peter Weiss, is then an anarchist-surrealistic 'rebellion against everything normative'.[16]

This shallow image of Nietzsche also compromises Habermas' critique of Foucault, which always tends to slip into abstract normative reasoning: his decisive reproach is that Foucault, with his monistic concept of power, does not do justice to the importance of communication-oriented action, its norms and values, and cannot capture the increase in legal certainty, subjective freedom and autonomy in modernity.[17] To this criticism Foucault can respond easily that the Habermasian assumption of norm-guided communicative relations supposedly beyond social relations of power belongs to the realm of 'utopia'.[18] Whereupon the Habermasian criticism adds that Foucault cannot justify his critique of power normatively, to which Foucault can respond by stating his basic wish to destroy just such a normative critique. To the extent that the debate spins around the opposition of 'power' and 'norms', and it does so to a large extent,[19] Foucault always seems to be the tortoise already at the finish line, while the hare Habermas still has to make long detours: was it not Foucault who, instead of appealing to norms, developed a concept of power as 'normalisation'? And did not the late-period Foucault, with his 'peculiar turn'[20] to ethics and the subject, preempt the Habermasian accusations of a

---

15   Habermas 1990, pp. 97, 107, 120, 126, 353, note 8.
16   Habermas 1990, p. 123.
17   Habermas 1990, pp. 335 et sqq.
18   Foucault 2001b Nr. 356, pp. 1545 et sq.
19   Cf. for example the overview in Honneth (1990, pp. 12 et sqq.); for the strongly moral philosophically oriented Anglo-Saxon discussion see e.g. the contributions in Hoy (1986) and Ashenden/Owen (1999). In contrast, see the much more substantial ethico-politcal argumentation of Nancy Fraser (1989, pp. 35 et sqq.).
20   Honneth 1990, p. 17.

lack of normative foundation for his approach to critique? The debate is certainly more complex and shall not be followed further here. But the staging of a dispute between the 'norms-philistine' Habermas and the 'anarchist' Foucault is theoretically fruitless and misleading: it bypasses the real, and also ethical, problem of Foucault's Nietzscheanism.[21]

But in view of the countless books in which the heritage of the postmodernist Nietzsche is received approvingly and passed on, the criticisms of Foucault inspired by Jürgen Habermas and Axel Honneth, and more so by the 'hermeneutic' approach of Manfred Frank, at least have the historical merit of articulating Foucault's Nietzscheanism as a theoretical problem. This becomes evident when one compares them with the silence of the Althusser School in this regard. Indeed, it was the Althusserians who believed that an alliance with Foucault could be formed on the basis of a critique of the subject, of anthropology and humanism, inspired by Nietzsche and Heidegger. When, for example, Dominique Lecourt sees essential similarities between Foucault's archaeology of knowledge and historical materialism, then this is because of a conception of history perceived as a 'process without a subject structured by a system of laws ... radically anti-anthropologistic, anti-humanist, and anti-structuralist'.[22] Disagreement arises at the point where Foucault rejects the Althusserian concept of ideology and replaces it with the concept of knowledge. Its limitations lie in his 'archaeological circle', i.e. the inability to think the specific 'régime de matérialité' of discourse, their interlocking [embrayage] with the 'ideological state apparatuses', as well as their determination by class struggles.[23] This critique is indeed illuminating, but the Nietzschean-Heideggerian foundations of Foucault's approach remain unchallenged. In 1989 Balibar looks back on the debate from an 'irreversible post-Marxist philosophical horizon',[24] which he tries to mitigate by withdrawing most of his previous objections – there is no desire to scrutinise the problematic foundations of Foucauldian Nietzscheanism. It's as if the capacity of the Althusser school to criticise is paralysed here by its 'theoretical anti-humanism', which itself is owed to a combination of Marx, Nietzsche, and Heidegger.[25]

---

21   Characteristic for the shifted debate is the anecdote about an obviously unsuccessful dinner the two had together in 1983, during which, without preliminary warning, Foucault showed Habermas his shark's teeth in a broad grin and said in a sarcastic tone: 'C'est peutetre que je suis un anarchiste?' (Veyne, quoted in Eribon 1994, pp. 291 et sq.).

22   Lecourt 1975, p. 189; 'processus sans sujet structuré par un système de lois ..., radicalement antianthropologiste et antihumaniste', Lecourt 1972, p. 101.

23   Lecourt 1972, pp. 108 et sq., 122, 127 et sq.; Lecourt 1975, pp. 194 et sq., 205, 208 et sq.

24   Balibar 1991, p. 61.

25   Cf. for this Waite 1998, pp. 2 et sq., 398 notes 8–10, 419 note 137.

These blind spots of Marxist critique have contributed significantly to the fact that the left faces a postmodern, refreshed Nietzscheanism with theoretical helplessness. A large number of works in the literature on Foucault try to connect Foucault's approach with Marxist-inspired theories, while at the same time playing down his Nietzscheanism, or recounting it in a purely descriptive manner, so to speak with a shrug of the shoulders. We will discuss this tendency with the example of Thomas Lemke, who reduces Foucault's Nietzscheanism to a 'war hypothesis', which is then replaced (beginning around 1976/77) by the 'productivity' of power (see below Chapter 3.2).[26] In turn, a conservative 'new-humanist' counter-movement, most notably conducted in France by Luc Ferry and Alain Renaut, fills the empty space of theoretical critique.[27] Their criticism of postmodernist Nietzscheanism, regarding Foucault as its main proponent, is at the same time presented as a reckoning with the thinkers of the '68ers' in general, under whom they subsume among others Derrida, Althusser and Bourdieu.[28] Of course this stance is politically overdetermined. Had the authors been concerned with an analysis of the thinking of the '68ers', to be consistent they would have had to include the strong influence of Sartre, whose existentialist humanism would certainly have spoiled their 'anti-humanist' enemy stereotype. Ferry and Renaut practice an over-generalisation which levels out Foucault's differences with other '68er'-directions and obscures the specific nature of his Nietzscheanism, rather than illuminating it. A similar political overdetermination can be observed with the example of Richard Wolin, who puts postmodernism in the same bag as the movement of the'68ers and criticises both in the name of the 'Enlightenment', 'humanism', the 'normative core' of Western democracy and finally 'American' values.[29]

In the following, the early Foucault's reception of Nietzsche will be investigated exemplarily, with reference to one of his best-known books prior to 1968, the *Order of Things*.

---

26   Cf. Lemke 2019, pp. 86 et sqq., 101 et sqq., 124 et sqq.
27   Luc Ferry later became Minister of Education from 2002 to 2004 in the cabinet led by the conservative Prime Minister Jean-Pierre Raffarin. In January 2019 he demanded the utilisation of military force against the Yellow Vests.
28   Ferry and Renaut 1990, pp. 69 et sq., 123 et sq., 153 et sqq.
29   Cf. Wolin 2004, pp. XIV, 278, 301, 313; for a critical analysis, see Rehmann 2005a.

2 The 'Age of History' and the 'Anthropological Sleep'

Foucault conceived the *Order of Things* as a positive counterpart to his study *Madness and Society* (1961): whereas the latter undertook a 'history of the other', of those excluded from modern civilization, now Foucault writes a 'history of the same' in the sense of an archaeological analysis of the knowledge of our modernity.[30] In the centre is the critique of the 'anthropological' and 'historicist' paradigm of the human sciences of the nineteenth century. It starts with the thesis that 'man' is only a young invention of about 200 years – 'no more than a kind of rift [déchirure] in the order of things', a 'new fold [pli] in our knowledge' – and ends with the announcement of his impending death, through which he 'would be erased, like a face drawn in sand at the edge of the sea'.[31] What created man as the epistemological subject of the human sciences was the collapse of the 'representation system' of the Enlightenment at the end of the eighteenth century. What causes man to disappear is a new constellation of knowledge that is foreshadowed, e.g. in structuralist ethnology and Lacanian psychoanalysis. The possibilities of a new thinking 'in the void left by man's disappearance' [dans le vide de l'homme disparu] had been opened up especially by Nietzsche, in particular through his teaching of the 'overman' and the 'Eternal Return'.[32]

This argument, influential for the manifestation of 'theoretical anti-humanism' in France, will be inspected in the following. To this end it seems to me necessary to dissect it into different strata, which in turn refer us to different manifestations of Nietzscheanism: the critique of 'anthropology', mediated primarily via Heidegger, leads us into an anti-humanistic critique of Kantian subject-philosophy; the use of 'eternal recurrence' and of the 'overman' leads us directly to Nietzsche's elaboration of a new religion, with whose aid he wanted to leave Christian morality as well as idealistic philosophy behind. In order to be able to understand the use of Nietzsche as a herald of a new thinking, we must first attempt to comprehend the way Foucault constructs the 'anthropological' paradigm as a homogeneous unity, and why he finds it so problematic that he wants to see it overcome entirely by means of Nietzsche's 'overman'.

Unlike other poststructuralists (e.g. Derrida) Foucault has the subject of modernity begin not with the 'representation system' of the Enlightenment, but only after its collapse at the end of the eighteenth century.[33] He distin-

30 Foucault 1994, p. xxiv, Foucault 1966, pp. 15 et sq.
31 Foucault 1994, pp. xxiii et sq., 362, Foucault 1966, pp. 15, 398.
32 Foucault 1994, p. 342, Foucault 1966, p. 353.
33 Cf. among others Frank 1989, pp. 135 et sqq., 140 et sqq., 146 et sq., 149.

guishes three different periods: up until the seventeenth century, the Renaissance system of thought dominated, in which words and things were connected by a system of similarities;[34] in the transition to the Enlightenment, this tripartite (ternary) system of signifiant, signifié, and mediating 'conjoncture' is replaced by a 'binary' system in which a universal reason constructs the relation between the signified and the signifying as a transparent relationship of representation: words have the task and the power of 'representing thought'.[35] Finally, in the period between 1775 and 1825 the static order of the classical system of representation is dissolved and superseded by the paradigm of 'history', which from then on structures the space of knowledge.[36] The emerging human sciences are characterised by the search for an irreducible structural element *behind* the visible, namely *labour* in economics, the *organisation* in biology, and the grammatical *inflection system* in the conception of language.[37] The philosophy of Kant marks 'the threshold of our modernity' by asking about the transcendental apriori beyond all experience, an apriori from which representations become possible.[38] Foucault conceives the 'age of history' as an 'anthropological sleep' in which 'man' sets out in search of his hidden essence, whose truth he has projected into the future.[39]

It is widely acknowledged that Foucault's critique of the 'anthropological age' is influenced over long stretches by Heidegger's critique of humanism.[40] This is especially true with regard to Heidegger's investigation titled *Kant and the Problem of Metaphysics*, from 1929, whose argument resurfaces partly verbatim in the *Order or Things*, without Foucault indicating it.[41] Therefore, the 'death of man' must be understood in the sense of Heidegger: 'le thème de la mort de l'homme consiste purement et simplement à célébrer la victoire du *Dasein* sur la conscience de soi, sur le *Bewusstsein*'.[42]

---

34 Foucault 1994, p. 46, Foucault 1966, p. 57.
35 Foucault 1994, p. 78, Foucault 1966, p. 92. This corresponds to Descartes' utopia of a universal language, with which the representative value of the words is so exactly fixed that with their assistance the peasants could judge better of the truth of things than the philosophers today (Foucault 1994, p. 205; cf. pp. 63 et sq., 66 et sq., 79, 81 et sqq., 206, Foucault 1966, p. 217; cf. pp. 77 et sq., 80 et sq., 93, 95 et sqq., 219).
36 Foucault 1994, p. 219, Foucault 1966, p. 231.
37 Foucault 1994, pp. 237 et sq., Foucault 1966, pp. 249 et sq.
38 Foucault 1994, pp. 242 et sq., Foucault 1966, p. 255.
39 Foucault 1994, pp. 340 et sqq., Foucault 1966, pp. 351 et sqq.
40 Cf. Dreyfus and Rabinow (1983, pp. XXI, XXVII, 11, 38), Frank (1989, pp. 102, 104, 190, 199 et sq.), Fink-Eitel 1990, p. 377, Forst 1990, pp. 161 et sqq., Schmid 1991, pp. 130 et sqq.
41 Ferry and Renaut 1990, pp. 101 et sq.
42 Ferry and Renaut 1985, p. 139; Ferry and Renaut 1990, p. 98.

Foucault himself says in 1984 in retrospect that without Heidegger he might not have read Nietzsche: 'Nietzsche alone did not say anything to me! Whereas Nietzsche and Heidegger, that was the philosophical shock'.[43] The strong influence of Heidegger is visible, for example, in the 1954 introduction to Binswanger's *Dream and Existence*, in which Foucault conceives of 'being human' as the content of that 'which ontology analyzes as the transcendental structure of *Dasein*, of presence to-the-world', and he certifies the book by Binswanger as having accomplished 'the passage from anthropology to ontology, which seems to us from the outset the major problem of the analysis of Dasein'.[44] The fact that Nietzsche will gain preponderance over Heidegger (c' est Nietzsche qui l' a emporté), as Foucault also notes in retrospect in 1984, cannot yet be ascertained at the time he wrote *The Order of Things*: almost all of the approving references to Heidegger in *Dits et écrits* date from 1966.[45] A first distancing occurred in 1969, when Foucault demanded the abandonment of the metaphysical 'figure of the same' reaching from Plato to Heidegger,[46] and in 1972 he criticised Husserl and Heidegger for questioning the foundations of knowledge starting from an 'origin' [à partir de ce qui est originaire], rather than like Nietzsche by means of a historical analysis of the 'positivist' type.[47] The fact that a tension exists here between Nietzsche and Heidegger was probably not evident to Foucault until the preparation of his essay *Nietzsche, Genealogy, History* in 1971, whose critique of 'origin' can also be understood as an implicit polemic against Heidegger's interpretation of Nietzsche.

3   Borrowings from Heidegger's Critique of Humanism

Heidegger seeks to demonstrate two things above all with his critique of Kant: firstly, that Kant wants to found the possibility of an ontology on the level of the subject, of 'the subjectivity of the human subject', thus making it a question of anthropology, and secondly, that this kind of 'inquiring into the subjectivity of the subject' can only lead us into darkness and is thus improper as an ontological foundation.[48] He demonstrates this with the example of the 'faculty of imagination' [Einbildungskraft], which Kant determines in a con-

---

43   Foucault 1988b, p. 250, Foucault 2001b, Nr. 354, p. 1522.
44   Foucault and Binswanger 1986, pp. 32, 73 et sq.
45   Cf. Foucault 2001a, Nr. 39, p. 570; Nr. 40, p. 573; Nr. 41, p. 579; Nr. 42, p. 581.
46   Foucault 2001a, Nr. 64, p. 798.
47   Foucault 2001a, Nr. 109, p. 1240.
48   Heidegger 1997, pp. 144, 150.

tradictory manner: on one hand it appears in the *Critique of Pure Reason* as an 'indispensable function of the soul, without which we should have no cognition whatever';[49] only through 'pure imagination a priori' does the schema of sensuous conceptions emerge (e.g. figures in space), the synthetic conjoining of the manifold perceptions, as well as the formation of the conceptions of the understanding;[50] and here, Heidegger summarises (while simultaneously translating Kant's approach into his own key), it forms 'the look of the horizon of objectivity [Gegenständlichkeit] as such in advance, before the experience of being', and without depending on the presence of beings.[51]

On the other hand, in the treatise written ten years later, Kant shows in *Anthropology from a Pragmatic Point of View* (1798) that the 'productive' imagination is not 'creative', 'namely not capable of producing a sense representation that was never given to our faculty of sense'.[52] However great an artist, indeed a sorceress, the imagination might be, she 'must get the material for its images from the senses'.[53]

Heidegger interprets this discrepancy as meaning that in the *Critique of Pure Reason* imagination is 'grasped in a way that is fundamentally more original', whereas the Kantian *Anthropology* is only related 'empirically' to experiencing beings, and is not sufficient for the transcendental problem.[54] However, the transcendental imagination, which is to produce the original unity of perception and thinking,[55] remains 'homeless' in Kant.[56] He looked briefly through it 'into a to us unknown root', that is to say into an 'original time', but he 'retreated' from it, by switching over in the second edition of *The Critique of Pure Reason* to a more 'logical' reflection.[57] He could not do otherwise than retreat because he attempted an ontological foundation within the framework of an anthropology in which this is not possible. The three fundamental philosophical questions of the *Critique of Pure Reason* – What can I know? What should I do? What may I hope?[58] – are dissolved in Kant's introduction to his lecture on logic into the

---

49   Kant 1984, p. 78; Kant 1974, B 103.
50   Kant 1984, pp. 111, 119; Kant 1974, pp. 162, 181.
51   Heidegger 1997, p. 92.
52   § 28, Kant 2006, p. 61; Kant 1980, p. 168.
53   Ibid.; Kant 1980, pp. 168 et sq.
54   Heidegger 1997, pp. 93, 144.
55   It is the 'mediating center' of sensuality and understanding, their 'original, unifying center', 'root of both stems' (Heidegger 1997, pp. 124, 137).
56   Heidegger 1997, p. 95.
57   Heidegger 1997, pp. 112 et sqq., 119 et sq., 137, 141.
58   Kant 1984, pp. 456 et sq.; Kant 1974, B 832 et sq.

fourth question, 'What is man?'.[59] Thus he expresses the 'fundamental tendency of man's contemporary position with respect to himself', namely to place himself into the 'center of beings':[60] 'Anthropology seeks not only the truth about human beings, but instead it now demands a decision as to what truth in general can mean'.[61] Heidegger claims to solve the question of origin raised by Kant at the point where his anthropology cannot 'reach', that is to say, with a 'metaphysics of Dasein' or in a 'fundamental ontology', whose task is the 'unveiling of the constitution of the Being of [Dasein]'.[62]

Foucault presented a similar line of argument already in 1961 in his introduction to Kant's *Anthropology from a Pragmatic Point of View*, submitted as a 'complementary thesis'. He questions the 'philosophical anthropologies' which present themselves as the 'natural access to the fundamental' and the 'anthropological illusion' by which philosophy 'locked itself into subjectivity'. But the thesis culminates with Nietzsche, who was able to undertake a 'veritable *critique* 'of the anthropological illusion by demonstrating that 'it is in the death of man that the death of God is realized'.[63] Therefore, the fourth question of the 'anthropological "quadrilateral"' (What is man?) reaches its end 'in the response which both challenges and disarms it: *Der Übermensch*'.[64] In the *Order of Things* he demands the destruction of Kant's 'anthropological quadrilateral' right down to its fundamentals.[65] Mind the justification: 'to recall it [philosophical thought] to the possibilities of its earliest dawning' in order to recover a 'purified ontology' or a 'radical thought of being'.[66] This indicates that Foucault also took over from Heidegger the 'fundamental-ontological' response. In addition, the dating of the 'anthropological age' as the period after the late eighteenth century has already been made by Heidegger.[67] Foucault's concluding statement that man will vanish like a face in the sand on the shore[68] is an echo of the Heideggerian thesis, that 'mankind's being a subject is not the only possibility of the primal essence of historical humanity there has ever been or ever

59   Kant 1992b, p. 538; Kant 1968c, p. 448.
60   Heidegger 1997, pp. 145 et sq., 146 et sq., 149 et sq.
61   Heidegger 1997, p. 147.
62   Heidegger 1997, pp. 162 et sqq.
63   Foucault 2008b, pp. 121, 123 et sq.
64   Foucault 2008b, p. 124.
65   Foucault 1994, pp. 341 et sq., Foucault 1966, pp. 352 et sq.
66   Ibid.
67   Since the end of the eighteenth century, Heidegger wrote 1938 in 'The Age of the World Picture', there has been an 'ever more exclusive rooting of the interpretation (Heidegger 2002, p. 70; cf. pp. 75 et sq.).
68   Foucault 1994, p. 387, Foucault 1966, p. 398.

will be', but is nothing more than a 'shadow of a passing cloud over a hidden land'.[69] Foucault adopts from Heidegger the perspective that modern thinking represents an increasing displacement of being [Seins-Verdrängung] through the 'self empowerment of the subject', and here he sees a way of thinking being prepared with which to understand history as a succession of configurations of knowledge of whole epochs, in which the subject is just an effect, a 'fold' of knowledge.[70]

The borrowings from Heidegger's fundamental ontology are not disputed in the Foucault literature, but there is little discussion about whether and how it affects Foucault's theoretical approach. A question of this kind is often precluded by an uncritical reading of Heidegger. For example, Dreyfus and Rabinow, who play a crucial role for the Anglo-American Foucault reception, suppose that they can describe Heidegger's hermeneutics with the 'idea' 'that human subjects are formed by the historical cultural practices in which they develop'.[71] With a representation of this kind, which almost turns Heidegger into a precursor of cultural studies, the central concern of his 'fundamental ontology', namely the transcendental position of 'Being' as opposed to the cultural practices of 'beings', is made invisible at the outset. Classifications like the following are characteristic: Foucault 'is clearly in a line of thinkers such as Nietzsche, Weber, late Heidegger, and Adorno'.[72] It is in no way so 'clear' that such a 'line' exists, since it was precisely Adorno who said of Heidegger's concept of fateful thrownness [Geworfenheit] that it 'was according to the taste of fascism'.[73] In the so-called 'critical' Foucault reader the two authors are carried away by the platitude that 'like Heidegger, Foucault wants to change our world',[74] without it crossing their minds that Heidegger understood such a world change above all in the sense of support for the Nazistate. For example, Rainer Forst moves in a similarly platitudinous pattern of reception when he reports that Foucault's and Heidegger's analyses are connected in their 'critical interest'.[75]

On such a level, one is far from grasping the contradictory impulses of Heidegger's philosophy. Its fascination for critical intellectuals rests above all on the metaphysics-critical argument that the essence of the human being reveals itself in its 'being-in-the-world'. Heidegger's strongest objection to Kant's

---

69   Heidegger 2002, p. 84.
70   Cf. Frank 1989, pp. 190 et sqq.
71   Dreyfus and Rabinow 1983, p. XXI.
72   Dreyfus and Rabinow 1983, p. XXVI.
73   Adorno 2003, p. 81.
74   Dreyfus and Rabinow 1986, pp. 117 et sq.
75   Forst 1990, p. 147.

anthropology is this shift towards exploring human relationships to the world: 'In [his] comportment toward beings which he himself is not, he already finds the being as that from which he is supported, as that on which he has depended, as that over which ... he can never become master. Depending upon the being which he is not, man is at the same time not master of the being that he himself is'.[76] The individuals, one could paraphrase with the help of the young Marx, find their 'essence' not inwardly as an 'inner, mute, general character which unites the many individuals in a *natural way*';[77] they can realise it only by entering the 'world', which they encounter and which they depend upon, and by adopting a part of its contained meanings and possibilities. That this is to be understood as a practical activity can also be found in some parts in Heidegger's works, for example when he speaks of 'a way of being as care [Besorgen]', which he describes as 'having to do with something, producing something, attending to something and looking after it, making use of something ... undertaking, accomplishing, evincing, interrogating, considering, discussing, determining'.[78] That as individuals we cannot arbitrarily dispose of the 'existent' outside of us, that is, of the given world of things and tools – in Heidegger's jargon the 'equipment' [das Zeug] –[79] as well as of social relations, is obvious; that even we ourselves are 'powerful' only in a limited sense can hardly be denied, for example in view of the Freudian discovery of the unconscious. Here we see an operational realism at work which seduced Lucien Goldmann to the formulation that between the theses of Heidegger and Marx's *Theses on Feuerbach* there is 'no basic difference'.[80]

There is, of course, a fundamental difference, and it lies in the fact that Heidegger has purified the being-in-the-world of the 'contingencies' of the objective world and has determined it as the 'transcendence of Dasein'.[81] Although there are passages that hint at the dependency of the concept of 'world' or 'equipment' on practice, his Dasein possesses 'neither a *body*, nor *hunger*, nor *gender*', noted Günther Anders.[82] Heidegger's fundamental onto-

76   Heidegger 1997, pp. 159 et sq.
77   Marx 1845, p. 4, Marx and Engels 1957-, Vol. 3, p. 6.
78   Heidegger 1998, pp. 82 et sq.
79   Cf. for this term Heidegger 1998, pp. 96 et sqq.
80   Goldmann 1977, p. 37.
81   Heidegger 1997 p. 165.
82   Anders 2001, pp. 83, 280. Anders worked out the 'illusory concreteness' [Schein-Konkretheit] of the Heideggerian 'world' in 1948, whose examples '[come] from the rural shoemaker's workshop' (Anders 2001, p. 80): 'The area of Heidegger's concreteness begins behind hunger and stops before the economy and the machine: in the center the "Dasein" sits around hammering with his "equipment", and in this way demonstrates "care" and

logy wants to go back behind the subject-object dichotomy, but not by exploring reality from the point of view of 'sensuous human activity', 'subjective'
practice, as Marx proposes in his First Thesis on Feuerbach,[83] but by splitting
a 'Being' off from 'beings' with its manifold 'behaviours' [hantieren] and setting up a new beyond. 'Being' is a 'transcendens', a 'transcendental universal', as
is written in the first determinations of *Being and Time*.[84] Sartre turns against
this transcendentalisation when he defines existentialism as the precedence
of existence before essence ['l' existence précède l' essence'] and – close to the
First Thesis on Feuerbach – deduces from it that 'subjectivity must be our point
of departure'.[85] In the *Letter on Humanism* Heidegger had ascertained that this
expression of existentialism has 'nothing at all in common' with his fundamental ontology.[86] Where Sartre wants to philosophise on the level of human
relationships, Heidegger counters with the supposedly deeper level, 'où il y a
principalement l' Être': 'Man stands ek-sistingly ... in the destiny of Being'.[87]

What this means can be shown best with the mode of 'thrownness', with
which we exist in Being. With this category, which is devoid of any practice,
Heidegger wants to express the 'in its whence and whither veiled ... Being character of Dasein', its 'that it is and has to be'.[88] What is at issue is that 'existence
... may accept the thrownness of its own "there" in a way that is more free
from Illusion'.[89] In this disposition the 'project' [Entwurf] is clearly subordinated to 'thrownness', or rather 'delivered over' [überantwortet], as Heidegger
puts it,[90] for Dasein involves not a 'free-floating self-projection', but rather is
'determined by thrownness as a Fact of the entity which it is'.[91] After all, in

---

the new beginning of ontology' (Anders 2001, p. 83). Anders sees Heidegger's philosophy
as characterised by an erasure of human neediness: 'Dasein is very busy of course: it
hammers and cobbles about and, in this concern "understands" its shoe last. But *why* it
concerns itself: he mentions the source of the concern at most casually and without drawing philosophical conclusions from it..... Because the truth is that life is 'concern', because
it is *hunger*. .... Man [is] so ontic that he must incorporate onticness, in order to be ontological, that is, to be there' (Anders 2001, p. 63).

83   Marx 1845, p. 3; Marx and Engels 1957-, Vol. 3, p. 5.
84   Heidegger 1988, p. 22. So the 'mundane facticity' of existence does not really come into
      play, but is 'pushed aside' in favour of the transcendental concept of world, notes Pocai
      (2001, p. 51).
85   Sartre 2007, p. 20.
86   Heidegger 1977, p. 209.
87   Heidegger 1977, pp. 213 et sq., 216.
88   Heidegger 1988, pp. 173 et sq.
89   Heidegger 1988, p. 443.
90   Heidegger 1988, p. 188.
91   Heidegger, 1988, p. 321.

the *Letter on Humanism* the project itself is disclosed as 'essentially a thrown', for 'what throws in projection is not man but Being itself, which sends man into the ek-sistence of Da-sein that is his essence'.[92] As Susanne Lettow has shown,[93] Heidegger's thrownness can be understood as a passive turn-about of what Marx and Engels had addressed in the *German Ideology* with the verb 'to find as given' [vorfinden] when writing that 'every individual and every generation' ... 'finds in existence as something given' a 'sum of productive forces, capital funds and social forms of intercourse'.[94] In addition to this, Heidegger adds the idea that each individual also finds himself as something given. But he turns these deliberations into a passive arrangement by making the existing ensemble of production and reproduction disappear behind the concept of an 'underlying Being'. This applies also to the relations of generations and gender into which the individuals are not merely 'thrown' inorganically, but rather born and socialised. Since the determining factors are not conceived in their concrete contradictoriness, they cannot also be actively appropriated and practically transformed, but only taken over as fate.[95]

If this is to be a 'practical philosophy', then it is one 'which simply contains instructions for accepting positedness [Gesetztheit], never for action', remarks Bloch:[96] 'Infinitely remote and not even touched upon in this "ontology of the subject" is the tendency to found *rebellion* in despair, to find *hope* in rebellion'.[97] When Bloch argues on the first page of the *Principle of Hope* that the work of hope 'requires people who throw themselves actively into what is becoming, to which they themselves belong', the polemic against Heidegger's 'thrownness' is obvious: Hope 'will not tolerate a dog's life which feels itself only passively thrown into What Is'.[98]

The young Marcuse, who was still engaged in the endeavour to synthesise Marxism and Heidegger's fundamental ontology, tried to overcome the internal contradiction between turning towards the world and turning to a hereafter in Heidegger: He credits him with having discovered the 'concrete human being

---

92 Heidegger 1977, p. 217.
93 Lettow 2001, pp. 775 et sq.
94 Marx and Engels 1845b, p. 54; Marx and Engels 1957-, Vol. 3, p. 38.
95 This distinguishes Heidegger's specification of the 'thrownness' from progressive uses of the term, for example by Sartre, Marcuse, Tillich, Hannah Arendt and Althusser. Regarding these usages and the criticisms of the concept by Bloch, Lukács, Adorno and O'Brien see Lettow (2001, pp. 777 et sqq.).
96 Ernst Bloch 1991 p. 282.
97 Ernst Bloch 1991, p. 283.
98 Bloch 1986, 1. For a discussion of Bloch's critique of Heidegger, cf. Fahrenbach 2017, pp. 245 et sqq., 294 et sqq.

in his concrete historical situation' as a philosophical starting point, but adds right away that there is nowhere even the hint of a 'breaking through' to the problems of the 'material constitution of historicity'.[99] If one raises such questions about the 'Dasein as such', they are 'empty, i.e. without commitment or obligation', and thus no real existential questions.[100] Adorno observed in his *Negative Dialectics* that Heidegger transforms historical primacy into an 'ontological precedence of "Being" pure and simple over all ontical and real things'.[101] What presents itself as if it had its place in the theatre of the world 'before the Fall of both subjectifying and objectivfying metaphysics – will turn, contre coeur, into a stark "in itself"'.[102] If Being is detached from beings, 'the attempt to break out of idealism is revoked and the doctrine of Being turned back into one of thought'.[103] According to Habermas, Heidegger's 'overcoming' of Kantian subject philosophy consisted basically in transferring the transcendence it contained into an ontological concept of Being which is removed from 'beings' (entities).[104] These 'beings' (entities) which Habermas understands as a term for 'lifeworld', also contain elements of 'care', creating, handling, but as far as they go beyond the individual, these are devaluated as 'inauthentic' Dasein, as everyday occurrences under the rule of the 'they' [des 'Man'].[105] The 'authentic' Being is not afflicted by such inauthentic attributes of the 'they' [das Man]. According to Heidegger's *Letter on Humanism*, a thinking which attends to the clearing of Being [Lichtung des Seins] is 'a deed that also surpasses all praxis'.[106]

    The problem with Foucault's reception of Heidegger lies not in the fact that he let himself be inspired by his questioning of anthropological transcendental philosophy. Rather, it lies in an uncritical reading that overlooks the turn of Heidegger's critique of metaphysics to the 'beyond' of a new metaphysics. Thus Foucault talks himself into a fundamental theory that more effectively removes the viewpoint of social practice from philosophical thinking than was the case in Kant's 'anthropology'. The remark made by Marx on idealism in general in

---

99   Marcuse 1928, pp. 60, 62.
100   Marcuse 1928, p. 61.
101   Adorno 1973, p. 67.
102   Adorno 1973, p. 70.
103   Adorno 1973, p. 87.
104   Habermas 1990, pp. 139 et sq., 143, 146.
105   Habermas 1990, pp. 149 et sq. Cf. for 'care' [Besorgen] §§14–24 of *Being and Time* in Heidegger 1998, pp. 91, 63–150; to 'they' [das 'Man'] cf. §§25–7, pp. 150–69. 'The "they" is the "subject of everydayness"' (Heidegger 1998, p. 150) and with its averageness causes a '"levelling-down" [Einebnung] of all possibilities of Being' (Heidegger 1998, p. 165).
106   Heidegger 1977, p. 239.

his First Thesis on Feuerbach holds true here as well, namely that it has the advantage, compared to merely contemplative materialism, of developing the '*active* side', albeit abstractly.[107] Marx's 'philosophy of praxis' includes here the project of turning the abstractly conceptualised into the concrete social, and grasping it as 'subjective', both as the determined as well as the transformative activity of social individuals. The possibility of such a 'translation' is subverted and foreclosed by the application of Heidegger's fundamental ontology. It is replaced with the dead space of a 'cult of authenticity',[108] in which nothing real moves anymore.

Such lack of practice and movement also haunts Foucault's critique of the 'anthropological age'.

4   The Reductionist Construction of an 'Anthropological' Age

Foucault's periodisation will not be examined empirically here, but inspected as a theoretical arrangement that is characterised by a contradictory principle of construction: on one hand, the transitions between the different paradigms of knowledge are presented as ruptures whose social foundations are left unstated. Sartre argued that Foucault thus withheld from us what is most interesting, namely how thinking was constructed, originating from its respective social conditions, and how humankind traversed from one paradigm to the next. To accomplish this, Foucault would have had to introduce the concept of practice, and thus of history, and that's exactly what he had to refuse within the framework of his anti-historical approach: 'Il replace ... le mouvement par une succession d'immobilités'.[109] In fact, Foucault developed his critique of the 'anthropological' constellation of knowledge at a level of abstraction that makes the social forces and movements that are interested in specific knowledge, their living conditions and forms of practice disappear. With the elimination of social practices, the connection between the objects of knowledge and the actual problems to be solved through knowledge and thinking has been lost.

In contrast to a rupture between the different periods, on the other hand, each period presents itself as a homogeneous range in which all opposites of thinking are flattened to mere variants of the same knowledge paradigm. In the 'classical age', Foucault claims, the various fields of knowledge are 'perfectly

---

107   Marx 1845, p. 3; Marx and Engels 1957-, Vol. 3, p. 5.
108   Adorno 2003, p. 3.
109   Sartre 1966, p. 87.

coherent and homogeneous', because they are determined by representation: it 'commands' the mode of being for language, individuals, nature and need itself, it forms the 'common ground ... upon which the history of the sciences figures as a surface effect'; thus it has a 'determining value' (valeur déterminante) for all empirical domains.[110] In the modern era this fundamental determining function is then assumed by *History*: With *Histoire* (capitalised) Foucault explicitly means not something to be explored empirically, but rather a 'fundamental mode of being' that determines the birthplace of the empirical and 'prescribes their destiny to all empirical beings, to those particular beings that we are'; it is 'the foundation [fond] from which all beings emerge into their precarious, glittering existence;' it will 'impose its laws (!) on the analysis of production, the analysis of organically structured beings, and, lastly, on the analysis of linguistic groups'.[111]

This contradictory principle of construction introduces a kind of double binding into the argumentation: whereas, in the confrontation with Hegelianism, Marxism, and Existentialism Foucault reverts again and again to an anti-deterministic and anti-reductionist rhetoric, his own manner of research is characterised by a determinism in which different fields of knowledge and approaches of thought are reduced to one principle. In the grammar, the natural history, and the analysis of riches at the beginning of the nineteenth century 'an event [took place] that is of the same type in all these spheres',[112] namely the discovery of truth *behind* the visible. When Adam Smith discovers the basis of value generation in *labour*, Jussieu and Lamarck conduct the classification of living things on a non-visible principle of *organisation* and in linguistics the grammatical inflection system is revealed as the internal mechanism of languages, there is always the 'same break': a 'behind-the-scenes-world' is created, to which the representations are linked. What is sought is a 'point, which drives down, beyond our gaze, towards the very heart of things', the things give themselves their own 'internal space' and withdraw to their own 'essence'.[113]

But this essentialism of the humanities is essentialistically constructed by Foucault himself. The main effort consists in bringing the heterogeneous approaches of thought under general terms in such a manner that their temporal-spatial coexistence is secretly transformed into a unitary essence. For example, Foucault identifies each finding of structural principles that are not directly

---

110   Foucault 1994, pp. 208 et sq., Foucault 1966, p. 221.
111   Foucault 1994, pp. 219 et sq., Foucault 1966, p. 231 (translation modified).
112   Foucault 1994, p. 237, Foucault 1966, p. 249.
113   Foucault 1994, p. 239, Foucault 1966, p. 252.

visible as 'metaphysics of the object' and of 'depths', without engaging with the respective scientific logic of the subject matter.[114] He then takes this general term, subsumes it under the category of 'objective "transcendentals"' and thereby associates it with the quite different problem of the Kantian transcendental subject: by designating 'labour', 'the organisation' and the 'inflectional system' as 'transcendentals' on the side of the object, he has arranged them as 'corresponding' with the discovery of a transcendental field by Kant.[115] In a similar way, 'history' is assigned to essentialism, although it is precisely historicisations which have the anti-essentialist potentials to dissolve a priori assumptions behind the phenomena, to defamiliarise and dissolve solidified identities. Finally, from the objective as well as the subjective 'transcendentals' Foucault derives an 'anthropology' which pursues a human 'essence' in order to restore it from 'alienation' (Marx) or the 'unconscious' (Freud).[116] In Foucault's stance against the 'human', which will be reflected in his later criticism of the 'repression thesis' of Freudo-marxism, the differences between passivating and activating dispositives, between ideological subject-effects and intervening actions from below, are eradicated. Foucault's essentialist paradigm of modern 'history' and 'anthropology' is a homogenised artificial product that is purged of all fractures and oppositions.

Foucault's periodisation of ages is homogenising in yet a further sense, reaching out beyond the *Order of Things*: it repeats itself almost identically both in his previous and ensuing publications. In *Madness and Civilisation* (1961), at the time of the Renaissance the 'fools' were still integrated as a dark and tragic truth of life. Their exclusion sets in with the transition to the 'classical age' (key date 1656: the foundation of the Hôpital géneral in Paris); the constitution of madness as mental illness takes place finally at the end of the eighteenth century, intertwined with the emergence of 'anthropological thinking'.[117] Accordingly, in *The Birth of the Clinic* (1963) modern medicine begins 'in the last years of the eighteenth century', and also here the 'founding role of origin' is ascribed to anthropology.[118] In *The Archaeology of Knowledge* (1969) the theoretical considerations claim to supersede the notions of historical con-

114 Isabelle Garo observes a strict determinism which does not relate to the respective object of knowledge (e.g. the economic development), but merely to the 'épistémè d'ensemble' (Garo 2011, pp. 114 et sq.).

115 Foucault 1994, pp. 244 et sq., Foucault 1966, pp. 257 et sq.

116 Foucault 1994, pp. 248, 327, Foucault 1966, pp. 261, 338.

117 Cf. Foucault 1965, pp. 28 et sqq, 38 et sqq.; Foucault 1961, pp. 37 et sqq., 56 et sqq., 541 et sqq. On the controversy in France (primarily with Gauchet and Swain) see Ferry and Renaut 1985, pp. 90 et sqq.

118 Foucault 2003a, pp. xii, 197; Foucault 1963, pp. VIII, 201.

tinuity through a radical decentring of history, a multiplication of the ruptures and discontinuities, and Foucault introduces an extensive apparatus of differentiating discourse-analytical categories for this purpose. But as soon as the discursive 'rules of formation' are related to history and especially to the history of ideas, they serve to reproduce theoretically the same era classification: Renaissance-Classic-nineteenth century.[119] In *Discipline and Punish* (1975), the end of the eighteenth century, or the exact period between 1760 and 1840, is the historical moment when the public spectacle of execution disappears and the 'birth of the prison', along with its new disciplinary power which penetrates the whole society, is supposed to take place: also here in close relation to the 'anthropological' view of the human sciences.[120] At the same time, in Foucault's *History of Sexuality* (1976) the different strategies of power operating on the lustful body merge together and are consolidated in a modern 'sexual dispositive', which, with its constraints on speech and conscience, has constructed a 'truth' of the human being in which psychoanalysis and Freudo-marxism have helplessly entangled themselves.[121] And finally, just in this period the primacy of a new type of power directed at the regulation of the population also develops, which Foucault refers to in different contexts as either 'biopower' or as 'governmentality'.[122]

The *double binding* between a rhetoric of differences and discontinuities on one hand, and a homogenising and deterministic paradigm construction on the other, is repeated here as a contradiction between the rhetorical staging of a permanent remodelling of theory and a constant and static basic structure of the investigations actually conducted. Foucault's comments in interviews and discussions, accompanied by public self-criticism, give the impression of a permanent new invention of theoretical concepts: from the epistemes of knowledge to power-knowledge, from power as an exclusionary system to the 'productivity' of power and to 'biopower', from the 'archaeology' to the 'genealogy', etc. – the abundance of innovations presented keeps the Foucault researchers short of breath in their endeavour appropriately to divide the work into its different periods. At the same time, in all the books from 1961 to 1976 there is always the same historical pattern of consecutive periods, which constitutes

---

119   Cf. Foucault 1972, pp. 157 et sqq., 166 et sqq.; Foucault 1969, pp. 205 et sqq., 216 et sqq.
120   Foucault 1995, pp. 15, 22, 29, 191, 225 et sq., 255 et sqq., 276 et sq., 297, Foucault 1975, pp. 22, 30, 38, 224, 262, 295 et sqq., 323, 346.
121   Foucault 1978, pp. 103 et sqq., 115 et sqq.; Foucault 1976a, pp. 136 et sqq., 152 et sqq.
122   Cf. to biopower Foucault 1978, pp. 135 et sqq.; Foucault 1976a, pp. 181 et sqq.; Foucault 2003c, pp. 242 et sqq.; Techniques of 'Gouvernementality' have developed already since the sixteenth century, however they become unfrozen only in the eighteenth century: see Foucault 2007, pp. 102 et sq., 109, 364.

a kind of meta narrative of the genealogy of the modern workings of power. Foucault's discursive mobility is laid onto an immobile pattern of historical succession. In it history surely does not proceed 'onward', but all the more in lockstep, without it becoming possible to determine or reflect contradictions of 'non-contemporaneity' within the respective forms of knowledge and thinking.[123] Gramsci's analysis of the heterogeneity of 'common sense' as a composite of different historical strata from the 'Stone Age' to the most advanced science, 'prejudices from all past phases of history ... and intuitions of a future philosophy',[124] finds no place here, despite all avowals of historical 'discontinuity' in this succession of epochs.

5   The Overcoming of Marxian Utopia by the Overman

Marx belongs to the 'anthropological' paradigm that is centred around the concept of *labour* as 'irreducible, absolute unit of measurement'.[125] It is first the distinction of use-value and exchange value, introduced by Smith, which connects work with the need-structure of humans, and thus with the 'anthropology' of the nineteenth century.[126] Ricardo then made this more consistent as the distinction between abstract and useful labour, thus constituting labour as a 'transcendental' that is removed from the grasp of 'representation' (i.e. the circulation of commodities):[127] only now can one see 'the emergence of a great linear, homogeneous series, which is that of production'.[128]

Foucault here touches upon an issue which Marx treated in the introduction to the *Grundrisse* in the context of the methical status of abstract concepts and that he spelled out using the example of the 'modern' concept of labour: on one hand labour appears as the abstract expression for the simplest and most primal relationship between humans and non-human nature, on the other the indifference toward the respective kind of labour implied in this abstraction presupposes a very developed totality of real kinds of work. The example shows strikingly 'that even the most abstract categories, despite their being valid ... for all epochs, are, in the determinateness of their abstraction, just

---

123   The concept of 'non-contemporaneity' was coined by Ernst Bloch (cf. Bloch 1991, pp. 97 et sqq.).

124   Gramsci, 1971, p. 324; Gramsci 1975, Q. 11, § 12.

125   Foucault 1994, p. 223, Foucault 1966, p. 235.

126   Foucault 1994, pp. 222 et sq., Foucault 1966, p. 234.

127   Foucault 1994, pp. 253 et sqq.; Foucault 1966, pp. 265 et sq.

128   Foucault 1994, p. 255; Foucault 1966, p. 267.

as much a product of historical conditions and retain their full validity only for and within these conditions'.[129] Seen in the context of this analytical distinction, Foucault's observations refer to an aspect of the abstraction process through which a concept of labour as such is distilled from the variety of concrete labour and constituted into the subject of political economy. However, Foucault addresses this procedure neither as a conceptual abstraction nor in connection with the real abstraction of bourgeois commodity-production. Instead, a discursive generation of the activities themselves is suggested, as if working and producing were actually created anew only now. Because 'man' in the eighteenth/nineteenth centuries came into a 'dialectic of production', '[he] lost the truth of his direct needs in the movements of his labour and in the objects which he created with his hands', Foucault writes in 1963, in an obituary for Bataille.[130] Foucault does not explain how human need satisfaction and sheer survival without work should have been possible before this modern 'Fall of Man'. The commonsense fact – formulated by Marx – that any nation which stopped working for only a few weeks 'would perish'[131] would be, in his concept of discursive reality creation, only one piece of evidence for the fact that the economy is based on an 'anthropology of [the] natural finitude' of man.[132]

Foucault constructed his paradigm of economic knowledge in such a way that the differences between Marx and his political-economic forerunners are only 'of little importance'.[133] Whether Ricardo sees humans overcoming their lack gradually through intensifying labour, or Marx conceives the relationship between humans in bourgeois society and labour as 'alienation', which is to be sublated then in a communist society, is insignificant, because it concerns only 'the two possible ways of examining the relations of anthropology and History as they are established by economics through the notions of scarcity and labour': 'At the deepest level of Western knowledge, Marxism introduced no real discontinuity', but found its place as a 'full, quiet, comfortable … form'. 'Marxism exists in nineteenth-century thought like a fish in water: that is, it is unable to breathe anywhere else'; the struggles between bourgeois and revolutionary economics are only 'storms in a children's paddling pool'; Foucault slammed them all together as types of 'utopias of ultimate development', which

129   Marx 1857a, p. 42; Marx and Engels 1957–, Vol. 13, p. 636.
130   Foucault 1998a, p. 84 (translation modified); Foucault 2001a, Nr. 13, p. 276.
131   Marx 1868, p. 68; Marx and Engels 1957-, Vol. 32, p. 552.
132   Foucault 1994, pp. 258 et sq., Foucault 1966, pp. 269 et sq.
133   Foucault 1994, p. 261, Foucault 1966, p. 273.

on the promised evening let the 'anthropological truth ... spring forth in its stony immobility'.[134]

This attribution is especially absurd with regard to Marx, who, in his *Theses on Feuerbach* had outlined the programme to no longer conceive of the 'essence' of the human being as immobile, an 'abstraction inherent' in each individual, but rather to decipher it from the respective conditions of realisation in the 'ensemble of the social relations'.[135] By taking this 'essence' out of the domain of theological and philosophical speculation and putting it into society, Marx deconstructs the subject as a 'transcendental', while at the same time reconstructing it as a multitude of social-historical subjects. A 'terrain change from the theory of knowledge [Erkenntnistheorie] to an epistemology of practice' is carried through,[136] which also challenges the dichotomy of subject and object criticised by Foucault.

Despite this possible point of commonality, Foucault's critique of humanism is directed with special sharpness against a competing subject and ideology critique originating from Marx. Foucault finds 'all these forms of leftist and warped reflection' (gauches et gauchies) particularly ridiculous, i.e., all those 'who still wish to talk about man, about his reign or his liberation', all those, who 'refuse to think, without immediately thinking that it is man who is thinking'.[137] Foucault's polemical overdrive prevents him from recognising that what is stored in historical configurations of knowledge and discourse also had to be 'thought' at one time by human beings, and that what is previously given in knowledge configurations also has to go through the brains of actual thinking individuals if it is to be 'thought'. With the dismissal of 'man', the human location in a system of domination is delegitimised, and wherever Foucault hears talk of 'liberation' he interprets it in essentialist terms as a search for the origins projected into the future.[138] But this is just his own projection. What is questioned is the capacity for anticipation of a better life, without which no viable culture of resistance can develop and survive.[139]

With Nietzsche's 'end of man' Foucault has found the pivot point which allows him to flip the immobile homogeneity of his knowledge paradigm into its abstract opposite, into the rhetoric of a total break:

---

134   Foucault 1994, pp. 261 et sq., Foucault 1966, pp. 274 et sq.
135   Marx 1845, p. 4; Marx and Engels 1957-, Vol. 3, p. 6.
136   Haug 1999a, p. 409.
137   Foucault 1994, pp. 342 et sq., Foucault 1966, p. 354 (translation modified).
138   Foucault 1994, pp. 332 et sqq., Foucault 1966, pp. 343 et sqq.
139   Cf. Rehmann 2012.

> [Nietzsche] took the end of time and transformed it into the death of God and the odyssey of the last man; he took up anthropological finitude once again, but in order to use it as a basis for the prodigious leap of the super-man; he took up once again the great continuous chain of History, but in order to bend it round into the infinity of the eternal return. ... It was Nietzsche, in any case, who burned for us ... the intermingled promises of the dialectic and anthropology.[140]

The passage becomes obscure as soon as one tries to understand it: with the 'end of the time' Foucault intends to point to the 'utopia of causal systems of thought',[141] which he also previously ascribed to Marx. The term 'utopia' applies here to the idea that one day an immovable and at the same time oppressed 'essence' of man will be liberated. But if he were concerned about deconstructing this 'essence' through a radical historicisation, it would still have to be explained how Nietzsche's figure of the 'last man' could help him in this. Why does Foucault, in order to overcome the conception of an historical continuity, want to rely on the idea of eternal recurrence, with which the 'continuous chain' is not broken open, but, as he says himself, only 'bent' (courbé)? Why does he want – of all things – the aid of the 'infinity' of the eternal recurrence to overcome the 'finiteness' of man? Does he, as does Nietzsche in the *Zarathustra*, 'lust for eternity'?[142] How does the proclaimed 'end of man', which Foucault understands as 'absolute dispersion' in language,[143] fit with Nietzsche's 'overman', who is supposed to be characterised as 'synthetic man' precisely by the fact that in him the '*multiple* man' whom we have today '[is] to be bound unhesitatingly into the yoke of a *single* goal'?[144] At the latest with such an overman, whom Nietzsche created as an 'allegory' for a stronger type of man, for a 'higher form of aristocratism',[145] the postmodern fun and games with the 'decentring of the subject' would have to stop. And how has Foucault not recognised that Nietzsche painted the overman with increasing clarity as 'legislator' and 'physician' of the future, who in the name of ascending life demanded 'the most ruthless suppression and sequestration of degenerating life'?[146]

---

140   Foucault 1994, p. 263, Foucault 1966, p. 275.
141   Foucault 1994, p. 263, Foucault 1966, p. 275.
142   see Nietzsche 2006, pp. 184 et sq.; Nietzsche 1999a, Vol. 4, pp. 287 et sq.
143   Foucault 1994, p. 385, Foucault 1966, p. 397.
144   Nietzsche 1999a, Vol. 12, p. 404.
145   Nietzsche 2003b, p, 177; Nietzsche 1999a, Vol. 12, p. 463.
146   Nietzsche 1968a, pp. 99, 131; Nietzsche 1999a, Vol. 6, pp. 134, 174; cf. Nietzsche 1999a, Vol. 10, pp. 530, 372; Nietzsche 1999a, Vol. 11, p. 542; Nietzsche 1999a, Vol. 12, pp. 425 et sq., Nietzsche 1999a, Vol. 13, p. 18.

Not to take a close look here is part of good manners in the Foucault literature, including the supposedly 'critical' one. Foucault's style is so esoterically
extravagant that a critic who wants to butt in here runs the risk of conducting
himself as a philological pedant, and making himself look ridiculous by taking
all this with inappropriate seriousness. But the argumentation is so typical of
Foucault's writings of the 1960s[147] that we need to take it seriously, i.e., to submit it to a 'symptomatic reading'.[148] The allegedly playful flirt with the gesture of
the Nietzschean pronouncement is itself a gesture which is to be reconstructed
in the context of its epistemological environment.

It is noticeable that Nietzsche's deployment against 'man' is itself celebrated
as a kind of religious event. This observation can be divided into two questions,
namely, first, why does Foucault invoke Nietzsche in particular at the point
where he starts to recast his ideology critique into his own eternity-religion
with the doctrine of the eternal recurrence, which is designed to overcome both
Christianity and the philosophical critique of religion? And secondly, why does
Foucault do this in a religious mode and without the slightest criticism of the
religious form?

But before turning to Nietzsche's doctrine of the eternal recurrence, I am
going to focus on the controversal issue of his relationship with anti-Semitism
and racism. For that, I choose a particular entry point, namely Nietzsche's reading of the theologian and orientalist Julius Wellhausen, which in turn reveals
his adoption and reworking of Christian anti-Judaism.

6   Excursus: Nietzsche's Reworking of Cultural Protestant
       Anti-Judaism – the Example of Wellhausen

Julius Wellhausen and Friedrich Nietzsche: with these two I am linking figures
who have little in common at first glance. One, a liberal theologian, Cultural
Protestant, biblical scholar and founder of an influential exegetical school, the
other, a sharp critic of religion and declared anti-Christian. Nietzsche's early
criticism of David Strauss was already a reckoning with the 'philistinism' of
German Cultural Protestantism, which, with reference to Hegel and Schleiermacher, sought to combine Christian faith with modern science.[149] In the 'Law

147   Cf. e.g. Foucault's Bataille obituary *Préface à la transgression* of 1963, Foucault 1998a, pp. 69
      et sqq., Foucault 2001a, Nr. 13, pp. 261 et sqq., or the review of Klossowski's *La prose d'Actéon*
      of 1964 (Foucault 1998a, pp. 123 et sqq.; Foucault 2001a, Nr. 21, pp. 354 et sqq.).

148   Cf. Althusser and Balibar 2009, pp. 28–9.

149   Nietzsche 2003a, p. 36; Nietzsche 1999a, vol. 1, p. 191.

against Christianity', which Nietzsche appended to *The Antichrist*, he demanded that action be taken more harshly against Protestants than against Cathol-
ics, and here again 'harsher with liberal Protestants than with orthodox ones'.
Reason: 'The criminality of being Christian increases with your proximity to
science'.[150]

And yet Nietzsche read Wellhausen's writings thoroughly in his late period,
especially his *Prolegomena to the History of Ancient Israel 1957* (1883) and his
Sketch of the History of Israel and Judah 1891 (1884), and, without any critical
or distancing gesture, he incorporated excerpts into his conception of a Jewish
'transvaluation of values'. As Robert C. Holub has observed, 'Wellhausen was
indeed the most important source for Nietzsche's expanded remarks on Jewish
history' in *The Antichrist*.[151]

At the same time, Nietzsche undertook a transformation of Protestant anti-
Judaism which provides relevant insights for his discourse strategy and specifically for the controversies surrounding his anti-Semitism or anti-anti-
Semitism. First, I would like to outline how Wellhausen arranges the religious
history of the Hebrew Bible as a descending line of degeneration from the
strong, monarchical Israel under David and Solomon to the Jewish priestly
religion in and after the Babylonian exile. Second, I would like to reconstruct
how Nietzsche adopted this anti-Judaic arrangement from Wellhausen, modified it, and finally applied it to early Christianity, so that the latter was itself
characterised as 'Jewish' in the sense of a slave and resentment morality. And
finally, I would like to draw some conclusions for the controversies surrounding Nietzsche's anti-Semitism or anti-anti-Semitism. Does redirecting Cultural
Protestant anti-Judaism further onto Christianity mean that Nietzsche had
now become 'philo-Semitic' in his late phase, as a large number of Nietzsche
scholars try to prove, or is it an 'exponentiated anti-Semitism' (potenzierter
Antisemitismus)?[152] Or did the organising standpoint from which Nietzsche
arranged the ideological material lie on another level that cannot be adequately
grasped in the anti-Semitism/philo-Semitism dichotomy?

6.1   Wellhausen's Anti-Judaic Construction

In the introduction to the *Prolegomena* Wellhausen reported that even as a
young student he was fascinated by the historical books of the Hebrew Bible,
especially the stories about Saul and David. However, the Torah, the Mosaic
'law', always gave him trouble: 'my enjoyment of the latter was marred by the

---

150   Nietzsche 2005, p. 67; Nietzsche 1999a, vol. 6, p. 254.
151   Holub 2016, p. 194.
152   Cancik 1995, pp. 144, 147.

law, it did not bring them any nearer to me, but intruded itself uneasily, like a ghost'. But then he heard that a colleague (Karl Heinrich Graf) was of the opinion that the law was written only later, in and after the Babylonian exile. This lifted a great burden from the Protestant exegete's soul: 'almost without knowing his reasons for the hypothesis, I was prepared to accept it; I readily acknowledged to myself the possibility of understanding Hebrew antiquity without the book of the Torah'.[153]

This already indicates the goal of Wellhausen's hermeneutical work: the elaboration of an authentic, genuine religion of ancient Israel 'without the Book of the Torah', the proof that the 'Law' was written only later by a Jewish priesthood in and after the Babylonian exile and projected back into the time of origin. He could rely on the fact that modern Protestant biblical scholarship of the nineteenth century had developed a method, namely the method of 'source separation', with which it attempted to determine what was written earlier and what later, what was 'genuine' and what had been 'constructed' from the point of view of later constellations.

One can see here how certain critical impulses from an Enlightenment critique of religion were absorbed into Protestant biblical scholarship and incorporated into a modernised bourgeois theology. This 'passive' incorporation, which takes the critical sting out of the critique of religion, is one of the most important ideological efforts of the modernisation of Cultural Protestantism.[154] The biblical exegete no longer proclaims the Word of God revealed in the Scripture, but instead critically disentangles what is credible and what is myth from the sources.

I am not concerned here with methodological questions of source differentiation in general,[155] but with the ideological construction that undergirded Wellhausen's usage of this method: fundamental was the dichotomy between an ancient, authentic *Israel* on the one hand, and a later *Judaism* on the other. The path from *Israel* to *Judaism* was described as a descent in which religion

---

153 Wellhausen 1957, pp. 3 et sq. The common equation of 'Torah' and 'law', especially in Protestant theology, is misleading: Torah means 'instruction', but was passed on through the Latin translation as 'lex'.

154 Cultural Protestantism refers to an embourgeoisement of Protestantism, which 'can be described in terms of the history of ideas, both as an effect of the Enlightenment on theology and as a "passive revolution" of theology against the Enlightenment' (Rehmann 2015a, p. 296).

155 In Hebrew Bible research, there is an increasing tendency to 'later dating' all the writings of the Hebrew Bible to the time during and after the Babylonian Exile, so that the attempt to separate the sources into 'authentic' and back-projected ones is itself suspected of being an ideological back-projection.

is increasingly exposed to 'denaturalisation'. The line of descent ran: a) from the strong monarchical Israel under David and Solomon via b), the division of Israel into a northern kingdom and a southern kingdom (from 960 BCE) and to c), the end of all statehood through the conquest by the Babylonians in the 6th century. The result was that during and after the Babylonian exile (c. 587–39 BCE) a stateless Judaism under the rule of a priesthood emerged. In short, the degeneration took place in a kind of three-step process: unified empire – disintegration into two partial empires – stateless and at the same time priestly Judaism.

How is the starting point of this line of descent to be understood? Let us look at the predominant pattern in the respective scholarship. After Wellhausen had been criticised by theologians during his lifetime as a 'Hegelian', the interpretation that he belongs to a 'Romantic' lineage oriented towards Herder and the 'historical school' has largely prevailed. Perlitt has characterised this romanticism as a view of ancient history as 'national history', a preference for the youth of peoples and their 'natural' growth, an 'organological' approach, anti-rationalist and anti-internationalist.[156] However, 'romantic' is a very vague label, and it leads to a misunderstanding if one associates it with the view that Wellhausen had oriented himself toward the 'origins' of Israel *before* the emergence of the monarchy.[157] What remains unnoticed is *how* Wellhausen construed these origins, namely not as a pre-state, nomadic idyll, but on the contrary as monarchical statehood or, insofar as he spoke of pre-state society, as an immediate and longingly anticipated preliminary stage toward monarchy. Wherever in the Hebrew Bible there is a warning against monarchy, its costly court, the expected plundering of the countryside, as for example in the Book of Samuel,[158] Wellhausen decided that such an idea 'is the offspring of exilic or post-exilic Judaism', is 'unhistorical' and contradicts 'genuine tradition'.[159] For 'in the eyes of Israel before the exile the monarchy is the culminating point of the history, and the greatest blessing of Jehovah. It was preceded by a period of unrest and affliction, when every man did what was right in his own eyes ...'[160] This had nothing to do with a romantic longing for origins as such. The decisive

---

156   Perlitt 1965, pp. 172, 179, 211 et sqq.
157   According to Andrea Orsucci, Wellhausen was oriented towards an original agrarian religion of the Canaanite culture (1997, p. 319). Ahlsdorf believes that he favours a creative originality of the individual over the institutionalised constraints of modern statehood and that his concept of naturalness is romantically oriented towards pre-state society (1997, pp. 83, 147 f.).
158   cf., 1 Sam 8: 11–18.
159   Wellhausen 1957, p. 255.
160   Wellhausen 1957, p. 253.

factor was the monarchical state as an ideological value par excellence. It constituted the 'holiness' that Wellhausen established and from which he criticised the biblical claim of another, 'higher' and 'more original' holiness: the holiness of the covenant with Yahweh, who led the people out of slavery in Egypt.

Let us look at the second station of the line of descent. After the collapse of the unified kingdom of Israel, prophecy developed, which Wellhausen portrayed ambivalently: on the one hand, he saw Isaiah as the representative of a 'prophetic reformation' that strove for the restoration of the Davidic monarchy through a future Messiah.[161] On the other hand, and more important for Nietzsche's reception, was the negative aspect, which Wellhausen identified in particular in Amos and Hosea, the prophetic critics of monarchical rule, namely a 'reversal' in which the nation was opposed to the *ideal*: by elevating the deity above the people, the prophets cut the 'natural bond' between God and the people and replaced it with a 'morally conditioned relationship'. The bond was 'natural' when Yahweh was still an organic expression of the whole of the people, but now he had 'outgrown the nation' and stood opposed to it as the 'God of justice'. He was the God of Israel only *insofar as* Israel met his demands. Thus the traditional order of the two fundamental articles of faith – God and people – was reversed, and this corresponded to the mood of a declining people.[162]

Finally, the loss of sovereignty through the Babylonian conquest in the sixth century led to the development of a priestly Judaism. According to Wellhausen, during and after the exile a great regression took place: religion was alienated, worship was only an exercise in godliness, a pedagogical means of discipline, 'dead work', the God of the prophets 'pupated' into a 'petty salvation and breeding institution'[163] – a ritualistic, restorative dead end from which only Jesus Christ would find a way out. At the same time, 'Jewish eschatology' took the place of prophecy: the religious hopes lost all content of reality, became fantastic, utopian, rapturous and were also directed towards the 'establishment of universal world domination'; their God was the 'God of wishes and illusion. It paints itself an ideal on paper to which no bridge leads from reality'; there is 'a poorly concealed greed of pious desires'. Wellhausen's passionate rejection included attributions that Nietzsche will later bundle into the concept of *resentment*: the Jews, a 'sect, full of impotent hatred mixed with envy against

---

161 Wellhausen 1891, pp. 108 et sqq.; Wellhausen 1958, pp. 122 et sqq.
162 Cf. Wellhausen 1957, pp. 417 et sq.; Wellhausen 1891, pp. 88, 122; Wellhausen 1958, pp. 108, 113, 139.
163 E.g. Wellhausen 1957, p. 425; Wellhausen 1891, p. 223; Wellhausen 1958, pp. 175, 194.

the hostile world that surrounded them'.[164] This then, is again a Jewish impasse, this time a 'social revolutionary' and internationalist one, and this too is only overcome by the death and resurrection of Jesus Christ: 'The Jewish Messiah was indeed completely destroyed by the crucifixion, and another Messiah took his place'.[165]

According to Wellhausen, during the exilic and post-exilic periods the writings of the Hebrew Bible were subsequently reworked. The priestly editing applied a 'Jewish measure', in his opinion; the literature handed down was 'Judaised through and through', 'adapted to the needs and tastes of Judaism'.[166] According to the characteristics of Judaism described, this results in a double retrojection: what is projected back are on the one hand the 'priestly' provisions of the law, e.g. the cultic regulations, purity laws, eating regulations, and on the other hand, and this too falls under the theological construct of the 'law', the social provisions to protect the poor, the Sabbath rest, the cancellation of debts, the release of slaves in the Jubilee year. Wherever criticism of ancient kingship and elites is articulated in the Hebrew Bible, wherever Yahweh is defined by his significance in the liberation from the Egyptian slave house, Wellhausen saw Jewish-legal re-painting, over-painting, over-stamping at work.[167]

So we see that Wellhausen's concept of 'Judaism' was an ideological construct consisting of two components: *Jewish* was, on the one hand, the restorative, priestly-legal line that stifles religious freedom, and on the other hand, a messianic eschatology, which Wellhausen criticised for the this-worldliness of the hope of redemption, its utopian and subversive character. Both components were held together by the Lutheran concept of 'legalistic' and 'work-righteous' religion. At the same time, they represented the front positions of the contemporary Protestant bourgeoisie at the time of the German culture war against Catholicism and of the anti-Socialist Laws of 1878–90 (and afterwards): on the one hand, against the 'Restoration', which in turn had both Junker and Catholic connotations and could possibly also be directed against the 'orthodox' opponents of modernisation in the Lutheran Church, and on the other against democracy and especially social democracy. Judaism was the projection surface of this double frontline. The bipolar image of the enemy was part of the basic pattern of bourgeois Protestant anti-Judaism in Germany.

---

164   Wellhausen 1958, p. 417; Wellhausen 1891, pp. 214, 223; Wellhausen 1958, pp. 187 et sq,
         pp. 196, 286 et sq.
165   Wellhausen 1958, p. 369.
166   E.g. Wellhausen 1958, pp. 15, 186.
167   Wellhausen 1957, pp. 293 et sq.

6.2   Nietzsche's Adoption and Modification of Anti-Judaism

Before we consider Nietzsche's modification of this anti-Judaic arrangement, we must situate his reading of Wellhausen. When did Nietzsche read Wellhausen? It is known that he bought the *Prolegomena* in 1883, the same year it was published; a year later, on 28 October 1884, he bought the *Abriss der Geschichte Israels und Judas* (Sketch of the History of Israel and Judah), also in the year of its publication.[168] According to the editors of the *Kritische Gesamtausgabe*, Giorgio Colli and Mazzino Montinari, Nietzsche read the *Prolegomena* in February 1888, i.e. at the same time he was preparing *The Antichrist*.[169] Here one is on safe ground, because Nietzsche excerpted the last chapter of the *Prolegomena* at length during this time[170] – the excerpt was then incorporated, in a slightly modified form, into Aphorisms 24–6 of *The Antichrist*. But the late date of the excerpt does not rule out an earlier reading, and it is not very likely (though not impossible) that Nietzsche would rush to buy the *Prolegomena* and the *Abriss* (*Sketch*) in 1883 and 1884, respectively, immediately after their publication, and then wait for four and five years before dealing with them.

According to Holub, 'there is some evidence that Nietzsche began reading Wellhausen in 1887 and perhaps as early as 1886'.[171] In fact, there are several references to a Wellhausen reading *before* 1888, and the question of dating is not unimportant because it is linked to the question of the extent to which Wellhausen's Cultural Protestant anti-Judaism was involved in Nietzsche's concept of a Jewish resentment morality. In a small note between the summer of 1886 and 1887, for example, it states: 'History of the Jews typical of the emergence of the "idealist". "God and Israel" in a covenant. First refinement: only with the just Israel does the just God remain in league'.[172] This is a reformulation of Wellhausen's criticism, according to which the prophetic conception of the covenant idealistically replaced the 'natural' bond between God and the people with a 'morally conditioned' relationship.

The note in turn falls in the immediate vicinity of his well-known formulations on the Jewish 'revaluation (or transvaluation) of values' and the 'slave revolt in morality' that this initiated. Nietzsche coined these key terms first in 1886 in *Beyond Good and Evil*, then in 1887 in *The Genealogy of Morals*. In the first case, the re-evaluation of values is attributed primarily to the prophets, who had fused the terms '"rich", "godless", "wicked", "violent", "sensual", and for the

---

168   See the book lists in Nietzsche 1999a, vol. 10, p. 718 and vol. 11, p. 352; cf. vol. 14, p. 718.
169   Nietzsche 1999a, vol. 15, p. 170.
170   Nietzsche 1999a, vol. 13, pp. 169–74.
171   Holub 2016, pp. 182 et sq.
172   Nietzsche 1999a, vol. 12, p. 223.

first time coined the word "world" as a term of reproach'.[173] In the second case, it is the 'priestly people' of the Jews who had reversed the aristocratic equation of values and held this reversal 'with the teeth of the most abysmal hatred (the hatred of impotence)'.[174] In the secondary literature, this second passage is usually associated with Wellhausen, but the first with Ernest Renan, who in his *La vie de Jésus* had similarly described the prophets' critique of domination.[175] The borrowings from Renan are indeed striking,[176] but I see no reason to frame the issue as an either/or question. For one thing, Wellhausen also attested to the prophets' 'remarkable sympathy for the lower classes',[177] and for another, Renan lacks precisely the idea that such a preferential option for the lowly was a re-evaluation of values, since for him the 'popular spirit' characterised the Old Testament in general.[178] If one includes the note on the emergence of the 'idealists', which clearly refers to the prophets, one can assume that Nietzsche brought together a piece of Renan and a piece of Wellhausen in the aphorism from *Beyond Good and Evil*. This would mean that Wellhausen's construction of a Jewish denaturalisation was involved in Nietzsche's concept of a Jewish transvaluation of values from 1886 onwards.

Of course, Nietzsche had already set some fundamental way-markers for his conception of religion before he set out to read Wellhausen. The contrast between a Homeric-Greek aristocratic on-top-religion and a servile Judeo-Christian religion was already present in the young Nietzsche and formed the starting point from which he specifically accessed Wellhausen.[179] But from him he could learn that the contrast between 'strong', lordly religiosity and subaltern religiosity also runs through the Hebrew Bible itself. This enabled Nietzsche to adapt the history of Israel to the general model of a heroic aristocratic origin and a later democratic plebeian degeneration.

Both in the Wellhausen excerpt of 1887/88 and in Aph. 25 of *The Antichrist*, Nietzsche traced Wellhausen's line of descent precisely: 'Originally, particularly in the time of the kings, Israel too stood in a *correct*, which is to say natural

---

173   Nietzsche 1997, p. 63; Nietzsche 1999a, vol. 5, p. 117.

174   Nietzsche 1999a, vol. 5, p. 267.

175   E.g. Colli and Montinari in *Kommentar zu Jenseits von Gut und Böse*, Nietzsche 1999a, vol. 14, pp. 359 et sq. and Ahlsdorf 1997, pp. 88, 92 et sq.

176   'The prophets ... had ... a close relationship between the words "poor, meek, humble, pious" on the one hand and the words "rich, ungodly, violent, wicked" on the other' (Renan 1898, p. 115; Renan 1863, pp. 129 et sq.).

177   Wellhausen 1884, p. 52.

178   Renan 1898, p. 115; Renan 1863, p. 129.

179   Cf. e.g. Nietzsche 1999a, vol. 1, pp. 69 et sq.; Nietzsche 1999a, vol. 2, p. 473; Nietzsche 1999a, vol. 7, p. 83; Nietzsche 1999a, vol. 8, p. 81.

relationship to all things. Its Yahweh expressed a consciousness of power ... the god of Israel and *consequently* the *god* of justice'. This is followed by the prophetic autonomisation of the ideal, in the course of which a God of justice confronts the people, until finally 'priestly agitators' bring morality into opposition to life.[180] What Wellhausen criticised as a Jewish recolouration of the Bible was now presented in Aph. 26 as a Jewish-priestly 'falsification', with which the great royal period of Israel was stamped as a time of decay.[181]

Insofar as Nietzsche's treatment of Wellhausen is thematised in the literature, the focus is primarily on demonstrating that he misunderstood, simplified, vulgarised him. For example, Stegmaier argues that Nietzsche had immersed himself in Wellhausen's 'highly differentiated studies of the history of Israel' and yet 'speaks of "the Jews" ... without any distinctions, he shortens their history ... in such a way that all that remains of it is "Jewish hatred". ... To speak of the Jewish people in this way ... may have hurt himself most of all'.[182] This empathetic interpretation obscures the fact that Wellhausen's account contains discriminating anti-Jewish characterisations as well, and that Nietzsche understood Wellhausen's dichotomy, which is by no means 'highly differentiated', between a still healthy kingdom of *Israel* and a 'denatured' post-state *Jewry* very well, far better than a literature that sees in Wellhausen nothing more than a 'romantic'. What is remarkable, rather, is that he clearly grasps the logic of state domination at the core of the anti-Judaic historical construction and states it with his peculiar bluntness. Paraphrasing a well-known quote by Karl Barth, one could say that Nietzsche is 'not even very cunning, but only a little like a keen-eyed spy, who spills the whole esoteric secret of this whole priesthood urbi et orbi'.[183] In Barth's case, the quotation was directed at Ludwig Feuerbach, and by 'priesthood' he meant the theologians' guild of Cultural Protestantism in the nineteenth century, from Schleiermacher to Ritschl, who would have turned theology into an ethicising, psychologising, etc. 'anthropology'. But for the etatist and anti-Judaist orientation of Cultural Protestantism and the power bloc it represents, it is rather Nietzsche who is the 'keen-eyed spy', and in the sense of this hermeneutic sleuthing, reading him is downright enlightening. A Nietzsche criticism that allows itself to be distracted from deciphering the secret itself by indignation at the extremism of his betrayal of the secret remains itself uncritical. The actual scandal is not that Nietzsche exposed the logic of domination at the core of Protestant anti-Judaism, but

---

180   Nietzsche 2005, § 25, p. 22; Nietzsche 1999a, vol. 6, pp. 193 et sq.
181   Nietzsche 2005, § 26, p. 23; Nietzsche 1999a, vol. 6, p. 195.
182   Stegmaier 1994, pp. 109 et sq.
183   Barth 1926, p. 14.

rather the fact that he incorporated it – with enthusiasm for domination – into his own construction of history.

Of course Nietzsche separated himself from Wellhausen's Cultural Protestantism in that he did not welcome Christianity as redemption from Judaism, but denounced it as Judaism's continuation.[184] It is noteworthy here that the branching off did not yet occur with Jesus himself: Nietzsche's image of a child-like, peaceful, purely inner faith was, in substance, entirely within the framework of the Cultural Protestant paradigm. The agreement is obscured by the negative value-judgment by which Nietzsche made the Christian saviour an 'idiot' (in the double sense of the apolitical private person and the mentally ill) precisely because of the private inwardness ascribed to him.[185] But one must not let the sharpness of this polemical reinterpretation obscure the fact that Nietzsche took the underlying labels of 'idiocy' directly from Wellhausen. From him he could read that Jesus stands with his faith 'above and apart from the world' and knows himself 'in all tranquility' as a 'child of God' – 'before him no one felt like that'.[186] Nietzsche had marked this passage in his copy and transferred the image into his own representation: this faith is not a faith that has been fought for, but an 'infantilism that has receded into spirituality', characterised by 'the polar opposite of struggle', 'blessedness in peace', a 'completely "internal", a "true" world'.[187] Thus, even in the polemical reversal to 'idiocy', the anti-Judaic misinterpretation was retained, with the help of which the image of Jesus is cleansed of all 'Jewish' eschatology, although, as Ernst Bloch notes in *Atheism in Christianity*, 'philologically its credentials were excellent'.[188] Like the leading theologians of the nineteenth century, Nietzsche opposed Ernest Renan's 'vulgar' image of Jesus as a 'transcendental revolutionary' who went before the palaces and announced the arrival of his revolution to the rulers 'with an imperious tone' (d' un ton impérieux).[189]

Nietzsche's opposition to Cultural Protestantism is not to be found here, but in the first Christian communities, and then especially in Paul, the 'genius' of

---

184   Interestingly, when he criticises the idea that the Christian God is an 'advance' over the God of Israel as a 'simplicity' [Einfalt], he does not name Wellhausen directly, but the Christian theologians in general: 'even Renan does this' (Nietzsche 2005 § 17, pp. 14 et sq.; Nietzsche 1999a, vol. 6, pp. 183 et sq.).
185   Nietzsche 2005 § 29, p. 27; Nietzsche 1999a, vol. 6, p. 200.
186   Wellhausen 1884, p. 100.
187   Nietzsche 2005, pp. 26, 27, 29, 33 et sq; Nietzsche 1999a, vol. 6, pp. 199 et sq., 203 et sq., 207; on Nietzsche's markings in the outline cf. Sommer 2000, p. 302.
188   Bloch 2009, p. 114.
189   Renan 1898, p. 281; cf. pp. 108, 159. 'Whatever wore a cassock and could stir a quill fought against Renan, the bishops in the front row', reports Albert Schweitzer (1984/1906, p. 214).

resentment, at whom, as Jacob Taubes notes, the cannons have been pointed since Nietzsche's *Dawn*.[190] Let us observe how Nietzsche redirected the criteria for judging religion that he discovered in Wellhausen's exegesis and applied them to the early Christian communities. After Jesus' death on the cross, they behaved in a typically 'Jewish' way, and this in two respects: on the one hand, they retroactively inserted their feelings of revenge into the image of Jesus and thus brought a negating and at the same time deterministic trait into Christianity; on the other hand, they set about *to elevate* Jesus in an 'extravagant manner, distancing him from themselves: just as the Jews once took revenge on their enemies by separating off their God and raising him up into the heights ... both are products of *resentment*'.[191] The two elements of Wellhausen's anti-Judaic critique, the 'idealistic' exaltation of the prophets and the priestly 'recolouration' of the Old Testament, were taken up and transferred to the early Christians.

However, one aspect that played an important role in Wellhausen's enemy image was no longer operative, namely the priesthood itself, which did not play a role in early Christianity. Nietzsche took this into account by distinguishing in Aph. 27 of *The Antichrist* between a 'Jewish reality' and a 'Jewish instinct' and contrasting the two. 'Jewish reality' designates the rule of the Jewish priests, the 'Jewish church', i.e. the 'house on stilts' of the really existing 'hierarchy of society', against which the 'Jewish instinct' of the early Christians now turns, namely as a 'priestly instinct that could no longer tolerate priests for its reality'.[192] 'Jewish' in this sense means inciting the *chandala* 'within Judaism' to resist the privileged caste.[193] Nietzsche extracted the concept of the *chandala* via Louis Jacolliot (1876) from the context of Indian caste society, where it is supposed to denote the lowest level of the social hierarchy: the outcasts, the untouchables, whom Nietzsche referred to in *Twilight of the Idols* as 'unbred people' and 'human hodgepodge'.[194] Thus he split the concept of Jewishness along a simple caste opposition of privileged and underclasses. The concept of a 'Jewish reality' became irrelevant with the fall of the Second Temple and was of no further interest to him; the concept of a 'Jewish instinct', on the other hand, he continued to pursue and track down in the most diverse modern ideologies.

---

190   Taubes 1995, p. 109.
191   Nietzsche 2005, p. 37; Nietzsche 1999a, vol. 6, pp. 213 et sq.
192   Nietzsche 2005, p. 25; Nietzsche 1999a, vol. 6, pp. 197 et sq.
193   Nietzsche 2005, p. 25; Nietzsche 1999a, vol. 6, p. 198.
194   Nietzsche 2005, p. 184; Nietzsche 1999a, vol. 6, p. 100.

What then was the Nietzschean reworking of Cultural Protestant anti-Judaism? Four points of view seem to me to be important: 1) Seen immanently, described as a displacement in ideological grammar, it was a matter of an exchange of predicate and subject. In Wellhausen's case, priestly Judaism had various anti-royal, utopian, eschatological, even envious qualities, which could certainly be summarised with Nietzsche's concept of plebeian 'resentment'. But in the paradigm of Cultural Protestantism, this resentment belonged to the predicates of a Jewish 'legalism' and 'work-righteousness'. With Nietzsche, on the other hand, plebeian resentment became the logical subject through which what is 'Jewish' is defined from now on; 2) this means that *Jewish* in the sense of the 'Jewish instinct' directly designates a social position as well as a plebeian 'social moralism' arising from it; 3) 'Jewish' is no longer a religious concept as it was in Cultural Protestantism, and also not a biological concept, but is aimed from the outset at the *international* composition of the social movement. Christianity was 'Jewish' precisely because it was 'not "national"', not a function of race', but a 'whole movement of rejected and dejected elements of every type', an 'aggregate of decadent forms from everywhere';[195] 4) 'Jewish', finally, were the intellectuals who convey this kind of plebeian context religiously or morally. Their prototype was Paul, *'the wandering* Jew *par excellence'*.[196] In contrast to the 'idiot' Jesus, he is the 'genius' of the moral slave revolt who, with the formula of the 'God on the cross', found a symbol with which 'everything lying below, everything filled with secret rebellion' could be condensed into a tremendous power: 'the whole *ghetto-world* of the soul risen *to the top* in a single stroke!'[197]

Obviously Nietzsche was able, through the lens of his hostility, to perceive some specific qualities of resistance of early Christian communities and of Paul's theology in particular. Not dissimilarly to Friedrich Engels, who portrayed early Christianity as '"socialism" ... as far as it was possible at the time',[198] Nietzsche described early Christianity as a precursor to modern socialism. '*God on the cross* – have people still not grasped the gruesome ulterior motive behind this symbol? – Everything that suffers, everything nailed to the cross is divine'.[199] For Nietzsche, Christianity's eschatology was a 'vengeance against Rome' and its 'melancholy of eternal building': 'The crucified Jew as the

195   Nietzsche 2005, §51, p. 50; Nietzsche 1999a, vol. 6, pp. 231 et sq.
196   Nietzsche 2005, §58, p. 61; Nietzsche 1999a, vol. 6, p. 246.
197   Nietzsche 2005, §59, pp. 61, 63; Nietzsche 1999a, vol. 6, pp. 247 et sq.
198   Engels 1894–5, p. 447.
199   Nietzsche 2005, §51, p. 51; Nietzsche 1999a, Vol. 6, p. 232.

symbol of salvation was the deepest mockery of the magnificent Roman praet-
ors ...' who seemed to be 'the symbols of perdition and of a "world" ripe for
destruction'.[200]

With regard to Paul's theology, Nietzsche recognised several aspects that
remained absent in mainstream theology for a long time. For one, he did not cut
off Paul's theology from Jewish eschatology, as almost all Christian theologians
did before Albert Schweitzer published his ground-breaking *The Mysticism of
Paul the Apostle* (1911).[201] Instead, Nietzsche accused Paul of pushing the eschatological aspirations further and making them into a subversive weapon against
the Roman Empire; second, he recognised that Paul's critique of 'law' is not just
directed against the 'Jewish law', but against the *nomos* of the Roman Empire.
Jakob Taubes remarks that it is precisely on this point that he has learned more
from Nietzsche than from anybody else: the 'law' Paul tried to overcome was an
ideological formula for the Roman Empire that held together its multicultural-
ism from above – it was a general 'aura' that could be intoned in Greek, Roman
and Jewish.[202] With the keen eye of the adversary, Nietzsche recognised Paul's
hegemonic ability to transform the most ignominious stigma of the cross into
a charisma, and thus to reorient the Roman Empire's relations of loyalty (of
faith/fides) towards the crucified and resurrected Christ.[203] According to Karl
Barth, Nietzsche has done us a good service: by depicting Christianity as a 'typical Socialist teaching', he has hurled himself 'against the strongest and not the
weakest point in the opposing front' and thereby reminded us how uncondi-
tionally we must hold on to what he has been dismissing.[204]

Although it is clear that Nietzsche left the anti-Judaism of Protestant super-
sessionism behind with his distinction between 'Jewish reality' and 'Jewish
instinct', it is highly controversial in which direction he left it.

6.3   Anti-Semitism, Anti-Anti-Semitism – Revisiting a Stalled Debate

Following Nietzsche's formulation that Christianity is Judaism 'once again', and
'to a second potency' (in 'zweiter Potenz'),[205] Cancik argues that Nietzsche's
Antichrist is the 'exponentiated, the "spiritual-aristocratic" anti-Semite'.[206]

---

200   Nietzsche 2011, § 71, p. 52; Nietzsche 1999a, Vol. 3, p. 70.
201   Cf. Schweitzer 1998 (1911), pp. 3, 37, 225.
202   Taubes 1995, pp. 36 et sqq.; cf. the detailed analysis of Paul's concept of 'law' in Kahl 2010,
       pp. 6–11, 209–27.
203   For the evaluation of Nietzsche's astute perception of Paul's 'genius', cf. Rehmann 2005b,
       pp. 152 et sqq.
204   Barth 1960, p. 242.
205   Nietzsche 1999a, vol. 12, pp. 501, 563.
206   Cancik 1995, pp. 132, 137, 147.

Such a label is strongly contradicted by numerous Nietzsche scholars, and this not least with reference to the Aph. 27 of *The Antichrist* under discussion: did Nietzsche not evaluate the Jewish priesthood there considerably more 'positively' than Wellhausen, when he called it the 'stilt-house' of the Jewish people? Isn't Nietzsche's critique of Christianity much less anti-Judaistic than a Christian theology that treats Judaism as a sort of manure pile on which the white lily of Christianity happened to grow miraculously? Can his emphasis on the 'Jewish' character of Christianity not also be understood as a subversive polemic against an anti-Semitism that essentially developed on the basis of a Christian anti-Judaism?[207]

Let us follow this trail. As is well known, there are several examples where Nietzsche clearly stood out from the articulations of contemporary anti-Semitism. The best-known passage comes from *Human, All Too Human* of 1878, i.e., from Nietzsche's 'middle', so-called 'ideology-critical' period: to Judaism one owes the 'noblest human being', namely Christ, the 'purest sage', namely Spinoza, the 'most powerful book and the most effective moral law in the world', i.e., the Hebrew Bible and the Ten Commandments. Here it is clear that the positive evaluation of the 'law' was only possible before the Wellhausen reading. It goes on to say: in the Middle Ages, the Jews held up the banner of enlightenment against the 'band of Asiatic clouds'. While Christianity had done everything to 'orientalise' the Occident, Judaism had helped to 'occidentalise' it again and again, and that meant 'making Europe's task and history a *continuation of the Greeks*'. The nation states were to be overcome by 'engendering the strongest possible European racial mixture', in which 'the Jew is just as usable and desirable an ingredient as any other national remnant'.[208]

This is indeed a remarkable arrangement. The 'orientalist' dichotomy of Occident and Orient is still dominant,[209] but on the 'light' side are Enlightenment, Greek, Judaism, even Christ himself, and on the 'dark', 'oriental', 'unenlightened' side is Christianity. One should however not overlook the inconsistencies: at the same time as the middle-period Nietzsche praised the nomadic 'rootless' cosmopolitism of the Jews, he maintained the anti-Semitic stereotype of the "Börsen-Jude" (stock-exchange Jew) as the 'most repugnant invention of the whole human race'.[210]

---

207   E.g. Kaufmann 1974, p. 299, Ahlsdorf 1997, pp. 110, 205, 207, 211.

208   Nietzsche 1994, p. 229 (translation modified); Nietzsche 1999a, vol. 2, pp. 310 et sq.

209   See Said 2003 [1978].

210   Nietzsche 1994, p. 229; Nietzsche 1999a, vol. 2, pp. 309 et sqq.; cf. the analysis in Holub 2016, pp. 115 et sqq.

Although the anti-Jewish terminology intensified again in the transition to the late phase – not least as a result of his break with Paul Rée and Lou Andreas-Salomé – the 'European' perspective was maintained. This is shown, for example, by the 'proposal' to marry the noble families from the Prussian Eastern borderland to Jews in order to 'add' the Jewish genius for money, patience and spirit to the Junker art of commanding and obeying, for which one would probably first have to banish the anti-Semitic bawlers out of the country.[211] The polemic against the *anti-Semites* as evil, vengeful and themselves resentful elements runs through the entire late work, right up to the 'insane note' of January 1889, in which Nietzsche calls for all anti-Semites to be shot.[212]

However, the interpretation of Nietzsche as an anti-anti-Semite all too readily overlooks the fact that in the same aphorism in which Nietzsche wanted to unite Junkers and Jews to form a 'a new ruling caste for Europe', he demanded that the eastern borders be closed against the immigration of eastern Jews.[213] In the *Antichrist* he explained his disgust for the first Christians with reference to the uncleanliness of the 'Polish Jews': it is not worth raising 'objections' against them, 'neither of them smells good'.[214] Here the interpretation of Nietzsche as a philo-Semite comes into some difficulty: Is it perhaps no longer anti-Semitism if the anti-Jewish stereotypes are 'only' used against the impoverished Eastern Jews and the subversive Jewish intellectuals, and exclude the distinguished Jews worthy of co-option? As soon as one 'normalises' the fact that only a part of the Jews is denounced, one can no longer draw a justifiable line. A literature that accepts such a selection has capitulated to anti-Semitism from the outset.

In the face of such attempts at apology, Cancik seems to have a point with his attribution of an exponentiated, finer, less vulgar anti-Semitism.[215] But the term 'exponentiated' (potenziert) is no more than a quantitative statement; the notion that Nietzsche's anti-Jewish denunciations should be 'finer' and 'less vulgar' is hardly tenable; and with the assertion that Nietzsche was 'more' anti-Semitic than the others, it cannot be understood that his idea of a Prussian-Jewish master class in Europe would be a decidedly different project than that of persecuting or even exterminating Jews. Obviously, in reflecting on this debate, we encounter a contradiction: on the one hand to absolve Nietzsche of the accusation of anti-Semitism is utterly questionable, since he consist-

211   Nietzsche 1997, p. 116; Nietzsche 1999a, vol. 5, pp. 194 et sq.
212   Nietzsche 1986, vol. 8, pp. 433, 575; Nietzsche 2013a, pp. 109, 141 et sq.; Nietzsche 1999a, vol. 5, pp. 369, 407 et sq., vol. 13, pp. 365, 423.
213   Nietzsche 1997, pp. 115 et sq.; Nietzsche 1999a, vol. 5, pp. 193 et sqq.
214   Nietzsche 2005, p. 44; Nietzsche 1999a, vol. 6, p. 223.
215   Cancik 1995, p. 144.

ently resorts to anti-Semitic stereotypes to discriminate against segments of the population and to justify domination; on the other hand, the category of anti-Semitism, even with the addition of 'exponentiated', is not sufficient to locate Nietzsche's specific position in the ensemble of anti-democratic ideologies. Anti-Semitic, it seems, is very much the ideological discourse material in which and with which Nietzsche worked, but the category does not capture the way in which he accessed and arranged this material.

The controversy is inconclusive as long as it moves back and forth on the level of offsetting anti-Jewish and pro-Jewish quotations. Its theoretical weakness is that it does not differentiate analytically between Nietzsche's social standpoint and the discursive material through which it was articulated. The opponents have failed to realise that Nietzsche distilled a concept of 'Jewishness' out of the materials of Protestant anti-Judaism, which directly served him as a cipher for an international subaltern class. 'Jewish' stands for one side of the social conflict that cuts across both Greco-Roman antiquity and European modernity and, as we have seen, the history of Israel and Judaism itself.

Domenico Losurdo has proposed the concept of a 'transversal racism', which does not pit Germans against Jews, Aryans against Semites, but refers directly to the opposition between nobles and plebeians. It is characterised by a 'racialisation of the subaltern classes' (razzizzazione delle classi subalterni), their discursive marking and stigmatisation into a race.[216] Following discussions on the relationship between 'racism' and 'classism', one could speak of a direct and at the same time racially articulated *classism*, which uses mainly anti-Semitic discourse material for this purpose. It is a 'classism' that constructs modern society according to ancient patterns, and whose pathos of distance also oscillates back and forth between social meanings and those of a 'spiritual' aristocratism. Nietzsche imagined himself in a 'republic of geniuses', where the great spirits are in conversation with other great spirits from mountain top to mountain top throughout the millennia, leaving the social and political 'dwarfs' far below them.[217] He is at home in the higher spheres of the German mandarinate, and at the same time in its rebellious side branch, which claims to shine light into the 'underworld of ideals' and reveals their domineering character.

Nietzsche's radically 'domination-affirming critique of ideology'[218] could serve the self-understanding of elites, where one speaks plainly behind closed doors or also for the imaginary elevation of those who would like to participate intellectually in the symbolic capital of elites. Yet the main currents

---

216   Losurdo 2020, pp. 760–4, 782–85, 804–7.
217   Nietzsche 2003a, p. 151; Nietzsche 1999a, vol. 1, pp. 317, 808.
218   Haug 1993, p. 18.

of anti-Semitism in the late nineteenth century went in a different direction. As candidates for a reorganisation of bourgeois hegemony, they developed a right-wing populism that united the German nation state-PEOPLE ('Staats-volk') against a (Jewish) counter-PEOPLE ('Gegenvolk'). A cross-class project of this kind required significant ideological shifts, as a result of which social antagonisms were projected into another level of discourse. In Hitler's speeches, for example, it could be observed how the discourse shifted from the semantic level of an impending socialist revolution to the level of a 'Jewish world conquest'.[219]

Measured against these requirements, Nietzsche's 'transversal' fusion of racism and classism proves to be a 'de-ranged' undertaking. In terms of ideology theory, the 'derangement' consists in the fact that the ideological displacements from the social semantics of class and gender antagonisms to their anti-Semitic articulation, required for the Nazis to gain hegemony, are retracted. For a popular movement from the right, Nietzsche's aristocratic classism from above was not directly suitable, but for the imaginary of elite rule, be it fascist or neoliberal (and possibly with a postmodern superstructure), it was and is a seductive stimulant.

7   Nietzsche's Eternal Recurrence as Religion

Nietzsche described the thought of an eternal recurrence of the same as a religious conversion and shaped it according to the example of the conversion of Paul or the Lutheran tower experience: a sudden experience during a mountain hike in Sils-Maria in August 1881, '6000 feet beyond man and time', before a mighty pyramid-shaped stone boulder, from which he attempted to imagine infinite time 'back' and 'forward'.[220] A 'revelation' in the sense that something becomes audible, 'that shakes one to the last depths', 'like lightning a thought flashes up, with necessity ... – I never had any choice'.[221] Nietzsche interprets the event in various self-descriptions, which fall in the periods both of the preparation of the *Gay Science* (1882) and the *Zarathustra* (starting from 1883), as a cause and indication of a 'recovery' from sickness and depression,[222] which,

---

219 cf., PIT 2007, pp. 90 et sqq.
220 Nietzsche 1989, p. 295; Nietzsche 1999a, Vol. 6, p. 335; Nietzsche 1999a, Vol. 9, p. 494.
221 Nietzsche 1989, p. 300; Nietzsche 1999a, Vol. 6, p. 339.
222 'Often one could have seen me dance' is written, e.g., in *Ecce Homo*, 'in those days I could walk in the mountains for seven or eight hours without a trace of weariness' (Nietzsche 1989, p. 303; Nietzsche 1999a, Vol. 6, p. 341). The *Gay Science* seems 'written in the language

however, is only temporary and after the conclusion of *Zarathustra* is replaced again by collapses and lengthy diseases: 'One pays dearly for immortality: one has to die several times while still alive'.[223]

By referring to Heraclitus and the Greek mystery cults,[224] Nietzsche intends to create a religious myth, which overcomes both Christianity and the philosophical critique of religion from Kant to Feuerbach: on one hand he intends to replace the Christian doctrines, which divert the eternal value away from life into a beyond, with a new metaphysics that 'emphasises precisely this life with the heaviest accent';[225] and at the same time he proposes to work against the tendency to 'secularisation' which tries to cast the beyond and every 'background world' from the mind. The fruit of this 'political delusion' is socialism, which Nietzsche defines as the 'volatile individuals' wishing to capture their happiness through 'societalisation' ['Vergesellschaftung'].[226] Günther Anders called the doctrine of the eternal recurrence an 'exaggerated reaction to the concept of progress'.[227] As Losurdo made plausible, this reaction to democratic and socialist 'progress' systematised and radicalised a widespread pattern of the anti-revolutionary culture after 1789, and then especially after the Paris Commune of 1870/71.[228] As Ishay Landa shows, Nietzsche's atheism is to be understood as a 'retaliation against an atheistic tradition that preceded it', designed to replace socialism's humanistic optimism with a combination of social Darwinism and Schopenhauerian pessimism.[229] Nietzsche confronts the 'preachers of equality' ('the tarantulas') with a 'pessimistic, tragic, and conservative mode of secularization', epitomised by the 'madman' as a despairing, anxious figure, who in aphorism 125 of *The Gay Science* cannot find God and cries out that we are all God-murderers and as a result are condemned to stray through the empty space of an infinite nothing.[230]

---

of a thawing wind', writes Nietzsche in the preface to the second edition (1886), in the gratitude of the convalescent, who now 'all of a sudden is "attacked" by the hope of good health' (Nietzsche 2017b, p. 1; Nietzsche 1999a, Vol. 3, p. 345).

223 Nietzsche 1989, p. 303; Nietzsche 1999a, Vol. 6, p. 342.

224 On Heraclitus, e.g. Nietzsche 1989, pp. 273 et sq. (Nietzsche 1999a, Vol. 6, p. 313), on the Greek mystery cults e.g. Nietzsche 1999a, Vol. 10, p. 340. Cancik examines the picture of 'cyclic' antique thinking which is also widespread among Nietzsche critics and comes to the conclusion: the recurrence teaching 'is marginal in the antique culture, a thought experiment of some philosophers and not as Nietzsche wished, the dogma of a widespread religion' (Cancik 1995, p. 114).

225 Nietzsche 1999a, Vol. 9, p. 515.

226 Nietzsche 1999a, Vol. 9, p. 504.

227 Anders 1982, p. 101.

228 Losurdo 2020, pp. 478 et sq.

229 Landa 2005, pp. 463, 467.

230 Landa 2005, pp. 469 et sq., 479 et sq.; cf. Nietzsche 1998a, Vol. 3, p. 481.

In order to accomplish the double overcoming of Christianity and its critique, Nietzsche works intensively on a series of ideological subject-effects. He is interested above all in the practical effect of the new teachings, which are discussed in the literature generally as 'existential effect', 'ethical imperative', 'hypothetical iterative', 'ethically motivated ideal of super-humanity', among others.[231] What is meant is the demand to live such 'that we want to live again and live that way for eternity', together with the expectation that this lends a new 'gravity' to life and transforms the person.[232] In the *Gay Science* Nietzsche lets a demon appear, who confronts man with the (either crushing or exhilarating) question of the eternal repetition of life: would you curse this demon or 'hast thou once experienced a tremendous moment in which thou wouldest answer: ' "Thou art a god"?'[233] The prospect of a revaluation of one's own life is posed by a separation of the important from the unimportant according to the criterion of the desired eternal recurrence. At the same time, this means the promise of bringing the eternity-effect of religion better to bear than past religions by means of a 'religion of religions', which is above all better than the other-world religion of Christianity, which is filled with the hopes for salvation of the lower classes: 'Let us press the image of eternity onto our life!'[234]

This new 'heavy accent' on one's own life is to accompany a 'philosophy of indifference' toward 'humanity's' problems.[235] What in universalistic morals constituted the 'seriousness of life', 'is seen only as play' and enjoyed aesthetically.[236] A further effect of the doctrine of eternal recurrence should be an accent on the instant, since according to Nietzsche life is only to be repeated for the sake of certain 'highest instants': 'the value of the shortest and most fleeting one, the seductive gold flashing on the belly of the serpent of life'.[237]

Deleuze designated this as a practical rule 'as rigorous as the Kantian imperative'.[238] The postmodern flirts with the eternal recurrence aim to replace the generalising 'universalistic' moral philosophy of Kant with Nietzsche's particularistic 'art of living', instead of turning it toward the practical and, as for example Marx tried, concretising it as a categorical imperative of 'overthrow-

231 E.g. Jaspers 1997, pp. 359 et sq.; Schmid 1991, p. 327; Müller-Lauter 1999, p. 188, Ottmann 1999, pp. 369 et sqq.
232 Nietzsche 1999a, Vol. 9, pp. 494, 496, 503.
233 Nietzsche 2017b, p. 128; Nietzsche 1999a, Vol. 3, p. 570.
234 Nietzsche 1999a, Vol. 9, p. 503; cf. Ibid., pp. 505, 513, 515; Nietzsche 1999a, Vol. 11, p. 488.
235 Nietzsche 1999a, Vol. 9, pp. 494 et sq.
236 Nietzsche 1999a, Vol. 9, p. 494.
237 Nietzsche 1999a, Vol. 12, p. 348.
238 Deleuze 2013, pp. 63 et sq.; Deleuze 1962, p. 77.

ing' inhuman and debasing relations.[239] However, Nietzsche's new religion encounters the difficulty that the proclaimed ethical effect on the conduct of life is at odds with the fatalistic basic structure of the eternal recurrence, by which the change of behaviour to be achieved would also have to be predetermined. Jaspers pointed out the antinomy 'that the will expresses the freedom to bring forth what is yet to come, and that the will itself is after all the cycle that simply repeats what has been'.[240] Deleuze tries to avoid this contradiction by understanding the doctrine of the eternal recurrence in such a way that not one and the same are to return, but only the difference in itself.[241] However, with this kind of metaphorisation not only is nothing resolved (since how is the difference per se to return without that which differs from one another?), but also the eternity-effect attempted by Nietzsche vanishes and is forfeited.

More serious than the question of logical consistency is the fact that the postmodern reading of Nietzsche is not interested in questioning the presupposition of a fundamental eternity-greed. The intended ethical effects are based on the assumption that happiness presses in principle toward 'eternal' recurrence, because desire wants *deep, wants deep eternity*.[242] With Nietzsche the yearning for religious salvation has taken the form of a lusting after eternity.[243] In contrast, the young Walter Benjamin of the *Theological-political Fragments* develops the far more sustainable thought that in happiness the earthly also desires 'its demise',[244] i.e., also wants its passing. While Nietzsche in his insistence on desire for eternity tries to exclude the rhythm of passing, he expresses unwittingly that the desire for release itself is 'unresolved': 'The fulfilled moment is reconciled with the passing, even if the reconciliation passes again and again'.[245] Günther Anders explained Nietzsche's doctrine of the eternal recurrence as a 'repetition compulsion' transposed into philosophy, 'only that in this case the compulsion is not "to-act", but an "event compulsion" [Geschehniszwang] projected into the universe (as its mode of being)'.[246] When Nietzsche confronts the religious other-world with the demand to

---

239   Marx 1843, p. 182; Marx and Engels 1957-, Vol. 1, p. 385.
240   Jaspers 1997, p. 362. As a scientific theory the teaching of recurrence is today 'only with difficulty defendable', and it looks as if it means a 'determinism which destroys the normative and imperative sense' of thinking and here above all the moment of choice (Abel 1998, p. 256).
241   Deleuze 2013, pp. 43 et sqq; Deleuze 1962, pp. 52 et sqq.
242   Nietzsche 2006, pp. 263 et sqq.; Nietzsche 1999a, Vol. 4, pp. 402 et sqq.
243   Nietzsche 2006, p. 184 et sqq.; Nietzsche 1999a, Vol. 4, pp. 287 et sqq.
244   Benjamin 1920/22, *GS* II.1, p. 204.
245   Haug 1997, p. 1090.
246   Anders 1982, p. 100.

THE DEATH OF MAN AND THE ETERNAL RECURRENCE

'remain faithful to the earth' and not to despise the body,[247] this remains inconsistent as long as it does not also affirm the finiteness of the body and the earth, without having its eye on eternity.

Finally, there is evidence of an imminent contradiction in the new religion, which makes the construction of the 'overman' and his increasing elaboration as a despotic character structurally necessary: since Nietzsche aims his ideology critique against a Christian morality which separates humans into good and evil and the afterlife into heaven and hell, he must lay out his doctrine of recurrence – against strong aversions – as inclusive in the sense that everything returns without deduction, and must in *amor fati* also be loved in such a way, 'without departure, exception and selection'.[248] Thereby he creates the problem that with his doctrine he also fails to get rid of the 'little people', whose position in the Christian form of morality he combats. Because those he mocks as 'superfluous' and 'all too many', whom one would rather lure away from this life with eternal life,[249] must also return again and again with the eternal return. Matthew Sharpe sums up the paradox: 'If we are asked to will the eternal recurrence of all things ... this would seem to mean willing the recurrence of all weakness and reactive forces – the very things that we, as good Nietzscheans, know should never be willed, even once'.[250] With this vision *Zarathustra* is seized by the 'surfeit of human beings', everything living appears to him like a 'dirty river', 'rabble mish mash', 'human mould and bones and crumbling past': 'Oh, nausea! Nausea! Nausea!'[251]

It is the idiosyncratic pressure of this people-disgust which causes Nietzsche to introduce the category of the overman, whose concrete elaboration is again non-uniform: occasionally he is described rather as a free spirited hedonist who can answer the inquiry of the demon as to the desirability of the eternal recurrence with yes, who lives according to his own laws and separate from the rabble like an 'Epicurean god', and expressly does not want to rule.[252] If

247   Nietzsche 2006, p. 6; Nietzsche 1999a, Vol. 4, p. 15.
248   Nietzsche 1999a, Vol. 13, p. 492.
249   Nietzsche 2006, p. 31; Nietzsche 1999a, Vol. 4, p. 55.
250   Sharpe 2021, p. 7.
251   Nietzsche 2006, pp. 6, 177, 232 et sq.; Nietzsche 1999a, Vol. 4, pp. 15, 274, 357 et sq. The aversion to this inclusive version becomes evident in the fact that Nietzsche in an earlier version of 1881 will only ascribe the recurrence to those who also believe in it: 'those who do not believe in it must eventually *die out* according to their nature. Only he who holds his existence for eternally repeatable *remains left*: among *such* however a condition is *possible*, to which as yet no utopian has reached' (Nietzsche 1999a, Vol. 9, p. 573).
252   Nietzsche 1999a, Vol. 9, p. 604; Nietzsche 1999a, Vol. 10, p. 244.

this aspect of the overman turned out to be attractive for 'free spirits', then this would be not least for the fact that it presents a private-elite, and one-sidedly distorted, image of the liberated life. In this context also belong, for example, the abilities related to perspectival variety and flexible perspective change: 'from many eyes to see into the world', 'to for a time give oneself over [to] life and afterwards for a time to rest on it with the eye'.[253] But then Nietzsche reflects in the preparation to the third part of *Zarathustra* (autumn 1883) the '*transition* from *free spirit* and hermit to having to *dominate*',[254] and this in the self-understanding of unwillingly having to execute a necessity: 'Dominating? Forcing my kind onto others? Horrible! Isn't my happiness simply looking at many others? Problem'.[255] However, only with the overman as 'legislator' does the doctrine of eternal recurrence become for the first time 'bearable' for Zarathustra.[256] Precisely the dominating 'forcing' is now drawn up by the late Nietzsche to the point of a fantasy of a 'medical' destruction of the 'degenerating life'.[257] The high point both of the 'bliss', as of the 'desire', will now be 'to press your hand upon millenia as if upon wax – bliss to write upon the will of millenia as if upon bronze'.[258] The overman becomes now the 'parable' for the '*secretion of a luxurious surplus from mankind*', which develops on the 'substructure' of a highly technological 'economic administration of the earth' a 'higher form of aristocratism'.[259]

A critique of religion will not be content with exhibiting logical contradictions here, or with formulating a moral condemnation of elitist and inhumane assumptions. More useful is the question of the 'inner strife'[260] in both the given society and individual life conditions, which drives the ideological need for specific eternity effects. And here Nietzsche's biographical embeddings are so dense that the material almost forces a consideration of the doctrine of recurrence from a Nietzschean perspective, i.e. from the body. Its contradictory composition of vitalistic decisionism and fatalism, which appears on the level of philosophical thought as logically incompatible 'antinomy', can be understood more adequately against the background of the permanent alternation

---

253   Nietzsche 1999a, Vol. 9, pp. 494 et sq.
254   Nietzsche 1999a, Vol. 10, p. 516.
255   Nietzsche 1999a, Vol. 10, p. 529. Ottmann sees here the 'point of the turn from the ideal of the apolitical to the doctrine of dominance' (Ottmann 1999, pp. 239 et sq.).
256   Nietzsche 1999a, Vol. 10, p. 530.
257   Cf. Nietzsche 1968, pp. 99 et sqq., Nietzsche 1999a, Vol. 6, pp. 134 et sqq.; Nietzsche 1968, p. 131; Nietzsche 1999a, Vol. 6, p. 174.
258   Nietzsche 1999a, Vol. 10, p. 637; Nietzsche 2006, p. 172; Nietzsche 1999a, Vol. 4, p. 268.
259   Nietzsche 2003b, p. 176; Nietzsche 1999a, Vol. 12, pp. 462 et sq.
260   Marx 1845, p. 3, Marx and Engels 1957-, Vol. 3, p. 6.

of depressing illness and euphoric 'recovery': it is not least a history of a painful illness transposed into thinking.

Against this background, in particular the 'discovery' of the *amor fati* can be explained as a paradoxical form of hope that is weighed down under the conditions of an inevitably fateful malady. Nietzsche represents it as his 'greatest desire' to be able to see and love the necessary: no accusing, but 'to be at any time hereafter only a yea-sayer!'[261] Any resentment against illness is forbidden, he insists in *Ecce Homo*; what helps is only a 'Russian fatalism ... without revolt' with which the soldier lies down in the snow: 'Because one would use oneself up too quickly, *if* one reacted in any way, one does not react at all any more: this is the logic. Nothing burns one up faster than the affects of resentment'.[262] His inmost nature has taught him not only to bear, but also to love 'whatever is necessary – as seen from the heights and in the sense of a great economy', he puts it in his last writing, *Nietzsche contra Wagner*. Precisely his long illness, the most difficult years of his life, is responsible for his 'higher health':

> Only great, ... slow pain, in which we are burned with green wood, as it were ... forces us philosophers to descend into our ultimate depths and put away all trust ... in which formerly we may have found our humanity.[263]

I don't see any justifiable reason for excluding those impulses from his philosophy as 'only biographical' factors or 'psychologisms'. Nietzsche needs a lot of 'height' in order to be able to bear his illness (and other sufferings). His doctrine of the eternal return is definitely also a religion in the sense of what the young Marx described as a 'sigh of the oppressed creature'.[264] However, it is characterised by the fact that it turns this impulse back directly, and with all force, against the oppressed and suffering. This turning back is the mechanism over which Nietzsche's personal history is intimately crossed with the ideological dynamics of alienated socialisation. Nietzsche's philosopher-religion is intended to be neither a '*protest* against real distress', as with Marx,[265] because such a protest is supposed to be annulled by the *amor fati*, nor another '*opium* of the people',

---

261 Nietzsche 2017b, p. 103; Nietzsche 1999a, Vol. 3, p. 521.
262 Nietzsche 1989, p. 230, Nietzsche 1999a, Vol. 6, p. 272.
263 Nietzsche 1982, pp. 680 et sq.; Nietzsche 1999a, Vol. 6, pp. 436 et sq.
264 Marx 1843, p. 175; Marx and Engels 1957–, Vol. 1, p. 378. According to Losurdo Nietzsche's language is clearly religious and 'aims not only at the justification of the reality, but also at "redemption" of reality as a whole' (2020, p. 482).
265 Marx 1843, p. 175; Marx and Engels 1957–, Vol. 1, p. 378.

because the 'people' are not the addressee of the religious interpellations, but are carried along, perforce as it were, in the eternal circulation. But that does not preclude that Nietzsche's religion works as an intoxicant among the many isolated individuals living in a culture emptied of solidarity, who strive from subaltern positions for higher ones and imagine themselves as such 'higher' ones. In the sense of this isolation, Nietzsche's overman is for Walter Benjamin the first who 'knowingly begins to recognize and to fulfill the capitalistic reli-gion'.[266] *Zarathustra* was used extensively for the first time in the First World War, where it was intended quite un-metaphorically to produce the readiness 'to overcome man', namely both to kill the enemy as well as to disregard one's own being, which full of fear for its life seeks to preserve it.[267]

Instead of uncritically reproducing Nietzsche's doctrine of the eternal recur-rence, critical theory has the task of deciphering the ideological mode of its functioning. We must try to understand the contradictory dynamics through which suffering can be transformed into a generalised hate of suffering, which vents itself against the weak and drives the disgust for people up to the point of fantasies of exterminism. Such an uttermost estrangement is what is addressed when Adorno in 1950 describes the fate-glorifier Nietzsche as a prisoner of bourgeois society, who 'is able to do nothing else than to love the cell in which he is locked up'.[268]

8   Postmodern Reading of Nietzsche as Pious Retelling

It is not only Nietzsche's anti-Semitic stereotypes and his 'transversal racism' (Losurdo) that are absent in the postmodern reception. Also the biographical background of the 'eternal recurrence' is blanked out, its alienated character overlooked, the compulsive fascination for domination ignored, the extermin-ist turning of suffering against those who suffer repressed. According to Fou-cault's narration Nietzsche 'rediscovered the point at which man and God belong to one another, at which the death of the first is synonymous with the

---

266   Benjamin 2004, p. 260, Benjamin 1921, *GS* VII.2, p. 101.
267   Together with Goethe's *Faust* and the *New Testament* the *Zarathustra* 'was the most popu-lar work literate soldiers took into battle for inspiration and consolation. ... About 150,000 copies of a specially durable wartime *Zarathustra* were distributed to the troops' (Asch-heim 1992, p. 135). However its ideological effect in the misery of trench warfare seems to have used itself up particularly fast (pp. 136 et sq.). In the five war years between 1914 and 1919 in Germany 165,000 copies of Zarathustra were sold, whereas in the preceding 22 years only 100,000 were sold (Zapata Galinda 1995, p. 68).
268   Quoted in Horkheimer 1989, p. 120.

disappearance of the second'.[269] Nietzsche announced the 'death of the God murderer', the 'absolute dispersion of man'. The double death of God and man is invoked in the religious language of an eschatological break: when mankind disappears, 'new Gods, the same, ... are already swelling the future ocean', now there comes an 'explosion of man's face in laughter'; here is perhaps the first suggestion of 'the first glow' of a new day, where thought will 're-apprehend itself in its entirety'.[270] Thought is no longer deduced from certain epistemic formations, but 'in a transarchaeological manner', observes Manfred Frank.[271] Whereas Frank formulates his objection only in terms of the philosophy of language, we can extend it also to the religion-like form of the Foucauldian argumentation. In an obituary for Bataille in 1963 Foucault celebrates a 'transgression' which is supposed to open 'onto a scintillating and constantly affirmed world without shadow ... originally linked to the divine': since Nietzsche philosophy has been reintroducing 'the experience of the divine at the center of thought'.[272]

Let us try to peel away the different layers of the argument. Why is Nietzsche's famous statement that 'God is dead' to be understood as the 'death of man'? This interpretation, which became a kind of commonplace in postmodern Nietzscheanism, was developed particularly by the writer and former Dominican Pierre Klossowski, who introduced it in 1964 and 1972 at two famous Nietzsche conferences in France.[273] In his book *Nietzsche et le Cercle Vicieux* (1969), which Foucault claims is 'the greatest book of philosophy' that he ever read,[274] he writes that Nietzsche's eternal return is the awakening of the subject to an infinite duplication of itself. Since God guarantees the identity of the responsible I, his death brings the I to extinction and opens the soul to all the identities which are possible for it.[275]

---

269   Foucault 1994, p. 342, Foucault 1966, p. 353.

270   Foucault 1994, pp. 384; 306, Foucault 1966, pp. 396 et sq., 317; cf. Foucault 1994, pp. 342 et sq., Foucault 1966, p. 353.

271   Frank 1989, p. 154.

272   Foucault 1998a, p. 75, Foucault 2001a, Nr. 13, p. 267.

273   In July 1964 in Royaumont, in July 1972 in Cerisy-la-Salle with prominent participation of Deleuze, Derrida, Lyotard, Eugen Fink, Sarah Kofman, Jean-Luc Nancy, Philippe Lacoue-Labarthe, Karl Löwith, Bernard Pautrat (cf. Waite 1996, pp. 273 et sq.).

274   Quoted from Schmid 1991, p. 325.

275   'The "death of God" (the God who guarantees the identity of the responsible self) opens up the soul to all its possible identities' (Klossowski 2009, p. 57, Klossowski 1969, p. 94). 'It is the self, the *same* "self", that awakens to an infinite multiplication of *itself* and his own life' (Klossowski 2009, p. 66, Klossowski 1969, p. 104) The multiplication of the self is at the same time its extinction: I '"deactualise" my present self, in order to will myself in *all the other selves whose entire series must be passed through*', thereby 'I cease to be myself *hic et*

The argumentation is a kind of reversed and yet retained theism. In order to unhinge humanism, it falls back on a religious explanation that derives the identity of man from God's creation and his making of man in the image of God. But this derivation is not sustainable, both from the perspectives of the history of religion and of ideology theory. On one hand, the idea that God 'guarantees' to humans their homogeneous identities is an essentialist illusion. It blocks out the fact that God, also in his monotheistic form, represents a contested authority of antagonistic interpellations, and thus is himself permeated by various oppositions and differences. Ton Veerkamp expresses this diversity of identity when he describes 'God' as 'a concentration within the ideological fabric', 'in which the most diverse social loyalty strands converge': 'This concentration locus is available for antagonistic interpellations. It is invoked as the absolute guarantor of dominant relations, but it can also be called upon as a legitimising authority for attempts to revoke loyalty' – in open conflict one or both of the authorities become constituted as 'idols'.[276] Therefore, the extent to which religious interpellations produce homogenising or antagonising subject effects cannot be specified once and for all, but depends on the hegemonic constellations of force. Thus, for example, the liberal separation of religion and politics demanded during the English Enlightenment, was successful not least because during and after the English revolution the ruptured religious field was no longer able to guarantee citizens a homogeneous 'identity'.[277]

Similarly unrealistic is Klossowski's complementary idea that with the 'death of God' the identities disintegrate: it excludes the fact that individuals also struggle for the coherence of their different identities in non-theistic ways, something they must do every day in order to be capable of acting. The postmodernist claim to leave modern humanism behind feeds itself from premodern clichés, which have also been called into question within theology for a long time.[278]

Finally, what was lost in the whole speculation is the fact that Nietzsche was not at all concerned with the death of 'God' as such, but with that of the God of the 'mob', a certain Jewish-Christian God who can be called upon by the

---

nunc and am susceptible to becoming innumerable others', and this means 'to renounce being oneself *once and for all*' (Klossowski 2009, pp. 57 et sq., Klossowski 1969, pp. 94 et sq.).

276   Veerkamp 2001, p. 917.

277   Cf. Zaret 1989, pp. 170, 172.

278   So e.g. in the 'dialectic theology' of Karl Barth the faith in the biblical God is understood as a contrast to a homogeneous identity: it is a 'cavity', a 'condition in air', a 'shaken stop making' (Barth 1968 [1922], pp. 39, 42, 57, 94). Cf. the ideology-theoretical evaluation of Rehmann 2001, pp. 802 et sq.

subaltern classes who toil and are burdened: 'the *refutation* of God is actually only the disproval of the moral God', writes Nietzsche in 1885.[279] In 1888 he sees in himself the 'religious, i.e. God-forming instinct' becoming alive again: 'And how many new Gods are still possible!'[280] Nietzsche has no objection to a God as 'culmination moment' and 'high point of power' of 'existence'.[281] Indeed, throughout the different periods of his work, Nietzsche showcases his admiration for the 'strong' religions of domination, be it the ancient Greeks who imagined their gods as mirror images of their own existence as caste, so that the relationship was one 'between a lower and a higher nobility',[282] be it the 'law of Manu', which legitimised the separation of the 'pure' noble classes and the masses underneath,[283] or, as he learned from Julius Wellhausen, even Yahwe, who during the heroic time of the Israelite kings 'was the expression of a consciousness of power, of joy in oneself, of hope for oneself'.[284]

'The "new", "French" and "leftist" Nietzsche has never really broken out of this Klossowskian aporia, this exitless labyrinth', notes Waite.[285] 'Where can man find a guarantee of identity in the absence of God?', asks Deleuze.[286] From him Foucault could take over again the interpretation that Nietzsche's 'God-is-dead-concept' represents above all an overcoming of the 'dialectical historical view': it directs itself above all toward another God-death, with which one (like Hegel) celebrates the reconciliation of humans and God, or (like Feuerbach) the replacement of God by man.[287] Against this kind of anthropological overcoming of God stands Deleuze's objection that this human being is still 'reactive man, the slave, who does not cease to be slavish by presenting himself as God ... the subject of a weak and depreciated life'. 'At this point it seems that the whole of the dialectic moves within the limits of reactive forces'.[288]

One must pause here for a moment, in order not to miss the reckless absurdity and its far reaching consequences: Deleuze has actually assumed Nietzsche's standpoint, dispatching both the Christian religion and its 'dialectical' critique as 'reactive' life, as the 'resentment' of little people. Whereas Marx's categorical imperative demands *'to overthrow all relations* in which man is a

279 Nietzsche 1999a, Vol. 11, p. 624.
280 Nietzsche 1999a, Vol. 13, pp. 525 et sq.
281 Nietzsche 1999a, Vol. 12, p. 343.
282 Nietzsche 1999a, Vol. 8, p. 81.
283 Cf. § 56 and § 57 of the *Antichrist*, Nietzsche 1999a, Vol. 6, pp. 239 et sqq.
284 Cf. § 25 and § 26 of the *Antichrist*, Nietzsche 1999a, Vol. 6, pp. 193 et sqq.
285 Waite 1996, p. 275.
286 Deleuze 2000, p. 130; Deleuze 1986, p. 138.
287 Deleuze 2013, pp. 147 et sq., 149 et sq., Deleuze 1962, pp. 180, 182.
288 Deleuze 2013, pp. 150 et sq., Deleuze 1962, pp. 182 f.

debased, enslaved, forsaken, despicable being', Nietzsche strives to create precisely such oppressive conditions, 'for which the existential insignificance of humanity will serve as a presupposition'.[289] The 'man' whose postmodern death Foucault and Deleuze want to announce gets back his original Nietzschean meaning as 'little people', who are to be rubbed out by the 'overman'. Also, what interests Deleuze in this above all is that the overman has nothing in common 'with the species being of the dialecticians'.[290] In contrast to Heidegger, who treated the 'overman' as the realisation of human nature, for Deleuze it is important to distinguish it as that which is entirely different from human beings, also from the 'higher' man.[291]

Let us look more closely at Deleuze's disagreement with Heidegger: he proves Heidegger's interpretation of the overman with his *Who is Nietzsche's Zarathustra?* of 1953, in which it is stated, for example: '"Eternal return of the same" is the name for the Being of beings. "Overman" is the name for the human essence which corresponds to this Being'.[292] Deleuze neglects to communicate that Heidegger already formulated this thought in his Nietzsche lectures of 1940, in *The European Nihilism* and in *Nietzsche's Metaphysics*: it is not a special type of man who is forethought in Nietzsche's overman, but 'for the first time man in the essential shape of a "type"',[293] and his greatness consists in the fact that he puts the essence of the will to power into the 'will of a manhood, which wants itself as the master of the earth', as 'a kind of manhood, that for the first time wants to be a kind of its own'.[294] Heidegger's interpretation places both the will to power and the overman in the context of world domination and imperial 'spatial need', and is clearly formulated according to the requirements of the Nazi war of conquest.[295]

Since Deleuze does not want to speak about Heidegger's crucial role in fascising the interpretation of Nietzsche,[296] the debate is reduced to a commentary on his understanding of the overman as a being who defines himself as

---

289   Landa 2005, p. 473; cf. Marx 1843, p. 182.
290   Deleuze 2013, p. 154, Deleuze 1962, p. 188.
291   Deleuze 2013, pp. 154, 157 et sq., Deleuze 1962, pp. 188, 190 et sq.
292   Heidegger 1991a, vol II, p. 231, GA I.7, p. 122.
293   Heidgger 1991b, vol IV, p. 99, GA l. 6.2., p. 128.
294   Heidegger 1991b, vol. III, p. 234, GA l. 6.2., p. 281.
295   Cf. on Heidegger's Nietzsche lectures of 1940 e.g. Zapata Galindo (1995, pp. 158 et sqq.), Farias (1989, pp. 335 et sqq.), Losurdo (2001, pp. 182 et sqq.).
296   As Losurdo shows in detail, it was not Nietzsche's 'evil' sister Elizabeth who has transformed his philosophy into a kind of 'protofascism', but rather Heidegger and other philosophers who fascicised Nietzsche by merging his aristocratic radicalism with rightwing populism (cf. Losurdo 2020, pp. 711 et sqq., 775 et sqq.).

opposed to man, as having a completely new and different way of feeling, think-ing, and evaluating.[297] Both Heidegger and Deleuze take the fictional character of the 'overman' at face value, instead of deconstructing it. Therefore they over-look what is important for Nietzsche in his presentation of the shifting relation-ship between Zarathustra and the 'higher man': he pleads for the 'ideological estates',[298] which he intends to teach to free themselves from any consideration for the lower ones, and to become detached from the moral forms influenced by them (primarily compassion and charity), and at the same time articulates his disappointment that they always fall back into the old ideologies, become pious (pray to the donkey), become infected by the rabble (smell bad).[299] Niet-zsche's 'overman' is a figure of hope for radical domination: a model character for anti-democratic elites, their ideologues and would-be allies.

Compared with Heidegger, Deleuze has only seized upon a more abstracted and eerie overman-variant, with which the social subject of power remains in the dark. In turn, this obfuscation is a necessary condition for the connection of Nietzscheanism with postmodernism. Therefore the interpretation cannot concentrate on Nietzsche's enthusiastic painting of the 'overman' and his des-potic character, but seeks the common denominator in the 'end of man', whom Nietzsche had called the 'skin disease of the earth'.[300] History has always shown the same in Deleuze's opinion, which coincides with Nietzsche's view, namely that the Greek world was perverted by theoretical man, Rome perverted by Judea, the Renaissance perverted by the Reformation, and therefore it was hopeless to defend 'the strong against the weak', because against the pressure of the weak the strong cannot escape becoming weak. Nietzsche's deeper view reveals 'what is truly generic is the becoming reactive of all forces'.[301] Like Niet-zsche, Deleuze rejects the human 'species' because the 'weak' have too strong a voice in it.

For Nietzsche it was clear why he dismissed any notion of a human 'species': It is a central point of reference for the past moralities and the sciences depend-ent on them, which strive to identify a persisting human commonality which goes beyond the individuals, and to derive from this an 'equality' of humans. This is for Nietzsche a 'constructed phantom', to be explained with the fact that

---

297 Deleuze 2013, p. 154, Deleuze 1962, p. 188.
298 Cf. for this concept Marx, e.g. in Marx 1862, p. 197 (translation modified); Marx and Engels 1957-, Vol. 26.1., p. 274.
299 E.g. Nietzsche 2006, pp. 240 et sq., 253 et sq., 264, 266, Nietzsche 1999a, Vol. 4, pp. 369, 388 et sq., 405, 408.
300 Deleuze 2013, p. 159, Deleuze 1962, p. 194; cf. Nietzsche 1999a, Vol. 4, p. 168.
301 Deleuze 2013, pp. 158 et sq., Deleuze 1962, pp. 193 et sq.

the 'mass instinct' has also seized on the domains of knowledge.[302] In reality 'there is no species, but just different single entities'.[303] As opposed to this, 'his' movement wants the 'elimination of equality, the creation of mightier ones', who stand elevated 'over the entire species "humanity"'.[304] Even if the equality in the past moralities applied only before 'God', it must be eliminated: if Nietzsche in *Zarathustra* lets the rabble so much as 'blink', there would be no higher humans; because 'human is human, before God – we are all equal', the answer reads: 'Before God! Now, however, this God has died'.[305]

Deleuze and Foucault adopt this argumentation and omit at the same time what is at stake. Everything is there again, even if it sounds different: the criticism of the anthropological focus of the 'past moralities' and the 'human sciences', including the stance against 'equality' in morality as conformist universalism and the dismissal of normalisation in the name of 'individual choice' and 'difference'. 'To play the big game – to spare no effort so that the existence of mankind may perhaps reach something higher than the preservation of the species', notes Nietzsche in 1883 in a draft to Zarathustra's last speech.[306] The postmodern proclamation of the 'death of man' intends to reenact this 'big game' again.

In the next part there will be an examination of how this theoretical-political dispositif changes when at the beginning of the seventies Foucault gradually begins to replace the concept of episteme with that of power.

302   Nietzsche 1999a, Vol. 9, pp. 500 et sq.
303   Nietzsche 1999a, Vol. 9, p. 508.
304   Nietzsche 1999a, Vol. 10, p. 244.
305   Nietzsche 2006, p. 232; Nietzsche 1999a, Vol. 4, p. 356.
306   Nietzsche 1999a, Vol. 10, p. 372.

The Introduction of a Neo-Nietzschean Concept of Power and Its Consequences

1   New Coordinates

What changes first are some of the political coordinates. Under the influence of the movement of '68, Foucault executes a swing to the left, which completely surprises several of his contemporaries. It should be remembered that his most successful publication so far, *The Order of Things* from 1966, had been regarded by many as a book of the 'right' owing to the sharp reckoning with Marx. Sartre had called it 'the last bulwark ... that the Bourgeoisie could still erect against Marx'.[1] During this period Foucault also distanced himself from Althusser, who had significantly supported his past teaching activities and publications, by extending his criticism of humanism from the 'young' Marx to the entire Marx, and to the dialectic itself. In turn, Althusser refers to this generalisation of the humanism critique when in 1966 he denounces Foucault's 'crazy interviews [interviews déconnantes] on Marx'.[2] In the years 1965/66 he also worked on the Gaullist project of a university reform (Réforme Fouchet), and was almost named deputy director of the university in the ministry of education, had he not been rejected because of his homosexuality.[3]

However, in March 1968 he encounters a militant student movement at the University of Tunis, whose Marxism he perceives as a mobilising moral energy of the Sorelian myth type. With new interest he reads Trotsky, Rosa Luxem-

1   'Derrière l'histoire, bien entendu, c'est le marxisme qui est visé. Il s'agit de constituer une idéologie nouvelle, le dernier barrage que la bourgeoisie puisse encore dresser contre Marx' (Sartre 1966, p. 88).

2   Cf. Eribon 1994, pp. 333 et sqq. Althusser probably refers primarily to Foucault's interview in Foucault 2001a, Nr. 39, pp. 569 et sq.; with regard to the relationship between Althusser and Foucault generally, cf. Eribon 1994, pp. 313–50 and 1993 pp. 32 et sqq., 55 et sqq., 57 et sq., 68 et sqq., 128 et sqq. According to Eribon, Foucault's entrance into the French Communist Party was already in 1950 considerably affected by Althusser. He quit the party in 1953. Promoted by or mediated through Althusser e.g. were the first assistantship in Besançon (1950), the teaching position in Lille (1951–5) and the first book publication in 1954 (*Maladie mentale et personnalité*).

3   Cf. Eribon 1993, pp. 133 et sqq.

burg, Che Guevara and the writings of the Black Panthers.[4] Returning to Paris, he takes part in 1969 in the legendary 'battle at Vincennes' as dean of the philosophy department, and participates in the intellectual milieu of the 'Gauche prolétarienne'. When the organisation is forbidden in 1970, and numerous representatives of 'Gauchism' are in prison, he founds with other well-known intellectuals the 'Groupe d'information sur les prisons' (GIP), which records and publishes the inhuman prison conditions and life stories of the prisoners. Within a short time the group succeeds in building a network of up to 2,000–3,000 intellectuals and begins to support the revolts in the prisons with a publicly effective prison-critical movement. However, success is only short-lived: the prison revolts collapse in 1971/1972 and are partly – as in Attica/USA – bloodily beaten down, a wave of suicides intervenes, the solidarity movement encounters the refusal of the workers and their organisations, the newly created self-organisation of the prisoners (CAP) turns against the 'presumption' of the intellectual spokesmen to speak for them, and the GIP dissipates in December 1972.[5]

The prison movement is the starting point for the first large investigation into disciplinary power in Foucault's *Discipline and Punish* [Surveiller et punir, 1975], of his works the most strongly inspired by Marx. It also forms the background for what Foucault in 1976 will characterise as the 'coupling [couplage] together of scholarly erudition and local memories'.[6] This connection was meant to open the way to a 'rebellion of "subjugated knowledges"' [insurrection des savoirs assujettis], which however directs itself as 'anti-science' against the institutionalised sciences and here especially against the 'totalitarian' theories of Marxism and psychoanalysis.[7] Foucault will accent this frontline ever more sharply. *The History of Sexuality* [Histoire de la sexualité, vol. 1, 1976] is a reckoning with the 'repressive hypothesis' of Freudo-Marxism. One year later Foucault will refer 'totalitarianism' directly to Marx, when, in an enthused review of Glucksmann's *Master Philosophers*, he calls the victims of Stalinism the 'flayed truth' of Marxist theory (see below Chapter 5.5).[8]

4   Cf. for this the chronicle in Foucault 2001a, pp. 42 et sq. and Miller 1993, p. 171.
5   Cf. for the history of the GIP among others Defert/Donzelot in Foucault 1976b, pp. 7–15; Eribon 1993, pp. 224 et sqq., 234; Miller 1993, p. 185; Lemke 2019, pp. 57 et sq.
6   Foucault 2003c, p. 8, Foucault 1997b, pp. 9 et sq.
7   Foucault 2003c, pp. 7 and 8 et sq., Foucault 1997b, pp. 7 et sq. and 10.
8   Foucault 2001b, Nr. 204, pp. 278 et sq. Not least owing to the position on the *Nouveaux Philosophes* do the paths of Foucault and Deleuze separate; the two do not see each other from the end of 1977 onwards (cf. Eribon 1993, pp. 261 et sqq.).

Balibar described the struggle with Marx as one of the fundamental main-springs of Foucauldian productivity.[9] It fed on the connection, as well as from the opposition, to a formerly powerful 'Parisian Marxism'. As Isabelle Garo observes, this productivity manifests itself among other things in a 'faculté aiguë d'intervention', more strategic than that of most Marxists at the time, which enables him to become a major public intellectual.[10] It is not least the intimate opposition to Marxism which made Foucault's ascent in the canons of postmodernist thinking possible.

2   Survey of the Terrain: The Overcoming of Ideology Critique through the 'Diversity' and the 'Productivity' of Power

In the Foucault literature it is mostly the 'anti-economistic' and the 'anti-totalitarian' stance that is received. It can rely on Foucault's self-assessment that he has overcome the Marxist fixation on economics and the state through the discovery of a 'micro-physics' of power,[11] which 'is exercised from innu-merable points, in the interplay of nonegalitarian and mobile relations',[12] so that finally, as was claimed in an interview in 1977, proletariat and bourgeoisie no longer face each other, but we fight 'all against all' – 'and there is always something in us that fights against something else in us'.[13]

Let us take as an example Michèle Barrett's book *The Politics of Truth. From Marx to Foucault (1991)*, which combines different dismissals of Marx and lets them converge with Foucault. Barrett wants to show that the political lexis of discourse and power is to be preferred to that of 'ideology, social formation, class and so on'.[14] The enumeration with its hasty 'and so on' shows the urge to see the entire bloc of historical-materialistic concepts finished once and for all. A reliable indication of the overcoming of Marxism is, in her estimation, above all the retirement of the ideology concept. As does Foucault, Barrett assumes that ideology always functions as a counter-concept to truth, is humanistic-ally related to a subject and cannot be separated from the deterministic basis-superstructure structure of Marxism: 'The implication of an "infrastructure"

9   Balibar 1991, p. 40.
10   Garo 2011, p. 83.
11   Foucault 1995, p. 26; Foucault 1975, p. 35.
12   Foucault 1978, p. 94; Foucault 1976a, pp. 123 et sq.
13   Foucault 1980, p. 208, Foucault 2001b, Nr. 206, p. 311.
14   Barrett 1991, p. 126.

is always there'.[15] To the extent that Foucault replaces the ideology concept through the discourse concept, for Barrett he criticises 'the materialist mind-set that sees value only in the mute, grey world of the pre-discursive and treats with disregard the productive creations of discourse'.[16] The re-narration suppresses the fact that Marx already in the first thesis of his *Theses on Feuerbach* criticised such a notion of a 'pre-discursive' mute external world as a materialism of the 'object, or of contemplation' and opposed it with a 'new' materialism which proceeds from 'sensuous human activity, praxis'.[17] The next step in overcoming Marx consists then in Foucault's resort to Nietzsche, in his essay *Nietzsche, Genealogy, History* (1971), which allows him to replace the linear conception of history, stretched between the search for an origin and a teleological goal, with a decentred 'genealogy' which is interested in various 'beginnings' – 'to think of difference rather than resemblance, of beginnings rather than a beginning, of exterior accident rather than internal truth'.[18] On this basis, Barrett's Foucault finally developed a social-theoretical terminology which breaks completely with the paradigm of a determining social structure. His concept of power 'was truly in sympathy with his concern with the polymorphous play of dependencies', a play which is not to be located in apparatuses, but takes place in micro operations.[19]

One must search a long time in the Foucault literature before one finds authors who do *not* share this (or a similar) reading of Foucault's achievement in principle, whatever else they may then criticise about Foucault's conception. That the connection between power and knowledge, taken over from Nietzsche, 'is more radical and far reaching' than any Marxist analysis of the conditions of knowledge could ever be, is self-evident for Dreyfus and Rabinow, for example.[20] It is a foregone conclusion that Foucault has grasped a somehow 'deeper' level of reality than 'simple' ideology theory, since this allegedly knows only phenomena of consciousness. Thus Mark Poster greets the dismissal of the concept of ideology by the Nietzschean insight into the perspectivism of all discourses because thereby Marxism's universalistic claim to liberation can be overcome by a 'tendency toward pluralism'.[21] Barry Smart enthusiastically points out that with Foucault's 'multiple' concept of power the Gramscian

15   Barrett 1991, pp. 123 et sq., 168.
16   Barrett 1991, p. 131.
17   Marx 1845, p. 3; Marx and Engels 1957-, Vol. 3, p. 5.
18   Barrett 1991, p. 132.
19   Barrett 1991, pp. 131, 134.
20   Dreyfus and Rabinow 1983, p. 115.
21   Poster 1984, pp. 84 et sq.

hegemony-concept can be extracted from its still Marxist presentation in the basis-superstructure relationship and ideology critique.[22] And Thomas Lemke considers Foucault's concept of power, because of its centring on the body, to be 'more materialistic' than a theory of ideology, which he previously specified in terms of a 'primacy of consciousness'.[23]

It is characteristic of the attraction of this kind of Marx-overcoming that Foucault's achievements in this regard are also assumed by critics who accuse him of a 'monist conception of power'.[24] Honneth reads the micro-physics of power first as an 'action-theoretic model of relations' that despite its ambiguity is superior to both the Althusserian theory of Ideological State Apparatuses as well as the fixation of Horkheimer and Adorno on the central administrative machinery.[25] Honneth's criticism begins only where Foucault cannot explain the increasing stabilisation and institutionalisation of decentral power rela-tions and their successes because he lacks a meaning for the 'normative'.[26] Nancy Fraser, who likewise accuses Foucault of the absence of a consistent 'normative perspective', emphasises his merit in having pointed out, against the state-centred and economist conceptions of power, 'that modern power is "capillary", that it operates at the lowest extremities of the social body in every-day social practices'.[27] In both cases there is the presupposition of that which would first have to be examined, that is, that Foucault really can fulfil his prom-ise to conceptualise multi-layered everyday practices, their contradictions and struggles, with his concept of power.

The criticism of Foucault's power monism falls short if understood as only a neglect of the 'normative'. On one hand it is fixated on an aspect where Foucault's approach does indeed have certain strengths: there are good reas-ons to analyse the construction of norms and values capable of creating con-sensus with regard to the underlying social relations of forces on which their respective interpretations also depend. If one follows Bourdieu, for example, according to whom 'symbolic power' is characterised by the fact that it imposes meanings as legitimate, 'by concealing the power relations which are the basis of its force',[28] then the appeal to norms is not to be regarded as a beyond of power strategies, but as their integral component.[29] Seen from Bourdieu's field

---

22 Smart 1986, pp. 159 et sq.
23 Lemke 2019, pp. 87 et sqq.
24 Honneth 1991, p. 151.
25 Honneth 1991, pp. 155, 157 et sq.
26 Honneth 1991, pp. 160 et sq., 174.
27 Fraser 1989, p. 18.
28 Bourdieu and Passeron 1977, p. 4.
29 Cf. also for this e.g. Bourdieu (1982, pp. 36 et sq., 68; Bourdieu 2010, pp. 166, 167 et sq.; 1996, p. 16).

and habitus concept, the objection of power consolidation raised by Honneth would not be treated as a problem of 'normative communication', but rather on the level of strategies with which the social distinctions of power are accumulated materially and symbolically.[30] And on the other hand, the criticism of Foucault's theory in the name of the normative is half-hearted: the central problem of the Foucauldian power concept consists not only in the fact that it cannot conceive of 'normative' institutionalisation, but also, as Honneth noted in a different context, in a functionalism in which 'the historical phenomena of social conflict ... in general ... [have] disappeared behind the systematic process of the continuous perfecting of techniques of power'.[31]

The theoretical critique should not entrench itself behind the question of norms, but get involved in the very construction of the Foucauldian concept of power. Among other things, this is characterised by the following contradiction: on one hand, power is determined as a relation, as 'relational power' [pouvoir relationnel],[32] up to the well-known 'nominalistic' definition that it is only 'the name that one attributes to a complex strategical situation in a particular society.'[33] On the other hand, it emerges in the same breath as a subject to which a certain characteristic is assigned – be it that of a sublimated 'war' or then (in the 80s) of a mobile-reciprocal relation of forces, which is characterised by the quality of 'freedom'. It is not only 'omnipresent' but also in the position to penetrate into the core of all social areas without friction, as well as to 'produce' their objects and subjectivities.[34] It was Poulantzas, especially, who pointed out that behind the Foucauldian diversity-rhetoric there hides an essentialism which reconverts the 'relational' power concept into an all-powerful 'Power-Master' [Maitre-Pouvoir].[35]

The shiny word of power-diversity is frequently linked in the literature with the no less dazzling concept of power 'productivity', the discovery of which enabled Foucault to overcome the 'simple' Marxist critique of exploitation, domination and ideology. As example I would like to draw on the study by Thomas Lemke, which is characterised by its integrating various critiques of

---

30   Cf. the argumentation of Schwingel, who agrees with Honneth's criticism that due to his nominalism Foucault has difficulties explaining the increasing reinforcement of power, but criticises Honneth's explanation of an 'interruption of the struggle' through 'normatively motivated agreement' (Honneth 1991, p. 174) as premature, and contrasts it with Bourdieu's conflict model (Schwingel 1993, p. 169).

31   Honneth 1991, p. 175.

32   Foucault 1995, p. 177; Foucault 1975, p. 208.

33   Foucault 1978, p. 93; Foucault 1976a, pp. 122 et sq.

34   Ibid.

35   Poulantzas 2014, pp. 149 et sq.; Poulantzas 1978a, pp. 165 et sq.

Foucault's 'power monism' and then smoothing them away in a Foucauldian manner, that is, in the framework of Foucault's own self-criticism. The strategy consists in limiting the accusation of a one-sided power-functionalism to the early phase of a still 'repressive' power concept, which then, through the grow-ing discovery of the 'productivity' of power, will be gradually overcome.

Simplified, the picture looks as follows. In 1971, in *the Order of Discourse*, Foucault still thematised power primarily as external 'exclusion' and internal 'shortage', and thus still thought its relationship to discourse as a negative.[36] He takes a decisive step beyond the 'negative' concept of power in *Discipline and Punish* by showing how the disciplinary power unites together subjection and economic usefulness into a 'productive and strengthening cycle'.[37] But the shortcoming is that Foucault's 'strategic-positive conception' of power is still bound to the 'hypothesis of Nietzsche', according to which the power relation-ships in the long run emerged from 'war'.[38] The term was coined by Foucault himself, who dedicated his lecture of 1976, *Society Must be Defended*, to 'Niet-zsche's hypothesis'.[39] According to Lemke, Foucault is by the war hypothesis still bound to the 'repression thesis', which he actually wanted to overcome. His genealogy still pursues a 'monocausal explanatory model', puts the accent one-sidedly on submission processes and reduces subjectivity to an effect of 'discipline', which despite avowals of their productive character remain 'negat-ive' in the long run.[40]

However, according to this reading, Foucault in 1976, in the first volume of the *History of Sexuality*, revised 'Nietzsche's hypothesis' by deriving power no longer monocausally from war, but assumed 'that this multiplicity of force rela-tions can be coded ... either in the form of "war", or in the form of "politics"'.[41] Lemke sees therein a crucial step to understanding the 'productivity and posit-ivity' of power, which in the following studies on governmentality in 1978 and 1979 were further developed.[42] The term 'productive' marks for Foucault the opposite to 'repression' and is meant to express the fact that power does not exclude, suppress or mask, but first brings forth the fields of objects and know-ledge (such as, e.g., of 'sexuality' and 'sex') as well as the respective subjects and their attitudes. Beyond that, the term 'positive' refers to an increasingly positive

36   Lemke 2019, pp. 45 et sqq.
37   Lemke 2019, pp. 68 et sq.
38   Lemke 2019, pp. 101 et sqq.
39   Foucault 2003c, p. 16, Foucault 1997b, p. 17.
40   Lemke 2019, pp. 106 et sqq., 113 et sq.
41   Foucault 1978, p. 93; Foucault 1976a, p. 123.
42   Lemke 2019, pp. 141 et sqq., 194 et sqq.

evaluation of power, which Foucault now in the 80s differentiates from force as well as domination, and approximates to 'freedom' and 'ethics'.[43]

Lemke's amazingly linear picture of an increasingly 'productive' concept of power has led us into Foucault's late phase, which Honneth called his 'peculiar turn' toward morality,[44] and which in the literature is either celebrated as discovery of a 'post-teleological' model of ethics,[45] or criticised as a conservative return to an 'in-group-privatism' and privileged aestheticism.[46] There are valid arguments on both sides, but I am mostly interested in an aspect that is usually blotted out in this controversy, namely a peculiar abstraction in the Foucauldian concept of power, which is the basis for both the 'war hypothesis' as well as the 'ethic of freedom' hypothesis and makes their exchange possible: How can it be explained that Foucault understands modern power for many years in reversal of the saying of Clausewitz as 'continuation of war by other means',[47] and then defines it in terms of a reciprocity characterised by 'mobile, ... reversible and unstable relationships', without which no society can live, and whose center is the 'intransitivité de la liberté'?[48] It is of course possible to develop a positive, neo-Spinozian concept of power centred on the question of the social capacity to act. But why should it actually be an advancement of knowledge to determine power ever 'more productively', if in the end the structural relations of domination, together with the apparatuses of repression and administrative force that frame them, have fallen out of the analysis of power? Why would it be an advantage to apply a concept of power as a set of mobile-reversible relationships, for example to the obviously non-reversible relations in the prison which Foucault analysed in terms of disciplinary power? There is no reason why it would in principle be better to think power in the 'productive' paradigm of a reciprocal mating play than in the 'negative' paradigm of a sublimated 'war', if we don't consider the respective concrete kind of power. If we take Foucault's rhetoric of a 'relational' concept of power seriously, we need to conceptualise it from the respective social relations and their hegemonic conjuncture.

---

43   Lemke 2019, pp. 324 et sqq.
44   Honneth 1990, p. 17.
45   Schmid 1991, p. 307.
46   Kammler 1986, pp. 203 et sq.; Rochlitz 1989, p. 297. Renate Schlesier sees in Foucault's *The Use of Pleasure* and *The Care of the Self* the return to a traditional history of ideas of antiquity and the celebration of an individualistic male morality (1984, pp. 819 et sq., 823).
47   Foucault 2003c, p. 16, Foucault 1997b, p. 16.
48   Cf. the interviews of 1982 (Foucault 2000, pp. 341 et sqq., 347; Foucault 2001b, Nr. 306, pp. 1056 et sq., 1061) and of 1984 (Foucault 1997a, pp. 292, 298, Foucault 2001b, Nr. 356, pp. 1539, 1546).

It is high time to think about the intellectual and political price of Foucault's 'overcoming' of Marxism. In the following, I try to substantiate the thesis that the contradiction between diversity rhetoric and essentialism is connected with the fact that Foucault took his concept of power from the late Nietzsche. It is not convincing to reduce Foucault's 'Nietzscheanism', as Lemke does, to his 'war hypothesis', which is then overcome with the aid of a 'more productive' concept of power. The 'productivity' of power – exactly that *is* Nietzsche, namely in the sense that he conceived of his 'will to power' as the sole and omnipresent productive force in nature, in the individual and in society.[49] Foucault himself located Nietzsche's influence primarily in the connection of power and truth, in whose names he dismissed the Marxist critique of alienation and ideology, and which constituted the core of his concept of 'productive' power. On it is based not only the refutation of the Freudo-Marxist 'repression thesis' in the first volume of Foucault's *The History of Sexuality*, whose original French title revealingly says 'La volonté de savoir', but also the investigative disposition of the studies of the Greek, stoic and early Christian sexual discourses.[50] Foucault's Nietzscheanism in the 1970s lies above all in the replacement of ideology critique by a fictionalistic critique of the 'truth', and in the construction of a concept of power which underlies social relations as a 'deeper' level of being.

The following re-reading concentrates primarily on the formation phase of Foucault's power concept between 1969 and 1972. In this period, which is also the phase of left-wing radical engagement, Foucault meets with an early ideology concept of Althusser, and at the same time rejects it by dissolving it first into the category of 'knowledge', before merging it into the category of power by way of the Nietzschean connection of truth and will-to-power.

3   The Dissolution of Ideology into 'Knowledge'

In the passage which Barrett brought up Foucault summarises his refusal of the ideology concept by saying that the concept would always stand in a

---

49   That the concept of power, of all things, as 'productivity' stems from Nietzsche was clearly noticed e.g. by Honneth (1991, pp. 164 et sq.) and Fink-Eitel (1980, p. 77 note 62).

50   'The political question, to sum up, is not error, illusion, alienated consciousness or ideology; it is the truth itself. Hence the importance of Nietzsche', claims Foucault e.g. in 1977 (Foucault 2000, p. 133, Foucault 2001b, Nr. 192, p. 160). Cf. on the meaning of the power-truth connection e.g. Foucault 1978, pp. 11, 60, 77, 106; Foucault 1990, pp. 5 et sqq.; Foucault 1986, pp. 73 et sqq.

potential opposition to the truth, is related to a subject, and is subordinated to economics.[51] The pronouncement comes from June 1976. Six years previously, in 1970 in his essay *Idéologie et appareils idéologiques d'État* Althusser had refuted the three attributions made by Foucault point by point: opposing a traditional concept which counterposes ideology to truth as 'false consciousness', Althusser emphasised its 'material existence', embodied in practices, rituals and interpellations of material ideological apparatuses,[52] which are to be reconstructed going from the outside inward: 'Kneel down, move your lips in prayer and you will believe';[53] according to Althusser, ideology is not to be understood from the perspective of a 'subject' but is characterised in reverse by the fact that it constitutes the individuals by 'interpellation' to 'subjects', who are subjugated in the form of 'freedom';[54] and finally, Althusser grasped ideology no longer as something subordinate to 'economics', derived from it, a reflecting construct of ideas, but as a relatively autonomous material arrangement which is indispensable for the reproduction of the relations of production and of the labour force.[55]

Here we encounter Foucault's strategy to relegate the concept of ideology far behind the level of the theoretical discussion at the time, in order to be better able to distance himself and to profile his own power concept.[56] Actually, already in 1969 in the *Archaeology of Knowledge* he distanced himself from an early ideology concept of Althusser, which preceded his first formulation of a historical-materialistic ideology theory. Foucault encounters the ideology problem with his attempt to 'show positively how a science functions in the element of knowledge'. The ideological functioning of science is located 'where science stands out against knowledge' [se découpe sur le savoir], where it is 'localized' in it, finds its place in a 'discursive regularity', functions in a field of discursive practices, in short: where it exists itself as a 'discursive practice'.[57]

However, this determination of ideology is far from clear. This is shown already by the counter question, where then does science not exist as 'dis-

51 Foucault 2000, p. 119, Foucault 2001b, Nr. 192, p. 148.
52 Althusser 2014, pp. 184 et sq.; Althusser 1995, pp. 298 et sqq.
53 Althusser 2014, p. 186; Althusser 1995, p. 301. Free after Pascal's *Pensées, Oeuvres complètes* (1954), Aph. 469 (= Edition Brunschvigg, Aph. 250).
54 Althusser 2014. pp. 187 et sq.; 197 et sq.; Althusser 1995, pp. 302 et sq.; 310 et sq.
55 Althusser 2014, pp. 48 et sqq.; Althusser 1995, pp. 269 et sqq.
56 Poulantzas showed (Poulantzas 2014, p. 67) that such a back transfer of the ideological into the realm of 'ideas' is also the basis for the opposing of ideology and 'normalisation' in *Discipline and Punish*. He observes a similar reductionism with the concept of the state (Poulantzas 2014, pp. 36 et sq.).
57 Foucault 2010a, p. 185 (translation modified); Foucault 1969, p. 242.

cursive practice', and where is it not to be located in 'knowledge'? 'Knowledge' (savoir) designates with Foucault – similarly to the 'archive' – not an empirically available set of information and insights, but a more deeply lying level of determination, which as a set of 'rules' specifies 'what must be said ... if a discourse is to exist', and which constitutes the foundation 'on the basis of which coherent (or incoherent) propositions are built up ... and theories deployed'.[58] In this conceptual framework there is not science on one hand, knowledge on the other, and in their contact an ideology problem, but science is itself a 'knowledge' that has overstepped certain thresholds (e.g. of epistemologisation or formalisation).[59] There are actually good reasons to question the counterposing of 'science' and 'knowledge' and thus of epistemology and 'archaeology'.[60] But where is ideology left in this conceptual arrangement?

Foucault dismisses the ideology problem in the first introductory sentences before he even poses it. To pose it would mean asking for specific forms and functional modes both in 'knowledge' and in 'science', which strengthen the tendencies to a voluntary subjection to the respective relations of domination, which weaken the dispositions to resistance and block emancipatory perspectives and progressive solutions. An analytic question of this kind, which would dissect the discourse formations of a society into different dimensions, is however not possible in Foucault's 'archaeology' because it is not compatible with the status of his concept of generative 'rules'.

As Dominique Lecourt has shown, Foucault's text is an answer to 'some already old books' of Althusser, in which he had set out to oppose science and ideology on the basis of Bachelard's concept of a *coupure* or *rupture*.[61] Meant are *Pour Marx* and *Lire le Capital*, where Althusser treats ideology primarily in connection with the humanism of the young Marx, which he sees replaced from about 1845 onwards by the 'science' of historical materialism. However, a textual comparison shows not only where Foucault turns against the Althusserian opposition, but also that he first took over the concept of ideology exactly from there. In *Pour Marx* the ideological is not yet conceived of as material instance of the 'ideological state apparatuses' and a contested site of struggle, but generally as a necessarily imaginary, 'lived' relationship to the world. Thus ideology is connected with every social practice and so also indispensable for every society.[62] Althusser will maintain this concept of an omni-

---

58   Foucault 2010a, p. 182; Foucault 1969, pp. 237 et sq.
59   Foucault 2010a, p. 187; Foucault 1969, pp. 243 et sq.
60   Foucault 2010a, p. 179; Foucault 1969, p. 233.
61   Cf. Lecourt 1975, pp. 199 et sq.
62   cf. Althusser 1996a, pp. 232 et sq., 235 et sq.; Althusser 1966, pp. 239 et sq., 242 et sq.

present and eternal ideology, while at the same time complementing it with his theory of 'ideological state apparatuses'. Jacques Rancière points out that the methodological decision to develop a general definition of ideology prior to class-struggle and outside the realm of a Marxist analysis led to an uneasy combination of two heterogeneous conceptual systems: historical materialism and a Comtian/Durkheimian sociology, which argues on the general level of a bond or cohesion of the social whole, with the effect that the ideology (in general) 'is not posited, at the outset, as the site of a struggle'.[63] Indeed, Althusser's concept of 'ideology in general' is conceived of as an unsocial, anthropological natural characteristic. It functions as a 'system of representations' (pictures, myths, notions) and differs thereby from science, 'in that in it the practico-social function is more important than the theoretical function'.[64] The fact that Althusser identifies the ideological with the 'practical-social function' in general, whereas for the sciences only the subject-less 'theoretical practice' remains, belongs to the anachronisms of an 'anti-humanistic' ideology concept, which through its identification with subjective practice as such can gain no discriminatory analytic power.[65]

Against this background, it is important not to place Foucault's objection at the wrong point. It is in no way directed against Althusser's over-generalised ideology concept, but presupposes it by identifying the ideological functioning of science with its existence as 'discursive practice'. Only with the next step do the paths separate. Althusser refers to a passage in Marx's *Introduction to the Critique of Political Economy*, in which scientific thinking is defined as a mental 'assimilation and transformation of perceptions and images into concepts'.[66] He interprets these 'perceptions and images' as ideology (in the sense of a practically lived relationship to the world), which as raw material [généralité I] enters into the process of scientific treatment, and there, through the 'theoretical practice' of critique, can be replaced by a scientific 'mental concretum'.[67] The possibility of such an ideology-critical 'cleansing' is demonstrated using the example of Marx, who (in Althusser's reading) recognised the humanistic categories of the 'human' and its 'alienation', etc. as ideology and replaced it in the course of a 'theoretical revolution' with a new set of historical-materialistic concepts (relations of production, basis, superstructure, etc.).[68]

---

63   Rancière 2011, pp. 131 et sqq.
64   Althusser 1996a, p. 231. 'en ce que la fonction pratico-sociale l'emporte en elle sur la fonction theorique' (Althusser 1966, p. 238).
65   Cf. for a detailed critique, Rehmann 2013, pp. 155–160, 173–8.
66   Marx 1857a, p. 38; Marx and Engels 1957–, Vol. 13, p. 632.
67   Althusser 1996a, pp. 182 et sq; Althusser 1966, pp. 186 et sq.
68   Althusser 1996a, pp. 227 et sqq., Althusser 1966, pp. 233 et sqq.

For the purpose of our argument, we are not interested at the moment in the weaknesses of the opposition between ideology and science, which Althusser himself will criticise in his *Self Critique* as 'theoristic deviation',[69] but rather in those of the Foucauldian answers, which in a displaced and unclear way turn against the perspective of an analytical working through of ideological over-determininations in general. The claim that ideology is situated 'not exclusive of scientificity' is not a real objection.[70] That there is no 'pure' science is also emphasised by Althusser, who for this reason wants to seek out the ideological mode of functioning within science, and with the assistance of a 'materialistic dialectic' transform it into theoretical knowledge.[71] That ideology is not to be overcome by the correction of scientific 'errors' is self-evident from Althusser's psychoanalytically grounded concept of ideology.[72]

Foucault's claim to exhibit the ideological mode of functioning not by means of a demonstration of the contradictions, gaps and deficiencies, but on the level of its 'positivity', is implicitly directed against Althusser's concept of a 'symptomatic reading'.[73] But here too, the theoretical argument is trivialised beyond recognition. Althusser used the concept, which he developed from Marx's treatment of classical economics, not in the sense of a critique which from the outside points out the deficiencies and gaps, but instead to emphasise a kind of reading in which Marx locates the 'necessary connection' between the field of the detected and the not-detected, deciphers the not-seen (bévue) in the seen [vue], and as a form of seeing, discovers the not-known in the strongest evidence, the silence in the discourse.[74] 'Symptomatic' means here the procedure to read the lines of fracture in a text (e.g. an answer without a corresponding question) as symptoms of a latent second text. Thus ideology critique is exposed to the strongest demands of textual analysis: it is a critique 'from the inside', which sounds out the text on the logic of its standpoint and perspective.[75] Demanded is the high art of reading the text from its best sides, entangling it in its own contradictions, and out of this kind of confrontation reconstructing the social structuring of the configuration and its internal borders.

Foucault reduces this project of an immanent ideology critique to an exhibition of 'gaps' and 'deficiencies', which he intends to replace with his own

---

69   Cf. Althusser 1976, p. 105.
70   Foucault 2010a, p. 186; Foucault 1969, p. 242.
71   Althusser 1996a, pp. 171 et sq.; Althusser 1966, pp. 171 et sq.
72   Foucault 2010a, pp. 186 et sq.; Foucault 1969, p. 243.
73   Ibid.
74   Althusser and Balibar 2009, pp. 23 et sqq., 32, 35 et sq.
75   Cf. Althusser and Balibar 2009, pp. 34 et sq.

'positive' account. But this methodological framework, which Foucault himself characterises as 'happy positivism', eliminates any space for a critical analysis of science's social standpoint logic.[76] Foucault hides his suspension of critique with the radical sounding suggestion that one criticise the ideological functioning of a science by questioning it as 'discursive formation'.[77] But in so doing he only shifts the problem onto a different terrain. Because to 'call it into question' as a discourse and knowledge formation would mean in turn to analyse such a formation as a contradictory field, on which (and for which) different social positions struggle with each other. Foucault's suggestion is pseudo-critical because he has abandoned the contradictions in the apparatuses of science between the dimensions of a 'horizontal' production of knowledge and a knowledge based on domination and prone to commodification. The claim of developing an ideology-critical science itself is dispensed with.

Foucault's superannuation of a Marxist ideology-theory is facilitated by a fundamental weakness of Althusserianism, namely by its inconsistent combination of ideology critique and a 'neutral' concept of ideology. With Althusser, science strives against the omni-historical and pervasive 'ideological' subject form, 'but only at the price of the detachment from human life processes', according to a critique by the Berlin *Projekt Ideologietheorie*: 'The negation of the ideological by science remains abstract: without a viewpoint in human practice itself'.[78] When Foucault tears down this bastion, his move seems to be plausible. But Foucault in no way rejects the 'neutral', domination-unspecific ideology concept that Althusser borrowed from Lacan. Instead, this over-generalised concept of an omnihistorical ideology makes it possible for him not to pose the ideology-critical question about the ways science and knowledge contribute to the reproduction of capitalist domination. Foucault dissolves the concept of ideology into that of discourse formation and later power, while at the same time tacitly transcribing its central conceptual contents, e.g. the omni-historicity of ideology, its 'effects', the 'subject constitution', etc., onto his own concept of power. The Althusserians (with the important exception of the more Gramscian Poulantzas) can offer so little resistance to this expropriation

---

76   'If, by substituting the analysis of rarity for the search for totalities, the description of relations of exteriority for the theme of the transcendental foundation, the analysis of accumulations for the quest of origin, one is a positivist, then I am quite happy to be one' (Foucault 2010a, p. 125). 'Eh bien, je suis un positiviste heureux' (Foucault 1969, p. 164).

77   Foucault 2010a, p. 186; Foucault 1969, p. 243.

78   PIT 1979, p. 127; cf. Rehmann 2013, pp. 164 et sq. Cf. also E.P. Thompson's criticism of the intellectualist reduction of experiences to an unhistorical and passive 'ideological' raw material of theoretical production (Thompson 1995, pp. 9 et sqq.).

because Foucault himself operates with the equipment of a one-sided, mutilated and parasitic Althusserianism, which he plays off against the attempts at a materialistic localisation of ideology.

Instead of having overcome the Althusserian ideology theory, as the Foucault literature claims almost unanimously, Foucault has himself only branched off from an early version of Althusser's concept of an 'ideology in general' which not only preceded the elaboration of a materialistic and analytic ideology concept, but also later stood in its way. As soon as one compares Foucault's 'happy positivism' with Althusser's *Self-Criticism*, one can see that the latter maintains a much stronger awareness of the antagonistic character of knowledge and science, rejecting his own antithesis science/ideology because it did not take the meaning of the social struggles into consideration.[79] Althusser proposes to rework it from the point of view of a 'complex process of the "production" of knowledge, where the class conflicts of the practical ideologies combine with the theoretical ideologies, the existing sciences and philosophy'.[80] According to Michel Pêcheux, Foucault missed the task of analysing a discursive formation on two levels: on the one hand from a 'regional' standpoint, which identifies its internal relationships, and on the other hand from a point of view of class, which is able to explain why ideologies invoke the same higher values but 'under contradictory modalities that are connected to the class antagonism'.[81] 'Knowledge' is thus not to be understood as the result of a deep-structural system of rules, but as an integral component of oppositely structured social productions.

Foucault will no longer bother to confront this historical-materialistic elaboration of the ideology concept. Because he thinks of the ideological not as a material instance, he remains, as Lecourt shows, in an 'archaeological circle' which consists of the fact that, while claiming to search for the connections between the discourse formations and their institutional 'régime de matérialité', he actually encounters nothing but the regularities of the discourses.[82] 'The Archaelogy remains itself a theoretical ideology'.[83] Without mentioning Lecourt's criticism, Dreyfus and Rabinow also point to a 'methodological failure' of the *Archaeology*, which they explain with the oscillation between a descriptive and a prescriptive concept of 'rule': 'He must locate the productive power revealed by discursive practices in the regularity of these same of

---

79   Althusser 1976, pp. 106, 114 et sq., 119 et sq.
80   Althusser 1976, pp. 147 et sq.
81   Pêcheux 1990, p. 258.
82   Lecourt 1975, p. 205; Lecourt 1972, p. 122.
83   Lecourt 1975, p. 213; Lecourt 1972, p. 133.

practices ... regularities which regulate themselves'.[84] In their view, Foucault should better have limited himself to the description of discursive practices, instead of being concerned with a theoretical explanation for their determination.[85] Of course, this is an empiricist proposal which does not touch upon the important theoretical problem formulated by Lecourt of a connection between ideology theory and discourse theory.[86]

But now Foucault – contemporaneous with his radically left-wing turn in Vincennes – undertakes a renewed resort to Nietzsche, which makes it possible for him to posit a 'will to knowledge' as the basis for 'knowledge', which he then, by way of a 'will to truth', merges into 'power'.

4   The Neo-Nietzschean Alternative: 'Everything Is Fake'

At the same time that Althusser attempts to work out a materialistic concept of the ideological with the essay on Ideological State Apparatuses (written 1969/70, published 1970), Foucault begins reading Nietzsche again. In 1969 in Vincennes he gives a course, 'Nietzsche and Genealogy', from which then the essay 'Nietzsche, Genealogy, History' (1971) will arise; this is followed in the winter semester 1970/71 at the Collège de France by a further course with the title 'La volonté de savoir', which addresses Nietzsche's concept of a 'will to knowledge'; and in December 1970 he holds his Inaugural lecture at the Collège de France, 'The Order of Discourse', in which he introduces the concept of power for the first time.

Foucault had already formulated the basic idea in 1967 in a contribution, *Nietzsche, Freud, Marx*, in which he addressed Nietzsche's notion of the primacy of interpretation over the sign: there is 'nothing to interpret' (in the sense of an absolute first), because everything is always-already interpretation; 'au dessous de tout ce qui parle', thus *beneath* all language activity, a relationship of violence is hidden.[87] With this equating of the primacy of 'interpretation' and a 'relationship of violence' Foucault has already made an essentialist and highly speculative definition of 'all speaking', which only needs to be

---

84   Dreyfus and Rabinow 1983, p. 84.
85   Ibid.
86   Paul Henry and Michel Pêcheux have tried to develop a materialistic discourse theory, which combined Lacanian psychoanalysis with the Althusserian interpellation model, in order to be able to explain the social production of sense evidence (Cf. Pêcheux 1975, p. 137).
87   Foucault 1998a, p. 276; Foucault 2001a, Nr. 46, p. 600.

expanded in the course summary of *La volonté de savoir*. This 'will', which he now wants to use as a 'theoretical justification' to support discourse practices, is 'anonymous' and 'polymorphic', and yet Foucault knows exactly what he is dealing with here. Because Nietzsche had discovered that knowledge is an 'invention' behind which something completely different hides itself, namely a play of the impulses, desiring, and the will to appropriation. Knowledge emerges not from an equilibrium, but from the hate between these impulses; it is not tied to pleasure and happiness, as Aristotle assumed, but 'à la lutte, à la haine, à la méchanceté'; from them arises 'the distinction between the true and the false'; truth is nothing more than the 'effect of a falsification'.[88]

In Foucault's 'Nietzsche, Genealogy, History', Nietzsche is the one who had recognised that behind the truth lie thousand-fold and thousand-year old errors. Thus, the arrogance of rejecting error in its name and of opposing make-believe is also finished: exactly this kind of entitlement belongs to the 'history of an error we call truth'.[89] Because as soon as one questions the passion for truth more closely one encounters the 'will to knowledge', and this in turn means 'instinct, passion, the inquisitor's devotion, cruel subtlety, and malice'.[90] The historical analysis of humankind's great desire for knowledge [ce grand vouloir-savoir] makes clear that a ground for truth is not possible because each cognition is based on 'injustice'. The instinct for knowledge is evil in itself, murderous and can do nothing for the happiness of humans. Thus it is also decided that the desire for knowledge, instead of being connected with the affirmation of a free subject, gathers ever more instincts for violence in it.[91]

The assumption that the 'truth' is nothing more than sublimated violence, and that power spreads itself especially through the 'will to knowledge' into the microstructures of the society and the subjects, will fundamentally determine the Foucauldian power analyses of the 70s. Beyond that it has become a sort of basic formula, with which postmodernist intellectuals, with resort to Nietzsche, have succeeded in imputing both the Marxist ideology critique and Freudo-Marxism with a traditional fixation on a suppressed and masked truth, which could be brought to light again with the assistance of scientific critique. It would be a hasty conclusion to criticise this repression of ideology critique normatively, that is, from the standpoint of an actually good 'truth', as Foucault had insinuated of ideology critique. Because here, in the questioning of the truth-idealism of philosophy, there obviously lies a strength of Nietzsche's

---

88   Foucault 1998a, pp. 12 et sqq., Foucault 2001a, Nr. 101, pp. 1110 et sqq.
89   Foucault 2003b, p. 354; Foucault 2001a, Nr. 84, p. 1007.
90   Foucault 2003b, p. 366; Foucault 2001a, Nr. 84, p. 1023.
91   Ibid.

criticism, which makes equating truth and power appear plausible. Its 'truth effect' seems to lie precisely in the radicalism with which the question about the respective standpoint underlying our thinking and speaking is posed.

In Foucault's account, various thoughts are pushed together – as with Nietzsche himself – which need to be disentangled. Thus Foucault emphasises rightfully Nietzsche's merit in having recognised the 'ideal depth' of a true consciousness as an invention of philosophers.[92] The assumption of a 'knowledge per se' suppresses the active and interpreting forces, 'through which seeing first becomes a seeing of a something', argued Nietzsche: 'There is only seeing from a perspective ... and the more emotions [Affekte] we express concerning a thing, the more eyes, different eyes, we train on the same thing, the more complete will be our "idea" of that thing, our "objectivity"'.[93]

Surprisingly, the thought intersects with Gramsci's criticism of objectivism, in which he reinterprets the term 'objective' as 'humanly objective' and thus at the same time as 'historically subjective'.[94] Beyond that it touches a central moment of Marxist ideology-critique: to reconstruct the products of human thinking from the standpoint of underlying social practices. Nietzsche's insistence that we regard knowledge of those products not from the perspective of an abstract truth, but rather focus on their 'embodiment', their 'character as conditions of life',[95] could be fruitfully mediated with for example Brecht's proposal that we understand truth not so much as a category of morality but above all as one of 'ability': 'It must be produced. There are thus production modes of the truth'.[96]

Foucault has paid for his dismissing of the 'symptomatic' reading with a loss of critical awareness. He overlooks the fact that Nietzsche's emphasis on the standpoint-dependence of thinking and speaking jumps directly into two completely different registers of thoughts: namely on one hand into a particular 'anthropological' interpretation of the perspectival desire for knowledge, as will for appropriation, violence, hate, malice, etc., and on the other into the conclusion that truth, due to its perspectivism, is to be treated as 'fiction', 'deception' and 'lie'. Both conclusions are anything but logically conclusive, and an ideology-critical text analysis would have the task of locating the fracture lines at which the turn from one to the other 'text' takes place.

---

92   Foucault 1998a, p. 272; Foucault 2001a, Nr. 46, p. 596.
93   Nietzsche 2013a, p. 106; Nietzsche 1999a, Vol. 5, p. 365.
94   Gramsci 1971, p. 445; Gramsci 1975, Q. 11, §17.
95   Nietzsche 2017b, p. 74; Nietzsche 1999a, Vol. 3, p. 469.
96   Brecht 1967, Vol. 20, p. 189. On the truth concepts of Gramsci and Brecht cf. W.F. Haug (2001a, pp. 133 et sq.).

As an example, take the early essay 'On Truth and Lying in a Non-Moral Sense' of 1873, in which Nietzsche conceives of truth as a 'mobile army of metaphors, metonymies, anthropomorphisms, in short a sum of human relations', which 'after they have been in use for a long time, strike a people as firmly established, canonical, and binding ... coins which, having lost their stamp, are now regarded as metal and no longer as coins'.[97] This operational definition of truth is often treated as an early document of the modern linguistic-analytical turn in philosophy.[98] The location of truth, one might continue, in the sense of Wittgenstein's 'language game', is not to be found in a non-verbal beyond, but in 'the whole, consisting of language and the actions into which it is woven'.[99] A 'genealogy' of truth would then have the task of making the 'human relations', which have disappeared in the finished product of 'valid' truth, visible again. This presupposes that Nietzsche would envisage these relations as social relations and investigate them as conditions of the production of 'truth'.

The fact that this does not come into question for him is shown by the example of his comparison between the bee and the human 'architectural genius': the bee builds from wax, which she gathers from nature, the human however, 'with the far more delicate material of concepts which he must first manufacture from himself'.[100] Similarly to the famous bee-architect comparison in Marx's *Capital*, this is an allusion to Kant's *Critique of the Power of Judgement*, in which the specifically human 'art' is characterised as a 'production through freedom, i.e. through a capacity for choice that grounds its actions on reason'.[101]

Let us have a closer look at the differences between Marx and Nietzsche with regard to this reference. With Marx the architect is characterised by the fact that he 'builds the cell in his mind before he constructs it in wax'.[102] Marx's formulation is not unproblematic, because the anticipation of the results of working is not connected here with the cooperative character of the work, which Marx has of course examined in various contexts. Regarded in isolation, Marx's statement therefore appears top-heavy.[103] However, the transfer of the picture onto labour also contains an implicit criticism of Kants's opposing of 'freedom' and 'nature'. With Marx the natural object (here: the wax) has disappeared just

---

97   Nietzsche 2007, p. 146; Nietzsche 1999a, Vol. 1, pp. 880 et sq.
98   This is done by Manfred Frank, for example, who focuses on the 'language-philosophical reinterpretation of the transcendental subject' (Frank 1989, pp. 207 et sq.; cf. p. 129 et sq.).
99   Wittgenstein 1963, §7, p. 5.
100   Nietzsche 2007, p. 147; Nietzsche 1999a, Vol. 1, p. 882.
101   Kant 2002, p. 182; Kant 1968b, I.1, 2. Book, §43.
102   Capital, Vol. I, 1976, p. 284; Marx and Engels 1957–, Vol. 23, p. 193.
103   Cf. the criticism of Sève (1972, p. 10) and Neusüss (1985, pp. 34 et sqq., 132).

as little as the natural aspect of work itself, which Marx determines as the function of 'mediating the metabolism between man and nature'.[104] Not coincidentally, it is this 'metabolic relationship', or more precisely the metabolic 'rift' brought about by capitalism's 'Anthropocene', which became a starting point for an ecological re-reading of Marx's *Capital*.[105] In contrast, Nietzsche's architect builds nothing more than 'concepts', and these 'from himself', as if human 'architects' were not dependent on materials provided by nature, be it food, water, air or raw materials for production, on the social division of labour, the historical-social knowledge of cooperation. Nietzsche's critique of truth-idealism remains in the realm of idealism inhabited by the allegedly non-social, private individual, detached from nature.

Here we have the breaking point at which perspectivism flips into an unmasking of the truth as 'lie'. Nietzsche's standpoint is that of a disappointed truth-idealism. From this standpoint 'human relations' must represent a kind of soiling of the still heroic-individually conceived (or thus desired) knowledge. As it is stated in the *Gay Science*, since consciousness 'does not properly belong to the individual existence of man, but rather to the social and gregarious nature in him', and since it forms 'only' a connecting net between humans, it becomes 'shallow, meagre, relatively stupid'.[106] In the same passage, in which Nietzsche in 'On Truth and Lying in a Non-Moral Sense' introduced the truth as an anthropomorphic network, its human relationality allows him to impute to it illusion and deception. It is this relationality that he perceives as an obligation set up by society, to 'lie' according to a firm convention and, in an obligatory style, binding for all.[107] It thereby becomes the vehicle for a general human will to deception and fiction: 'Human beings themselves have ... an unconquerable urge to let themselves be deceived' and they are thereby 'as if enchanted with happiness'.[108]

Thus the groundwork is laid for exposing truths as the '*irrefutable* errors [of man]',[109] to declare illusion as 'the sole reality of things',[110] to regard 'the will to illusion' as deeper and more metaphysical than that to 'reality, to being',[111]

---

104   Capital, Vol. I, 1976, pp. 133, 283 et sq.; Marx and Engels 1957–, Vol. 23, pp. 57, 192 et sq.
105   For example, Foster et al 2010, pp. 45 et sqq., 76 et sq., and Jason Moore 2015, pp. 75 et sqq., 80 et sqq.
106   Nietzsche 2017b, pp. 140 et sq.; Nietzsche 1999a, Vol. 3, pp. 591 et sqq.
107   Nietzsche 2007, pp. 145 et sq.; Nietzsche 1999a, Vol. 1, pp. 880 et sq.
108   Nietzsche 2007, p. 151; Nietzsche 1999a, Vol. 1, p. 888.
109   Nietzsche 2017b, p. 101; Nietzsche 1999a, Vol. 3, p. 518.
110   Nietzsche 1999a, Vol. 11, p. 654; cf. Nietzsche 1997, pp. 1 et sq.; Nietzsche 1999a, Vol. 5, pp. 16 et sq.
111   Nietzsche 1999a, Vol. 13, p. 226.

and to ascribe to blindness and the lie a divine origin and a holy character.[112] The true world is considered by Nietzsche to be 'bare fiction, made of fictitious things'.[113]

Foucault appropriated the Nietzschean omnipresence of fiction early on and maintained it consistently. Thus he suggests in 1963 that we remove all 'contradictory words' of a confrontation of subjective and objective, inside and outside, reality and imaginary and replace them with a 'language of fiction' [langage de fiction].[114] Fiction, he claims in 1966, is the 'order of narration' itself [régime du récit], the grid [trame] which is the basis for the relationship between the speaking person and the spoken.[115] And to that extent he, too, has written nothing other than historical 'fictions' which he knows very well are not true.[116]

'Whatever is owed to constructive and correlating, ordering and interpreting operations of thinking, is to be treated as fiction', summarises Haug, who criticises this procedure as 'fictionalism', i.e. as a 'negative ontology of cognition, by which the fictional is expanded to include its counter, reality'.[117] The plausibility of fictionalism relies on an everyday life experience. Everyone tends to see primarily that in which they are practically interested, and 'the real is not to be had without fictive moments' – also not in science, which must transgress the limits of certain knowing through provisional assumptions, methodical abstractions, ideal types, hypotheses, extrapolations, emphatic exaggerations etc. But instead of identifying the contradictory standpoints and perspectives in the framework of an analysis of social relations, fictionalism is content with enshrining the perspectival as untrue. Foucault and Nietzsche do not challenge the philosophical ideologisation of truth (e.g. in its Platonic form) by an analysis of the organising social standpoint, but in a totalising manner with the fictionalisation of truth in general. Whereas Althusser's ideology-theory has revealed the materiality of the ideological, its existence as apparatuses, practices, rituals, is all dissolved here and merged with the ontological fictionality of 'everything is fake'.[118]

---

112   Nietzsche 2017b, p. 133; Nietzsche 1999a, Vol. 3, p. 577; Nietzsche 2013a, pp. 135 et sq.; Nietzsche 1999a, Vol. 5, pp. 401 et sq; Nietzsche 1968b, p. 190; Nietzsche 1999a, Vol. 6, p. 243.
113   Nietzsche 1999a, Vol. 13, p. 270; cf. Nietzsche 1999a, Vol. 13, p. 193.
114   Foucault 1998b, pp. 104 et sq., Foucault 2001a, Nr. 17, pp. 308 et sq.
115   Foucault 1998a, p. 137, Foucault 2001a, Nr. 36, p. 534.
116   Foucault 1996, pp. 300 et sq., Foucault 2001b, Nr. 280, p. 859; Foucault 2000, p. 242, Foucault 2001b, Nr. 281, p. 863.
117   Haug 1999b, pp. 449, 459.
118   Haug 1999b, pp. 449 et sq., 459 et sq.

It should be evident by now that neo-Nietzschean fictionalism did not 'overcome' the Marxist debates on ideology of the time. On the contrary, it fell back on positions which the various efforts of a historical-materialistic ideology theory in the 70s attempted to overcome. What united these different strands of ideology-theory, stretching from the Althusser school in France to Stuart Hall's Birmingham School of Cultural Studies and to the Berlin *Projekt Ideologietheorie*, was the double critique of an economistic reductionism considering ideology as a mere epiphenomenon and of a traditional ideology-critique that reduced ideology to 'false consciousness', 'illusion' and 'fiction', both of which proved insufficient to comprehend the stability of bourgeois hegemony.[119] The Nietzschean equation of fiction with violence, malicious 'lie' and 'deception' goes even farther back to Enlightenment concepts of 'priest deceit'.

According to Nietzsche, 'metaphysics, morality, religion, science – they are … considered only as different forms of the lie: with their assistance there is *faith* in life [wird an das Leben *geglaubt*]'.[120] Not only the differences between ideology and science are flattened out, but also those within each of the particular ideological formations. If critique in its original meaning (Greek *krinein*) signifies making distinctions, the fictionalist confiscation of every distinctiveness amounts to the destruction of critique itself. 'Fictionalism gobbles up cognition altogether', notes Bloch.[121] It transforms scientific concepts 'most usefully into share certificates which fluctuate according to the given situation' and 'makes the doubt about the Being graspable today into one about anything and everything. It thus runs through large parts of modern thinking, easy, comfortable, faithless'.[122] It is as if Bloch already anticipated the effect of postmodernist fictionalism: developing the gesture of a radicalising of critique in a way that corrupts the possibility of critique itself. The corruption consists in depriving it of the capacity for a differentiating 'determinate negation', and thus letting it run into emptiness.

5   Power as Dissimulation Machine

The transition from 'everything is fake' to 'everything is power' was already implied in the reduction of perspectival knowledge to appropriation, violence, hate, and malice. Fascinated by the pseudo-radical gesture, Foucault fails to see

---

119   Cf. Rehmann 2013, pp. 5 et sqq.
120   Nietzsche 1999a, Vol. 13, p. 193.
121   Bloch 1950, p. 24.
122   Bloch 1991, pp. 257 et sq.

that here Nietzsche projected an aggressive variant of bourgeois private egoism onto human nature per se. He also ignores the fact that Nietzsche's authoritarian concept of 'power' is the exact opposite of Spinoza's cooperative power of action (*potentia agendi*), whose capability of activity he tries to incorporate at the same time (see above Chapter 1.7). The 'will to power', which Nietzsche mentions for the first time in November 1882 in preparation for *Zarathustra*,[123] replaces the Spinozean term of 'self-preservation' he had used until then, and introduces the sharp verticalist turn of the late Nietzschean phase.[124] Its function is to synthesise all the tendencies of 'overwhelming, becoming master' over the less powerful,[125] of oppressing, raping, exploiting, and then to project them onto the 'nature of the living being' itself.[126] As later with Foucault, the will to truth is a central vehicle of its implementation. As *Zarathustra* puts it, 'And even you, seeker of knowledge, are only a path and footstep' of this will to power, that indeed '[follows] on the heels of your will to the truth'.[127] Several drafts of the planned book on the 'will to power' indicate that Nietzsche conceived the 'will to truth' as the first chapter.[128]

Foucault's *Order of Discourse* of 1971 gives us a first idea of how Nietzsche's coupling of 'will to truth' and 'will to power' caught on with Foucault. As Foucault reports it, there was a condition before the Platonic dichotomy of true and false, in which true discourse still coincided directly with power. With the Sophists of the sixth century BC true discourse was still that 'which dispensed justice and gave everyone his share', the 'precious and desirable discourse ... linked to the exercise of power'. Yet in the fifth century BC the Sophist is banished, the truth is displaced from the authorised 'act of enunciation, towards the utterance itself', and since that time in occidental history the 'will to knowledge' runs in the general form of a 'will to the truth'.[129] This 'will to truth' develops into the most important of three great excluding systems (in addition to censorship and the exclusion of madness), with which the power of the discourse is dammed

---

123   Nietzsche 1999a, Vol. 10, p. 187.
124   'Each thing ... strives to preserve in its being' (in suo esse perseverare conatur) (Spinoza 1996, p. 75, Ethics III, Prop. 6). In his 'middle', ideology-critical phase, Nietzsche referred several times to the Spinozean self-preservation principle (e.g. Nietzsche 1994, p. 68; Nietzsche 1999a, Vol. 2, p. 95, Nietzsche 2017b, pp. 74 et sq.; Nietzsche 1999a, Vol. 3, p. 471), which he will then attribute in the fifth book of the *Gay Science* to the 'consumptive' Spinoza (Nietzsche 2017b, p. 137; Nietzsche 1999a, Vol. 3, p. 585).
125   Nietzsche 2013a, pp. 62 et sq.; Nietzsche 1999a, Vol. 5, pp. 313 et sq.
126   Nietzsche 1997, p. 126; Nietzsche 1999a, Vol. 5, p. 208; Nietzsche 1999a, Vol. 13, p. 258.
127   Nietzsche 2006, p. 90; Nietzsche 1999a, Vol. 4, p. 148.
128   E.g. Nietzsche 1999a, Vol. 13, pp. 515 et sq., 537, 543.
129   Foucault 1981, p. 54; Foucault 1971, pp. 17 et sq.

and subjected. And although since its Platonic idealisation it is no more 'the discourse that answers to the demands of desire, or the discourse which exercises power', the discourse is traversed precisely by desire and power.[130]

Lemke locates the problem in the wrong place when he claims Foucault would still have addressed power here 'only along the lines of external "exclusion" and inner "rarefaction"'.[131] In this he follows Foucault himself, who in 1977 attests that his earlier concept of power was caught in 'negative' conceptions of a prohibiting law.[132] But this 'self-criticism' is misleading or at least unclear. Because in *The Order of Discourse* power is also and above all that which is to be excluded by truth: the prohibitions enacted by this 'prodigious machinery' of exclusion affect discourse,[133] and are precisely directed against its 'link with desire and with power';[134] 'discourse is the power which is to be seized' [le pouvoir dont on cherche à s'emparer].[135] The 'subjection of and by discourse' is to master its 'proliferation', in particular that which could be 'violent, discontinuous, pugnacious, disorderly as well, and perilous'.[136] As a counter-strategy Foucault suggests questioning our 'will to truth' and to restore to discourse its 'character as an event', that is, to 'conceive discourse as a violence which we do to things, or in any case as a practice which we impose on them'.[137]

Foucault's transition from discourse to power is generally appreciated in the Foucault literature as the successful breaking through of his 'archaeology circle'.[138] Even Habermas, who realises that Nietzsche's concept of power is 'utterly unsociological', asserts that Foucault's analysis has now gained a 'social-theoretical' quality.[139] Precisely this is questionable, because with the concept of power borrowed from Nietzsche, Foucault has not overcome the mysterious progenitor status of the discursive rule-system, but only rehashed it in modified terminology. Power now arises on both sides of the 'exclusion machinery': in the form of a subjugating 'truth' as well as in the form of the subjugated anarchic ('unordered') creative-violent potential, which Foucault links with an original 'sophistic' identity of truth and domination. Emerging on the heels of

---

130   Foucault 1981, p. 56; Foucault 1971, p. 22.
131   Lemke 2019, p. 45.
132   Foucault 1980, pp. 181 et sq.; Foucault 2001b, Nr. 197, pp. 228 et sq.
133   Foucault 1981, p. 56; Foucault 1971, p. 22.
134   Foucault 1981, p. 52; Foucault 1971, p. 12.
135   Foucault 1981, p. 53; Foucault 1971, p. 12.
136   Foucault 1981, pp. 53, 64, 66; Foucault 1971, pp. 12, 46, 52 et sq.
137   Foucault 1981, pp. 66 et sq.; Foucault 1971, pp. 53, 55.
138   E.g. Dreyfus and Rabinow 1983, pp. 104 et sqq. and Lemke 2019, p. 44.
139   Habermas 1990, pp. 248 et sq., 269; see Honneth 1991, p. 150.

a necessarily fictitious and malicious 'will to knowledge', Foucault's notion of power, like that of 'discourse', lurks, without qualification, in every direction. It is not being introduced as an analytical tool to decipher social relations and respective (in)capacities to act, but rather as a vague quality somehow attached to knowledge and truth-claims, no matter for whom, of what kind, to what end or practical purpose. We are dealing with an enigmatic force equally per-meating the strategies of immediate domination, hegemonic ideologies as well as the aspirations of the subaltern classes. Foucault has fastened, as it were, under his concept of 'knowledge' a still more fundamental concept of power, without ever developing the power/knowledge complex [pouvoir-savoir] out of the respective social relations. As with Nietzsche, his power concept functions as a 'dissimulation machine [Entnennungsmaschine]' that makes disappear all concrete social practices and their respective power potentials.[140]

The dissimulation effect becomes evident when we regard more closely the components of that which the 'truth' excludes. Foucault's starting point at a 'pre-philosophical' constellation, in which truth and exercise of power still coincide directly, reproduces Nietzsche's ideological construct of an 'idyllic' ori-gin of an unsublimated domination power in pre-classical antiquity. It belongs to the construction of a Dorian aristocratic ur-Greece, and is, as Cancik and v. Reibnitz have shown with much material, part of a romantic-reactionary tradi-tion in German phil-hellenism, which merged with the Aryan myth and was directed above all against the liberal-humanistic interpretations of classical antiquity.[141] Nietzsche located his concept of power on the side of a 'Soph-ist culture', which in his view stood against 'the morality-and-ideal swindle of the Socratic schools which was then breaking out everywhere'. The Sophists opposed this idealist 'swindle' with the strict realism of the 'older Hellenes', their 'agonal instinct', and 'value of the race'.[142] From here he wants, in a 'full set-tlement with antiquity',[143] to unmask the utopian tendencies in philosophical idealism, which made Christianity and thereby also modern socialism pos-sible.[144] He thus develops a particular ideology critique which is articulated

---

140   Haug 2006, p. 151.
141   Cf. v. Reibnitz 1992, pp. 106 et sq., 149 et sqq.; Cancik 1995, pp. 125 et sq.; Cancik-Lindemaier and Cancik 1999, pp. 95 et sqq. What is attacked above all is Winckelmann's 'liberal' orient-ation toward classical Greece. The image of a Dorian aristocratic ur-Greece can be traced back to the graecist Nietzsche in his school leaving thesis of 1864 (*On Theognis of Megara*). Nietzsche himself explains that he wants to explode the alliance between humanism and enlightenment with antiquity (Nietzsche 1999a, Vol. 8, p. 58).
142   Nietzsche 1968, pp. 118 et sq.; Nietzsche 1999a, Vol. 6, pp. 156, et sq.
143   Nietzsche 1999a, Vol. 8, p. 80.
144   'Christianity is Platonismus for "people"'. Nietzsche 1997, p. x; Nietzsche 1999a, Vol. 5, p. 12.

from the standpoint of immediate class domination. It directs itself against the ideological inasmuch as it is articulated in terms of a value-universalism, because this means a compromise formation in whose instances the lower classes are also represented and to which they can appeal.

Foucault ties into this rhetoric and transfers it into the discourse of the student protest movements. Also the historical critique in his work begins only at the point, where the 'tricks' and 'paradoxes' of the sophists are banned and power has assumed the form of 'truth', which is disguising it.[145] What fascinates him (as Nietzsche) is the unsublimated and undisguised power of violence, which as such is portrayed as a rebellious, anti-ideological potency. Here the fact that Foucault drew his concept of power not from Spinoza, but from Nietzsche takes its toll. He reproduces Nietzsche's suppression and overwhelming of the Spinozean *potentia agendi* and therefore cannot differentiate analytically between a cooperative power of action from below and a dominating power from above. The Sophist's right of the more powerful flows indistinguishably together with the combative-violent dimension, which 'we' would have to recover now in our discourses.

This indistinctness, held in abeyance, is the precondition for Foucault's strategy to connect his Nietzscheanism with a Parisian 'Gauchism' in which class-reductionistic articulations of the 'question of power' cross with spontaneist approaches to new subject-experiences. Before we examine this combination (see below Chapter 3.7), we turn to the essay 'Nietzsche, Genealogy, History' and observe how Foucault, with the assistance of an extremely doubtful philology, organises a re-coding of Nietzsche into the precursor of an alternative and radically decentralised culture.

6   Nietzsche's 'Genealogy', or, the Violent Construction of an 'Alternative Nietzsche'

Foucault's 'Nietzsche, Genealogy, History' is based on the assumption of a dichotomy between the term of *Ursprung* [origin] and of *Herkunft* [descent] in Nietzsche, and can be summarised in the thesis that Nietzsche turned primarily against a historiography which was oriented toward the uncovering of a metaphysical *Ursprung* of morality and truth, as well as toward a continuous line of development. Against this concept of 'history', Nietzsche's 'genealogy' was characterised by the search for the *Herkünfte* and *Anfänge* [beginnings] of morality

---

145   Foucault 1981, p. 65, Foucault 1971, p. 48.

in the *Niederungen* [low areas], in the ridiculous, the discontinuous.[146] Because it was interested in the 'lower', the 'gray' of life, in 'coincidences' of struggle and in the body, it liberated history from the metaphysical and anthropological model and made from it a 'countermemory'.[147] This interpretation is clearly part of Foucault's strategy of connecting Nietzsche's approach with relevant themes of the post-68er movements. Nietzsche, so it appears, is the pioneer of an everyday history from below, which has set out to bring into the light what was supressed by traditional historiography: the small, the local, the ordinary.

Let us consider first the philological finding of a contrasting use of *Ursprung* [origin] and *Herkunft* [descent] in Nietzsche, from which Foucault's interpretation draws a large part of its plausibility. Foucault seems to argue here in the mode of textual criticism: he quotes the terms in the German original, differentiates between different usages, and supplies a quantity of references in the footnotes. The philological analysis appears precise, nuanced, and respectable. In addition, there comes a strong pathos of scientific precision. Already in the first section the 'patience and a knowledge of details' and a 'rigorous method' are invoked. Genealogy demands 'relentless erudition'.[148] The appearance of verifiability appears to make verification redundant.

The few scholars who actually attempted verification so far came to the conclusion that Foucault projected his own terminology onto Nietzsche's texts, instead of developing it from there.[149] But this is an objection which receives scant attention in the Foucault literature: either Foucault's interpretation of Nietzsche is passed on unquestioned, or the question of philological reliability is declared irrelevant. To the first variant belong interpretations which justify the agreement of Foucault and Nietzsche summarily with the 'critical' function of genealogy, without asking about the standpoint and perspective of the critique.[150] To the second variant belongs that of Brieler, for example, who

---

146 Foucault 2003b, pp. 353 et sq.; Foucault 2001a, Nr. 84, pp. 1007 et sq.
147 Foucault 2003b, p. 365; Foucault 2001a, Nr. 84, p. 1021.
148 Foucault 2003b, pp. 351 et sq.; Foucault 2001a, Nr. 84, p. 1004.
149 Cf. Cook 1990; Pizer 1990.
150 Edward Said justifies the agreement between Nietzsche and Foucault with their 'antidynastic' criticism of the origin (1985, pp. XII et sq., 290, 301; cf. 1988, p. 6). 'Foucault's use of the term continues Nietzsche's', is asserted without evidence in the *Routledge Encyclopedia of Philosophy*, because for both genealogy is 'a form of historical critique' (Hill 1998, p. 1). Also for Cronin, a philological examination of the agreement is unnecessary, because 'Foucault quite clearly adopts Nietzsche's claim to use history for critical purposes' (Cronin 2001, p. 283) On the other hand, there is a short reference in the introduction by Prado to the fact that, although 'Nietzsche, Genealogy, History' 'is exegetic', Foucault 'effectively articulates the basic conception of his own genealogy in expounding Nietzsche's' (Prado 2000, p. 33). Although Mirjam Schaub recognises that Foucault's *Nietzsche, Genealogy, His-*

rebuffs Pizer's detailed philological refutation of the Foucauldian reading with the remark: 'As if philological attachment to tradition would be of concern to Foucault!'[151] There seems to be an unwritten law that one should limit oneself to a positive representation of the Foucauldian 'concern', and omit critical questions about its argumentative justification. No historian or sociologist could afford Foucault's sovereign gesture claiming to be entitled to distort Nietzsche at will, and forgo a 'historical and philological reconstruction', notes Losurdo.[152] Dreyfus and Rabinow also profess abstention from any historical-critical reconstruction – 'We plead neutrality concerning the textual accuracy of Foucault's reading' – which weighs all the more heavily as they accord the essay 'Nietzsche, Genealogy, History' the importance of containing 'all the seeds' of the Foucauldian work of the 1970s.[153] Bernard Harcourt assumes that in this text 'Foucault deploys Nietzsche's writings in a linguistic modality',[154] without ever asking whether this 'linguistic modality' is based on an accurate textual analysis. When it comes to Foucault, any philological negligence seems to be legitimate. In what follows, we will confront Foucault's interpretation with the references he himself selected.

6.1   'Ursprung' versus 'Herkunft' with Nietzsche?

Foucault makes clear at the beginning that Nietzsche is not by any means consistent in opposing *Ursprung* and *Herkunft*: in a general use of terminology Nietzsche uses both terms synonymously; but in a second, 'exactly determined' usage, 'Ursprung' is the opposite of 'Herkunft', namely in the First Aphorism of *Human, All Too Human*, in some passages of *The Dawn* and *The Gay Science*, and in the preface to the *Genealogy of Morals*. Then follows the restriction that in the last paragraphs of the preface to the *Genealogy* Nietzsche returns to a neutral and indiscriminate use, and a footnote informs the reader that *Ursprung* and *Herkunft* in the *Genealogy* are 'frequently [used] indiscriminately (de manière à peu près équivalente')'.[155] So Foucault has every reason to reduce his thesis to the fact that Nietzsche 'at least on certain occasions' [au moins en certaines occasions] rejected the search for the origin.[156] If one adds the aforementioned

---

tory concerns a 'revaluation of the Nietzschean genealogy concept', she cannot make clear wherein this 'revaluation' lies, because she has already inserted the Foucauldian interpretation in her own description of Nietzsche's argument (Schaub 2001, pp. 223 et sq., 225).

151   Brieler 1998, pp. 285 et sq., n. 2.
152   Losurdo 2020, pp. 732 et sq.
153   Dreyfus and Rabinow 1983, p. 106.
154   Harcourt 2021, p. 3.
155   Foucault 2003b, pp. 352 et sq. and 368 note 9; Foucault 2001a, Nr. 84, p. 1006 and note 2.
156   Foucault 2003b p. 353; Foucault 2001a, Nr. 84, p. 1006.

text references together, one sees that according to Foucault's own representation most Nietzsche passages speak for a synonymous usage, and this equally for the earlier text *Human, All Too Human* of 1878 as well for the later text of *The Genealogy of Morals* of 1887.

But even the 'occasionally' different usage claimed by Foucault becomes doubtful when one considers more closely the already narrow textual basis for an opposition of *Ursprung* and *Herkunft*. First off, all those text passages which Foucault portrays as an 'ironic' treatment of *Ursprung* are not valid for the point he is trying to make:[157] when Nietzsche explains that the origin of morality and the moral judgement of the other as 'bad' lies in the fallacy that what is doing me harm is a lasting characteristic of the other, is to be dealt with as inimical per se,[158] then what is criticised is obviously not the notion of *Ursprung*, but its 'fallacious' understanding. When Nietzsche opposes the traditional explanations that the *Ursprung* of religion lies in a revelation or in a metaphysical need (Schopenhauer) with the statement that religion is in reality to be traced back to a 'mistake', or an 'invention',[159] he attacks again only certain theo-philosophical interpretations of origin; in none of these passages does the term *Herkunft* appear, in some not even the term *Ursprung*.[160] 'Ursprung is not itself the butt of the ironic and deceptive tone', summarises Cook.[161] Apart from that, it seems questionable to regard the aforementioned text passages as 'ironic': as we have seen (see above Chapter 3.4), it is a consistent tendency with Nietzsche to explain ideological phenomena with concepts of false consciousness ('error') or priestly deceit (invention, lie).

Therewith the textual basis is narrowed to the first aphorism of *Human, All Too Human* and to the preface to the *Genealogy of Morals*. In the first case Nietzsche is not concerned with the opposition between *Ursprung* and *Herkunft*, but with that between a 'metaphysical' and an 'historical' philosophy. The former is characterised by the assumption 'that the more highly valued things [had] a miraculous origin, directly from out of the heart and essence of the "thing in itself"', the latter stands in close connection with the natural sciences and is therefore equipped to destroy the metaphysical conceptions of unegoistic activity, by drawing on the assistance of a '*chemistry* of moral, religious,

---

157   Foucault 2003b, p. 352; Foucault 2001a, Nr. 84, p. 1005.

158   Nietzsche 2011, p. 70; Nietzsche 1999a, Vol. 3, p. 90.

159   Nietzsche 2011, p. 45 et sq.; Nietzsche 1999a, Vol. 3, p. 62; Nietzsche 2017b, pp. 87 et sq., 139; Nietzsche 1999a, Vol. 3, pp. 494 et sq., 589.

160   Nietzsche 2013a, pp. 34 et sqq.; Nietzsche 1999a, Vol. 5, pp. 281 et sqq.; Nietzsche 1968a, pp. 64 et sq.; Nietzsche 1999a, Vol. 6, pp. 95 et sq.

161   Cook 1990, p. 303.

aesthetic ideas and feelings'.[162] As in real chemistry, also this moral 'chemistry' would come to the conclusion that the most splendid colours are obtained from 'base, even despised materials'. The aphorism ends with the supposition that not many are interested in such investigations, since humanity prefers to put 'the questions of Herkunft [descent] and Anfänge [beginnings] out of mind'.[163] When Foucault uses this concluding passage as proof of a fundamental opposition between *Herkunft* and *Ursprung*, simply because the word *Herkunft* is used there, his interpretation is, to say the least, far-fetched. Not only had Nietzsche shown no interest in setting the terms in relation to each other, he also did not speak of *Ursprung* [origin] in general, but of a 'miraculous origin' ['Wunder-Ursprung']. Instead of establishing an opposition between *Ursprung* and *Herkunft*, he juxtaposes 'miracle origin' and 'origin': '"Wunder-Ursprung" is the antithesis of "Ursprung"'.[164] As Deborah Cook observes, 'Foucault's interpretation of this first section of *Human, All Too Human* … is, unfortunately, seriously flawed'.[165]

Let's look at the preface to the *Genealogy of Morals*, which Foucault considers to be the most important for his thesis. The reasoning is somewhat complicated: according to Foucault, Nietzsche specifies that the subject of the *Genealogy of Morals* is the Herkunft [descent] of moral prejudices, and the first provisional formulation (according to Nietzsche) is in *Human, All Too Human*. Looking back yet further, Nietzsche recalls a 'first philosophical writing exercise' as a 13 year old, in which he proved God to be the father of evil. Foucault's presentation of Nietzsche is applicable up to that point.[166] Now, however, comes a first intervening interpretation: Nietzsche now laughs at this juvenile argumentation, and 'properly characterises it as a search for the origin'.[167] However, that is not Nietzsche's reasoning, who indicates that he would have learned through historical and philological training no longer to seek the origin of evil '*behind* the world'.[168] Instead of laughing about the fact that evil could have an origin, Nietzsche sets about looking for it *in* the world, and for him this means to examine under what conditions humans 'invented' the good-evil dichotomy.[169] Foucault's second interpretive intervention refers to the fact

---

162   Nietzsche 1994, pp. 13 et sq.; Nietzsche 1999a, Vol. 2, pp. 23 et sq.
163   Nietzsche 1994, p. 14; Nietzsche 1999a, Vol. 2, p. 24.
164   Pizer 1990, p. 473.
165   Cook 1990, p. 301.
166   Cf. Nietzsche 2013a, pp. 4 et sq.; Nietzsche 1999a, Vol. 5, pp. 248 et sq.
167   Foucault 2003b, p. 352; Foucault 2001a, Nr. 84, p. 1005.
168   Nietzsche 2013a, pp. 6 et sq.; Nietzsche 1999a, Vol. 5, p. 251.
169   Nietzsche 2013a, pp. 6 et sq.; Nietzsche 1999a, Vol. 5, pp. 251 et sq.

that Nietzsche thinks he has prepared his 'descent-hypotheses' [Herkunftshy-pothesen] in *Human, All Too Human*, although there with regard to the prehistory of morality, asceticism, justice and punishment 'the word used was always origin'.[170]

But why should the circumstance that Nietzsche speaks at times of *Ursprung* and at times of *Herkunft*, be of any importance at all? It appears so to Foucault: 'It would seem that at this point in the *Genealogy* Nietzsche wanted to validate an opposition between Herkunft and Ursprung that he had not put into play ten years earlier'.[171] This assumption is unconvincing for several reasons: on one hand the only argument of Foucault's worth mentioning for an opposition between descent/beginnings and miracle-origin comes straight from *Human, All Too Human*, where it is now suddenly supposed to play 'no role'. And on the other hand Foucault himself pointed out that in the *Genealogy of Morals* origin and descent are usually used synonymously. There is neither a development between an earlier 'origin' and a later 'descent' with Nietzsche, nor a break between them.[172] In not a single one of the text passages presented by Foucault is Nietzsche interested in this sort of terminological opposition. In fact, he is actually interested in the opposition between a metaphysical and a 'real' moral history, which is based on the 'grey, by which I mean documentary evidence, that which is capable of definite proof, that which has actually existed',[173] but this is not attached to the terminological use of origin or descent – not even 'occasionally'.

That which Foucault claims to read out of Nietzsche, he has read into him. But while it is simple to point out his philological deception, it is to some extent

---

170   Foucault 2003b, p. 352; Foucault 2001a, Nr. 84, p. 1006. Also this statement is philologically not accurate. An examination of the references in the preface to the *Genealogy of Morals* (cf. Nietzsche 2013a, pp. 6 et sq.; Nietzsche 1999a, Vol. 5, p. 251) shows e.g. that the aphorism 45 on the double prehistory of good and evil does not use the term 'origin', but that of the 'Vorgeschichte' (prehistory) (Nietzsche 1994, p. 46; Nietzsche 1999a, Vol. 2, p. 67). On the other hand, 'origin' is used e.g. in the *Human, All Too Human* aphorisms 92, 96, 100 (1994, pp. 64, 66 et sq., 69 et sq.; Nietzsche 1999a, Vol. 2, pp. 89 et sq., 93, 97, 412), but again not in *Human, All Too Human* aph. 136 (1994, p. 94; Nietzsche 1999a, Vol. 2, p. 130), not in *Der Wanderer und sein Schatten* Aph. 22, 26 and 33 (Nietzsche 2013b, pp. 164 et sqq., 169, 172 et sqq.; Nietzsche 1999a, Vol. 2, pp. 555 et sqq., 560, 564 et sqq.) and also not in *Dawn* Aph. 112 (Nietzsche 2011, pp. 78 et sqq.; Nietzsche 1999a, Vol. 3, pp. 100 et sqq.). 'Out of the ten quotations Nietzsche makes of his own work in Section 4 of the "Preface", the word "*Ursprung*" is used only four times' (Cook 1990, pp. 307 et sq.).
171   Foucault 2003b, pp. 352 et sq.; Foucault 2001a, Nr. 84, p. 1006.
172   'The contrast that Foucault attempts to demonstrate between the earlier use of "*Ursprung*", and the later use of "*Herkunft*" is ill-founded' (Cook 1990, p. 307).
173   Nietzsche 2013a, p. 9; Nietzsche 1999a, Vol. 5, p. 254.

difficult to explain it. In fact, Foucault's terminology is already fixed, before he takes the trouble to legitimise it on the authority of Nietzsche with the help of an allegedly sophisticated philology. 'Origin' and 'utopia' are already considered in the *Order of the Things* as characteristics of anthropological thinking, whose overcoming was introduced by Nietzsche's 'death of man'.[174] Contrary to the common periodisation 'archaeology-genealogy', also the concept of genealogy is not a recent discovery in *Nietzsche, Genealogy, History*, but is already to be found in the middle of the 'archaeological' period – together with the challenge to every 'original foundation'.[175] To that extent Foucault's 'philology' functions as an enforced adaption of the Nietzschean terminology to his own. It is as if he wanted to demonstrate in practice what he a short time previously in the Inaugural Lecture at the Collège de France laid out theoretically: to conceive discourse as a 'violence' which we do to things.[176] The need to construct a Nietzschean line of tradition and to fit into it stands in strange contrast to the anti-linear and anti-authoritarian gesture of his genealogy. The opposing of origin and descent is at the same time a displaced dissociation from Heidegger, who interpreted Nietzsche's will to power as an original 'essential will' [Wesenswille].[177]

Foucault could just as well have followed Walter Benjamin, who in *The Origin of German Tragic Drama* treated 'Entstehung' [genesis] as a signifier of a linear conception of history, and set 'Ursprung' [origin] in opposition to it as discontinuously 'emerging': an 'eddy' which 'in its current swallows the material involved in the process of genesis'.[178] Actually Nietzsche polemicised in the *Birth of Tragedy*, to which Benjamin refers here, against the 'crude, unscientific ... assertion' of an 'Entstehung' of tragedy from the choir, and countered it with a more comprehensive derivation from the 'religious origins' of Dionysic music.[179] However, caution is also advised here, because on one hand Nietzsche knows also the idea of a 'hybrid', thus nonlinear 'Entstehung',[180] but on

---

174   Foucault 1994, pp. 262 et sq. and 328 et sqq.
175   Foucault 2010a, p. 13. Cf. also Foucault's remark from 1967 that his 'archaeology' in *The Order of Things* owes more to the Nietzschean genealogy than to actual structuralism (Foucault 1998a, pp. 293 et sq., Foucault 2001a, Nr. 48, p. 627).
176   Foucault 1981, p. 67; Foucault 1971, p. 55.
177   Cf. Heidegger GA I.6.1., pp. 57 et sq.; GA I.6.2., p. 237. See above Chapter 1.4 as well as Chapter 2.2 and 2.3.
178   Benjamin 2003, p. 45; GS I/1, p. 226.
179   Nietzsche 2007, pp. 36 et sqq., 114 et sq.; Nietzsche 1999a, Vol. 1, pp. 52 et sqq., 153 et sq. See for this and details critically v. Reibnitz (1992, pp. 179 et sqq.). A similar opposition is in Nietzsche 1999a, Vol. 2, p. 540.
180   Nietzsche 2007, pp. 93 et sq.; Nietzsche 1999a, Vol. 1, pp. 125 et sq.

the other hand occasionally he also uses *Entstehung* [genesis] and *Ursprung* [origin] synonymously.[181] Foucault could have avoided the errors of his construction had he differentiated between 'term' and 'concept': instead of settling rigidly on the false opposition of certain words, it would have been appropriate to proceed from Nietzsche's claim of an anti-metaphysical moral history (or genealogy) through changing terminologies.

In the following I would like to establish the thesis that Foucault, with the assistance of his opposition of *Ursprung* and *Herkunft*, repressed another opposition which runs through the Nietzschean text material he used: the misleading construction presented with the high pathos of philological precision covers up a sharp verticalisation toward an unfettered domination, which took place during the transition from the 'middle' to the 'late' Nietzsche.

6.2   Points of Support for the Foucauldian Interpretation in the 'Middle' Nietzsche

Foucault's portrayal of a Nietzsche who attempts to detect the beginnings of morality in the 'low areas' is by no means groundless. This approach has its location above all in the so-called 'middle' period, usually said to be between Nietzsche's break with Wagner in 1876 and the drafting of *Zarathustra* around 1882/83. It is characterised by the connection of ideology critique and a naturalistic materialism, which Nietzsche obtained primarily through reading Friedrich Lange's *History of Materialism* (1866).[182] In *Ecce Homo*, Nietzsche himself characterised the phase in retrospect (i.e. in 1889) as the liberation from an 'idealism' filled with the 'opiate' Wagner.[183] According to the autobiographical report, the title of *Human, All Too Human* announces the program in advance: '"where you see ideal things, I see what is – human, alas all-too-human!"'. Its characteristic is 'a merciless spirit that knows all the hideouts where the ideal is at home – where it has its secret dungeons and, as it were, its ultimate safety ... With a torch whose light never wavers, an incisive light is thrown into this underworld of the ideal'.[184] In order to be rid of the idealism of the 'higher swindle' and the 'beautiful feelings', he wants to rely on the natural science of his time.[185] The passage, which Foucault uses as proof for his opposi-

---

181   For example, Nietzsche 2011, pp. 45 et sq.; Nietzsche 1999a, Vol. 3, p. 62.
182   The significance of Lange for Nietzsche's middle phase has been thoroughly examined: for the reception of antique materialism by Lange see Cancik (1995, pp. 3 et sq., 18, 67); for the reception of the French moralists by Lange see Donnellan (1982, pp. 1 et sq.); generally, see Salaquarda (1978) and Stack (1983).
183   Nietzsche 1989, pp. 283, 286 et sq.; Nietzsche 1999a, Vol. 6, pp. 322, 325.
184   Nietzsche 1989, p. 283; Nietzsche 1999a, Vol. 6, pp. 322 et sq.
185   Nietzsche 1989, pp. 286 et sq. and 288; Nietzsche 1999a, Vol. 6, pp. 325 and 327.

tion between *Ursprung* [origin] and *Herkunft* [descent], actually belongs in this context: the project of a moral 'chemistry', which is to extract 'the most glorious colours ... from base, even despised substances'.[186]

Here, in 'middle' Nietzsche, which includes in addition to *Human, All Too Human* also *Dawn* and books 1–4 of *The Gay Science*,[187] we actually encounter an ideology-critique which comes closest to the pathos of a 'rooting in the low areas' conveyed by Foucault. The 'gladdening and dazzling errors' of the metaphysical age are counterposed to the 'little, humble truths' which were 'discovered by a strict method'.[188] The fact that the moral-critical art of 'psychological dissection' subjects human souls to 'belittling and doubt' is justified as a requirement of science.[189] To suggest that humans have a divine origin has become a forbidden path, 'because before its gate stands the ape along with other heinous beasts, grinning knowingly'.[190] The 'origin' (sic) of morality is to be found in 'disgraceful petty inferences' and 'accidental relations',[191] the 'exaltation of the "Entstehung"' (sic) is explained as the effect of a 'metaphysical after-drive [Nachtrieb]'.[192] The diversity of the sources of morality is addressed in the work programme of the *Gay Science*, in which Nietzsche asks about the varieties of the 'moral climate': 'on what account does this sun of a fundamental moral judgement and standard of highest value shine here – and that sun there?'.[193]

What Foucault erroneously ascribes to the term *Herkunft* is actually this ideology-critical dimension of the 'middle' Nietzsche. But it is already in the second sentence of his essay that Foucault lets himself be enticed by the late Nietzsche into a misleading confrontation: 'Paul Rée was wrong to follow – like the Englishmen – the tendency in describing the history of morality in terms of a linear development', as if there hadn't been invasion, battles, subterfuge.[194]

---

186   Nietzsche 1994, p. 14; Nietzsche 1999a, Vol. 2, p. 24.
187   The fifth book of *Gay Science* as well as the Preface and the 'Songs of the Prince Vogelfrei'
       are added only in the second edition of 1887 and belong thus into the late phase (see. e.g.
       Nietzsche 1999a, Vol. 14, p. 231; Nietzsche 1999a, Vol. 15, p. 162). Cf. for the dating among
       others Donnellan (1982, pp. XI–XII), Ottmann, who pleads for a relatively late dating for
       the autumn of 1883 (Ottmann 1999, pp. 239 et sq.), Losurdo, who connects the transition
       to the late phase with Nietzsche's protest against Bismarck's social politics (Losurdo 2020,
       pp. 326 et sqq., 329 et sqq., 336 et sq.).
188   Nietzsche 1994, p. 15; Nietzsche 1999a, Vol. 2, p. 25.
189   Nietzsche 1994, pp. 39 et sq.; Nietzsche 1999a, Vol. 2, pp. 59 et sq.
190   Nietzsche 2011, p. 38; Nietzsche 1999a, Vol. 3, p. 54.
191   Nietzsche 2011, p. 70; Nietzsche 1999a, Vol. 3, p. 90.
192   Nietzsche 2013b, p. 151; Nietzsche 1999a, Vol. 2, p. 540 (translation modified).
193   Nietzsche 2017b, p. 28; Nietzsche 1999a, Vol. 3, p. 379.
194   Foucault 2003b, p. 351, Foucault 2001a, Nr. 84, p. 1004 (translation modified).

What is amazing is not only how uncriticallyFoucault passes on Nietzsche's collective designation 'the Englishmen', but also the characterisation of Rée. Because when the 'middle' Nietzsche sets out to design his morality critique in *Human, All Too Human*, he refers directly to Rée, whom he praises as one of 'the keenest and coolest thinkers' and places at the side of the honored La Rochefoucauld and the other 'French masters in examining the soul'.[195]

Let's have a closer look here as well. The relationship to Rée can be used as a kind of signpost, which can lead us through both Nietzsche's 'middle' phase and the paradigm change to the late phase. Rée was a friend of Nietzsche's, with whom he had spent the autumn and winter of 1876/77 in Sorrento. From the intensive exchange of ideas during the common residence, Rée's *On the Origin of Moral Feelings* (1877) and Nietzsche's *Human, All too Human* (1878) arose simultaneously. Contrary to the wide-spread image held until today, which has Rée appear beside the 'genius' Nietzsche as a mediocre and flat ('linear') thinker, his intellectual influence on Nietzsche's ideology-critical phase can hardly be overrated. Through him Nietzsche encountered the philosophy of Spinoza, through and with him he familiarised himself with the French moral critics ('moralists') Montaigne, La Rochefoucauld, Vauvenarges, La Bruyère and Stendhal, and there are many indications that Nietzsche loses a piece of his earlier anti-Semitism through the friendship with the Jewish intellectual, at least temporarily.[196] Accordingly, not only Richard Wagner traces Nietzsche's falling away from him back to the harmful influence of Rée; so too do other contemporaries, who perceive the critique of ideals in *Human, All Too Human* as a disconcerting aberration.[197] The 'worried' letters of the sister and Nietzsche's circle of friends reveal a confluence of anti-feminist and anti-Semitic stereotypes.[198]

---

195   Nietzsche 1994, pp. 39 and 42; cf. p. 92; Nietzsche 1999a, Vol. 2, pp. 59, 61; cf. 127.

196   On Rée and Spinoza cf. Wurzer (1975, p. 53) and Ottmann (1999, p. 211), for the mediation of the French moral critics see among others Janz (1978/79, Vol. I, p. 755) and Donnellan (1982, p. 8), for the perception Rées as a 'Jew' see Janz (1978/79, Vol. I, pp. 642 et sq., 783) and Losurdo, who comes to the conclusion: 'There can be no doubt that the relationship of respect and friendship with the brilliant Jewish intellectual had helped to undermine Nietzsche's previous Judeophobia' (Losurdo 2020, p. 261).

197   Cf. Janz (1978/79, Vol. I, pp. 752, 819 et sq., 826), Janz (1978/79, Vol. II, p. 99).

198   Many of these letters can be read as the struggle of the 'milieu' for winning Nietzsche back from the 'ideology-critical' period: the blame for Nietzsche's misfortune is with the 'raging egoism' and 'immorality' of Lou Salomé (Elizabeth Nietzsche) in connection with the harmful influence of Rée's 'corrosive reason', which won the upper hand over Salomé's 'idealism' (v. Meysenburg): 'Behind it now stands Dr. Rée ..., indeed somewhat Mephistophelian, undermining everything' (Ludwig Hüter; quoted in Pfeiffer 1970, pp. 252, 286, 310).

But as described above (Chapter 1.6), the friendship between Nietzsche and
Rée is impaired by the fact that both fall in love with Lou Andreas-Salomé.
Toward the end of 1882 it comes to a break, which is at the same time a break
between Nietzsche and Salomé. The crisis of unfortunate love coincides with
the draft of *Zarathustra*, through which Nietzsche, as he writes in a letter to
Overbeck, '[has] elevated himself "vertically" from this low point to [his] altitude'.[199] This new and precarious 'altitude' will characterise the Nietzschean
late phase up to the collapse in 1889.

One must consider Rée's biographical and intellectual significance for Nietzsche's 'middle' phase in order to understand the disassociation dynamics in
the late phase. In the *Genealogy of Morals*, Rée emerges as a cipher in a double
sense: on one hand he represents a moral critique, which Nietzsche summarises under the heading 'the Englishmen', and which he uses as a foil for his new
approach in the *Genealogy of Morals*, while on the other hand he gives Nietzsche the opportunity to set himself off from his own moral explanations in the
'middle' phase without having to make this specific.

Let us consider Nietzsche's argumentation in the preface to the *Genealogy
of Morals*, on which Foucault relies primarily. In Rée's, 'precocious little book',
namely the *Origin of Moral Feelings* (1877), he encountered a 'perverse and
absurd kind of genealogical hypotheses, ... actually English in origin', he says
here, and perhaps he had never read anything that elicited such an emphatic
rejection.[200] Nietzsche's representation suggests that the opposition was clear
already with the first encounter, and already in *Human, All Too Human* he had
replaced Rée's 'improbable' explanations by 'a more probable theory'.[201] Reference points follow from *Human, All Too Human*, *Mixed Opinions and Maxims*
(1879), *The Wanderer and His Shadow* and *Dawn*, which are to document the
early disagreement with Rée – these are what Foucault erroneously brings up
as proofs for the origin-descent opposition.[202] In fact, Nietzsche has gathered
some aphorisms in which he treats the development of the morally 'good',
unlike Rée, not as a problem of the emergence of 'unegoistic' actions, but as
agreement with the law of 'custom', or as the product of opposing 'tables of
value'.[203] However, the representation of such differences as opposites stands

---

199   Nietzsche 1975–, Vol. III, 1, p. 324. 'If I don't find this alchemist trick to transform these
      feces into *gold*, I am lost', he writes on 25 December 1882 (ibid., p. 312).
200   Nietzsche 2013a, p. 6; Nietzsche 1999a, Vol. 5, p. 250.
201   Ibid.
202   Nietzsche 2013a, p. 7; Nietzsche 1999a, Vol. 5, p. 251.
203   Cf. above all *Human, All too Human*, Nietzsche 1994, pp. 46 et sq., 66 et sq.; Nietzsche 1999a,
      Vol. 2, pp. 67 et sq., 92 et sq.

in contradiction to other passages from *Human, All Too Human*, as well as those from the posthumous fragments, which show that the 'middle' Nietzsche believed himself to be in agreement with Rée's moral genealogy, and a dissociation took place at the earliest in the spring-summer of 1883, thus briefly after the break of the friendship.[204] Nietzsche works intensely on the homogenisation of his own intellectual trajectory, and the backward projection of a theoretical opposition with Rée represents, as it were, the backside of the construction of an unbroken continuity between *On the Genealogy of Morals* and *Human, All Too Human*. He is concerned expressly with the proof that at that time he already had 'the same thoughts' which from the beginning developed in him 'not in an isolated, arbitrary or sporadic' way, but out of a 'common root ... from a ... *fundamental will to* knowledge calling from my innermost depths': 'That is the only state of affairs that is proper for a philosopher'.[205]

6.3   The Late Nietzsche's Verticalisation and Its Suppression by Foucault

So far it looks as if the urge to 'linear genesis', which Foucault attributes to Rée, is primarily to be found with Nietzsche himself, and that this is additionally connected with the same concept of philosophical 'depth' to which the postmodernist Nietzsche-interpretation is so vehemently opposed. Furthermore, Foucault misrepresents the Nietzschean criticism of Rée and the 'Englishmen'. For Nietzsche does not criticise so much the 'linearity' of their moral genesis as their tendency to the 'belittling' and the 'humiliating' of humans:[206] that is precisely what he himself in *Human, All Too Human* has lauded as the heroic task of 'science'.[207] Rée and the 'Englishmen' are occupied incessantly with pushing the 'partie honteuse of our inner world', for example, the utility, the habit, the forgetfulness, into the foreground.[208] In this way the pride of the 'higher man' is to be humiliated, his self-esteem 'undone'.[209] The derivation is for him not

---

204   E.g. in agreement with Rée, the derivation of good and bad in Aph. 39 of *Human All Too Human* (Nietzsche 1994, pp. 43 et sqq.; Nietzsche 1999a, Vol. 2, pp. 62 et sqq). 'The joy over Rée's psychological observations is one of the greatest', notes Nietzsche in the summer of 1878 (Nietzsche 1999a, Vol. 8, p. 555). A first dissociation takes place with the remark in the spring-summer of 1883 that Rée would not know much about morality and 'that mostly through hearsay: and finally he was of the opinion that morality itself is hearsay' (Nietzsche 1999a, Vol. 10, p. 243). The criticism is then developed further in a longer note in the autumn of 1883, under the heading 'my differences with Rée' (Nietzsche 1999a, Vol. 10, pp. 503 et sqq.).

205   Nietzsche 2013a, p. 4; Nietzsche 1999a, Vol. 5, p. 248 (translation modified).

206   Nietzsche 2013a, pp. 13 and 15; Nietzsche 1999a, Vol. 5, pp. 257 and 259.

207   Nietzsche 1994, pp. 39 et sq.; Nietzsche 1999a, Vol. 2, pp. 59 et sq.

208   Nietzsche 2013a, p. 13; Nietzsche 1999a, Vol. 5, p. 257.

209   Nietzsche 2013a, p. 15; Nietzsche 1999a, Vol. 5, p. 259.

only 'unhistorical', but is itself the expression of a *plebeianism* of the modern spirit, which is of English origin', it emerges from the 'decay of aristocratic values'; in it the 'herd instinct' and the 'democratic prejudice' of the modern world articulate themselves.[210]

This polemic leads us into a wide network of references. What Nietzsche describes as 'English' moral derivation is primarily a compilation of statements from Rée's *Psychological Observations* (1875) and from his *Origin of Moral Sensations* (1877). Whereas the former was modelled after the example of the *Maximes* of La Rochefoucauld, which also played an important role in the discussions between Rée and Nietzsche in Sorrento,[211] the latter is occupied above all with the 'Englishmen' Hutcheson, Hume, Mill, Darwin and Helvetius, who, although actually a Frenchman, is declared by Nietzsche to be the forerunner of the 'boring theories' of the English utilitarians.[212] As already in the *Maximes* of La Rochefoucauld, both books are primarily concerned with the demonstration that behind morality only a private egoistic immorality hides itself.[213] For the moral genealogy this means the assumption that the 'egoistic instinct is the older and stronger, and the non-egoistic instinct is the later and the weaker'.[214] If it were the other way around, 'then communism would not only be possible, it would already be present at hand'.[215] Also morality has its origin in 'utility', more precisely in utility for others: one describes non-egoistic behavior as good 'because it is good for others', but this practical origin is then forgotten, so that the opinion develops that the non-egoistic is good in and of itself.[216] In addition comes the illusion of the free will, on the basis of which one makes oneself and others morally responsible for one's own and their actions, respectively.[217] The argument is directed against Kant and Schopenhauer, who understand morality as 'revelation from the transcendent world'. A philosophical explanation of this kind is 'deeper' than the object to be explained, and explaining an object

---

210 Nietzsche 2013a, pp. 16 et sq.; Nietzsche 1999a, Vol. 5, pp. 260 and 262.
211 Cf. Donnellan (1982, p. 8).
212 Cf. Rée 1877, pp. VII et sq., l et sq., 5, 23, 25 et sqq. For Nietzsche's commentary on Helvétius, cf. *Beyond Good and Evil*, Nietzsche 1997, pp. 95 et sq.; Nietzsche 1999a, Vol. 5, pp. 164 et sq., Nietzsche 1997, pp. 95 et sq., similarly in Nietzsche 1999a, Vol. 11, pp. 432, 500, 523 et sq.
213 'He who has, to him will be given, because he can return', 'we forgive people their errors, but not the knowledge of our errors', 'the convicts are not worse than other humans: They only counted more badly', 'the best actions have often unappetizing entrails', etc. (Rée 1875, pp. 21, 28, 47, 64).
214 Rée 2003, p. 96, cf. Rée 1877, p. 13.
215 Rée 2003, p. 97, cf. Rée 1877, p. 16.
216 Rée 2003, pp. 161 et sq., cf. Rée 1877, pp. 135 et sq.
217 Rée 2003, pp. 162 et sq., cf. Rée 1877, pp. 136 et sq.

'too deeply' is worse than explaining it 'too shallowly'.[218] Rée questions not only metaphysics, but also the idea of moral progress: 'It is remarkable that people, while egoistic, selfish, and envious in their actions, should assert the reality of moral progress as soon as they themselves start to philosophize'.[219]

The young Marx described this kind of a discrepancy as an 'estrangement' in which 'each sphere applies to me a different and opposite yardstick – ethics one and political economy another'.[220] And in *On the Jewish Question*, he observes that modern politics splits the human being into, on the one hand, an egoistic private individual of bourgeois-civil society, 'withdrawn ... into the confines of his private interests and private caprice, and separated from the community', and on the other into the moral person of the citizen of the political state, who is 'only abstract, artificial man, man as an *allegorical, juridical person*' and 'deprived of his real individual life and endowed with an unreal universality'.[221]

However, the comparison with Marx also shows the limits of Rée's moral philosophy: what Marx analysed as a specific alienation of modern bourgeois society and its subjects, is transposed by Rée onto the level of humankind per se.

At bottom it is this universalising of the private bourgeois egoist that the late Nietzsche rightfully rejects as 'unhistorical'. But since he articulates his criticism from the fictitious standpoint of an original aristocracy, he attacks it as an 'English', democratic-plebeian diminishment of higher man. The dissociation from Rée is at the same time a self-criticism, displaced and made unrecognisable. The fact that the motives of humans are of 'not much value' because they can all be attributed to 'self-love' had been described by Nietzsche in 1878 as a pleasurable discovery inspired by Rée, which freed him from his 'metaphysical period'.[222] Also in *Human, All Too Human*, the impossibility of 'unegoistic' actions and the illusory character of human free will are constant topics.[223] Almost identically to Rée, the middle Nietzsche also derives moral feelings from useful and harmful actions whose practical origin is later

---

218   Rée 2003, p. 99, cf. Rée 1877, p. 19.
219   Rée 2003, p. 164, cf. Rée 1877, p. 140.
220   Marx 1844a, p. 310; Marx and Engels 1957-, Vol. 40, p. 551.
221   Marx 1844b, pp. 154, 164, 167.
222   Nietzsche 1999a, Vol. 8, pp. 555 et sq.
223   Cf. on the egoism among others Nietzsche 1994, pp. 13, 41, 59, 60 et sq., 92; Nietzsche 1999a, Vol. 2, pp. 23, 60, 83, 84 et sq., 127 and *Gay Science*, Nietzsche 2017b, pp. 31 et sq.; Nietzsche 1999a, Vol. 3, p. 387; for the criticism of the free will see among others Nietzsche 1994, pp. 44 et sq., 69, 71, 73 et sqq., Nietzsche 1999a, Vol. 2, pp. 63 et sq., 96, 99, 102 et sqq.

forgotten and erroneously shifted into the nature of human beings[224] – thus exactly the sequence of what in the *Genealogy of Morals* is characterised as 'idiosyncratic traits of the English psychologist'.[225] This sequence is also present in 1880, in aphorism 40 of *The Wanderer and his Shadow*, where it is expressly determined that morality is 'originally social utility, which has had great difficulty in prevailing against private usefulness and in making itself more highly regarded'.[226] Also knowledge developed from 'errors' of which some proved to be 'useful and preservative of the species' is still written in 1882 in the *Gay Science*.[227]

No, answers the late Nietzsche, the source of origin of the concept 'good' lies not in any kind of 'utility' for others, but it is 'the good men', that is, the noble, the powerful, those of higher status who experienced 'that they themselves were good, and that their actions were good, that is to say of the first order': the 'pathos of distance' opposite all the low and low-minded ones – '*this* is the origin of the opposition of "Good" and "Bad"', and also the origin of 'language itself' is to be understood as an 'expression of the power of the masters'.[228] As Stegmaier observes, Nietzsche tries to raise morality out of its humiliation inflicted by moral critique and to conceive of it as 'higher' again.[229] However, it is a 'highness' which Nietzsche, contrary to the value heaven of traditional religious and moral ideologies, wants to understand directly 'in the social [ständisch] sense'.[230]

The dissociation from the 'diminishing' moral critique of the 'Englishmen' is again closely connected with the rejection of Spinoza, which we examined in Chapter 1.6 as an indicator of the transition to the late phase. When the late Nietzsche criticises Spinoza's 'self-preservation', he does so not least because of its linkage with 'usefulness', and thus as the 'basis of English utilitarianism'.[231] Both 'self-preservation' and the Darwinian category of the 'struggle for survival'

---

224   Nietzsche 1994, pp. 43 et sq., Nietzsche 1999a, Vol. 2, pp. 62 et sq.
225   Nietzsche 2013a, p. 14, Nietzsche 1999a, Vol. 5, p. 259.
226   Nietzsche 2013b, p. 178, Nietzsche 1999a, Vol. 2, p. 571.
227   Nietzsche 2017b, p. 73, Nietzsche 1999a, Vol. 3, p. 469.
228   Nietzsche 2013a, p. 15, Nietzsche 1999a, Vol. 5, pp. 259 et sq.
229   Stegmaier 1994, p. 99. Stegmaier thinks that Nietzsche thereby conceives of the moral from the point of view of the 'particular individual' (ibid.), which, however, dissimulates the core of Nietzsche's argumentation, which has to do with domination.
230   Nietzsche 2013a, p. 17, Nietzsche 1999a, Vol. 5, p. 261.
231   Nietzsche 1999a, Vol. 11, p. 224. Cf. for Nietzsche's critique of the self-preservation principle also Nietzsche 1997, pp. 9 et sq., Nietzsche 1999a, Vol. 5, pp. 27 et sq.; Nietzsche 1999a, Vol. 9, pp. 518, 559; Nietzsche 1999a, Vol. 11, p. 233; Nietzsche 1999a, Vol. 12, p. 131; Nietzsche 1999a, Vol. 13, p. 301.

appear to him now as developed by 'humans in states of distress' – they are therefore unable to grasp the aggressive dynamics of the 'will to power'. He explains the strong influence of these terms with reference to the origin of most scientists from the 'people', from the 'suffocating air of over-crowded England', the 'odor of humble people in need and in straits'.[232]

Ironically, the late Nietzsche criticises Rée (and actually himself) for exactly what Foucault wants to attribute to his alternative Nietzsche: for rooting in the nether regions and locating the historical beginnings in 'the lower'.[233] Although the same word is used, the 'Ursprung' (origin) is now no more that which the middle Nietzsche had sought in the everyday low areas of the 'disgraceful petty inferences' and 'accidental relations'.[234] In between them lies a particular ver-ticalisation, which is extinguished in Foucault's tailoring of an alternative Niet-zsche. Nietzsche found in his imagination of a heroic original aristocratic rule the pivot point from which he arranged anew the different elements of the earlier moral criticism. If morality is 'first the self glorification of the power-ful ones and the dominant caste', he argues in his critique of Rée in 1883, it will also be possible to transfer the critical deciphering of an underlying 'egoism' into a positive quality of morality: 'I fight the thought that egoism is harmful and despicable: I want to create the egoism of good conscience'.[235]

The 'altitude' of the new standpoint seems to have exercised an enorm-ous cohesive effect on Nietzsche. It makes it possible for him to hook up with his early idealistic phase, and at the same time to integrate the moral-critical instruments of the middle phase. The ideology-critique developed there is not simply dropped, but reformulated from the perspective of an unsublimated power of domination: it turns against the value universalism of the ideological (of Christian religion, morality, the philosophical truth, etc.), not because it helps to reproduce the relations of domination, but because it entails a com-promise formation, in whose instances the lower classes are represented and to which they can appeal.

The misconstructed opposition between *Ursprung* (origin) and *Herkunft* (descent) is like a smokescreen, which hides Nietzsche's turn toward a radical 'domination-affirming ideology critique'.[236] Foucault praises the perspectival view of Nietzsche's conception of history, which 'knows from where it looks

---

232 Nietzsche 2017b, p. 137, Nietzsche 1999a, Vol. 3, pp. 585 et sq.
233 Foucault 2003b, pp. 354 et sq.; Foucault 2001, Nr. 84, pp. 139 et sq.
234 Nietzsche 2011, p. 70, Nietzsche 1999a, Vol. 3, p. 90.
235 Nietzsche 1999a, Vol. 10, pp. 503, 505.
236 Haug 1993, p. 18.

and what it looks at',[237] but he conceals from us where this perspective of the late Nietzsche really is. But this silence has its own ideological function: it is 'necessary' in order to be able to join Nietzsche with the antiauthoritarian domination critique of the social movements after '68. Foucault organises it with a procedure which he himself denounces vehemently, namely with a homogenisation that makes the shifts and breaks in Nietzsche's intellectual trajectory unrecognisable. What emerges is a unified neo-Nietzschean line, which is held together by the empty pathos of a discontinuous, diverse and fragmentary monotony.

With the concept of genealogy developed in *Nietzsche, Genealogy, History* and the concept of power developed in the *Order of Discourse*, Foucault created for himself the theoretical preconditions for connecting his alternative Nietzsche image with the protest culture of French gauchism.

7   The Affiliation with Left-Wing Radicalism in Paris

An initial practical political application of the concept of power takes place in a discussion with high school students in November 1971, which is published under the Nietzschean title *Beyond Good and Evil* (*Par-delà le bien et le mal*). Foucault explains the exclusionary function of the knowledge presented in schools with reference to the fact that the popular movements are always represented only as those being driven by hunger, but never as movements which are fighting for power.[238] This is due to the fact that the event and the power are excluded from the 'knowledge' of our society.[239] For this exclusion, Foucault specifies two levels: on one hand, Roman law, by establishing a sovereign right to property, has already subjugated the 'will to power'; on the other hand, it is humanism that for Foucault contains 'everything in Western Civilisation that restricts the desire for power'.[240] It is now time to blow up this restriction, on one hand through a 'de-subjection [désassujettissement] of the will to power', i.e. through a political struggle which is waged as class warfare, and on the other hand by a cultural destruction of the subject, i.e. by abolition of sexual taboos, through common life, and the abolition of the prohibition of drugs.[241]

The course of the discussion shows how Foucault's 'alternative' Nietzscheanism polemicises right past the student's need for theory. What can be intro-

237   Foucault 2003b, p. 362; Foucault 2001a, Nr. 84, p. 1018 (translation modified).
238   Foucault 1977, p. 219; Foucault 2001a, Nr. 98, p. 1092.
239   Foucault 1977, p. 221; Foucault 2001a, Nr. 98, p. 1094.
240   Foucault 1977, p. 221; Foucault 2001a, Nr. 98, p. 1094.
241   Foucault 1977, p. 222; Foucault 2001a, Nr. 98, p. 1095 (translation modified).

duced in place of this system, asks one, and another objects that the present movement is in need of a utopia and theoretical reflection, in order to go beyond lived experiences which are always only piecemeal. On the contrary, answers Foucault, one must 'reject theory and all forms of general discourse', since they belong to the system from which one has had enough; instead the utopia is to be opposed by 'actual experiences' and experimentation.[242] The student's objection that experience alone is still 'partial' is not taken seriously. The experiences from which Foucault wants to let a future society emerge are: 'drugs, sex, communes, other forms of consciousness, and other forms of individuality'.[243] But the students understand from their own realistic experience that this is an unsustainable compilation: 'The politicised students continue their studies; those who take drugs leave school altogether'.[244] Another continues to insist: he cannot believe that the movement is to remain with this 'vague, unsubstantial underground ideology', which refuses 'to endorse any form of social work or community service, any action that requires going beyond the immediate group. It's unable to assume the responsibility for the whole of society, or it may be that it's incapable of conceiving of society as a whole'.[245]

This is the keyword for Foucault: the idea of *the whole of society* [l' ensemble de la societé] developed in the Western world and on the historical line, which led to capitalism; it is therefore 'precisely that which should not be considered except as something to be destroyed. And then, we can only hope that it will never exist again'.[246] Foucault's Nietzscheanism manifests itself through his attempt to introduce into the protest movement a particularistic kind of critique, which undermines the development of an ethical responsibility for the whole. The reasoning follows a totalising logic which wraps up a historical 'line' or even an entire ideological mega-construct like 'Western civilisation' into a homogeneous unity.

The 'particularistic' criticism we can see in Foucault's argument gives us some indication of his ambiguous relationship to neoliberalism, which is usually discussed in the context of a later period from the late 1970s and early 1980s onwards (see below Chapter 5.6).[247] But we can see here that it was already in the midst of Foucault's earlier radical 'gauchist' discourse that he anticip-

---

242   Foucault 1977, p. 231; Foucault 2001a, Nr. 98, p. 1102.

243   Foucault 1977, p. 231; Foucault 2001a, Nr. 98, p. 1102.

244   Foucault 1977, p. 226; Foucault 2001a, Nr. 98, p. 1098.

245   Foucault 1977, p. 232; Foucault 2001a, Nr. 98, p. 1103.

246   Foucault 1977, p. 233; Foucault 2001a, Nr. 98, p. 1103.

247   Cf. Zamora 2016a, pp. 2 et sq., Behrent 2016, 29; see also Garo 2011, pp. 141 et sqq., 150 et sqq.

ated the neoliberal destruction of an overall societal 'ensemble', epitomised in Thatcher's famous saying that 'there is not such a thing as society'. Indeed, whatever Foucault's intention might have been, his 'apotheosis of fragmentation' could only be realised in an alliance with neoliberal 'representatives of the free market and the lean state, of a creative work ethic and an optimised consumption'.[248]

Let us go back again to Foucault's 'gauchist' period. In the same month as the debate with high school students (November 1971), Foucault discusses with Noam Chomsky on Dutch television the question of whether the resistance against bourgeois society is to be based on a standard of justice or on the necessities of class struggle. Chomsky proceeds from a concept of justice which he sees anchored in a 'human nature', i.e. in fundamental qualities of human creativity. From here, he intends to develop yardsticks for both the criticism of ruling injustices and for the development of a responsible leftist politics. Without a valid goal of justice, the project of social liberation is as empty of content and as destructive as the war in the trenches of the First World War.[249] Chomsky's argumentation moves in the philosophical paradigm that Foucault characterised in the *Order of Things* as that of the transcendental 'anthropological' and 'humanist' apriori: on one hand, he claims that justice has an unhistorical foundation, on the other hand, he defines the elaboration of just criteria of critique as a historical task. Obviously, the 'anthropological' foundation of Chomsky's concept of justice is also connected with the neo-Kantianism of his grammar theory.[250] The strength of his orientation toward justice criteria lies in the political experience that almost all appealing popular movements are inspired by a massive perception of 'injustice' and include a 'moral economy' of justice.[251] In addition, Chomsky takes into consideration the violent practices of state terror during the Stalinist era, which separated itself from fundamental postulates of justice.

---

248   Reitz 2003, p. 83.
249   Foucault and Chomsky 1974, pp. 162 et sq., 175 et sq., 185 et sq.; Foucault 2001a, Nr. 132, pp. 1362, 1366 et sq., 1373 et sq.
250   Chomsky also conceives of the development of the sense of justice according to the neo-Kantian 'schematism' of innate organising principles (de principes organisateurs innés), which allow the child to develop a comprehensive linguistic competence out of coincidentally heard language sequences (Foucault 2001a, Nr. 132, pp. 1340, 1343). For a critique of Chomsky's neo-Kantian approach from the point of view of a Gramscian concept of grammar, cf. Ives 2001, pp. 935, 942 et sq.
251   For the term 'moral economy', see e.g. E.P. Thompson (1971), for its historical and theoretical elaboration see above all Barrington Moore (1978).

Foucault answers with a radical-leftist strategy of 'unmasking', which misses the contradictory potentials of the concept of justice and its importance for hegemonic struggles. His counter-position consists of delegitimising the question of justice in the name of a 'question of power', which he justifies with a mixture of class warfare rhetoric and Nietzsche's will-to-power: we live in a class dictatorship, 'which imposes itself by violence, even when the instruments of this violence are institutional and constitutional'. This class power based on violence must be detected in apparently independent institutions (family, school, university, medicine).[252] With reference to Nietzsche, he explains that the idea of justice itself was 'invented' as 'instrument of a certain political and economic power' or as weapon against it.[253] Now, however, the proletariat declares 'war' on the ruling class not because this is just, but 'for the first time in history it wants to take power'.[254]

Chomsky senses the danger of this kind of abstract power rhetoric detached from any social capacity to act, from human rights and legal protections: if he had to assume that a proletarian seizure of power led to a police state of terror, he would try to prevent it.[255] Foucault rejects Chomsky's demand for a connection between socialism and human rights by dissolving the question of violence into the 'class question': there is nothing wrong with a dictatorial, even bloody exercise of power by the proletariat against the vanquished classes, and if the power turns against the proletariat, this only shows that it is not the proletariat which has taken power, but rather 'a class outside the proletariat' or a bureaucracy or petit bourgeois elements inside the proletariat.[256] This however is itself Stalinist logic, which adjusts the evaluation of the correct politics and ultimately the question of the subjects' lives and deaths by the attribution or denial of a correct class basis.

We can conclude from the two debates of 1971 that Foucault's introduction of the concept of power did not by any means serve the overcoming of a Marxist power-and-class reductionism, but was done *initially* in connection with one of its most dogmatic and sectarian variants. Foucault's argumentation is based on the equation of class-violence-power, whereby the latter is characterised only by the fact that its true class and force character is hidden behind the appearance of independence and neutrality.[257] The relationship of the classes

---

252   Foucault and Chomsky 1974, p. 170; Foucault 2001a, Nr. 132, p. 1363.
253   Foucault and Chomsky 1974, pp. 184 et sq.; Foucault 2001a, Nr. 132, pp. 1372 et sq.
254   Foucault and Chomsky 1974, p. 182; Foucault 2001a, Nr. 132, p. 1371.
255   Ibid.
256   Ibid.
257   Foucault and Chomsky 1974, p. 170; Foucault 2001a, Nr. 132, p. 1363.

to ideology is conceived of in a strictly instrumentalist way, so that the actual effectiveness of the ideological, its cross-class capacity to condense social antagonisms into 'compromise formations', is lacking from the start.[258] Gramsci's distinctions of force and consent, *società politica* and *società civile* remain just as unconsidered as Althusser's modifying distinction between repressive and ideological state apparatuses. The rhetoric of the 'class dictatorship' eliminates the qualitative difference between bourgeois democracy and fascist dictatorship. Finally, Foucault's statements about post-revolutionary violence reveal a sectarianism that falls far behind the level of the PCF discussions at that time about Stalinism, left alliances and democratic popular front politics.

This initial introduction of the concept of power is interesting, not only for biographical but above all for theoretical reasons. Looking at the lectures in 1975/76 at the Collège de France, published under the title *Society Must Be Defended* (Il faut défendre la société), one can observe that Foucault resumes the reductionistic treatment of the ideological developed in his radically left-wing phase without a break, even after he dropped the *class*-reductionistic frame of reference. As it is put in the lectures, 'In the West, the law is the right of the royal command', e.g., it functions as an 'instrument' of domination and implements it directly.[259] But this is a hasty, instrumentalist assessment, which overlooks the fact that the legal system is also a contested site where social struggles are fought out, however asymmetrically. After Foucault has lumped the law overall onto the side of the 'sovereign power', he confronts it on the opposite side with a discourse of 'war' and 'race war', which in the sixteenth and seventeenth century is supposed to include both the heated acts of revenge of the people and the nostalgia of the declining aristocracies, both of which are portrayed as a 'counter history' (see below Chapter 5.4).[260] Now the universalism of ideology is opposed by *war* as 'a force relation laid bare', as well as the 'subject who is fighting a war', who is interested in 'a law marked by dissymmetry'.[261] Again 'open', 'honest' domination and war receive the charisma of the rebellious. The 'below' which Foucault opposes to the universalistic ideologies is a construction in which 'right', 'left' and in part also sado-masochistic myths of immediacy flow together: 'a series of brute facts, which might already be described as physico-biological facts: physical strength, force, energy, the proliferation of one race, the weakness of the other', 'intertwining bodies, passions, and accidents', 'a seething mass which is sometimes murky and sometimes

---

258   Cf. Rehmann 2013, pp. 254 et sqq.
259   Foucault 2003c, pp. 25 and 28, Foucault 1997b, pp. 23 et sq. (translation modified).
260   Foucault 2003c, pp. 57 et sq., 65, 270, Foucault 1997b, pp. 49, 57, 242.
261   Foucault 2003c, pp. 46 et sq., 53 et sq., Foucault 1997b, pp. 40, 46.

bloody', over which a fragile rationality rises.[262] Foucault follows the Nietz-schean mode of ideology-critique which reduces the ideological to the value heaven of a claimed universalism and humanism, and criticises it as masked power. By treating violence and war as anti-ideology, he overlooks that they also can be part of the real functioning of ideological socialisation (both on the basis of the entanglement of repressive and ideological apparatuses, as well as because of the ideological appeal of violence and war). And he fails to recognise that universalistic ideologies also contain aspirations of the subaltern classes, which a critical ideology-theory has to identify, liberate and translate into com-ponents of co-operative agency.

8   The Enigmatic Issue of Power and Its Anchorage in War

Habermas characterised Foucault together with the *Nouveaux Philosophes* as disappointed Maoists, who found in the power theories of bourgeois pessim-ism from Hobbes to Nietzsche the 'receptors' for their left apostasy.[263] We have to add that Foucault's Nietzscheanism is far older and constant than the short period of his radical left-wing commitment. Nevertheless, Habermas' political localisation points to a dynamics which is repressed in the prevailing Foucault reception like a 'low' beginning: Foucault's first 'overcoming' of Marxism con-sists in 1970/71 in replacing the concrete analysis of the relations of force in state and civil society with a pathetic 'combatism', in which Nietzsche's will to power and Mao Zedong's 'power from the barrel of a gun' are eerily entwined. One cannot jump over this political context if one wishes to understand Foucault's further development of the concept of power: it is not a matter of a plural over-coming of Marxism, but is concretely related to the question of how Foucault comes out of the dead-end of his own radically leftist paradigm.

In a discussion with Deleuze in March 1972, for the first time a modific-ation becomes visible, which makes possible the detachment of the power concept from class reductionism without a political break: Marx has in the nineteenth century discovered 'exploitation', but today we do not know a great deal about what 'power' is: this 'enigmatic thing which we call power, which is at once visible and invisible, present and hidden, ubiquitous'.[264] Terms like 'ruling class' and 'state apparatus' are not sufficient in order to understand that

---

262   Foucault 2003c, p. 54; Foucault 1997b, p. 47. Regarding the significance of sadomasochism for the Foucauldian concept of power, see the extensive material in Miller 1993.

263   Habermas 1987, p. 257 A 26.

264   Foucault 1996, p. 79; Foucault 2001a, Nr. 106, p. 1180.

'under the ancient theme of meaning, of the signifier and the signified', there is the 'question of power, of the inequality of powers and their struggles'.[265] To the class and its state Foucault now adds a multiplicity of new centres of power: the caretaker, director of the prison, judge, union representative, editor-in-chief (ibid.). A kind of division of labour between proletarian class politics and power critique is proposed: if one fights against exploitation, one must join the leadership and the ideology of 'the proletariat', yet in the struggle against power everyone can participate locally, thereby entering into the revolutionary process as an ally of the proletariat. 'The generality of the struggle specifically derives from the system of power itself, from all the forms in which power is exercised and applied'.[266]

The emphatic reference to 'the' proletariat, to its 'leadership' and 'ideology', belong to the gauchist class-warfare paradigm from which Foucault is just beginning to detach himself. This detachment contains two characteristics which will determine his concept of power from now on: 1) 'power' is introduced as its own reality, which is in juxtaposition to the 'exploitation' analysed by Marx, and whose criticism is to make an alliance between intellectuals and workers possible; 2) it designates at the same time a reality which is to be found *under* meaningful human behaviour and its signifiers, and which, due to this basis-position ('sous-sol') allows the struggle to become 'general'.[267] Foucault's rhetoric of power's 'diversity' is inseparably connected with the claim to have found 'power' located at a level of reality *beside* and *beneath* social production and reproduction, as well as gender relations and relations of domination in general.

It is worthwhile to take a closer look at this methodological separation. Following primarily Marx and Gramsci, Nicos Poulantzas presented already in 1968, thus before the Foucauldian introduction of the concept of power, a 'relational' conception of power: according to it, the power of a class is to be understood not as firm possession or class essence, but as a capacity to assert its own interests – a capacity which is constituted on the field of social practices and is determined by the respective relations of force with the other classes of the social formation.[268] This power field is therefore 'strictly relational [strictement relationnel]'.[269] Capitalistic relations of production and the appropriation of

265   Foucault 1996, p. 79, Foucault 2001a, Nr. 106, p. 1181.
266   Foucault 1996, p. 81, Foucault 2001a, Nr. 106, p. 1183.
267   Power functions as the 'foundation' and 'sous-sol' of civil egalitarian rights, is written e.g. in *Discipline and Punish* (Foucault 1995, p. 222).
268   Poulantzas 1978b, pp. 99 et sqq.; Poulantzas 1968, pp. 101 et sqq.
269   Poulantzas 2014, p. 147; Poulantzas 1978a, p. 161.

surplus labour organised in them are therefore to be examined as a specifically tightly woven 'power network' [réseau de pouvoirs] of the society.[270] What
Poulantzas explicitly formulates here can be shown to be an implicit procedure with Marx, whose *Critique of Political Economy* is a critique of the accumulation and alienation of social power. It applies a genetic-reconstructive
method: instead of conceiving of the bourgeois 'economy' as an 'eternal natural form of social production', it reconstructs it – e.g. through the analysis of
the value form – as a historical form of social practices. Economic categories
are translated back into societal forms of practice and relations and from there
explained functional-historically.[271] The Marxist analysis of capitalist production relations is applied as a specific analysis of power, which concentrates
primarily on the bourgeois-capitalistic type of impersonal and reified powers,
the 'dull compulsion of economic relations', which runs in the juridical form of
the freedom of contract.[272]

Since the 'economy' itself represents a crystallised form of power relationships (albeit not the only one),[273] the Foucauldian juxtaposition of 'power'
and 'exploitation' is untenable, especially from the standpoint of a 'relational'
concept of power. Until approximately 1976, the 'beside' and 'beneath' of power
with regard to societal practices is secured with the assistance of an ontology
of war, which Foucault designates as 'hypothesis of Nietzsche': the relations of
power emerge from 'war', so that one could say in reversal of the Clausewitz
saying that 'politics is the continuation of war by other means'.[274] In *Nietzsche, Genealogy, History*, Foucault derived this 'hypothesis' from Nietzsche's
vivid descriptions of the creditor's claim against the debtor.[275] We find this war-
ontology in 1973 as an alternative to the Marxian critique of exploitation: 'At
the heart of power is a warlike relationship and not one of appropriation'.[276]

270   Poulantzas 2014, p. 32; Poulantzas 1978a, p. 40.
271   Regarding the concept of a 'functional-historical analysis' elaborated in Holzkamp's *Crit-
      ical Psychology* see Maiers (1999, pp. 1133 et sqq.), for the concept of 'genetic reconstruction'
      see Haug (2001b, pp. 264 et sqq.).
272   Marx and Engels 1845b, pp. 77 et sq.; Marx and Engels 1957–, Vol. 3, p. 74; Marx 1867, p. 726;
      Marx and Engels 1957–, Vol. 23, p. 765.
273   'In fact, production relations were also, for Marx, power relations' (Losurdo 2020, p. 983).
274   Foucault 2003c, p. 16; Foucault 1997b, pp. 16 et sq.
275   Cf. Nietzsche 2013a, pp. 51 et sq.; Nietzsche 1999a, Vol. 5, pp. 300 et sq. The master's law
      is the 'calculated pleasure of relentlessness. It is the promised blood, which permits the
      perpetual instigation of new domination [le jeu de la domination]', instead of mankind
      progressing to a 'universal reciprocity', humanity installs 'all its violences in a system of
      rules and thus proceeds from domination to domination' (Foucault 2003b, p. 358; Fou-
      cault 2001a, Nr. 84, p. 1013).
276   Foucault 1976b, pp. 114 et sq.

According to *Discipline and Punish*, an 'eternal struggle' lies at the base of the 'microphysics of power', which therefore is not to be analysed as 'appropriation' but as 'strategy'.[277] And in *Society Must be Defended*, Foucault makes clear that power is to be understood neither as 'surrender', 'contract' or 'alienation', nor in functional categories of the reproduction of production relations, but as 'conflict, confrontation, and war'.[278]

The war discourse has the double function for Foucault: to remain in touch with the 'combatist' rhetoric of the gauchist milieu, and at the same time to substitute the Marxist analysis of appropriation and alienation by an allegedly 'more radical' alternative. Here we need to differentiate: an extension of the analysis of power beyond a Marxist critique of 'appropriation' is justified and fruitful, but their opposition is problematic and misleading. Even the creditor-debtor relationship claimed by Nietzsche as 'original', from which Foucault derives his war ontology, is essentially a relationship of 'appropriation', which is enforced and secured by the described burning of the debt markers into the debtors' bodies. And is not the appropriation of the surplus product also a field of combat, in which those involved develop opposing 'strategies'? There are both strategies of appropriation and appropriations of strategies which constitute a majority of the business of politicians competing against each other. And does Foucault really want to say that wars are waged only for the sake of war?

9   Outlook: The Suppression of the Structurally Anchored Power Relations

Here the intellectual price of the Foucauldian overcoming of Marx becomes visible: the justified claim to extend the analysis of power beyond the appropriation paradigm flips over into essentialism, with which power is positioned *behind* social relations.

This essentialisation is something other than what Lemke has in mind when he talks about the concept of 'negative' power, which characterised the Foucauldian approach from 1971 to 1975, and which Foucault has overcome with a more 'productive' concept of power from 1976 onward. On the contrary, what is meant is a systematic excluding of structurally anchored power-relations, which continues to define Foucault's approach also after he gives up his 'war hypothesis' in 1976.

---

277   Foucault 1995, pp. 26 et sq.; Foucault 1975, p. 35.
278   Foucault 2003c, p. 15; Foucault 1997b, p. 16.

The scope of this methodological decision is hardly to be underestimated. We confine ourselves to an example from the first volume of the *History of Sexuality*, which shows that the methodical exclusion concerns not only the power relations anchored in the capitalistic 'economy', but also those from 'gender relations'. This concept became common in ethnologist, social-historical and feminist investigations 'for critically investigating the structural role that genders play in social relations in their totality'.[279] In contrast, Foucault in a 'rule of the constant variations' specifies that the question 'who within the range of sexuality has power (the men, the adults, parents, the physicians), and who is robbed of it (the women, ... the children, the patients)' plays no role in the investigation; instead it may only be asked which 'pattern of modifications' the relations of force imply 'by the very nature of their process' [par leur jeu même].[280] Thus Foucault's allegedly 'relational' concept of power is robbed of its relations; the 'relations of force', which 'by their process itself' constitute power, must have nothing to do with the real relations of force between the genders. In this paradigm neither the diversity of 'sexual' power relations, nor their solidification into structurally asymmetrical gender relations, can be conceptualised.

Similar to the knowledge constellation of the *Order of Things*, we stand before the phenomenon of a strange double binding: Foucault's rhetoric of the most diverse micro-structures is based on the essentialist concept of an all-powerful 'Maître-Pouvoir'.[281] Foucault's power concept is characterised by the fact that throughout its different periods it abstracts from the various relations which it conjures up. This abstraction is the basis for both the 'war hypothesis' as well as the later 'freedom/ethics'-hypothesis and made their succession possible.

---

279   F. Haug 2005, p. 279. Frigga Haug proposes examining gender relations in connection with Marx and Engels' *German Ideology* as 'relations of production' in the broad sense, i.e. as relations of the 'production of life' (Marx and Engels 1845b, pp. 29 et sq.; Marx and Engels 1957-, Vol. 3, pp. 29 et sq.), which include the social organisation of child-raising and care (F. Haug 2005, pp. 282 et sqq., 299 et sqq.; cf. 2002, pp. 45 et sq.).

280   Foucault 1978, p. 99; Foucault 1976a, pp. 130 et sq.

281   Poulantzas 2014, pp. 148 et sq.; Poulantzas 1978a, pp. 163 et sq.

CHAPTER 4

From Prison to the Modern Soul – 'Discipline and Punish' Revisited

The investigation *Discipline and Punish*, published in 1975, is the first study in which Foucault pursues his project of a *genealogy* of power and subjectivity on a historical subject. As we have seen in Chapter 3.6, he drew this genealogical project from his interpretation of Nietzsche in 'Nietzsche, Genealogy, History': the Nietzschean body-power-truth nexus is now applied to historical material as the leading question. *Discipline and Punish* is a study which in parts is inspired by Marxist investigations of the development of capitalistic relations of production, and at the same time claims to supplement these and give them a new foundation with a genealogy of the 'disciplinary power'.

The prevailing tendency to present the Foucauldian discourse and power concept as a successful overcoming of Marxist social theories can also be observed in the commentaries on *Discipline and Punish*. Dreyfus and Rabinow see Foucault's achievement in the fact that he analyses punishment and prison as a 'complex social function', and thus overcomes their being viewed as instruments of repression or reflections of the social structures.[1] Poster welcomes the fact that Foucault, with recourse to Nietzsche's concept of genealogy, develops a perspective in which the mode of production no longer stands at the centre.[2] Also Michèle Barrett sees the achievement of Foucauldian disciplinary power in its 'sidelining' of the Marxist fixation on social structures. Thereby it is particularly important to her that from the beginning Foucault works outside of the basis-superstructure model, instead of still trying to modify it with polymorphous causality concepts, as do the Althusserians.[3] According to John Ransom, Foucault, using the example of the prison inmates, cleared out the naive anthropology of Marxist theoreticians, including the Frankfurt school, who held that despite all deformations there would still be a better world 'in the wings': 'The inmates' true selves are not repressed; rather, their "true selves" are created, manufactured by one or several technologies of power'.[4] Lemke thinks

---

1   Dreyfus and Rabinow 1983, p. 143.
2   Poster 1984, p. 95.
3   Barrett 1991, p. 138.
4   Ransom 1997, pp. 21 et sq.

the advantage of *Discipline and Punish* is that the 'relative autonomy' of the power relations is taken seriously and in this way the 'reductionist ... essentialist and economistic models of explanation' are replaced with 'social analysis carried out in historically concrete terms'.[5]

Precisely these attributions of anti-reductionism and historical concretion prove to be untenable when investigated more closely. This does not mean calling into question that Foucault has provided valuable impulses for the study of modern penitentiary systems and disciplining projects. The criticism is directed rather toward a theoretical arrangement which deprives the historical material of its concreteness and subjects it to a totalising framework. Of course such a totalising procedure cannot be read off from the Foucauldian rhetoric of power diversity, but shows up in the operational strategies with which he arranges the material.

Foucault's argumentation is saturated with historical examples to an extent that makes it difficult to uncover the 'perspectivism' of his selection and arrangement. In order to defamiliarise the Foucauldian account, I will bring in a classical text with which *Discipline and Punish* overlaps and at the same time contrasts. It is a study which Foucault himself called a 'great work',[6] namely *Punishment and Social Structure*, published in 1939 by Georg Rusche and Otto Kirchheimer.

1   An (All Too) Cursory Meeting with 'Critical Theory'

Rusche and Kirchheimer's study is the first publication of the 'Institute for Social Research' in the USA. Both authors belong to the periphery of the Frankfurt School, although in different ways. Rusche, who emigrated to London, completed an initial manuscript of the book in 1934, and eventually came into increasing disagreement with Horkheimer.[7] Because he was 'not availabale' for a revision, as Horkheimer reports in the preface to the study,[8] the book is revised, supplemented and finished by Kirchheimer, who belongs to the insti-

---

5   Lemke 2019, p. 70.
6   Foucault 1995, p. 24; Foucault 1975, p. 32.
7   Cf. Melossi (1980, p. 57) and Steinert (1981, p. 316). The theoretical conflict between Rusche and Horkheimer rests among other things on opposing interpretations of German fascism: is it the last stage of developed monopoly capitalism or the completion of the pure positivist rationality of the economic, manifested in an authoritarian irrationalism? (cf. Zander 1980, p. 206).
8   Rusche and Kirchheimer 2009, p. x.

tute in New York, beginning in 1937. The two authors never worked together and did not know each other. Rusche, from whose publications in 1930 and 1933 the original version can partly be reconstructed, is apparently disappointed with the final result.[9] The study is almost ignored for a long time and then becomes an insider tip at pertinent conferences towards the end of the 1960s, as sociological approaches enter the domain of criminology. The book becomes a 'myth',[10] and it is considered an 'indispensible precondition for the discussion of a political economy of criminal law';[11] the pair of names becomes the 'smiling sun of the anti-prison movement'.[12] According to Steinert, Foucault's *Discipline and Punish*, with its 'elegance and eloquence', then pushed the book 'for some time into the background', and made it appear 'dry and pedantic, ... with no imagination ... in its "economism", which appeared to be overcome by Foucault's theory of diffuse power'.[13]

Let us consider first the reporting in *Discipline and Punish* itself. Foucault talks first of Rusche and Kirchheimer's methodological principle, that of explaining the penitentiary systems, not directly from the respective crimes, but as independent 'social phenomena' in themselves.[14] The thought follows that the punitive measures are 'not simply "negative" mechanisms that make it possible to repress, to prevent, to exclude, to eliminate', but are connected to 'positive and useful effects'. Obviously here the well-known disassociation from a purely negative 'repression thesis' is being heard, which Foucault will then work out primarily in the first volume of the *History of Sexuality*. However, according to Foucault, Rusche and Kirchheimer related the different penitentiary systems directly to the respective 'system of production', so that the slave-owner society had the punishment of enslavement, feudalism physical corporal punishment, mercantile 'trading society' the penitentiary and the industrial system corresponded to '"corrective" detention' (détention de fin corrective).[15] As an alternative to these 'strict correlations' Foucault suggests writing the history of the punishments on the basis of a 'micro-physics of power', which is based on

---

9   In a letter to Horkheimer from 14 June 1939 Rusche writes: 'I am sorry to have to say that there are a number of weaknesses in the work of Dr. Kirchheimer, which do not belong in the book and which I regret here' (quoted in Steinert 1981, p. 314). Regarding the complex historical development and the contradictory character of the book cf. among other things Zander (1980, pp. 204 et sqq.) and Steinert (1981, pp. 314 et sqq).
10   Steinart 1981, p. 332.
11   Rausch 1975, p. 218.
12   Schumann 1981, p. 64.
13   Steinert 1981, p. 332.
14   Foucault 1995, pp. 24 et sq., Foucault 1975, p. 32; cf. Rusche and Kirchheimer 2009, p. 5.
15   Foucault 1995, p. 25; Foucault 1975, p. 33.

a '"political economy" of the body', while concentrating primarily on the constitution of 'power/knowledge relations'.[16]

So this seems to be the point at which Foucault, with his concept of power,
overcomes what Lemke described as one of the 'reductionist, essentialist, and
economistic models of explanation'.[17] However, Foucault's reporting is hardly
helpful for an understanding of the methodical differences. This already results from the fact that he refers exclusively to five pages from the introduction written by Kirchheimer,[18] whose explicit theory remains behind the far
more complex implicit theory of the historical chapters of the development
of the bourgeois penitentiary system. It was precisely from these that Foucault, without making it recognisable, took over results which are among the
most interesting of *Discipline and Punish*. This questionable handling of the
'great book' leads to several inaccuracies: there is no 'strict correlation' between
punishing and production systems with Rusche and Kirchheimer. Thus, for
example, 'feudalism' is divided into an 'early' and a 'late' middle age, to which
again completely different penitentiary systems are assigned, and also, within
the 'industrial system' of capitalism, the authors differentiate different kinds of
punishing – from solitary confinement to the 'prison factory' up to the fine –
which partly complement each other, partly compete with one another. This is
primarily because of the fact that they have chosen as their point of reference
not the respective modes of production but primarily the fluctuations of the
labour market. And finally, it is Foucault himself who is heading his investigation into a 'corrective' system for the purpose of improvement, not Rusche and
Kirchheimer, who instead observe between approximately 1875 and 1932 a general decrease of the terms of imprisonment and their replacement by fines. In
the chapters rewritten by Kirchheimer this 'commercialization of the penal system' is treated as an appropriate expression of modern capitalistic 'rationality',
and in this sense as 'rationalisation' of the civil penal system.[19] Thereby Foucault's discussion deprived the study by Rusche and Kirchheimer of its point.
This is all the more amazing, since he too understood his book as an investiga-

---

16   Foucault 1995, pp. 25 et sq.; Foucault 1975, pp. 33 et sqq.
17   Cf. Lemke 2019, p. 70.
18   Rusche and Kirchheimer 2009, pp. 3–7.
19   Rusche and Kirchheimer 2009, pp. 103 et sqq., 173, 175, 206. It can be assumed that Kirch-
      heimer formulated this rationalisation thesis based on Max Weber's concept of modernity,
      in disagreement with Rusche, in whose writings (Rusche 1930; 1933) the concept plays no
      role. In addition to the introduction, Chapters IX–XIII are from Kirchheimer (Schumann
      1981, p. 66).

tion of western 'rationality',[20] so that a debate over the different rationalisation concepts (disciplining and/or commercialisation) would have almost offered itself.

Since Foucault's account does not give reliable information, we must reread Rusche and Kirchheimer in order to be able to evaluate both the borrowing Foucault made and his theoretical modifications and departures.

2   The Socio-Historical Approach of Georg Rusche and Otto Kirchheimer

Let us first look at the general theoretical framework of Rusche/Kirchheimer's socio-historical analysis, which is inspired by some insights of Marx's *Critique of Political Economy*. According to Marx, capitalist relations of production are characterised by the tendency to produce a 'population surplus in relation to capital's average requirements for valorization'.[21] There are three main reasons for this. First, since capitalist enterprises are bound to strive for profits and to compete with each other, they are obligated to increase their investments more and more in ever faster and more efficient technologies, at the expense of their investments in living labor. They have to increase their constant capital in relation to their variable capital.[22] Second, capitalist development is always irregular and crisis-ridden; it oscillates between expansion and contraction. Capital, therefore, needs a 'surplus population' as a buffer. When production contracts, capital needs to get rid of workers whose labour power is no longer needed for profits, and when production expands again, capital needs a pool from which to draw fresh supplies of labor. Third, an 'industrial reserve army' is needed to curb the aspirations of those who have a job and to weaken their negotiating power: if they go on strike for higher wages or even to defend their current life conditions, workers risk losing their jobs and sinking down into the mass of redundant paupers.[23] Marx describes this as an uttermost alienation: the working population 'produces both the accumulation of capital and the means by which it is itself made relatively superfluous'.[24] The employed segment of the

---

20   The subject matter of *Discipline and Punish* is not the history of the prison or of punishment per se, but 'la ratio qui a été mise en oeuvre dans la réforme du système pénal', it is an historical analysis 'de la raison punitive' (Foucault 2001b, Nr. 277, pp. 832 et sq.).
21   Marx 1976, p. 786.
22   Marx 1976, pp. 781–3.
23   Marx 1976, p. 792.
24   Marx 1976, p. 783.

working class is overburdened, and it is exactly by its overwork that it produces the very means by which it is made superfluous: 'Its over-work swells the ranks of its reserve', and conversely, the industrial reserve army competes with the employed working class and conditions its submission to overwork. One part of the working class is overworked while the other part is condemned to 'enforced idleness'.[25] This dichotomy is for Marx a telling example of the fundamental irrationality of capitalism. It can only be overcome by 'planned co-operation between the employed and the unemployed',[26] who both demand a shortening of labour time so that everyone has a job. But for the capitalist class it is of great importance that the working class is split into two competing and hostile camps.

Rusche/Kirchheimer's investigation focuses on the relationship between the size of this surplus population and the development of the penal system. Their 'historical-sociological analysis of penal methods' begins with the 'early Middle Ages', which is described as a period of slight social tensions and relatively favourable living conditions for the lower classes.[27] For the containment of feuds and the maintenance of the public peace the criminal justice system concentrated on private conciliation by fines, which among the insolvent lower classes were replaced by physical corporal punishment.[28] However, the 'late Middle Ages', starting from the fifteenth century, are described as a period of enclosures, the penetration of capital and the increasing impoverishment of the lower classes.[29] In order to secure the practice of dispossession and its devastating effects, a cruel system of execution and mutilation was introduced, which was directed primarily against property offenses committed by those without possessions.[30] The death penalty, which up until the fifteenth century was hardly used, became in the sixteenth and seventeenth centuries the 'most common method of punishing'; the authorities continually came up with new means for making the executions even more painful: 'We find removal of the hands, whole fingers, or phalanges, cutting off or tearing out of the tongue, putting out of eyes, severing of ears, and castration'.[31]

Here we come upon the first overlapping with Foucault: the display of the executions and mutilations, which Rusche and Kirchheimer treat in connec-

---

25   Marx 1976, p. 789.
26   Marx 1976, p. 793.
27   Rusche and Kirchheimer 2009, p. 4.
28   Rusche and Kirchheimer 2009, pp. 8 et sqq.
29   Rusche and Kirchheimer 2009, pp. 11 et sqq.
30   Rusche and Kirchheimer 2009, pp. 14 et sqq.
31   Rusche and Kirchheimer 2009, pp. 19 et sq.; cf. p. 22.

tion with the so-called 'primitive accumulation of capital' (Marx), correspond
to the 'torture spectacles' which are described in detail in the first part of
Discipline and Punish. However, in Foucault's presentation the socio-historical
connection with the early capitalistic deterrence of pauperism, which Marx
described as 'bloody legislation against the expropriated',[32] is no longer visible.
The tortures appear as characteristic of a 'sovereign power', which is described
as the conduct of a ritualised war.[33] Later Foucault will define this 'sovereign
power' as royal 'right of seizure' [droit de prise] of the bodies of the subjects
and oppose it with the modern forms of 'disciplinary power' and 'bio-power'.[34]

However, Rusche and Kirchheimer concentrate on a development for which
there is no correspondence with Foucault, namely, the tendency in the mercantilism of the seventeenth century to exploit the labour of prisoners by galley
slavery, deportations and forced labour.[35] A decrease in population and a shortage of labour led in the seventeenth century to high real wages and prevented
the formation of a 'reserve army', which the increasing factories desperately
needed. The mercantile states reacted on one hand with intensive measures for
the increase of the total population (populationism) – an aspect that Foucault
will later summarise under the concept of 'bio-power' and will shift into the
late eighteenth century –[36] on the other hand with the socio-political strategy
of reducing the shortage of labour by integrating the poor into production
without permitting wages to rise.[37] In this context the 'house of correction' is
introduced. The *Rasphuis* in Amsterdam, opened in 1596, serves as the model
for the founding of numerous houses of correction. In Paris the first 'Hôpital
General' is founded in 1656 and then, on the initiative of the Jesuites Cha-
raud, Dunod and Guevarre, institutions of this kind spread into the whole
of France.[38] Generally, there is a combination of poorhouse, work house and
penal institution, which functions primarily as a factory, and thus as a direct component of capitalistic development; its inhabitants are beggars able
to work, vagrants, prostitutes and thieves; its major aim is 'to make the labour
power of unwilling people socially useful'.[39]

Against this background Rusche and Kirchheimer explain the emergence of
the prison as a further development of the mercantilist house of correction:

---

32   Marx 1867, pp. 723 et sqq.; Marx and Engels 1957-, Vol. 23, pp. 761 et sqq.
33   Cf. Foucault 1995, pp. 40 et sq., 49, 57; Foucault 1975, pp. 51 et sq., 59, 69.
34   Foucault 1978, p. 136; Foucault 1976a, p. 178.
35   Rusche and Kirchheimer 2009, p. 24.
36   Foucault 1978, pp. 139 et sq.; Foucault 1976a, pp. 183 et sq.
37   Rusche and Kirchheimer 2009, p. 35.
38   Rusche and Kirchheimer 2009, p. 42, Note 84, p. 43.
39   Rusche and Kirchheimer 2009, pp. 42, 50 et sq.

'The early form of the modern prison was ... bound up with the manufacturing houses of corrections', which served not so much 'the improvement' of the
worker, but rather had the primary functions of worker exploitation and the
training of new worker reserves.[40] However, they identify a second genealogy
of the prison, namely from the Catholic Church, which was not permitted to
carry out death sentences, and which, therefore, earlier than the state, turned
to punishing religious deviation and clerical criminality with imprisonment.[41]
This was implemented primarily as solitary confinement, and aimed at repent-
ance and internal conversion – the exploitation of labour played hardly a role
here.[42]

But beginning with the second half of the eighteenth century, the mixture of
offenders, poor, orphans, prostitutes and the mentally impaired in the houses
of correction, as well as the increasing pauperisation of the institutions, are criticised as despotic arbitrariness by various representatives of the 'enlightened'
penal reform movement. The critique is based on a concept of justice that has
predictability as its main content and insists on a strict correlation between the
crime and the punishment.[43] In addition, there is reflection on the dangerous
effect of the public executions, because 'the frequent and unjust execution of
domestic servants for the pettiest thefts led to dangerous disturbances'.[44] Mod-
erating the punishments also serves the defence against the revolution[45] – an
aspect we also find with Foucault.[46]

According to Rusche and Kirchheimer, the critique of the 'enlightened' penal
reform movement is successful because it intersects with the crisis of mercantile penitentiary labour: on one hand, the second half of the eighteenth
century experiences a surplus of workers and thus their pauperisation – the
'relative overpopulation' desired by the dominant classes is now reality –[47] on
the other hand the mechanisation of industry makes it 'increasingly difficult
to keep able-bodied inmates of the poorhouses at profitable work'.[48] Whereas
mercantilism had a strong need for cheap convict labour, this is now attacked
'vehemently ... by the working class and employers alike'.[49] Thus the 'repress-

---

40   Rusche and Kirchheimer 2009, pp. 62, 63, 65 et sq., 68.
41   Rusche and Kirchheimer 2009, pp. 70 et sqq.
42   Rusche and Kirchheimer 2009, pp. 70 et sq.
43   Rusche and Kirchheimer 2009, pp. 74 et sqq.
44   Rusche and Kirchheimer 2009, p. 76.
45   Rusche and Kirchheimer 2009, pp. 76 et sq.
46   Foucault 1995, pp. 57 et sqq., 74; Foucault 1975, pp. 69 et sqq., 88.
47   Rusche and Kirchheimer 2009, p. 86.
48   Rusche and Kirchheimer 2009, p. 91.
49   Rusche and Kirchheimer 2009, p. 111.

ive, deterrent side [comes] to the fore', prison work becomes a method of torture without productive sense: 'Prisoners carried huge stones from one place to another and then back again, they worked pumps from which the water flowed back to its source, or trod mills which did no useful work'.[50] Imprisonment becomes 'the chief punishment throughout the western world at the very moment when the economic foundation of the house of correction is destroyed by industrial changes'.[51]

The generalisation of detention together with the simultaneous crisis of the house of correction is what Foucault describes as the 'birth of the prison', although he does not deal with the separation of the prison sentence from the 'productive' work in the penitentiary. Whereas he concludes that there is a comprehensive prison system which penetrates the entire social body so that it is transformed into a 'disciplinary society', Rusche and Kirchheimer trace a contradictory development in which – depending upon labour market situation and socio-political constellation – different models of punishment compete with one another.

The differences between the US-American and the European systems are remarkable. In the USA the Philadelphia system, which was introduced by the Quakers in the 1830s and included strict solitary confinement, was increasingly replaced, under the conditions of an acute lack of workers, by the 'Auburn system' that limited solitary confinement to nights, combined with common work in the workshops by day. With good work performance, the prisoners could earn themselves a reduction of sentence.[52] Supported by the computations of Beaumont and Tocqueville from 1833, Rusche and Kirchheimer show that the incomes from prison work soon exceeded maintenance costs.[53] 'The prisons became busy factories once again and began to produce goods on a profitable basis',[54] until the pressure of the labour movement toward end of the nineteenth century led again to an extensive restriction of prison work, 'causing much suffering to the prisoners'.[55]

The development in Europe took place differently. Between 1780 and 1830 pauperisation intensified; behind the rising crime rate there was fear of social

---

50   Rusche and Kirchheimer 2009, p. 112.
51   Rusche and Kirchheimer 2009, p. 102.
52   Rusche and Kirchheimer 2009, pp. 128 et sqq.
53   Rusche and Kirchheimer 2009, p. 131. 'À Auburn, pendant les deux dernières années (thus starting from 1830; JR), les recettes provenant des traveaux ont excédé les dépenses d'entretien' (Beaumont and Tocqueville 1836a, p. 333).
54   Rusche and Kirchheimer 2009, p. 130.
55   Rusche and Kirchheimer 2009, p. 132.

revolution.[56] Primarily under the rule of Napoleon and the European Restoration from 1815 onwards, this led to a dual modification of the penitentiary system: on one hand there was an attempt to return to the cruel physical punishment of the Ancien Régime, for example to a partial restoration of whip, pillory, and branding iron;[57] on the other hand a forced expansion of the prison system with a corresponding rise in prison sentences took place. Unlike in the USA, the European punishment experts at the international congress on prisons in 1846 in Frankfurt/Main came out by a large majority for the Philadelphia model. The positive incentives for work found under the Auburn system were criticised as too indulgent; for 'reasons of discipline' solitary confinement was preferred as a reformatory institution.[58] With it 'the entire force of the authorities as well as the very architecture of the jail could be brought to bear on a single inmate'[59] – a thought which Foucault will elaborate in his analysis of 'Panopticism'. Under these conditions the work of prisoners became unproductive and was transformed into pure punishing work. In England, for example, handmills or treadmills (the 'crank') were introduced, which did not propel anything but were used only from motives of cruelty.[60]

For Rusche and Kirchheimer the priority of deterrence is connected with the existence of a large industrial reserve army in Europe and the corresponding fear of revolution: 'What European society, with its industrial reserve army, needed was a punishment which would strike fear into the hearts of the starving'.[61] It is above all in this 'European' constellation of the early nineteenth century in which Foucault locates his 'birth of the prison'. What according to him represents the germ cell from which the disciplinary society develops, is, however, with Rusche and Kirchheimer only one phase of the bourgeois penal system. They contrast it with a 'modern prison reform' which begins in approximately 1875 and lasts with short interruptions up to the world economic crisis.

---

56   Rusche and Kirchheimer 2009, pp. 95 et sq.
57   Rusche and Kirchheimer 2009, pp. 95, 99.
58   Rusche and Kirchheimer 2009, pp. 131 et sq.; Rusche and Kirchheimer 1981, pp. 131 et sq., 135.
59   Rusche and Kirchheimer 2009, p. 134.
60   Rusche and Kirchheimer 2009, pp. 135 et sq.
61   Rusche and Kirchheimer 2009, p. 132. Beaumont and Tocqueville had considered the application of the 'productive' US model to Europe problematic in 1833 because of the poverty of the working class: due to the lack of workers and the high wages in the USA there is no danger that the prison labour threatens free labour; the low wage level in Europe on the other hand creates a fatal competition, in which the prison enterprises have the advantage that with worse economic situation the state must pay for the maintenance of the prisoners (Beaumont and Tocqueville 1836b, 108–11; cf. Rusche and Kirchheimer 2009, p. 112).

Due to higher real wages and the stronger participation of the workers in mass consumption there is a general decrease in criminal offenses,[62] and in view of the 'maximum absorption of labor power' the 'senseless imprisonment of individuals ... is out of step with the times'.[63] Reformers (for example Liszt in Germany, Prins in Belgium) develop a 'sociological' approach, according to which crime is primarily to be fought using socio-political measures.[64] The goal should be through fines, probationary sentences and removal of the social ills, to remove as many delinquents from the prisons as possible, as well as to reduce the duration and severity of the sentences.[65] The conditions in the prisons did in fact become more bearable: the suicide and the death rate declined, and from 1882 to 1932 an increase of the fines in approximately 50 percent of the theft and fraud cases is registered.[66]

The nuanced investigation by Rusche and Kirchheimer has among other things the advantage of allowing characteristics of the fascist penal system to become visible. In the economic crisis of 1929–33 the prisons are again occupied to capacity.[67] At the same time, when the Nazi government waives the rule of law and again makes massive use of the death penalty the prison sentences increase in number and duration; the living conditions in the prisons worsen rapidly; the approaches to professional training and rehabilitation are dropped.[68] The Nazi propaganda against the 'Weimar prison paradise' is a component of a racist accentuation and intensification of the 'moral' distinction between the 'poor but honest' and the criminals – an intensification which Rusche and Kirchheimer call 'ideology construction'.[69] The moralising accompanies the elimination of sociological approaches from criminal procedure: the 'Gerichtshilfe' (court assistance), which in the Weimar Republic had supplied the court with information about the social environment and the personal history of the delinquents, is partly suppressed, partly subordinated directly under the public prosecutor's office – the crimes are isolated from their social basis and treated as betrayal of the community.[70] The culpable individual is not to be measured based on the average human being, but

---

62   Rusche and Kirchheimer 2009, pp. 138 et sq.
63   Rusche and Kirchheimer 2009, p. 140.
64   Rusche and Kirchheimer 2009, pp. 140 et sq., 143.
65   Rusche and Kirchheimer 2009, pp. 145 et sq.
66   Rusche and Kirchheimer 2009, pp. 147 et sq., 166.
67   Rusche and Kirchheimer 2009, p. 177.
68   Rusche and Kirchheimer 2009, pp. 185–91.
69   Rusche and Kirchheimer 2009, pp. 182 et sqq.
70   Rusche and Kirchheimer 2009, pp. 183 et sqq.

according to an 'ideal picture which has been constructed' of the 'strong-willed Volksgenosse'.[71]

The periodisation proposed by Rusche and Kirchheimer has been confirmed on the whole in the literature on the social history of the penal system.[72] However, the authors overlooked, as did later Foucault, the 'racialisation of prisons' in the USA after the abolishment of slavery, whereby primarily in the South the white prison population was replaced by a disproportion of black prisoners.[73] Michelle Alexander has traced a continuous line of racist oppression stretching from the convict lease system during the Jim Crow era and the road crew system (chain gangs) to the 'New Jim Crow' of neoliberalism's incarceration system.[74] Racial oppression is at the same time a form of class oppression: the modern US prison system does not target African Americans equally as such (as during Jim Crow), but rather specifically the poorest and most precarious segments of black communities.[75] What is needed, then, is an approach that accounts for the 'overdetermination' of class and race relations, which are in turn overdetermined by political and ideological transformations.[76]

Some scholars have therefore raised the objection that Rusche/Kirchheimer's correlation between punishment and the labour market is insufficient for the explanation of the non-profitable prison systems, and that it underestimates the role of the state and the relative autonomy of the political.[77] Dario Melossi argued that instead of correlating the penal system to the actual number of unemployed, the function of the prison system should be correlated to the living conditions of the working class in general: that is, to declining wages, increased pressures at the workplace, increased levels of inequality, the weakening of trade unions, and so on. With these modifications, Melossi argues,

71 Rusche and Kirchheimer 2009, pp. 184 et sq. On the significance of the intensive articulation of the role model [Vor-bild] in fascism, cf. W.F. Haug (1986, pp. 146 et sqq.).

72 Cf. for France, above all the study of J.-G. Petit (1990) as well as the anthologies he published (1984 and 1991). The approach of Rusche and Kirchheimer is continued and developed further among others by the study of Melossi and Pavarini (1981) and in Germany by the work of Steinert and Treiber. For particular historical objections see Steinert and Treiber (1978) and Schumann (1981, pp. 68 et sq.).

73 The 'racialisation of prisons' takes place for example, through Black Codes, which already imposed prison sentences for 'loitering' and work absenteeism (James 1996, p. 33). 'The abolition of slavery ... corresponded to the authorization of slavery as punishment' (Angela Davis 1998, p. 99).

74 Alexander 2001, pp. 188 et sqq.

75 Cf. Forman (2012, pp. 131–6) and Reed (2013, pp. 52–4).

76 Cf. Rehmann 2015b, p. 308.

77 Steinert 1981, pp. 324, 328. Cf. Melossi and Pavarini 1981, p. 17, Schumann 1981, pp. 72, 76.

the model of Rusche and Kirchheimer is still useful if applied to long cycles of roughly fifty years.[78]

Karl Schumann has argued that Rusche and Kirchheimer's approach cannot be reduced to a 'job market thesis'. Including the essays of Rusche, he has made distinctions between a 'degradation thesis', a 'job market thesis' and a 'fiscal thesis'.[79] The latter refers to the obligation of the penal institutions to finance themselves and their expenses as far as possible through the optimal use of prisoner employment (for example through a private contract system). The degradation thesis is described by Rusche as a 'formal' principle, according to which the prison must fall below the living conditions of the poorest proletarian layers in the society in order to function as a deterrent.[80] The ideological production of subjects who voluntarily submit themselves to a dominant order can only function when it is framed by a repressive-deterring treatment of the 'bad' subjects who refuse such subordination. The labour market thesis says nothing more than that high unemployment favours a predominantly repressive deterrence system, while a shortage of workers has effects in the direction of economic exploitation.[81] The general correlation is modified by the respective socio-political regulation. Thus, for example, Rusche elaborates that in Europe after the First World War the criminalisation of the lowest layers was retarded by an extensive unemployment welfare scheme, so that the prison numbers did not rise over the level of pre-war times; in reverse, it was the lack of this kind of social programme that in the USA during the world economic crisis led to a 'dramatic collapse of the humane penal system', with a rapid increase in crime, repression and prison revolts.[82]

As soon as one looks beyond Kirchheimer's introduction, on which Foucault bases his entire interpretation, one sees that the implicit theory of the historical chapters, as well as the corresponding essays by Rusche, are not by any means reductionist. This is shown in the careful differentiation both of the genealogy of the prison (penitentiary and church) and its contradictory functions (deterrence, exploitation, 'improvement'). It also becomes clear to what extent the position of prison work was dependent on the political influence of the labour movement, which usually demanded its prohibition. In any case, the weakness of the study is not that it grasps the relationship of mode of produc-

---

78   Melossi 2008, pp. xxv–xxxii.
79   Schumann 1981, pp. 66 et sq.
80   Rusche 1933, pp. 301 et sq.
81   Rusche 1933, pp. 303 et sq.
82   Rusche 1933, pp. 310 et sq., 312 et sq.

tion and penitentiary system as 'strict correlation', as Foucault claims.[83] It is of course true that in 1939 the authors did not have the analytic equipment at their disposal to elaborate the state-theoretical and ideology-theoretical implications of their approach. The attractiveness of the Foucauldian approach consists not least in occupying this gap.

3   Advancement or Abandonment of a Social History of the Penitentiary System?

3.1   *From Function to Aspects of Functioning*

Let us begin with some aspects which can be understood as a fruitful advancement of a social history of the penitentiary system. One of them is that the prison is conceived of as part of social disciplining, which in the coordinate system of Rusche and Kirchheimer does not emerge as its own topic. Melossi and Pavarini, who try to combine both approaches, give Foucault credit for working out discipline as a 'functional connection' between prison and factory.[84] A further strength lies in his interest in the forms and material arrangements of disciplining. Where Rusche and Kirchheimer asked the prison about its social *functions*, Foucault concentrates on aspects of its *functioning*: public enactments, spatial arrangements, visual perspectives, temporal structuring, modes of subjecting and subject constitution. According to Loïc Wacquant, Foucault is right when he insists that the penal system does more than 'repress', that it is also 'productive' in the sense that it engenders 'new categories and discourses, novel administrative bodies and government policies, fresh social types and associated forms of knowledge across the criminal and social welfare'.[85] What the prison 'produces', is, for example, disciplined subjects who are shaped by a specific interweaving of usefulness and subjection (docilité-utilité).[86] And it produces the field of a 'delinquency' which represents the complementary counterpart to the moralising of the lower classes in the nineteenth century:

---

83   Foucalt 1995, p. 25; Foucault 1975, p. 33.
84   According to Melossi, 'the functional connection between the prison and the factory is made in the concept of *discipline*', and Foucault shows convincingly that the production of the individual as labour-power is a 'bodily' process (Melossi 1979, pp. 91 et sq.). In the prison it is not so much a matter of the production of goods, but about the 'production of subjects for an industrial society ... the production of proletarians by the enforced training of prisoners in factory discipline' (Melossi and Pavarini 1981, p. 144).
85   Wacquant 2016, p. 121; Wacquant 2009b, p. 295.
86   Foucault 1995, pp. 136 et sq.; Foucault 1975, p. 161.

the 'decent' workers need to be split off from 'social banditry' and the lumpen-proletariat in general.[87]

But whereas Rusche and Kirchheimer are concerned to reconstruct the prison historical-sociologically in connection with the relations of force in the labour market and social politics, Foucault accords it the significance of an 'elementary form of the disciplinary society'.[88] To be explained is nothing less than the comprehensive social disciplining of modern bodies, the development of the modern 'scientific-legal complex' with a new universalistic 'system of truth', the common 'matrix' of criminal law and human sciences, as well as 'a piece of the genealogy ... of the modern "soul"'.[89] From the birth of the prison we arrive at the 'birth to man as an object of knowledge for a discourse with a "scientific" status',[90] which Foucault had already decribed in the *Order of Things* for the same period. Discipline directly 'produces' 'individuals' and an 'individuality' which is cell shaped, organic, evolutionaryand combinatorial.[91]

It is above all this grandiose explanatory claim which lent to the book the fascination of a 'major coup'. As soon as we compare Foucault's 'holistic' claim with the preceding 'de-totalising' tendencies in Marxism, we can see that this reception is not without paradoxes: after Althusserianism and other strands of Marxist ideology-theory set out to criticise the 'derivations' of (state) power from the economy as a Hegelianising thinking of an 'expressive totality' and to concentrate on the relative autonomy of the ideological instances, Foucault seemed to have found a way to unite the different functional levels of the society from the architecture of 'panopticism' up to the 'innermost' of the individual, as it were at one blow. Add to this the fact that this derivation is accompanied by the rhetoric of a decentralised 'micro-physics of power' with multiple lines of descent, which seems to weaken any suspicion of a new reductionism.

3.2   A Neo-Nietzschean Framework

In 1978, in a discussion with historians, Foucault explained that with *Discipline and Punish* he wanted to take up once again the topic of Nietzsche's *Genealogy of Morality*.[92] This brought him the accusation that he had written a 'philo-

---

87   Foucault 1995, pp. 255 et sq., 276 et sq., 283 et sqq.; Foucault 1975, pp. 295 et sqq., 323 et sq., 330 et sqq.
88   Breuer 1986, p. 61.
89   Foucault 1995, pp. 22 et sq., 28; Foucault 1975, pp. 30 et sq., 38.
90   Foucault 1995, p. 24; Foucault 1975, p. 32.
91   Foucault 1995, pp. 167, 170, 192 et sq.; Foucault 1975, pp. 196, 200, 225 et sq.
92   Foucault 2000, p. 224; Foucault 2001b, Nr. 278, p. 840. Already in 1975, with the publica-

sophical book' that used the historical material only as illustration, in order to apply Nietzsche's derivation of morality from the mnemonics of physical punishment to the development of modern disciplines.[93] In the second part of the *Genealogy of Morals* Nietzsche had based the development of 'conscience' and 'guilt' on the mnemonics of the torture marks which are burned into the body of the insolvent debtor. Only in this way was it possible to stamp a memory into this '[savage mind] ... incapable of grasping or retaining anything'.[94] The derivation of the 'crucible of moral concepts' from the 'delight' of the powerful ones, 'de faire le mal pour le plaisir de le faire' is, as we have seen (see above Chapter 1.3), tied into the myth of aristocratic origin, which ontologises the relationship between creditor and debtor as the 'oldest and most basic personal relationship'.[95]

Similarly, in Foucault's representation of the 'torture spectacles' the sovereign power is characterised by the compulsory burning of the 'mark'. The punishment must mark the victim: 'by the scar it leaves on the body ... [it] must brand the victim with infamy; ... it traces ... on the body of the condemned signs that must not be effaced. In any case, men will remember public exhibition'.[96] The punishment ritual is the function of a power which would 'exert itself directly on bodies', which was 'exalted and strengthened by its physical manifestations' and was 'not entirely unconnected with the functions of war'.[97] As we have seen, Foucault calls this derivation of power from war the 'hypothesis of Nietzsche', which he elaborates in his lecture course in 1976, *Society Must Be Defended*.[98] He consistently follows Nietzsche's argumentation that punishment is not to be derived from any usefulness (e.g. deterrence), nor from revenge, but rather from a 'will to power' and to 'greater power'.[99] It is not a

tion of *Discipline and Punish*, he had written that if he were ambitious he would place his work under the title *The Genealogy of Morals* (Foucault 1980, p. 53; Foucault 2001a, Nr. 156, p. 1621).

93   Melossi and Pavarini 1981, p. 192.
94   Nietzsche 2013a, p. 46; Nietzsche 1999a, Vol. 5, p. 297.
95   Nietzsche 2013a, pp. 50 et sqq., 56 et sqq.; Nietzsche 1999a, Vol. 5, pp. 299 et sqq., 305 et sq.
96   Foucault 1995, pp. 34, 131; Foucault 1975, pp. 44, 155. Cf. on these and other parallels with Nietzsche's *Genealogy of Morals* e.g. Geiss (1993, pp. 37 et sqq.).
97   Foucault 1995, p. 57; Foucault 1975, p. 69.
98   Foucault 2003c, p. 16; Foucault 1997b, p. 17.
99   Nietzsche 2013a, pp. 62 et sqq.; Nietzsche 1999a, Vol. 5, pp. 313 et sqq. Nietzsche polemicised in this context primarily against Dühring, who derived the conceptions of law including the ideas of a transcendental justice from a retaliation impulse, 'which in its heightened form is called revenge. The sense of justice is substantially a resentment, a reactive feeling, i.e. it belongs with the revenge to the same class of feelings' (Dühring 1865, p. 219; cf. pp. 20, 71 et sq.).

matter of the re-establishment of an equilibrium, nor about the superiority of the law, but about the 'physical strength of the sovereign beating down upon the body of his adversary and mastering it'.[100] The central role of the confession points to the connection between power and the artfully regulated finding of the truth, which like a kind of 'duel' [une sorte de joute] is carried out between the executioner and the tortured.[101]

In fact, Foucault's *Discipline and Punish* can be read in parts as an application of the Nietzschean critique of civilisation to modern historical material. Also for Nietzsche it was a matter of a genealogy of the 'soul', which he locates where the strong man, 'imprisoned by the strictures imposed upon him by society to establish and preserve peace', can no longer discharge his instincts outside, but must turn inward.[102] The 'soul', like the bad conscience which accompanies it, is a symptom of the 'animal-man ... scared back into himself'.[103] Where Nietzsche treats the 'soul' as a side-effect of the taming of the 'strong' man, for Foucault the 'modern soul' appears as an effect of its subjection to the disciplines which in the seventeenth and eighteenth century became 'general formulas of domination'.[104] The great taming of humanity, which Nietzsche saw carried out in the dim and distant past, so to speak, in the 'transvaluation' from an aristocratically conceived, sovereign master's origin, to both the Greek polis democracy and to Judaism, is now transferred into the era of the emergence of bourgeois democracies. Here, in the transition from the eighteenth to the nineteenth centuries, more exactly between 1760 and 1840, a 'great transformation' occurs,[105] in which the public torture spectacle disappears and is replaced by a punishment which is to become 'the most hidden part of the penal process'.[106]

For Nietzsche life on earth was 'more cheerful' when 'mankind' (that is, the minority of the 'strong ones', who are of course male as well) was not yet ashamed of its cruelty, whereas with the introduction of the bad conscience a 'pathological coddling [Verzärtlichung]' began, under which modern society suffers until today.[107] Similarly, Foucault attacks a humanism which interprets the end of the torture spectacles as a 'progress' of humaneness, whereby in his

---

100   Foucault 1995, p. 49; Foucault 1975, p. 60.
101   Foucault 1995, p. 41; Foucault 1975, p. 51.
102   Nietzsche 2013a, p. 70, Nietzsche 1999a, Vol. 5, pp. 321 et sq.
103   Nietzsche 2013a, p. 92, Nietzsche 1999a, Vol. 5, p. 332.
104   Foucault 1995, p. 137; Foucault 1975, p. 161.
105   Foucault 1995, p. 15; Foucault 1975, p. 22.
106   Foucault 1995, pp. 9, 11 et sqq.; Foucault 1975, pp. 16, 18 et sqq.
107   Nietzsche 2013a, p. 53; Nietzsche 1999a, Vol. 5, p. 302.

view it concerns only a refinement of punishing power, which can now anchor itself 'down to the finest grain of the social body'.[108]

It is above all the project of applying the *Genealogy of Morals* to modernity that motivates Foucault to divide his historical investigation into two parts. Whereas Rusche and Kirchheimer distinguish between various phases and manifestations of corporal punishment, forced labour and prison, Foucault draws the different varieties together into a single 'great transformation' in the transition from the eighteenth to the nineteenth century. This lets history fall apart into one epoch prior, characterised by sovereign power, and one afterwards, characterised by disciplinary power. In both penal systems the body stands at the centre. Previously it is publicly tormented, afterwards subjected to a 'political anatomy' of body-disciplining – the short intermediate period of the 'ideologists', whose reform suggestions aimed directly at the 'soul', is practically without consequences and soon replaced by the prison system.[109]

According to Foucault, Rusche and Kirchheimer treated only the 'general and in a sense external reasons' (des raisons en quelque sorte externes) for the changes in the penal system, whereas he himself treats the 'function' of the punishments from a 'political economy of the body' and a respective truth/power relation which 'lies at the heart of all mechanisms of punishment'.[110] With this body/truth/power nexus, which already appears in the writing on Nietzsche from 1971,[111] Foucault believes himself to have found an 'internal' level of investigation. In the following is to be observed how the Nietzschean perspective affects the Foucauldian selection and arrangement of the socio-historical material. We focus both on the ideal-typical construction of Foucault's subject-matter and on the socio-economic and ideology-theoretical references from which he abstracts.

3.3   *The Abstraction from Forced Labour*

Foucault's exclusive fixation on the torture spectacles of the 'sovereign power' is already questionable, because this was no more than a visible demonstration and a relatively small part of the absolutist penal system. Foucault describes the terror that was staged for deterrence, and thereby takes note of a precarious ambivalence of state violence which, among other things, could easily lead, in the crisis of hegemony of the Ancien Régime, to the spectators taking the side

---

108   Foucault 1995, pp. 77, 80 et sqq.; Foucault 1975, pp. 93, 96 et sqq.
109   Foucault 1995, pp. 102 et sq.; Foucault 1975, p. 122.
110   Foucault 1995, p. 55; cf. pp. 25 et sq.; Foucault 1975, pp. 66 et sq., cf. pp. 33 et sq.
111   Cf. Foucault 2003b, pp. 356 et sq., 359 et sq.

of the victims.[112] As McNally confirms, 'rather than solemn rituals that impress the lower classes with the gravity of the law, public hangings had become occasions for turbulent displays of solidarity with the condemned by thousands of the London poor'.[113]

However, Foucault lets himself become fascinated to such an extent by the cruel torture spectacles of the 'sovereign power' and the 'physical force' exposed in them that he does not investigate its position in the overall system of punishments. Excluded are first of all the galley punishments, which in absolutist France were widespread at that time. They were 'royalised' in the seventeenth century under Louis XIV and Colbert and organised by the state: e.g. by means of forced slave purchase around the Mediterranean and at the Black Sea (les 'Turcs et Mores'), through the targeted persecution of the salt and tobacco smugglers, as punishment for deserting soldiers and protestants.[114] The galley punishments were abolished in 1748, but the hard labour is resumed in the punishment camps [bagnes], which were used in the seaside cities under the command of the navy for the building of ships and in the extension of harbour installations.[115]

It seems that Foucault refrains from considering the organisation of forced labour because it documents a continuity in the penal system right where he tries to establish a sharp break between old sovereign power and the new disciplinary power. The *bagnes* were not abolished in 1791 by the National Constituent Assembly because through intense lobbying the navy succeeded in maintaining its monopoly without any parliamentary control. Due to a Jacobin amnesty for smugglers and petty criminals, the number of forced labourers is reduced for a short time, but the Thermidor of 1795 reverses the trend through the inclusion of lesser offenders and vagabonds.[116] Around the middle of the

---

112   The public execution was 'suspected of being in some way linked with [the crime]' and becomes the hearth 'in which violence bursts again into flame' (Foucault 1995, p. 9; cf. pp. 57 et sqq., 74, 89). For illustration Foucault contrasts a failed execution at the end of the seventeenth century in Avignon, in which an angry crowd freed the condemned and strangled the hangman, with a 'clean' execution in 1775 in Paris, in which the theatrical aspect disappeared and soldiers effectively kept the people at a distance (Foucault 1995, pp. 63 et sqq.).

113   McNally 2011, p. 17. Cf. his analysis of the common practice of having the executed bodies dissected by surgeons for the purpose of anatomic research, the 'interconnection of power and knowledge', and the violent struggles about the corpses (ibid., pp. 18 et sqq.).

114   Cf. Zysberg (in Petit 1991, pp. 90 et sqq., 96 et sqq.). From 1680 to 1715 altogether 38,000 prisoners were sent to Marseille (Petit 1991, pp. 97 et sq.).

115   Cf. Zysberg, in Petit (1991, pp. 175 et sqq., 199 et sqq.).

116   According to Zysberg, between 1795 and 1812 the number rises from 4,000 to more than 10,000 (in Petit 1991, p. 194).

nineteenth century, the *bagnes* become unproductive through the introduction of new technologies in ship and harbour construction, but the forced
labour is continued – likewise under the command of the navy – in the form of
extensive deportations primarily to Guyana and New Caledonia up until their
abolition by the *Front Populaire* in 1938.[117]

In order to demonstrate the transition from the torturing spectacles to the
secret punishments of the disciplinary power, Foucault contrasts the 'chain-
gang', with which the prisoners were led chained through the cities and villages
of France, with the covered police van which replaced them around 1837.[118]
On a symbolic level it certainly makes sense to point out different 'econom-
ies' of the public representation of state power. But it would be a fallacy to
take the observed differences in the presentation of power for those of the
actual exercise of power in the execution of sentences. Ultimately, the prisoners in both transportation variants are brought to the same port cities to work
there in 'penal camp workshops' [bagne-arsenal], which function as integral
components of a large state enterprise – under quite profitable conditions and
frequently together with free workers.[119] Here Foucault could have easily found,
in addition to the old punishment instruments (chains, branding etc.), technologies of disciplining: not as manifestations of a diffusely enforcing new
'disciplinary power', but organised by a centralistic state apparatus; guaranteed
by a hierarchical military surveillance staff, which primarily in the Restoration
period is built up anew; maintained both by the direct violence of physical punishment as well as through more 'modern' means of the work premium as well
as differentiation according to achievement.[120]

3.4   *A Narrowed-Down Genealogy of the Prison*

That Foucault omitted the work houses and penitentiaries from his genealogy
of the prison is all the more surprising because in 1961 he himself in *Madness
and Civilisation* had treated the Hôpital Général in Paris as one of the answers to
the economic crisis in Europe.[121] As did Rusche and Kirchheimer, he analysed
the meaning for the labour market there – 'cheap manpower in the periods of
full employment and high salaries; and in periods of unemployment, reabsorp-
tion of the idle and social protection against agitation and uprisings'[122] – and

---

117   Cf. Pierre, in Petit (1991, pp. 231 et sqq., 256 et sq.).
118   Foucault 1995, p. 264; Foucault 1975, p. 308.
119   Cf. Zysberg in Petit (1991, pp. 194, 201 et sqq., 208 et sqq.).
120   Cf. Zysberg in Petit (1991, pp. 201, 204 et sq., 206, 208 et sq.).
121   Foucault 1965, pp. 49 et sqq.; Foucault 1961, pp. 77 et sqq.
122   Foucault 1965, p. 51; Foucault 1961, p. 79.

showed that compulsory labor was enforced at the same time in the form of a 'moral reform'.[123] To analyse the penitentiary as a combination of incarceration, forced labour and moral practice in the discipline of bourgeois wage labour is of course not new in the socio-historical literature. When Marx, for example in his chapter on the so-called 'primitive accumulation of capital' describes the 'bloody legislation' against the expropriated since the fifteenth century, the penitentiary – in addition to whipping, branding, galley work and executions – plays an important role in the apparatus of force used for the development of early capitalistic relations of production.[124] As the executive institution of the 'laws grotesquely terrible' against begging and vagrancy, it contributes to the adaptation of the pauperised former peasants to 'the discipline necessary for the wage system' – they are 'compelled to sell [their labour power] voluntarily'.[125]

By positioning the 'birth' of the prison in the transition to the nineteenth century, Foucault 'either missed the topic or gave the book a misleading subtitle', argue Treiber and Steinert.[126] Because in reality it was not about a 'birth' of the prison, but its 'acknowledgment by the judicial system'.[127] Whereas the work houses and penitentiaries had contained a heterogeneous mass of the impoverished, now criteria of legal punishment are implemented, according to which the prisoners were defined and sentenced as legal subjects. On the basis of this distinction, which was also proposed by other authors,[128] Foucault's thesis of a 'birth' of the prison in the nineteenth century can be justified in a paradoxical way only with the juridical argument of a new 'legality', which since the French Revolution is tied – at least as a claim – to the 1791 declaration of human rights. However, Foucault would reject this kind of 'legalistic' distinction since he considers the idea of 'progress' in the area of the rule of law to be a humanist misunderstanding of a refined power strategy.[129] On the other hand,

---

123   Foucault 1965, p. 60; Foucault 1961, p. 87.
124   Marx 1867, pp. 723 et sqq.; Marx and Engels 1957-, Vol. 23, pp. 762 et sqq.
125   Marx 1867, p. 726; Marx and Engels 1957-, Vol. 23, p. 765. Marx compares the 'ideal workhouse' for paupers with the factory (Marx 1867, pp. 281 et sq.; Marx and Engels 1957-, Vol. 23, pp. 292 et sq.). Cf. on the connection of compulsory labour and moralising, among others Sachße and Tennstedt (1986, p. 20) und Stekl (1986, pp. 119, 122 et sqq.).
126   Treiber and Steinert 1980, p. 82.
127   Treiber and Steinert 1980, pp. 89 et sq.
128   Cf. Nicole Castan in Petit (1991, pp. 58 et sq.).
129   Habermas criticises a series of one-sided abstractions, with which Foucault separates the penal jurisdiction first from the development of the constitutional state, then, while refraining from the general criminal procedural law, narrows it to the penal system and with this blends out again the aspects of juridification, so that finally all tendencies for increasing legal security are eliminated (Habermas 1985, pp. 290 et sqq.).

since he tries to demonstrate that civil liberties are dependent on the 'sub-structure' of disciplines, which in the 'foundation' [sous-sol] of formal juridical liberties guarantees the submission of bodies,[130] he would have to substantiate the new quality of the prisons as opposed to the penitentiary with regard to their disciplinary techniques. This is exactly what he does not do, because this kind of comparison would call into question both his 'birth'-thesis as well as his ideal-typical succession of sovereign and disciplinary power.

In Foucault's representation both the juridical differences between prison and penitentiary and their functional commonalities are faded out and covered over by the dichotomy of 'torture spectacle' and modern physical disciplin-ing. He designs his neo-Nietzschean concept of 'genealogy' in such a way that in the name of the 'coincidental', 'event-typical', 'discontinuous', a historical-critical reconstruction of historical connections is omitted.[131] It is methodically misleading to put the prison into relationship with all possible institutions for punishment, just not with the one that represents its precursor and functional equivalent.[132] What would Foucault's new power technology look like if he had compared the educational discourses of the prison directors with the no less pedagogical discourses of the penitentiary directors, instead of opposing it to the tortures of the executioner?

Whereas Rusche and Kirchheimer reconstruct the development of the prison both from the disciplining apparatuses of forced labour and from the solitary confinement practice of the Catholic Church, Foucault presents a narrowed-down prison genealogy, which, especially with the penitentiary, excludes the obvious functions of intimidating the 'dangerous classes' and for-cing them into a new factory discipline. These dimensions are not ended with the fall of the penitentiary, but pervade in different proportions also the his-tory of the modern prison up to and including the current manifestations of neoliberal hyper-incarceration.

3.5   Foucault's Elimination of Contradictions

The problem does not lie in the fact that Foucault would not mention the house of correction in *Discipline and Punish*, but that he does this in a way which makes Rusche and Kirchheimer's distinctions between penitentiary labour

---

130   Foucault 1995, p. 222; Foucault 1975, pp. 258 et sq.
131   Cf. Foucault 2003b, pp. 356, 360 et sqq., 365 et sq.
132   'The penitentiary cannot be considered as the successor to public executions', notes Spier-enburg (1984, p. 206), who also rejects Foucault's thesis that the ordeals and the pub-lic character of the punishment disappeared within a short time: 'Both elements slowly retreated in a long, drawn-out process over several centuries'. (Spierenburg 1984, p. VIII).

and prison sentence disappear. Thus, for example, he begins his listing of successful penal sentencing models with the Rasphuis penitentiary in Amsterdam, opened in 1596, which '[was intended] for beggars and young malefactors' and was based on the principle of common work.[133] The Maison de Force of Gent follows, in which the work is organised according to 'economic imperatives'.[134] Next he covers the 'English model' adopted by the prison in Gloucester, which 'adds on' isolation to the work principle as an essential condition.[135] However, the expression 'add on' (ajouter) proves misleading when reading on, because the underlying programme of 1775, formulated by Hanway, turns expressly against common work, because it would transform the prison too much into a manufactory, and promotes the single cell, which is then combined with the economically unreasonable solitary confinement work at the 'treadmill'.[136] Along these lines lies also the 'machine for altering minds' of the Philadelphia model.[137] After Foucault completes his enumeration of the different incarceration concepts, he summarises the difference loosely under the term 'reformatories', introduced by Hanway, or the 'apparatus of corrective penalty'.[138] So not only is a historical break glossed over, but also a functional contradiction which will shape the further development of the prison.

Foucault applies a similar method when he touches upon the difference between the single cell system of the Philadelphia model and the prison 'factory' of the Auburn model.[139] It is already misleading that both are discussed under the classification 'principle of isolation'.[140] According to Foucault, the optimal implementation of this principle was the sole topic of debate over Auburn and Philadelphia.[141] The information is surprising because Foucault in the following works out the opposition in part quite appropriately – and in agreement with Rusche and Kirchheimer: in Auburn it is a matter of a 'unification of the individuals from above' with the goal to 'rehabilitate the criminal as a social individual', in the solitary cell of Pennsylvania 'the only operations of correction were the conscience and the silent architecture that confronted it',

---

133   Foucault 1995, p. 120 et. sq.; Foucault 1975, p. 142.
134   Foucault 1995, p. 121; Foucault 1975, p. 143.
135   Foucult 1995, p. 122; Foucault 1975, p. 144.
136   Foucault 1995, pp. 122 et sq.; Foucault 1975, pp. 145 et sq.
137   Foucault 1995, p. 125; Foucault 1975, p. 148.
138   Foucault 1995, pp. 126, 128; Foucault 1975, pp. 150, 152.
139   Rusche and Kirchheimer 2009, p. 130.
140   Foucault 1995, p. 236; Foucault 1975, p. 274.
141   Foucault 1995, pp. 237 et sq.; Foucault 1975, p. 275.

here the 'myths of resurrection' are revived – 'Auburn was society itself reduced to its bare essentials', Pennsylvania was 'life annihilated and begun again'.[142]

Despite the speech prohibition maintained in the Auburn system a 'unification from above' is certainly not the same as solitary confinement, which according to Rusche/Kirchheimer meant for most convicts 'only illness, lunacy, and agony'.[143] Disregarding the debates about the profitability of the prisons, Foucault ends the section with a summary that buries the differences again: the 'heart of the debate' and 'primary objective' is 'coercive individualisation, by the termination of any relation that is not supervised by authority or arranged according to hierarchy'.[144] This is, however, an over-generalised description, which would probably apply to all punishing apparatuses and most educating apparatuses of the nineteenth century.

We can observe a peculiar argumentation that transforms complex and contradictory fields into prison 'principles', which are then added to each other. That which in the Philadelphia-Auburn debates was disputed, namely *labour*, functions as a second prison 'principle', and does this in a manner that avoids any qualitative specification. 'Whether it is a question of forced labour, reclusion or imprisonment, it [labour] is conceived, by the legislator himself, as necessarily accompanying it'.[145] Behind the abstraction of work in itself and its 'necessity', the functional differences not only disappear (for example profit, wage dumping, deterrence, punishment, rehabilitation), but also the concrete kinds of work and labour conditions which could possibly decide between life and death: for example, whether the prisoners draining a swamp are worked to death, whether they become dulled through senseless 'punishment' on the treadmill, or receive professional training which could make a new existence after release possible for them, is not considered in Foucault's argumentation.

In general, the material presented is stronger than the theoretical evaluation. Thus, for example, Foucault reports that a glove manufacturer, who wanted to establish a workshop around 1845 in the prison of Clairvaux, was prevented by the (free) workers of his manufactory by force; the worker newspapers fear a reconverting of the prison into a penitentiary (the old 'Hôpital General'), which, with the labour input of beggars and unemployed persons, would undermine the minimum standards of free wage labour; against this, govern-

---

142   Foucault 1995, pp. 238 et sq.; Foucault 1975, pp. 276 et sq.
143   Rusche and Kirchheimer 2009, p. 137. In Paris the large single cell prison Mazas was commonly called the 'prison-tombeau' because of its high number of suicides (Petit 1991, pp. 132 et sq.).
144   Foucault 1995, p. 239; Foucault 1975, p. 278.
145   Foucault 1995, p. 240; Foucault 1975, pp. 278 et sq.

ment and administration assure us that the prison work is economically unproductive, its use has to do with the fact that it intervenes as a regulative factor 'by virtue of the effect it has on the human mechanism … it bends bodies to regular movements, it excludes agitation and distraction, it imposes a hierarchy and a surveillance'.[146]

This interpretation is also taken over by Foucault, and it is characteristic of his theoretical 'mode of production' that it can barely be distinguished where the representation of the argumentation of the prison administration ends and his own argumentation begins. The prison is not a workshop, he continues, it is 'a machine whose convict-workers are both the cogs and the products', its 'economic' effect consists simply in 'producing individuals mechanised according to the general norms of an industrial society'.[147] Supported by this metaphorical expansion of the concept of production, he comes to the conclusion that the work in the prison brings neither profit nor a 'useful skill', but only 'the constitution of a power relationship' and 'schema of individual submission' for adjustment to a production apparatus.[148]

With this definition Foucault has shut down all the contradictions that pervade the penal system on all fronts at the same time. This begins already with the premature dismissal of the profit principle. The statement that in the prison it would no longer be a matter of profit obviously confuses the calculus of private-capitalistic prisoner exploitation with the differently constituted question of the general economical productivity of the prison. Of course, work by prisoners can yield profits through the low cost of the labour, even if it drops back behind the average productivity level. Otherwise it would be incomprehensible why the private 'contract system' in the nineteenth century would become the most common prison form in the USA, which meant not least that by far the largest part of the day for the disciplining of prisoners was organised directly by the private contractor for the purpose of maximum work performance. 'The re-educative dimension … tended to be subordinated to the needs of production pure and simple, even to the point of the physical destruction of the labour force'.[149] Also in France prison work in the nineteenth century is organised on the basis of state-private contracts, which allows private entre-

---

146   Foucault 1995, p. 242; Foucault 1975, pp. 280 et sq.

147   Foucault 1995, p. 242; Foucault 1975, p. 281.

148   Foucault 1995, p. 243; Foucault 1975, p. 282.

149   Melossi and Pavarini 1981, p. 134. The 'contract system' primarily on the plantations in the south of the USA was supplemented by a 'leasing system', with which usually black prisoners were lent to a private 'contractor' for a certain period of time (Melossi and Pavarini 1981, p. 134; cf. Sullivan 1990, p. 38).

preneurs the exploitation of the workers at the lowest possible wages and leaves the implementation of a corresponding work discipline up to them.[150]

The fact that prison work in the affected sectors frequently leads to undermining the standards of free work is obviously a real problem, one that is not to be speculated out of the world with the emphasis on the subject-'production' carried out in the prison. Foucault covers up here the contradictions of the social positions, which, for example, amount to the fact that worker resistance against prison work has quite real bases and at the same time is a corporatist effort directed against the interests of the prisoners. Marx sensed this problem when he criticised the social-democratic demand for the prohibition of prison work as the 'petty fear of competition' in the *Critique of the Gotha Programme*.[151]

Also with the second claim, namely that the prison results in no 'useful skill', Foucault closed off a contested terrain at the outset. Progressive prison reform approaches, above all since the late nineteenth century, have repeatedly tried, against the primacy of deterrence and retaliation, to implement rehabilitation and professional training projects which might be of actual use for the prisoners' agency before and after their release. Even if there may be reasons to consider such requirements for reform as mostly illusory, the criticism would have to point out at which constellations they fail.[152]

That Foucault is not interested in such differences is the consequence of a conceptual framework by which he subsumes prison 'reform', without a qualitative differentiation, under the concept of 'improvement', which he lets coincide directly with that of 'individual submission'.[153] In fact, all the 'principles' with which Foucault defines the prison are oriented according to the same logic. Whether single cell or prison factory, punishing work or professional training, wage system or psychotherapy – it is always only a matter of

---

150   Cf. Petit (1991, pp. 121 et sqq.), exemplary for this, who comes to the conclusion: 'L'État libéral et ses élites dirigeantes préféraient cette organisation basée sur le privé et ses contraintes économiques, plutôt que l'interventionnisme administratif' (Petit 1991, pp. 126 et sq.).

151   Marx 1875, p. 99; Marx and Engels 1957–, Vol. 19, p. 32. In any case in a general workers programme it would have to be 'clearly stated that there is no intention from fear of competition to allow common criminals to be treated like beasts, and especially that there is no desire to deprive them of their sole means of betterment, productive labour. That was surely the least one might have expected from Socialists' (Marx 1875, p. 99; Marx and Engels 1957–, Vol. 19, p. 32).

152   Cf. e.g. Sullivan (1990, p. 40), who shows how many vocational training projects of the 1970s years failed owing to the lack of technical equipment in the prison workshops, among other things.

153   Foucault 1995, p. 234; Foucault 1975, p. 271.

'improvement', that is, about 'operating transformations on individuals'.[154] For this, he sees the prison apparatus reaching back toward three great models: 'the politico-moral schema of individual isolation and hierarchy; the economic model of force applied to compulsory work; the techno-medical model of cure and normalization. The cell, the workshop, the hospital'.[155] The procedure of a system-theoretical functionalism, for which Foucault has been criticised by very different scholars, such as Honneth and Poulantzas,[156] can be observed here in concrete execution. Whatever happens in the area of the prison is brought into the 'simultaneous system' of a normalising subject-production.[157]

3.6   The Fixation of Critique on the Social-Pedagogisation of the Penal System

The pedagogical claim to improvement is not only the aspect which Foucault takes as the basis for all 'principles', but also that which he questions the most fundamentally and sweepingly. Here above all is where he sees the ideology of humanism embodied, which interprets the transition from the torture spectacles to the hidden prison sentence as a progress of 'humaneness'. Without doubt, Foucault's criticism of humanism's self-misunderstanding derives its plausibility from the tension between humanist ideologies and the realities of the penal system. But Foucault's anti-humanist polemic is abstractly radical on one hand, and on the other uncritical.

Let's start with the latter: without scrutiny, he takes the term 'improvement', to which he attaches his critique of disciplining, from the ideological texts of the punishing apparatuses, which tend to legitimise even the most repressive punitive measures as suitable means of moralising. Because he abstains from confronting this category with the real prison practices to which it refers, he presents disciplining 'from the one-sided perspective of the administration of society', and thus 'from the bureaucratic perspective'.[158] Instead of critically deciphering the discourses of the prison ideologists, he takes them at face value and nestles his own discourse into their ideologies.

On the other hand, where Foucault criticises 'improvement', the criticism is too general to be able to grasp the different meanings of the term in disciplinary and social-pedagogical discourses. It cannot be discerned whether 'improvement' functions as a cover word for subject destruction in solitary confinement

---

154   Foucault 1995, p. 248; Foucault 1975, p. 288.
155   Foucault 1995, p. 248; Foucault 1975, p. 288.
156   Cf. for example Honneth (1991, p. 195), Poulantzas (2014, p. 68).
157   Foucault 1995, p. 271; Foucault 1975, p. 316.
158   Treiber and Steinert 1980, pp. 77, 87.

and/or in exploitative convict labour, or rather as point of reference from which such a subject destruction could be criticised. This kind of bloated criticism becomes uncritical. 'Criticise everything' is merely the flip side of 'Anything goes'.[159]

With closer inspection it becomes evident that Foucault's critique is fixated primarily on the potentially progressive social-pedagogical aspects which are important in the critique of the deterrence and exploitation functions of the prison. When Foucault defines the 'teleological' requirement of a '"useful" transformation' and reintegration of the prisoners as an essential determinant of the prison,[160] he overgeneralises a trait that needs to be historically specified. According to Rusche/Kirchheimer, this kind of 'teleologically' aligned rehabilitation could prevail in Europe against the equivalence 'justice' of the deterrence principle only in the time of the prison reforms from about 1875 to 1932.[161] This is also the time in which imprisonment declines, conditions in the prisons improve, death and suicide rates sink.[162]

We also understand now why Foucault is not interested in the oppositions between the social-pedagogically oriented approaches to prison reform on the one hand, and eugenic, proto-fascist and fascist orientations on the other hand. The 'social democratic' constellation on which he concentrates his normalisation critique is at the same time that which in Germany was denounced by the Nazis as 'Weimar prison paradise'.[163] But a critique which directs its fire at social-pedagogical rehabilitation projects and thereby overlooks their fascist abolition and replacement with the liquidation of the 'abnormal' ones and the uttermost pauperisation of the prisoners, has lost the connection to actual battle lines and proves empty.

3.7   Foucault's 'Dispositif' and the 'Political Economy' of the Body

Taking up the question of this chapter's title, namely whether or in what regard Foucault advances or abandons the insights of a social history of the penitentiary system, we can see that the yield is ambivalent. As we observed in Chapter 4.3.1., the transition from an analysis of the social function of the prison system (regarding the labour market, for example) to its 'productive' function-

---

159   Resch 1989, p. 518.
160   Foucault 1995, p. 244; Foucault 1975, p. 283.
161   Rusche and Kirchheimer 2009, pp. 138 et sqq., 143. In France the progressive projects of an 'improvement' through vocational training and therapy could not gain a foothold until the Third Republic (1875–38) (cf. Pierre, in Petit 1991, pp. 264 et sqq.).
162   Rusche and Kirchheimer 2009, p. 150.
163   Cf. Rusche and Kirchheimer 2009, p. 178, Note 4.

ing in terms of a new 'technology' has the potential to open up new areas of research that are relevant for a critical ideology-theory. One of the most inspiring aspects is expressed by Foucault's concept of 'dispositifs de normalisation' (usually mistranslated in English as 'mechanism'). By this he means institutionally fixed spatio-temporal arrangements which subjugate the subjects to the technologies of power, for instance detailed timetables, barracks, administrative buildings, hospitals, schools.[164] Indeed, Foucault's attention to spatial arrangements and temporal structuring can sharpen our perspective on the socialisation forms in repressive and ideological apparatuses, which have a structural predominance in relation to the transmitted 'contents'. The *Projekt Ideologietheorie* (*PIT*) has, therefore, proposed to adopt Foucault's concept of '*dispositif*' to designate the ideological as an 'external arrangement' of ideological powers that organise subjection and consent from 'above'.[165] But what could contribute to a fruitful extension of a critical social history is done by Foucault in a reductionist way, which falls back behind the social-historical reflection and differentiation level of Rusche and Kirchheimer.

We can observe a similar ambivalence with regard to the body. When Foucault emphasises the 'physical nature' of the disciplining of bodies,[166] he touches upon an aspect also emphasised by Bourdieu, namely that social action patterns (habitus) are not effective primarily on the cognitive-reflective level of subjects, but as 'incorporated' and thus deeply anchored dispositions.[167] But whereas Bourdieu attempts to analyse the 'incorporation' of social structures and fields,[168] Foucault tends to blend out the social determinations again. For this reason Michel Pêcheux has criticised Foucault's somatic materialism for its 'larval biologism',[169] and Étienne Balibar points out a 'vitalism' which prevents Foucault from thinking of the bodies in their class, sex, and cultural singularity as 'relations'.[170]

Despite the promising rhetoric, Foucault's attempt to overcome the merely 'external' treatment of the penitentiary system by Rusche and Kirchheimer with the assistance of a 'political economy of the body' does not bring up substantial results. This is due to the fact that he discusses the 'physicality' of punishment and disciplining primarily on the basis of ideological texts and

---

164   Foucault 1995, p. 306; cf. Foucault 1975, p. 358.
165   PIT 1979, p. 180; cf. Rehmann 2013, pp. 207 et sqq.
166   Foucault 1995, p. 26; Foucault 1975, p. 34.
167   Bourdieu 1990, pp. 68 et sqq.
168   Bourdieu 2000, pp. 169 et sqq.; cf. Beate Krais (1993, pp. 215 et sqq.) and Sünne Andresen (2001, pp. 50 et sqq.).
169   Pêcheux 2014, p. 21.
170   Balibar 1991, pp. 62 et sq.

programmes, and not on the basis of real bodily practices and patterns in the prison. Relevant information could be gathered, for example, from nourishment statistics, labour requirements, mortality rates, suicide numbers, and in particular from experience reports of the prisoners themselves. The physical immediacy of the Foucauldian body-discourse disguises the fact that it only concerns 'bodies' as far as they are represented in discourses, so that Joy James can say that Foucault shows how easy it is to evaporate the body while concentrating one's discourse on it.[171] This explains the paradox that on one hand Foucault's investigation could be attributed to a 'biologism' whose categories extract themselves from the actual social relations, and on the other hand to a 'secret idealism', which misses the real practices of the penitentiary system.[172] Eagleton speaks of a 'magical kind of materialism'[173] which indulges in an elaborate 'body talk' and elegantly omits the reality of slaving, malnourished bodies: 'For the new somatics, not any old body will do. If the libidinal body is in, the labouring body is out. There are mutilated bodies galore, but few malnourished ones'.[174]

4   The Panoptical Nucleus of the Disciplinary Society

4.1   The Panopticon as Diagram of Modern Hegemony?

The significance of Bentham's panopticon for Foucault's argumentation can hardly be overrated. Firstly, it is the 'architectonic form' in which the power techniques of the disciplines which Foucault has derived from the plague quarantines towards the end of the seventeenth century consolidate themselves and are applied to the 'space of exclusion'.[175] According to Foucault's account, the dark dungeon [cachot] with its densely packed masses of prisoners has been replaced with the single cell and its isolated prisoner-individuals, who can be seen completely from the central tower without seeing their observer. Secondly, for Foucault the panopticon completes and embodies the process in which both the individualising and normalising disciplines become 'general formulas of domination'.[176] By means of its 'endlessly generaliseable mechanism', it 'unlocks' the disciplines [désenfermer] and lets them spread out

---

171   James 1996, p. 25.
172   E.g. Treiber and Steinert 1980, pp. 77 et sq.
173   Eagleton 1996, p. 70.
174   Eagleton 1996, p. 71.
175   Foucault 1995, p. 199; Foucault 1975, pp. 232 et sq.
176   Foucault 1995, p. 137; Foucault 1975, p. 161.

diffusely, polyvalently into the entire social body.[177] It is 'the diagram of a mechanism of power reduced to its ideal form'.[178] In this capacity it serves Foucault as a connecting link between the prison and a 'disciplinary society', which he constructs as a homogeneous 'great carceral continuum'.[179]

And finally, the panopticon represents the spatial 'dispositif' in which the prisoners internalise the power relations, so that the subjected subjects become the 'principle of [their] own subjection'.[180] It is here, for example, that Foucault enters directly the area of ideology theory. In the continuous, yet mostly implicit argument with Althusser, the panopticon claims a central place in the analysis of self-subordination. Whereas the prison is conceived in Althusser's ideology theory as a component of the 'repressive state apparatus' which represents the armour of force for the work of the different 'ideological state apparatuses', in Foucault's 'panoptic' concept of power it becomes a model of modern hegemony in general.

Foucault's treatment of Bentham's model of a panopticon surely has the merit of directing attention to the disciplinary underside of a philosopher widely considered 'democratic' and 'radical', and thereby also to an important component of the bourgeois imaginary with respect to the control and moralising of the 'dangerous classes'. But I would like to show in the following that his theoretical evaluation is impaired by a problematic generalisation which smoothes out the differences between force and ideology as well as between subject production and subject destruction, and in addition is supported by an extremely selective and thus misleading reading of Bentham's panopticon writings.

4.2   The Levelling of Repressive and Consensual Socialisation

Let us begin with the passage in which Foucault explains the active internalisation of power by the individualised prisoners. Accordingly, their subjection comes from a 'fictitious relationship' which consists of the fact that they are permanently to be seen, even when they are not being directly supervised. Therefore one can 'do without the means of force': the panoptical mechanisms are amazingly 'informal', there are no lattice gates, no chains, no 'heavy locks', instead a 'simple geometry' with 'clean separations' and 'real openings'. The effectiveness of power has passed over to the 'target', as the subjects take it over, interiorise it, play it off against themselves, and make themselves into the

177   Foucault 1995, pp. 208 et sqq., 215; Foucault 1975, pp. 239 et sqq., 251.
178   Foucault 1995, p. 205; Foucault 1975, p. 239.
179   Foucault 1995, pp. 268, 297; Foucault 1995, pp. 244; 348 et sq.
180   Foucault 1995, p. 203; Foucault 1975, p. 236.

principle of their own subjection.[181] Power imposes itself no longer 'from the outside, like a heavy rigid constraint', but 'spontaneously and without noise'.[182]

This is the 'diagram' of the dis-individualised and at the same time individualising power which enables Foucault to dismiss the 'traditional' critiques of class and state domination and sexual oppression as juridical and negative 'repression theses', of which Foucault comments that 'we still have not cut off the head of the king'.[183] Obviously, the Foucauldian attempt to distinguish the new panoptical 'power' from violence is based on a very narrow concept of the direct use of physical violence. It is not to be seen why the 'architecture and geometry' of the panopticon should not be a kind of institutionalised *violence*, chiselled in stone, particularly since it is actually not possible for the prisoners to leave the institution of their own free will. Foucault seems to have forgotten that prison architecture has not only a 'geometry', but also insurmountable walls, locked doors with real locks. His thesis of the active internalisation of disciplinary power covers up a decisive difference to the 'voluntary' ideological subjection which Althusser explained by the model of a subject-constituting 'interpellation'. A 'recognition' of imposed subjection as one's 'own', self-intended, is surely not the primary effect of the Benthamian panopticon, but would be perceived by fellow prisoners and prison administration instead as a pathological misperception of reality. Those imprisoned have a clear awareness of the compulsive character of their situation, even if they may have differing opinions concerning the 'legitimacy' of the compulsion to which they are subjected. One could speak of an ideological subjection if the prisoners received keys that allowed them to leave cell and prison, but had no motivation to do this because they preferred to be 'good' prisoner subjects.

Foucault's notion that panoptical power is not perceived as an 'oppressive weight' from outside is pure fantasy. The numerous experience reports of prisoners, who describe solitary confinement as the most terrible punishment, show this.[184] Foucault's interpretation of the panoptical system as a 'dispositif' of moral subject *'production'* overlooks the fact that especially the supervised single cell has the specific purpose of destroying the (old) subject through the withdrawal of all connections to social practice and language, a procedure that in the literature is described among other things as 'self-mortification',

---

181   Foucault 1995, pp. 202 et sq.; Foucault 1975, p. 236.
182   Foucault 1995, pp. 206 et sq.; Foucault 1975, pp. 240 et sq.
183   Foucault 1978, pp. 88 et sq.; Foucault 1976a, p. 117.
184   It is again and again referred to as 'the most horrid punishment' [le plus affreux supplice] by Beaumont and Tocqueville in their collected interviews (1836b, pp. 168 et sqq.; cf. Melossi and Pavarini 1981, pp. 166 et sqq.).

'disculturation', 'desocialisation' or 'role dispossession'.[185] Through the expropriation of social embedding and of any space for oneself the individual is to be thrown back on a naked interior, in order to then produce in the de-socialised empty space inside a new subject through bible reading and pastoral ministry. This tabula rasa conception of moralisation is by no means as modern as Foucault assumes, but stands in a long religious tradition. It is also controversial in the prison literature of the nineteenth century, since instead of destroying the 'evil' in humans, the isolation often destroys the subjects' capacity to act at all (insanity or suicide). Foucault's assumption of a propagation of the panoptical disciplinary power throughout the entire society thus skips over substantial differences between enforced and consensual socialisation, subject interpellation and subject destruction.

4.3   The Real-Imaginary of the Panopticon

Foucault rests his expansion thesis directly upon Bentham's statement that his 'simple architectural idea' is independent of any concrete objective and applicable to all social institutions: 'Morals reformed, health preserved, industry invigorated, instruction diffused, public burthens lightened, economy seated as it were upon a rock, the gordian knot of the Poor-Laws not cut but untied – all by a simple idea in Architecture!'[186] However, this claim shows nothing more than Bentham's advertising strategy, with which he tries to convince the English government for 20 years to entrust him with the building and direction of a panoptical prison. His requests are finally rejected in 1813.

In order to be able to discuss Foucault's argumentation, it is important to distinguish between 'panoptism' as a general principle and Bentham's specific panopticon project: the utopia (or rather dystopia) of an installation of one-sided visibility is as old as hierarchic monitoring itself, theologically concentrated in the 'deus absconditus', who sees everything without being seen, and as the technology of power sought by rulers of all kinds.[187] However, the spe-

---

185   Cf. Goffman (1961, pp. 13 et sq.), who analyses the strategies of subject destruction among other things by the admission rituals in the prison (expropriation, stripping naked, convict clothing, change of clothing, sometimes name loss): precisely the actions are destroyed 'that in civil society have the role of attesting to the actor and those in his presence that he has some command over his world, that he is a person with, "adult" self-determination, autonomy, and freedom of action' (Goffman 1961, p. 43).

186   Bentham 1787, Vol. IV, pp. 39, cf. p. 66.

187   According to Treiber and Steinert the utopia of a knowing and punishing apparatus, which Foucault sees embodied in Bentham's Panopticon, is to a good part already implemented in early medieval monasteries, and this almost completely without separate monitoring staff (Treiber and Steinert 1980, pp. 61, 65).

cifically Benthamite Panopticon does not even materialise in the building of prisons, or is at most only very partially implemented there. Foucault's assumption that 'in the 1830s, the Panopticon became the architectural programme for most prison projects' is misleading.[188] It is correct at best (and here only partially), inasmuch as one considers 'projects' to mean *theoretical* projects. It becomes influential in theoretical concepts of punishment, debated in specialist conferences, architecture magazines, administrative measures, as well as with some exemplary buildings.[189] As J.-G. Petit has demonstrated with much material, because of cost factors it was scarcely realised in the actual building of prisons in the nineteenth century: in France the initial enthusiasm for the panoptical prison is soon replaced by the myth of the 'healthy' agricultural labour – beginning approximately 1848, the 'earth' became the central point of reference of the penal-imaginary.[190] The fact that after the French Revolution the prisoners were often placed in secularised monasteries or former penitentiaries led to an 'architectonic confusion' of new and old elements, 'un fouillis de murs, de cours, d' étages, un enchevêtrement de bâtiments anciens et nouveaux, où s' affirme la volonté d' occuper l' espace au maximum'. What was new in the development since the Restoration, from 1815 onwards, was primarily the additional establishment of the large parallel lines of the workshops.[191] Prevailing is a compromise between two different economic strategies: on one hand disposing of the prisoners in the most inexpensive manner by overcrowding the old buildings, on the other, one of adding on workshops in order to be able to occupy the prisoners as profitably as possible.[192] The director of the prison administration must admit in 1885 that the single cell system remained purely theoretical.[193]

Contrary to a widespread prejudice in the Foucauldian literature, Foucault is not dealing with the 'materiality' of the Benthamite panopticon, but rather with the *idea* of such a materiality.[194] Of course this does not mean that this 'idea' is meaningless. It shows the importance of the panopticon for the ima-

---

188   Foucault 1995, p. 249; Foucault 1975, p. 289.
189   E.g. Joliet in Illinois, La Petite-Roquette in France. Cf. Perrot 2001, pp. 85, 89, 91; Petit 1990, pp. 64, 242, 247 et sq.; Semple 2003, pp. 312 et sq.
190   Petit 1990, pp. 248 et sqq.
191   Petit 1991, pp. 127 et sq.
192   Petit 1991, pp. 128 et sq.
193   Petit 1991, pp. 133 et sq.
194   This difference is overlooked by, for example, Lemke (2019, pp. 89 et sq.), who considers Foucault's concept of power to be 'more materialistic' than that of ideology. Also with Warren Montag it looks as if Foucault had understood Althusser's thesis of the 'materiality' of the ideological better than he himself (Montag 1995, p. 75).

ginary of certain fractions of the bourgeoisie and their intellectuals. 'Imaginary' here does not mean unreal, but designates an ensemble of pictures and projections, in which conditions of reality are perceived and solutions are presented. The question is then whether Foucault's evaluation really applies to the 'real imaginary' of the panopticon. For this we must leave the text-immanent level of our analysis and use the Benthamite panopticon writings as comparison.

4.4   'Economy Ought To Be the Prevalent Consideration' (Bentham)

First of all, a central characteristic must be added, one which is not evaluated in Foucault's representation: what differentiates Bentham's system from competing models of his time, are above all the explicit principle of an almost unlimited prisoner exploitation in the contract system, and the extraordinary powers of the private contractor, for whose position Bentham applies in his requests to the government.[195] 'To come to the point at once, I would do the whole by contract. I would farm out the profits ... to him who ... offered the best term'.[196] Accordingly, the contractor is to be equipped with 'all the powers that his interest could prompt him to wish for, in order to enable him to make the most of his bargain'.[197] Here Bentham turns against the dominant legislation in England, which in his view presumes to prescribe penal work while ignoring all 'pecuniary productiveness'.[198] After all, he objects, the sense of the punishment consists precisely in that the right to freely sell their labour power is taken from the prisoners. 'The confinement ... preventing his carrying the work to another market, subjects him to a monopoly, which the contractor, his master, like any other monopolist, makes, of course, as much of as he can'.[199] Therefore Bentham rejects a legal maximum limit for prison work: 14 or 15 hours would not be too much, since one could also take the meal times into account as rest periods.[200] Economically seen, the system is only favourable because where else is there an entrepreneur 'that can reduce his workmen, if idle, to a situation next to starving, without suffering them to go elsewhere?'[201]

We can therefore see what abstractions Foucault makes use of when out of Bentham's panopticon writings he only reads a new paradigm of 'normalising'

---

195   'The contractor was the key to Bentham's scheme' (Himmelfarb 1968, p. 58). Cf. for this also Ignatieff 1978, pp. 109 et sqq., Melossi and Pavarini 1981, pp. 41 et sqq., Semple 1993, pp. 122 et sqq., 134 et sqq, Perrot 2001, pp. 77 et sq, 96, 98 et sq.
196   Bentham 1787, p. 47.
197   Bentham 1787, p. 48.
198   Bentham 1787, p. 51.
199   Bentham 1787, p. 54.
200   Bentham 1791, p. 163.
201   Bentham 1787, p. 56.

subjection. Moral 'improvement' is more a matter of rhetoric than of substance, which is expressed in the following blunt assertion: 'Economy ought, in every point of management, be the prevalent consideration'.[202] The dominance of this criterion also shows up when one compares the 'Panopticon Letters', written in 1787, with the 'Postscript' of 1791: in the letters Bentham was still of the opinion that it was possible to combine the contract system with the single cell, which is to be monitored by the panoptical installation. 'Solitude is in its nature subservient to the purpose of Reformation', he explains,[203] and also Foucault makes this claim when he characterises the cells as 'small theatres' in which 'each actor is alone, perfectly individualised and constantly visible'.[204] But in the 'Postscript' Bentham understood that the single cells were not only too expensive, but also – despite the perfect monitoring – had a negative effect on the work performance, which required the co-operation of the prisoners with each other.[205] Therefore he now suggests the enlargement of the cells so that up to four prisoners can be accommodated therein.[206] Where the economic advantage is apparent, the proof of the moral advantage is not long in showing itself: Bentham now discovers the fact that long-term solitary confinement is 'barbarian' and that instead there must be an emphasis on the ties of 'friendship, the sister of the virtues'.[207] In order to keep this 'friendship'-virtue under control, he falls back on a kind of informer system: naturally, the supervisor will assemble the prisoners in such a way 'that there may checks upon one another, not assistants, with regard to any forbidden enterprise'.[208]

However, such an enlargement of the cells for the purpose of increasing the productivity results again in making the isolating effects of the panoptical monitoring 'dispositif' emphasised by Foucault ineffective. Even the visibility would only be ensured to a limited extent. It is obviously not possible in Bentham's system to combine the contradictory requirements of intensive control, moral 'improvement' and economic productivity.[209] This inconsistency, glossed over by Foucault, also contributed to the fact that Bentham's requests to the English and French governments for the building of a panopticon (and his own appointment as 'contractor') eventually failed. Where the religious ideology of the single cell system prevails, as in England, Bentham's project is rejected with

---

202   Bentham 1791, p. 123.
203   Bentham 1787, p. 47.
204   Foucault 1995, p. 200; Foucault 1975, p. 233.
205   Bentham 1791, pp. 71, 74.
206   Bentham 1791, p. 71.
207   Bentham 1791, p. 74.
208   Bentham 1791, p. 76.
209   Cf. Melossi and Pavarini 1981, pp. 40 et sq., 46.

the reasoning that the private prisoner exploitation contradicts the desired moral improvement.[210] On the other hand, where the private contract system is practiced, one falls back rather on the whip, which is touted by Elam Lynds, an influential representative of the Auburn system, as the 'most efficient', 'most humane' and 'healthiest' form of punishment.[211]

4.5   Bentham as Visionary of 'Disciplinary Neoliberalism'

Contrary to the Foucauldian interpretation, it seems to me that the fascination of the Benthamite panopticon lies precisely in the perfection with which it is drafted as a 'mute' repressive apparatus for the profitable organisation of intensively supervised forced labour. The contract system was not only typical for the workhouse and the penitentiary, but was also the usual procedure with which, for example, the transport of slaves into the USA was organised.[212] Bentham's Panopticon writings were originally inspired by a manufactory which his brother Samuel established in the south Russian city of Krichev; Prince Potemkin Pottier wanted to make it a model of industrialisation in Russia. The problem of perfect monitoring, which Bentham wants to solve with his 'architectural idea', developed here directly in the context of the refusal of rural workers to submit to the prescribed industrial discipline. The matrix of the panopticon is a 'Russian labour camp, realised by an English engineer', notes Michelle Perrot.[213]

Contrary to the 'teleological' perspective of a reintegration into the society problematised by Foucault, Bentham thought out an ingenious system designed to hold the prisoners in despotic conditions even after their release: either they can prove themselves to have a place in the army or navy or find themselves an entrepreneur who deposits an annual endorsement of 50 pounds for 'good behaviour' (an extraordinarily large sum, which brings the former prisoner into complete dependence), or they are taken on by other 'panoptical' systems, which are operated at best by the same contractor.[214] 'A man serving even a brief sentence would be, literally, in bondage for life', notes Himmelfarb.[215]

Beyond that, in 1797 Bentham develops in his text 'Pauper Management Improved' a comprehensive plan for the internment of up to 500,000 poor

---

210   Cf. for this Ignatieff 1978, p. 112 and Perrot 2001, p. 84.
211   Cf. Beaumont and Tocqueville 1836b, p. 191.
212   Semple 2003, p. 135.
213   Perrot 2001, p. 78.
214   Bentham 1791, pp. 165 et sq.
215   Himmelfarb 1968, p. 57.

people in 250 'industry houses', which, following the model of the East India Company, are to be under the direction of a single corporation, the 'National Charity Company'.[216] The immediate goal is 'the extradition of labour to as great a value as may be';[217] beyond that it is a matter of a better regulation of the job market,[218] and the elimination of begging.[219] All persons without possessions and livelihood are to be incarcerated.[220] Every citizen is to have the right to deliver beggars to an industry house, from which they can only be released if a wealthy taxpayer vouches for them.[221] All those interned (including the children) can attain their liberty only after they have balanced the costs of their maintenance through their own work.[222]

Foucault both felt and misjudged the fascination of the Benthamite panopticon. It did not lie in the invention of a new power-diagram, detached from the principles of force and of profit, but in the promise to get the old and recurrent problem of mass pauperism under control and to solve it unnoticed as well as profitably on the basis of a modernised monitoring architecture. Bentham is the 'forerunner of the application of modern free-market ideology' in the penitentiary system, as Semple (with apologetic intention) emphasises.[223] He anticipated the privatisation tendencies such as those undertaken since the end of the 1970s in the neoliberal project of a radical dismantling of the welfare state with simultaneous forced development of a system of 'hyperincarceration'.[224] As the direct failure of Bentham's prison and workhouse plans shows, the desired connection of monitoring and productivity in the context of his 'architectonic idea' was not to be resolved convincingly. Nonetheless, panopticism in the broader sense plays a central role in 'disciplinary neoliberalism':

---

216 Bentham 1797, p. 369.

217 Bentham 1797, p. 383.

218 Bentham 1797, pp. 397 et sq.

219 Bentham 1797, pp. 401 et sq. As Polanyi observed in 1944, this is about a gigantic project to compensate capitalistic economic cycles: 'Bentham's plan amounted to no less than the levelling out of the business cycle through the commercialization of unemployment on a gigantic scale' (Polanyi 1975, p. 107).

220 Bentham 1797, p. 370.

221 Bentham 1797, pp. 401 et sq.

222 Bentham 1797, p. 382.

223 Semple 2003, p. 134.

224 In the USA, the 'Federal Prison Industries Enhancement Act' of 1979 permitted the formation of state-private 'joint ventures', under which heading can be distinguished on the one hand state 'prison industries', which sell their products only to other government agencies, and on the other hand the fast increasing purely private prison industry, which by 1999 covered seven percent of the population in detention (cf. Parenti 1999, pp. 217 et sqq., 230 et sqq.; Wacquant 2009a, pp. 58 et sqq., 80).

through the technological advancement of monitoring technologies with the assistance of video cameras, electronics and computer technologies it is possible to decouple the control power from a certain architectural form.[225]

It can now be observed how Foucault's selective and over-generalising evaluation of the historical material is reflected in his theory of disciplinary power, by which it is in return affected.

5   Foucault's Disciplinary Power in a Double-Bind between 'Microphysics' and Omnipresent 'Phagocytic Essence' (Poulantzas)

5.1   *The Hidden Contradiction*

The success story, widespread in the Foucault literature, that Foucault has overcome Marxist 'reductionism' with the assistance of a polycentric and polyform concept of power, conceals a contradiction which is characteristic of his method. On one hand, he actually introduced his concept of power, primarily in a demarcation from Althusser's 'ideological state apparatuses', as a 'microphysics' which does not have a centre of power and cannot be located in state instances, but represents a complex net of multiform processes with multiple genealogies.[226] On the other hand, there is not much more to see of the announced diversity when it comes to Foucault's explanation of a 'society penetrated through and through with disciplinary mechanisms'.[227] As soon as the new disciplinary dispositif asserts itself, its propagation functions 'uniformly' and with 'continuity';[228] the 'great carceral network' extends from the compact institutions over the charitable societies and workers' housing estates 'seamlessly' [sans rupture] into the most remote areas and penetrates the entire social body.[229] The formation of the disciplinary society exhausts itself in a 'motion of extension'.[230] It is as if the historical linearity against which Foucault introduced the Nietzschean concept of genealogy has reasserted itself behind his back.

Given this double-bind, we will focus our critique on both the theoretical inconsistency of the multiple 'micro-physics' of power and on the smoothness with which it is supposed to permeate the entire society.

225   Cf. Bakker and Gill 2003, pp. 136, 181, 188, 200, 207 et sqq.
226   Foucault 1995, pp. 26 et sq., 138, 215 et sq., 231 et sq.; Foucault 1975, pp. 34 et sq., 163, 251 et sq., 268.
227   Foucault 1995, p. 209; Foucault 1975, p. 243.
228   Foucault 1995, p. 299; Foucault 1975, p. 350.
229   Foucault 1995, pp. 298 et sq., 305; Foucault 1975, pp. 348 et sq., 355.
230   Breuer 1986, p. 61.

5.2   The Diversity of Power and the Problem of Its Accumulation

Let us begin with the first pole, a genealogy of the disciplinary power, which Foucault derives from a 'multiplicity of often minor processes, of different origin and scattered location'.[231] Foucault concentrates primarily on the disciplining of the soldier's body in the late eighteenth century and the 'analytical' monitoring system during the plague toward the end of the seventeenth century,[232] but his examples refer also to schools, colleges, hospitals, enterprises and other institutions.

That disciplines develop variously and at the most different points of a society is, first, a quite plausible assumption, and it is linked, among other things, with the ambiguity of the meaning of the word 'discipline', which originates in Latin *discere* (learn: teaching, education, instruction, training). There are the most varied disciplines, e.g. the monastery, the royal court, the guilds, as well as the urban middle class. The latter develops a set of disciplined attitudes, which both Werner Sombart and Max Weber (again differently) characterise as the 'spirit of capitalism';[233] there are the most varied attempts at a 'disciplining' of the lower classes, as well as the oppositional attempts at a 'self disciplining' in the labour movement for the purpose of a democratic self-socialisation. In authoritarian state socialism and in particular in Stalinism this changed again into despotic-hierarchical rule. Therefore 'discipline' may be defined from opposite perspectives, it is ambiguous and contested: 'Discipline can be just as revolutionary as the offence against discipline'.[234]

Against the background of such a contradictory semantic field, Foucault's stress on the multiple origins of the disciplines is both uncontested and quite pointless. He is not at all interested in the qualitative differences between the disciplines. A substantial social analysis would need to differentiate between, for example, a handicraft notion of discipline in terms of a use-value point of view, a capitalistic asceticism geared towards the accumulation of profits, and the self-organisation of social movements of subaltern classes. But Foucault's concept of anonymous, self-reproducing 'power' does not allow for any analytical distinction. Thus diversity itself becomes a rhetorical figure which does not unlock the contradictory field of the disciplines, but instead hides it.

In addition, the diversity rhetoric is incapable of explaining the proclaimed development of the disciplines into 'universal forms of domination' in the

---

231   Foucault 1995, p. 138; Foucault 1975, p. 162.
232   Foucault 1995, pp. 135 et sqq., 195 et sqq.; Foucault 1975, pp. 159 et sqq., 228 et sqq.
233   For a comparison of Sombart's and Weber's genealogy of a 'capitalist spirit', cf. Rehmann 2015a, pp. 338 et sqq.
234   F. Haug 1995, p. 789.

seventeenth and eighteenth centuries. This becomes clear when Foucault's genealogy of the disciplines is confronted with the investigations of modern 'social disciplining', inspired primarily by Max Weber and Gerhard Oestreich.[235] According to these studies, what is crucial is the transition from the 'self-disciplining' of certain social groups to an 'external disciplining' which asserts itself in two large thrusts: beginning with the urban regulation of begging and paupers of the late Middle Ages, it is first imposed primarily by the army and the administration of the absolutist state, which generalise it into the programme of a 'basic discipline'.[236] In a second wave, the expanding capitalistic market and its corporations produce a new reified and predominantly anonymous type of domination, which Marx analysed as an 'objective power' over the society, characterised by the 'dull compulsion of economic relations'.[237] According to Stefan Breuer, Foucault's account of the generalisation of discipline needs to be explained by the 'totalisation of abstract labour' and the accompanying increase of the abstract-linear time to 'system time'.[238]

Max Weber, who put the concept of discipline very near to that of domination,[239] summarises these two thrusts under the heading 'disciplining and objectification [Versachlichung] of the forms of domination'.[240] Thereby he works out that the modern increase of discipline prevailed militarily 'on the basis of an increasing concentration of the means of warfare in the hands of the warlord' and economically on the basis of 'the "separation" ... of the workers from the material means of administrative organization'.[241] Thus, in the areas of the military, of the bureaucratic state in general, as well as the 'economically

---

235   Cf. for this as overview still the anthology of Sachße and Tennstedt (1986, pp. 13 et sqq.), also in critical argument with Foucault Treiber and Steinert (1980, pp. 90 et sqq.) as well as the work of Stefan Breuer (1978, pp. 411, pp. 430 et sqq.; 1983, pp. 261 et sqq.; 1986, pp. 52 et sqq., 55 et sq.; 1987, pp. 324 et sqq., 336 et sq.).

236   Oestreich 2008, pp. 271 et. sq.

237   Cf. the *German Ideology* (Marx and Engels 1845b, p. 77; Marx and Engels 1957–, Vol. 3, p. 74), the *Grundrisse* (Marx 1857b, pp. 84 et sq.; Marx and Engels 1957–, Vol. 42, pp. 81 et sq.) and *Capital*, Volume 1 (Marx 1867, p. 726; Marx and Engels 1957–, Vol. 23, 765). Above all the dependence of the workers on the continuous and uniform movement of the machine calls for the 'strictest discipline' (Marx 1867, p. 414, cf. pp. 373, 426 et sq.; Marx and Engels 1957–, Vol. 23, p. 433; cf. pp. 390, 446 et sq.)

238   Breuer 1987, p. 336.

239   Weber introduces discipline not in connection with his concept of a 'sociologically amorphous' power but with that of domination. Discipline is to designate the probability that 'by virtue of habituation a command will receive prompt and automatic obedience in stereotyped forms, on the part of a given group of persons' (Weber 1978, p. 53, cf. Weber 1980, p. 28).

240   Cf. Weber 1980, pp. 681 et sqq.

241   Weber 1978, p. 1154, Weber 1980, pp. 685 et sq.; Weber 1946, p. 82, Weber 1980, pp. 825 et sq.

large-scale enterprises', the social penetration of the disciplines is accompanied by an enormous (and also by no means nonviolent) concentration of power.

We can see now that both sides (and periods) of this power concentration are blanked out in Foucault's genealogy of disciplinary power. In principle Foucault is aware of the possibility that the micro-physics of power-relations might form 'a chain or system', a 'dense web that passes through apparatuses and institutions', which can be integrated and codified in state-power.[242] However, as Bob Jessop observes, Foucault 'faced difficulties in moving from the amorphous dispersion of micro-powers to their class-relevant overdetermination in and through the central role of the state'.[243] What is missing in particular are the analytical tools to grasp *how* the micro-physics of power can be assembled and accumulated in such a fashion that they build strategic axes of economic, state, and patriarchal domination. In this regard Bourdieu's emphasis on the modes of 'conversion' between different kinds of power, or, in his terminology, between economic, cultural, social and symbolic 'capital', is a fruitful contribution that helps to fill this gap. Whereas Foucault's concept of power leaves the question of *how* to ascend from a micro-physics of power to class- and state-domination unresolved, Bourdieu demonstrates how power-resources are anchored in different social fields, how the 'capital' attained in one field can be 'converted' into the 'capital' of other fields, so that the dominant milieus especially in the economic field are able to appropriate and accumulate power.[244] As soon as one asks the question of the accumulation of power concretely, one encounters the instances of the economic, the state and the ideological which Foucault excluded from his concept of power.

Looking at the examples Foucault presents for the new power diagram, we can see that they point in a quite different direction. Both the 'system of permanent registration' of plague control and the disciplining of soldiers' bodies are intimately connected with the development of the modern territorial states, and therefore cannot be isolated from an analysis of the state apparatus.[245] As Andreas Kalyvas has shown, the historical material presented by Foucault contradicts his explicit theory of power: the examples suggest 'that the new techniques of power did in effect come from one central strategic terrain, the state, to spread all over the social field during the creation of the modern bourgeois nation state and the first phases of capital accumulation'.[246]

---

242 Foucault 1978, pp. 92, 96.
243 Jessop 1990, p. 238.
244 Cf. Swartz 1997, pp. 79 et sq., Schwingel 1993, pp. 169 et sq.
245 Foucault 1995, p. 196; Foucault 1975, p. 229.
246 Kalyvas 2002, pp. 117 et sq.

Poulantzas has observed that Foucault, in order to set off his concept of power from that of the state and outside of its range, takes as a basis the narrow concept of the state which Gramsci has overcome: hospitals, lunatic asylums, sports apparatuses, and other institutions of this sort, which Foucault locates outside of the state, belong to 'the apparatus of asylums and hospitals' [appareil santé-asiles] and are thus part of an integral state.[247] Poulantzas notes a similar reductionism with regard to both the economic and the ideological: insofar as Foucault separates 'power' from the economy, he no longer sees the latter as a dense 'network of powers' [réseau de pouvoirs], as an ensemble of practical relations of power/powerlessness, but transforms it back into the pre-Marxist form of economic 'factors'.[248] Foucault's juxtaposition of disciplinary power and ideology is only possible because he conceives of the latter again traditionally in the sense of ideas. Thus it remains unconsidered how practical forms and 'matrices' of dominant ideology enter into the process of normalisation.[249] Foucault's 'micro physics' grasps neither the real, antagonistically reclaimed diversity of power, nor its appropriation and accumulation by the ruling power bloc. It is precisely by cutting out the social concentration of power through capital, state and ideological apparatuses that Foucault establishes a 'disciplinary power' which possesses the omnipotence to spread into the modern soul.

5.3   'The Limits of Social Disciplining' (Peukert)

We have arrived at the second pole of the Foucauldian concept of power, i.e. its totalising potency. Honneth accuses Foucault of a functionalism which is conceived 'according to the model of total institutions' and which regards social conflicts only as 'the everyday plain over which the systemic process paves the way'.[250] According to Habermas, Foucault's genealogy is reductionistic because it erases 'all traces of communicative actions entangled in life-world contexts' and thus eradicates the modern increase in subjective liberty.[251] As Breuer notes, Foucault's concept of power 'promises a new, non-totalising history and yet totalises itself, ... by dissolving all differences into the general fog

---

247   Poulantzas 2014, p. 37; Poulantzas 1978a, p. 41. 'Indeed, as Poulantzas correctly saw, all of Foucault's examples of the sites of the new power relations were in fact an integral part of the strategic field of the capitalist-liberal state: prisons, national armies, public education, and public health' (Kalyvas 2002, p. 117).
248   Poulantzas 2014, pp. 37 et sq., 68 et sq., 149; Poulantzas 1979a, pp. 39 et sq., 75, 163.
249   Poulantzas 2014, p. 67; Poulantzas 1978a, p. 73.
250   Honneth 1991, pp. 195 et sqq.
251   Habermas 1990, pp. 286 et sqq.

of "power"'. Breuer explains this totalisation with reference to a fundamental 'metaphysics of power' which Foucault took from Nietzsche.[252]

As Loïc Wacquant has shown, Foucault 'consistently conflated the blueprints of penal reformers and the prescriptions of theorists of confinement with the everyday reality of imprisonment'.[253] What this means for the treatment of historical material becomes clear in an exemplary manner in the criticism of Detlev Peukert, who worked out the 'limits of social discipline' in an investigation of the German youth welfare service from 1878 to 1932. According to him, relevant differences already become apparent at the level of discourses which remain unconsidered by Foucault, namely, on one hand, a norm setting and control discourse by the jurists, and on the other a 'classification discourse' by medical and psychological 'science', and, finally, the discourses of the educators, which again were split between an authoritarian traditionalist morality education, above all in church boarding schools, and a cultural-critical humanistic pedagogy developed by pedagogues connected with youth movements and focusing on an 'understanding reconstruction of the otherness of the lifeworld logic of young people'. As soon as one includes the point of view of the young people concerned, one must take the differences between these discourses seriously.[254] If the criticism overlooks the alternative tendencies within pedagogy that take the youngsters' life-world seriously and thus challenge the disciplinary discourses, then it ends up in 'fatalistic apology for power'.[255]

Foucault also misses the gap between the claims of the control discourses and a reality that was usually characterised by a 'regiment of deficiency, improvisation and resigned renunciation of the implementation of the pedagogical project', so that the utopia of control in almost all areas of the welfare state had 'their location in nowhere'.[256] In reality, the young people developed their own 'calculating methods' in handling the disciplinary technology, e.g. each spring a young person might escape the educational institution in order to drift around, and with the coming of cold in the autumn let himself be caught again to enjoy for some months the advantages of a warm room and sufficient food,

---

252   Breuer 1987, p. 324.
253   Wacquant 2016, p. 124; cf. Wacquant 2009b, p. 296.
254   Peukert 1991, p. 326; cf. Peukert 1986, pp. 23 et sq.
255   Peukert 1991, pp. 326 et sq.
256   Peukert 1991, p. 326. Léonard had argued something similar: 'M. Foucault exagère la rationalisation de la société française dans la première moitié du XIXe siècle. Il minimise, en plusieurs domaines, la résistance des habitudes du passé, et il sous-estime l'importance du désordre, du laisser-aller, de la jungle, de la pagaille en somme.' (Léonard 1977, p. 166) Cf. also the references by Michelle Perrot in Foucault 1980, pp. 162 et. sq.; Foucault 2001b, Nr. 195, pp. 205 et sq.

'until in spring the freedom of the highway lures again'.[257] 'Each suburban pub, each clique and each cinema deny the pedagogue the validity of their illusion of omnipotence', and one should be careful not to 'fall for the self-hubris of the erudite pedagogical text producers and overlook "life", which does not only oppose in Nietzschean emphasis the dry plans of the scholarly world, but also in simple source-saturated diversity'.[258] Consequently, according to Peukert, in the period that he investigated (1878–1932) there was no expansion of social discipline, but at the end of the 1920s the 'licentiousness' of maladjusted youth subcultures seemed 'far more threatening' than 50 years earlier.[259]

In short: Peukert considers Foucault's approach heuristically fruitful when it comes to deciphering the disciplinary and control function lying behind the 'humanistic self-interpretation' of pedagogy; however, he turns against a generalisation which reduces the subject to a 'global discourse of disciplining'.[260] Foucault applies a 'philosophical' method of source selection which filters out everything that might resist the assumed smooth penetration of reality by disciplinary discourse.[261] Here the historian cannot help raising the suspicion that Foucault's method of presentation and his subject matter have entered into 'a strange elective affinity'.[262]

5.4   The Removal of the 'Topography' from the Theory of Society (Althusser)

The described contradictions in the Foucauldian concept of power represent not simply a logical inconsistency, but are connected with one another. This becomes clear when one considers the discursive strategies which produce them. We find with Foucault both a 'de-localisation' discourse, in which he attempts to prove that power can be thought neither from the state and its ideological apparatuses, nor from class relationships, and at the same time a discourse of 're-localisation', which relocates power, because of its connection with 'war', with 'knowledge' and the 'body', in a position 'underneath' that of the social relations from which it was previously abstracted.[263] Both discourses

---

257   Peukert 1991, p. 327.
258   Peukert 1991, pp. 327 et sq.
259   Peukert 1991, p. 328. 'Rather, capitalist free wage labour produced not only all the disciplining elements, but also the historically new scale of "disciplinelessness" to which social policy responded with calls for new control systems' (Peukert 1986, p. 67).
260   Peukert 1991, pp. 325, 329 et sq.
261   Peukert 1991, p. 330.
262   Ibid.
263   It functions as a 'base' and 'sous-sol' of bourgeois juridical liberties (Foucault 1995, p. 222; Foucault 1975, p. 258), moves underneath the ideologies and apparatuses (Foucault 2003c,

have in common that power – contrary to Foucault's claim – is treated not as a real relational concept, 'pouvoir relationnel',[264] but in a neo-Nietzschean way as a subject with almost unlimited producer status.

When Althusser was confronted with the charge of reductionism, he turned the tables and claimed that the analytical distinction between societal 'instances' such as base/superstructure or economy/politics/ideology represents, despite its metaphorical weaknesses, a heuristic precondition for a non-reductionist analysis of society. As soon as one removes the 'topography' from social theory, one falls back on Hegelian notions of an 'expressive totality', i.e. on the logic of expanding spheres and circles, and finally lands at the 'delirious idealist notion of producing its own material substance'.[265] Foucault's concept of power is indeed a good example to use for confirming Althusser's thesis: Foucault's 'micro-physical' dis-localisation of power, its extraction from the functional connection of the instances, turns into the omnipotence of power, by which it now can penetrate the topical levels to the inmost and 'produces' them.

In a different way, Poulantzas thematises this paradoxical connection between power-diversity rhetoric and totalisation. Foucault regards power, no longer as a relation between social practices, but as something that has only itself as basis. It becomes pure 'situation', in which sense there has always been power.[266] In this manner the qualitative question of which power is involved and what it does is excluded from the analysis.[267] This means that the points of resistance which Foucault conjures up cannot be justified theoretically. Because there is no basis for the resistance, there is nothing that could limit power.[268] So through the back way the result is an all-powerful 'Master Power [Maître Pouvoir]', which has always been the basis for struggles: instead of a relation, we get an 'ensnaring substance' [substance qui attrape], 'a voracious,

p. 33; Foucault 1997b, p. 30) and comes 'from below', from 'the moving substrate of force relations' (Foucault 1978, pp. 93 et sq.; Foucault 1976a, pp. 122, 124).

264 Foucault 1995, p. 177; Foucault 1975, p. 208.
265 'délire idéaliste de produire sa propre matière (Althusser 1974, pp. 77 et sqq.; Althusser 1976, pp. 141 et sqq.).
266 Power is not possessed or appropriated, but is something 'which is exercised' [s'exerce] (Foucault 1995, p. 26; Foucault 1975, p. 35), it exists only 'in the execution' [il n'existe qu'en acte], is not conducive to the reproduction of economic conditions, but is an 'in itself, a relationship of force' (Foucault 2003c, p. 15; Foucault 1997b, p. 15), something 'which is exercised from innumerable points' (Foucault 1978, p. 94; Foucault 1976a, pp. 123 et sq.).
267 Poulantzas 2014, pp. 148 et sq.; Poulantzas 1978a, p. 163.
268 'For Foucault, the danger is that the specificity of different social relations is dissolved through their common use of the same technique of power', notes Jessop 1990, p. 231.

self-reproducing machine' [une machine autoreproductible et dévoratrice], a 'scavanger cell' [essence phagocyte], which contaminates all resistances.[269]

6 Foucault's Metaphorisation of the Prison and the Reality of Neoliberal Hyperincarceration

For Foucault the prison network does not have an 'outside' any longer because in the panoptic society imprisonment represents an 'omnipresent armature', which can scarcely be distinguished from the 'therapeutic-educational institutions'.[270] It forms the 'greatest support of ... the normalising power', which is produced by the various categories of intellectuals in the same way: 'We are in the society of the teacher-judge, the doctor-judge, the educator-judge, the "social worker"-judge; it is on them that the universal reign of the normative is based'.[271]

This equating of force (confinement), ideology (normalisation), healing and education leads to another contradiction of the Foucauldian argumentation. The prison dispositif, which morphed into a disciplinary and normalisation power penetrating the entire society,[272] finally makes itself redundant. Since the 'normalisation networks' of medicine, psychology, education, public assistance, 'social work', etc. become ever denser, the hinge of the prison loses its significance.[273] The contradiction consists in the fact that Foucault stylises a partial aspect of the coercion apparatus into the hegemony model of modern society altogether and then sublimates it into the 'normative', as if the deterrence function of the prison, and with it the repressive apparatuses in general, had disappeared from bourgeois society completely. The overgeneralisation of the aspect of coercion leads to its imaginary abolition. The erasure of both state violence and of what Marx analysed as the 'dull compulsion' of capitalist relations of production is the pivot point at which the 'middle' Foucault of *Discipline and Punish* can smoothly segue into the power concept of the 'late' Foucault. Instead of analysing repression and power-'productivity' in their mutual relationships, Foucault defines, for example, his concept of modern 'bio-power' as being bent on 'generating forces, making them grow, and ordering them', whereas the repressive 'right to death' is relegated to a

---

269 Poulantzas, 2014, pp. 150 et sq.; Poulantzas 1978a, pp. 165 et sq.
270 Foucault 1995, pp. 301, 303; Foucault 1975, pp. 352, 354.
271 Foucault 1995, p. 304; Foucault 1975, p. 356.
272 Foucault 1995, p. 211; Foucault 1975, p. 246.
273 Foucault 1995, p. 306; Foucault 1975, p. 358.

former 'right of the sovereign'.[274] We will see a similar abstraction with regard to his writings on 'governmentality', 'liberalism' and 'neoliberalism' (see below Chapter 5.3).

Foucault covers over the contradiction between the omnipresence of the prison dispositif and its dissolution in the normative through a metaphorical use of the term 'prison'. This can be observed in the example of the much discussed passage in which Foucault understands the 'soul' as a product of the disciplinary power and articulates it as 'the prison of the body'.[275] Presumably it is a matter here, as Judith Butler suggests, of an allusion to the Aristotelian concept of the soul as form and principle of the body.[276] Butler discusses the Foucauldian manner of speech as a figure of subjectivation per se, with which 'every "identity," insofar as it is totalizing, [seems to act] as precisely such a "soul that imprisons the body."'[277] Of course, one could ask, what would remain of Foucault's celebration of the body if it were to be deprived of the 'soul' whose 'materialist' dimension can be observed in – for example – the Hebrew word *ruah*, i.e., the breath. But what needs to be brought into question here is the ideological function of Foucault's prison metaphorisation itself: all those who see themselves restricted in the realisation of their possibilities for action are invited to feel themselves as victims of the same normative 'prison' as those who are actually locked up. It is the appeal to a political self-understanding which in imagination abolishes the differences between those 'inside' and those 'outside'.

This contradiction also impacts the level of political strategy. On one hand, *Discipline and Punish* is laid out as a 'history of the present' and corresponds directly with the political experience of the prison revolts in the post '68 movement.[278] At the same time, it reacts to the defeat of the prisoner movement in a way that amounts to a retreat from this area of struggle. For Foucault, it is not about whether the penal system could be humanised, so that it contributes to healing and reintegration (this would be a possible application of reform proposals), and also not about the question of 'whether we should have prison or something other than prison' (this amounts to a radical, 'abolitionist' challenge), but about the 'steep rise in the use of these mechanisms of normalization' per se.[279] To the extent that Foucault dissolves the prison into the

---

274   Foucault 1978, p. 136.
275   Foucault 1995, pp. 29 et sq.; Foucault 1975, p. 38.
276   Butler 1997, pp. 90 et sq.; cf. 1993, pp. 33 et sqq.
277   Butler 1997, p. 86.
278   Foucault 1995, p. 31; Foucault 1975, p. 40.
279   Foucault 1995, p. 306; Foucault 1975, p. 358.

flexible 'norm', he gives up on struggles against the repressive detention systems of bourgeois society.

According to Loïc Wacquant, 'Foucault misread the historical trend of modern Western penality when he prophesied the vanishing of the prison at the very moment it was entering a phase of rapid expansion and wholesale solidification'.[280] Indeed, shortly after the publication of *Discipline and Punish*, the transition from a 'Fordist', Keynesian 'welfare state' to neoliberalism generated a new penal policy, which in particular in the USA caused the numbers of incarcerations to rise precipitously. Whereas the number of convicts had fallen to 380,000 by 1975, the trend was completely reversed after Ronald Reagan's election in 1980: by 1985 the prison population had already doubled to 740,000, by 1995 it passed 1.5 million, and by 2000 it amounted to 2 million. In twenty-five years, from 1975 to 2000, the prison population saw a fivefold increase. In 2009 the United States became the biggest incarcerator on the planet, with an incarceration rate of about 750 inmates per 100,000 inhabitants – a rate that stands six to twelve times higher than that in the countries of the European Union.[281] But also in Europe, after a longer period of sinking prison numbers, in the quarter-century following the publication of *Discipline and Punish* the incarceration rate doubled in France, Italy, and Belgium and nearly tripled in England, Sweden, and the Netherlands.[282] In short, 'penal confinement has made a stunning comeback and reaffirmed itself among the central missions of Leviathan, just as Foucault and his followers were forecasting its demise'.[283]

Against the backdrop of neoliberalism's hyperincarceration, other aspects of Foucault's assessment turned out to be erroneous as well. Already the Foucauldian thesis of the disappearance of the torture spectacle at the beginning of the nineteenth century had overlooked not only the cruel practices of punishment in the European colonies, but also the lynching murders of African Americans after the American Civil War and the spectacular exhibition of the mutilated body.[284] The 'spectacle of the scaffold' has not been supplanted by the panopticon, but moved to the '*Court TV* and the profusion of crime-and-punishment "reality shows" that have inundated television ..., not to mention the use of criminal justice as fodder for the daily news and dramatic series'.[285] Also the 'devices for normalization' anchored in the carceral institution have

---

280   Wacquant 2016, p. 124; Wacquant 2009b, p. 296.
281   Cf. Wacquant 2009a, pp. 58 et sqq.
282   Wacquant 2016, p. 122; cf. for France the statistics of Faugeron in Petit 1991, p. 337.
283   Wacquant 2016, pp. 121 et sq.; Wacquant 2009b, p. 296.
284   James 1996, pp. 29 et sq.
285   Wacquant 2016, p. 124; Wacquant 2009b, p. 298.

not spread equally through the social order, but targeted 'essentially the denizens of the lower regions of social and physical space', 'so that the state may check the social reverberations caused by the diffusion of social insecurity in the lower rungs of the class and ethnic hierarchy'.[286] The prison is both part of a repressive system that ensures the overdetermined antagonisms of class and race, and also part of an ideological mechanism that construes an abject 'outside' of otherness, with whose assistance the 'inside' of US-American civil society is held together. Foucault's normalisation thesis overlooks the fact that the ritualised exhibition of police force plays an important role in control of the 'dangerous classes'.[287] Fixed on the welfare state integration and therapeutic rehabilitation models of the late 1960s, he did not take note of the bifurcation between bourgeois self-regulation and the supervised exclusion of a Helot class. A part of the surplus population needs to be sacrificed to keep the others complacent and under control, and this sacrifice is enacted by a theatrical spectacle of control that keeps viewers both in fear of and fascinated by state power.[288]

Foucault lacks the analytic instruments for grasping the neoliberal connection between the 'atrophy of the welfare state' and the 'hyperthrophy of the penal state'.[289] Precisely here, as we have seen, were the strengths of Rusche and Kirchheimer's historical-sociological approach. Foucault's criticism is directed one-sidedly against a social-pedagogisation of the penitentiary system, such as was typical for the 'social-democratic' age of the Fordist welfare state. He wanted to prove that the reformers who claimed to replace the deterrence function of punishment with a more 'humane' project of 'improvement' did not implement anything more than a refinement of social control. This fixation led him to leave unconsidered the position of the prison in the 'armour of coercion', as well as its function in the social politics of bourgeois society.

---

286   Wacquant 2016, pp. 123, 127; cf. James 1996, p. 24; Angela Davis 1998, p. 98.
287   Parenti 1999, p. 135.
288   Taylor 2001, pp. 49, 60, 105 et sq.
289   Wacquant 2009a, p. 58.

Forays into the Late Foucault

The term 'forays' in the title of this chapter is carefully chosen. It would be pre-posterous to try to cover the works of the 'late Foucault' in their entirety and in all their facets. I decided from the outset not to engage Foucault's research on subjectivities and ethics from ancient Greece through the Roman Empire to early Christianity; this evaluation would have required a thorough reading of the sources he used and of the secondary literature he consulted. I will focus instead on reconstructing two trajectories: on the one hand, the transform-ation of his concept of power after the development of 'disciplinary power' discussed in Chapter 4. This reconstruction begins with Foucault's introduction of the concept of biopower or biopolitics, moves through his studies of differ-ent varieties of governmentality, and gauges the potentials of the widening of his power concept towards techniques of the self. On the other hand, I will trace a political trajectory that leads Foucault first to a staunch anti-socialism (and in particular anti-Marxism) and then to an affiliation with neoliberalism, which includes a critique of the security system of the Fordist welfare state. The conceptual and the political levels interact intensely, but cannot be reduced to each other. One question at issue is to what extent the opening of Foucault's power concept towards the strategies of self-conduct is overdetermined by his encounter with neoliberal theories, in particular with Gary Becker's concept of 'human capital'.

1   Biopolitics – A New Power Enters the Stage

It was primarily the investigation of the modern transformations of the Cath-olic confession of sexual secrets in the *History of Sexuality* (Vol. 1) that led Foucault to envision the emergence of a new type of power. The confession had been codified in the Lateran Council in 1215, and intensified during the Counter-Reformation after the Council of Trent (1525–63).[1] It was subsequently taken up, disseminated, and transformed during the eighteenth and nineteenth century: for example through a 'clinical codification' that combined confession with examination, a 'medicalisation' which placed sex under the rule of the nor-

---

1   Foucault 1978, pp. 18 et sq., 58.

mal and the pathological, or through an economic 'socialization of procreative behavior' that targeted the fertility of the 'Malthusian couple'.[2] Foucault calls this new type 'biopower' (also biopolitics) and defines it as 'the entry of life into ... the order of knowledge and power'.[3]

Let us look at how Foucault juxtaposes this new type of power to the two types he had introduced before: to 'sovereign power', which we discussed already with the example of the 'torture spectacles' that preceded the emergence of the prison (see above Chapter 4.3.2.), and to disciplining power, which according to *Discipline and Punish* permeated the whole fabric of modern society (see above Chapter 4.5). Whereas 'sovereign power' is characterised as the 'old power of death' that wields 'the right to *take* life or *let* live', biopower operates as the power 'to make live and let die'.[4] Due to the increase in agricultural productivity and to demographic growth during the eighteenth century, 'the period of great ravages from starvation and plague had come to a close before the French Revolution'. Death was ceasing to 'torment life so directly', and 'Western man was gradually learning what it meant to be a living species in a living world'.[5] By adjusting the accumulation of people to that of capital and to the expansion of productive forces, biopower became an indispensable component in the development of capitalism.[6]

Whereas disciplinary power, emerging in the seventeenth and eighteenth centuries, targets the individual body, biopower, emerging in the second half of the eighteenth century, focuses on the 'species body' (corps espèce) of the population and targets its 'life': 'As for population controls, one notes the emergence of demography, the evaluation of the relationship between resources and inhabitants, the constructing of tables analyzing wealth and its circulation'.[7] It operates as a 'power of regulation' that manages the ratio of births to deaths, fertility, mortality rates, morbidity, public hygiene, and medical care in order to medicalise the population and insurance systems.[8] Working with forecasts, statistical estimates, calculations of probability, thus intervening 'at the level at which these general phenomena are determined', it aims at the establishment of an equilibrium.[9]

---

2   Foucault 1978, pp. 65, 67, 104 et sq.
3   Foucault 1978, pp. 141 et sq.
4   Foucault 1978, pp. 138.
5   Foucault 1978, p. 142.
6   Foucault 1978, pp. 140 et sq.
7   Foucault 1978, pp. 139 et sq.
8   Foucault 2003c, pp. 243 et sq., 247.
9   Foucault 2003c, pp. 246, 249.

As Thomas Lemke observes, Foucault's terminology 'is not consistent and constantly shifts meaning in his texts'.[10] The terms 'biopolitics' and 'biopower' are frequently used interchangeably, but sometimes 'power over life' seems to be the generic term encompassing the two basic forms of disciplinary power and biopolitical 'regulations of the population'.[11] Sometimes, the term 'biopolitical' is replaced with the term 'regulatory'. In any case, 'regulatory' biopolitical power does not exclude disciplinary power, but 'dovetails into it', integrates and infiltrates it, while it is also embedded in existing disciplinary techniques.[12] For example, this interaction applies to the rationally planned town, in which working-class housing estates control bodies which are also embedded in 'regulatory mechanisms' such as health-insurance systems, old-age pensions, rules on hygiene, etc. Sexuality exists at a 'point where body and population meet', and is thus a matter for both discipline and regulation; medicine can be applied to both the individual body and the 'body' of a population.[13]

It appears that Foucault has accepted some of the criticisms targeting the 'expressive totality' of his all-powerful disciplinary 'Maître Pouvoir'. In his lecture on 17 March 1976, he articulates a first implicit self-criticism with regard to his method of deriving modern normalisation uniquely from the paradigm of disciplinary power: 'The normalising society is therefore not ... a sort of generalised disciplinary society whose disciplinary institutions have swarmed and finally taken over everything ... [It] is a society in which the norm of discipline and the norm of regulation intersect along an orthogonal articulation'.[14] The spatial metaphor of a mutual 'orthogonal' articulation would of course need some more explanation, but it could in principle open up a social analysis that investigates how different techniques of power combine, superimpose and overdetermine each other, or – what is still left out in Foucault's deliberations – how they confront and contradict each other.

But again, Foucault's types of power are eerily detached from social relations and their underlying conditions of 'life'. The notion that ancient power is merely about the sovereign's 'right to *take* life or *let* live' abstracts from the fact that these regimes also had to deal with the necessity of allocating people to the given modes of production and distribution. Plato, for example, deliberates in detail on how the philosopher-rulers of the state manage to systematically arrange marriages for the sake of obtaining the best 'breed of people', while

10   Lemke 2011, p. 34.
11   Foucault 1978, p. 139.
12   Foucault 2003c, p. 242.
13   Foucault 2003c, pp. 250 et sqq.
14   Foucault 2003c, p. 253.

secretly having the 'inferior' ones killed.[15] Obviously, 'positive' and 'negative' eugenics were combined, and the notion of a planned regulation of the 'population' was not absent in the imaginary of ancient powers. Giorgio Agamben has a point, therefore, when he argues that 'the production of a biopolitical body is the original activity of sovereign power',[16] which secures a separation of bare life (*zoé*) and political existence (*bios*). We don't need to follow his proclamation that the camp is the 'biopolitical paradigm of the modern', or that modern biopolitics necessarily coincides with 'thanatopolitics'[17] – a simplistic and reductionist assumption which eliminates the contradictions between democracy and fascism.

Referring to both Foucault and Agamben, Achilles Mbembe introduced the concept of 'necropower', and thereby brought back to the (post)modern era what Foucault tended to relegate to pre-modern times, namely the systematic exposure to social and civil death, for example (in the case of the 'splintering occupation' of Palestinian lands by the Israeli government) through territorial fragmentation. This includes a network of fast bypass roads, bridges, and tunnels that weave over and under one another in an attempt at maintaining the Fanonian 'principle of reciprocal exclusivity', as well as waging 'infrastructural warfare' by uprooting olive trees, demolishing houses and cities, and destroying electricity transformers:[18] 'While the Apache helicopter gunship is used to police the air and to kill from overhead, the armored bulldozer (the Caterpillar D-9) is used on the ground as a weapon of war and intimidation'.[19]

On another frontline, Michael Hardt and Antonio Negri argue that Foucault's biopower only describes a power 'over' life, without considering the aspect of life-power itself. Due to his 'functionalist' epistemology, he fails to grasp the 'bios' that actually drives the system, and thus 'the real dynamics of production in biopolitical society'.[20] 'Biopolitical production' is at work, for example, in the 'immaterial nexuses of the production of language, communication, and the symbolic that are developed by the communications industry'.[21] Whereas biopower 'stands above society … and imposes its order, biopolitical production … is immanent to society and creates social relationships and forms

---

15   Plato, Politeia, 458d–461c.
16   Agamben 1998, p. 6; cf. the comparison of Foucault's and Agamben's concepts of biopower in Genel 2006.
17   Agamben 1998, pp. 10, 117, 123, 142, 175.
18   Mbembe 2003, pp. 28 et sq.
19   Mbembe 2003, p. 29.
20   Hardt, Negri 2000, p. 28.
21   Hardt, Negri 2000, p. 32.

through collaborative forms of labor'.[22] Used interchangeably with 'immaterial labor', biopolitical production 'creates not only material goods but also relationships and ultimately social life itself'; it operates as today's hegemonic form of labor 'in qualitative terms', characterised by 'continuous cooperation among innumerable individual producers'.[23]

According to Alberto Toscano, Hardt and Negri try 'to infuse the fire of living labor into Foucault's biopolitics', but they do this through a juxtaposition of two unmediated totalities ('biopower' from above, 'biopolitical production' from below), and thus remove the dialectics from class struggle.[24] Indeed, Hardt and Negri posit that the 'multitude' has an ontological priority and organises its biopolitical production in an increasingly autonomous way, so that the Empire is just an 'apparatus of capture that lives only off the vitality of the multitude'.[25] This notion of a quasi-autonomous biopolitical production underestimates the formative power of high-tech capitalism and eliminates the manifold contradictions within the 'multitude'. The related idea that the multitude is already 'thoroughly political' and constitutes itself 'on the plane of immanence without hegemony',[26] fails to recognise the relative autonomy of politics, and overlooks the specific difficulties of a political 'translation' and condensation of social struggles and movements.[27]

The debate is affected by the problem that also the critics tend to accept Foucault's notions of biopolitics or biopower without challenging their over-general nature. Foucault's examples stretch from mercantilist population policy to mandatory school attendance and to modern social security, insurance and health care systems. They designate heterogeneous developments that cannot be placed in one bag. They would need to be reconstructed in the context of the respective transformations of capitalism and the accompanying social struggles. The invocation of 'life' as either a regulated domain, or, in the case of Hardt/Negri, as the 'lifeblood' of both the Empire and the multitude, substitutes philosophical speculation for the task of a historical-materialist analysis. Furthermore, Foucault seems to ignore the fact that at about the same time as he develops his concepts of biopower and biopolitics, the United States see the emergence of a vibrant biotech industry, which

---

22   Hardt, Negri 2004, pp. 94 et sq.
23   Hardt, Negri 2004, pp. 109, 187.
24   Toscano 2007, pp. 113, 116.
25   Hardt, Negri 2000, p. 62.
26   Hardt, Negri 2009, pp. 169 et sq.
27   For a critique of Hardt/Negri's concept of 'multitude', see Rehmann 2019a, pp. 81 et sqq.

then becomes a dynamic part of a 'neoliberal revolution'.[28] What is missing in both Foucault's deliberations on biopower and in the debate about this concept are the actual advances of a 'biocapitalism' which, by combining biosciences, informatics and aggressive patenting strategies, creates new 'enclosures' for life forms, transforms the materials derived from human bodies and nonhuman living beings into commodities, and incorporates them into the domain of capitalist accumulation.[29]

2   Foucault's Distinction between Techniques of Domination and Techniques of the Self

Foucault's concept of power experiences another shift during the long and crisis-ridden period between the first volume of the *History of Sexuality* and the second and third volumes, that is, between 1976 and 1984. As we have seen in Chapter 4, in *Discipline and Punish* he had used the concept of power in the sense of a subtle and omnipresent formation of subjects that did not leave any room for subversion and resistance. Complementing disciplinary power, the concept of 'biopower' was specified as a power over 'life', this time not of the individual body, but of the body of the population. What he now discovers is the subjects' relationship to themselves. The ways in which they organise their lives and the 'techniques' they apply to themselves, to their attitudes, their bodies and their psyches become an important component of Foucault's late concept of power. The exercise of power acknowledges others in principle as acting subjects in their own right, 'having in front of them a field of possibility in which several conducts, several reactions, and various modes of behavior can take place'.[30] This includes the aspects of mutual influence and of the reversibility of power relations.[31] On the opposite side, 'domination' designates a 'strategic' fixation, in which power relations are no longer reversible, but rather blocked and ossified (*bloquées et figées*).[32]

The conceptual distinction between power and domination is indeed heuristically fruitful, because it allows us to analyse contradictory fields and dynamics of hegemonic struggles. As we have demonstrated in Chapter 1.7, the notion of power in both the Germanic and Romance languages (the German *Macht*

---

28   Cooper 2008, p. 11.
29   Cf. Lettow 2018.
30   Foucault 2001b, Nr. 306, p. 1056.
31   Foucault 2001b, Nr. 306, p. 1061.
32   Foucault 2001b, Nr. 306, p. 1062; Nr. 356, pp. 1529 f.

going back to the Gothic *mahts* and *magan*; the French noun to the verb *pouvoir* etc.) has its etymological roots in 'being *capable*'. According to Max Weber, the term is 'sociologically amorphous',[33] and can be found on opposite sides of class, gender, and race divides. Whereas power is in principle open to demo-cratisation, the concept of domination is formed around the ancient figure of the dominus ("master"), which marks the intersection of patriarchal and class rule and cannot be conceived without its constitutive meanings of social hierarchy and verticality. It is in this polarised space between the powers of domination and the agency of subaltern classes that the hegemonic struggles take place: on one side ideological apparatuses and ideologues manufacturing a consensus from above, on the other side, subaltern classes developing net-works of a 'horizontal' self-socialisation and solidarity. Of course, these poles are not to be understood as empirically separated entities, but as moving in continuous interaction. One of the major tasks of a critical ideology-theory is to analyse the dynamics of how the capacities and powers of the subaltern classes are constantly tapped and absorbed by the powers of domination.[34]

As soon as we confront the late Foucault with the potentials of his own dis-tinction between power and domination, we can see that he did not carry it through in a consistent fashion. In an interview in 1984 he was confronted with Hannah Arendt's differentiation between a collective power, in which individu-als gain a greater capacity to act than if they relied merely on themselves, and a power of domination, which might emerge from it or insert itself into it. Fou-cault responded that this is just a 'verbal' distinction.[35] Furthermore, he usually did not distinguish between the two concepts analytically, according to qualit-ative dimensions, but rather did so quantitatively, according to the criterion of size and scale, so that 'domination' described the macrostructure and 'power' described the microstructure. Whenever power became 'global', Foucault used the term 'domination', and whatever invaded and permeated immediate rela-tionships was defined as 'power'.[36]

But this is not a sustainable distinction. Domination is also capable of per-meating immediate human relations, including the most intimate ones. A case in point is patriarchal domination, whose ideological forms and patterns are permanently internalised and re-enacted by both genders. Furthermore, social movements such as, for example, the altermondialist movements of the World Social Forum, aim to build a democratic and anti-imperial power from

---

33   Weber 1978, p. 53, cf. Weber 1980, p. 28.
34   Cf. Rehmann 2013, pp. 241 et sqq.
35   Foucault 2001b, Nr. 341, p. 1408.
36   Foucault 2001b, Nr. 306, p. 1062; Nr. 356, p. 1529.

below on a 'global' level, and maintain that it must not flip over again into a new form of uncontrolled domination. Foucault misses the opportunity to re-conceptualise his concept of power from its etymological roots as 'ability' or 'capability'. His fascination with Nietzsche's elitist *will to power* keeps prevent-ing him from taking up Spinoza's concept of power as a cooperative capacity to act (*potentia agendi*). The late Foucault now includes the aspects of self-conduct and techniques of the self in his concept of power, but he does so in an individualistic manner which fails to grasp the potentials of collective agency and self-determination. As we will see later (below, Chapter 5.6.5), it is at this point that Foucault's 'care of the self' intersects with the ideological conjunc-ture of neoliberalism.

But rather than focus on the weaknesses of Foucault's approach, I would like to concentrate first on its possible (though unrealised) potentials. Between the 'techniques of the self' and the fixated blocs of domination, Foucault assumes an intermediary level which he calls 'governmentality'. He differentiates three levels of his analysis of power: 'the strategic relations, the techniques of gov-ernment, and the techniques of domination that are applied to the others and to the techniques of the self'.[37] Within this multilayered concept of power, 'governmentality' designates the 'encounter' between the techniques of domin-ation and the techniques of the self.[38] Foucault defines the term as a 'conduct of conducts'. The expression is based on an ambiguity of the French verb *conduire*, which signifies on the one hand 'directing' someone (*conduire quelqu'un*), and on the other hand the way in which one conducts oneself (*se conduit*), com-ports oneself, behaves, so that governmentality means '*conduire des conduits*' – conducting people's conduct.[39]

The distinction between techniques of domination and techniques of the self enables Foucault to develop a sense for subtle forms of resistance which did not yet play a role in *Discipline and Punish* or the first volume of *The His-tory of Sexuality*. He now looks at revolts of conduct articulated in the will 'to be conducted differently', or 'to escape direction by others and to define the way for each to conduct himself'.[40] An example of such 'insubordination' (insoumission) or 'counter-conduct' was medieval asceticism, which Foucault describes as an 'exercise of self on self ... in which the authority, presence and gaze of someone else is, if not impossible, at least unnecessary'. It is a 'reversed obedience' or 'excess', by which certain themes of religious experience are util-

---

37   Foucault 2001b, Nr. 356, p. 1547.
38   Foucault 2001b, Nr. 363, p. 1604.
39   Foucault 2001b, Nr. 306, p. 1056; Nr. 340, p. 1401; cf. Foucault 2007, p. 193.
40   Foucault 2007, pp. 194 et sq.

ised against the structures of power.[41] The religious communities are in part based on the 'refusal of the pastor's authority and its theological or ecclesiological justifications', replacing the clergy-laity dimorphism with 'relationships of reciprocal obedience', or, during the Reformation, by the priesthood of all believers.[42] In mysticism, the soul is not offered to the other for examination by a system of confessions, but 'sees itself in God and … God in itself' and thereby 'short-circuits' the pastoral hierarchy by replacing it with an immediate communication.[43] Counter-conduct can also manifest itself in a return to Holy Scripture.[44] Eschatological beliefs disqualify the pastor's role by claiming that the times are by themselves in the process of being fulfilled.[45] Another case in point is the truth-speech (*parrhesia*) of ancient Cynicism, which manifests itself as an 'interpellation of the powerful in the form of the diatribe'.[46]

The concept of 'conducting conduct' could indeed open up promising research questions. Obviously, the conduct of life under contradictory conditions is a complex and complicated affair. The subjects have to balance different demands, prioritise them, bring them into a linear temporal sequence – a procedure which cannot be achieved without a certain degree of critical evaluation of the respective necessities of life and of self-discipline.[47] To the extent that an instance of domination or an ideological apparatus successfully connects with the strategies of self-conduct, speaks in their name, and mobilises them for certain purposes, it gains access to the structures of common sense, and thus finds a sounding board so strong that intellectual criticism is unable to counter it. Conversely, communities and individuals can only resist ideological socialisation 'from above' in a sustainable manner if they develop and practice capacities of self-conduct, both collective and individual.

It is tempting to read Foucault's concept of governmentality together with a Gramscian concept of leadership which, in contrast to violence, is characterised primarily by an aspect of consensus. Foucault's attempt to mediate techniques of domination and techniques of the self touches upon a central issue of bourgeois hegemony, namely its capacities to achieve an active and 'voluntary' subordination to domination. The desire to explain the efficacy and appeal of such a subordination, which is experienced as free and responsible subjectivity,

---

41   Foucault 2007, pp. 200 et sq., 204, 207 et sq.
42   Foucault 2007, pp. 208, 210 et sq.
43   Foucault 2007, p. 212.
44   Foucault 2007, p. 213.
45   Foucault 2007, p. 214.
46   Foucault 2010b, p. 344.
47   For a Marxist analysis of the contradictions of *Lebensführung* in a capitalist society, see Holzkamp 1995.

was the founding impulse of the ideology-theories that emerged in the 1970s and 1980s, first in connection with Louis Althusser in France, then with Stuart Hall in the UK and the *Projekt Ideologietheorie* (PIT) in Berlin. Foucault's question of how the techniques of domination and of the self are interconnected would then be located in what ideology-theories discuss in terms of an encounter between ideological apparatuses and common sense practices. Foucault's specific contribution would be the analysis of ideological patterns and self-conduct as particular 'technologies' of power and their 'governmental' assemblage as a hegemonic bloc.

But, of course, Foucault is convinced that he has overcome the approaches of a critical ideology-theory, which he has replaced with a 'positive' account of discourses (see above, Chapter 3.3).[48] This is why the promise to investigate the interactions of techniques of domination and of the self drops out of sight.

3   The Mysterious Concept of 'Governmentality'

The problem begins with the term 'governmentality', which sparkles in all directions, its floating meanings hardly to be determined. The French neologism seems to carry an enigmatic content which dissipates as soon as one tries to translate it into plain language. If one explains it according to two components 'government' and 'mentality', one gets something like the 'mentality of (the) government', or a way to 'think about government'.[49] However, this explanation was contradicted by Michel Sennelart, the editor of Foucault's lectures at the *Collège de France* of 1977–79, who let it be known that the term is not derived from the noun 'mentality', but rather emerged from the adjective 'gouvernemental' being transformed into a noun, in the same way as '*musicalité*' can be derived from 'musical'.[50] If this is accurate (Sennelart does not provide any philological proof), one could ask all the more whether the new terminological coinage is really worth the effort: taking the adjective '*gouvernemental*', which is itself derived from the noun '*gouvernement*', and then retransforming it into another noun by adding the new ending '*-ité*', does not yield anything more than 'government-like', or 'of the kind of government', none of which contains any explanatory power.

More importantly, Foucault uses the term in very different ways: on the most general level 'governmentality' designates 'the way in which one conducts the

---

48   Foucault 2010a, pp. 125, 186 et sq.; Foucault 1969, pp. 164, 243.
49   Dean 1999, pp. 16 et sqq.
50   Foucault 2007, pp. 399 et sq., n. 126.

conducts' of people,[51] that is to say, the 'conducting of conducts', which by its consensual components is 'different from "reigning or ruling", and not the same as "commanding" or "laying down the law", or being a sovereign, suzerain, lord', but instead is enacted as 'government of souls'.[52] It is on this level that 'governmentality' could be mediated with Gramsci's concept of hegemony.

On a second level, it describes a 'line of force' that traverses the history of the West and leads to the preeminence of 'government' over all other types of power.[53] It is the 'pastorate' of the Jewish-Christian tradition, that is to say a particular conception of leadership that understands itself in terms of the relationship of a shepherd to his flock, and has its origin 'in the East and in the Hebrews'.[54] According to Foucault, this leadership concept was foreign to Greek thought. However, this assumption is already challenged by his own counter-examples, according to which the king is addressed 44 times as 'shepherd' in the *Iliad* and 12 times in the *Odyssey*.[55] The Pythagoreans derived from *nomeus*, the shepherd, the word *nomos*, the law, and Nomios, the god-shepherd, which was the title of Zeus.[56] In Plato's *Critias*, *The Republic*, and *The Laws*, the good magistrate is seen as a good shepherd.[57] Plato's *Statesman* applies the shepherd-metaphor to the political leader as well. However, Plato subsequently shows this to be insufficient, because the specifics of the politician's activity must be grasped according to the model of 'weaving': just as the weaver joins the warp and the weft, the statesman binds together the 'virtues in their different forms', and 'different contrasting temperaments'.[58] Foucault's account is accurate, but the example does not demonstrate what he claims it does. Instead of proving that the shepherd-flock relationship is foreign to 'Greek thought', it shows, as Foucault himself admits, that Plato was critically scrutinising 'if not a commonplace, then at least a familiar opinion'.[59] Whereas Foucault confronts the 'oriental' figure of the shepherd with the Greek concept of the king as the 'good pilot', who governs not primarily individuals but the 'ship' of the city-state,[60] a philological evaluation published in the *Reallexikon für Antike und Christentum* comes to the conclusion that Hesiod, Aischylos, Sophocles, and

---

51   Foucault 2008a, p. 186.
52   Foucault 2007, pp. 115 et sq., 121, 192.
53   Foucault 2007, p. 108.
54   Foucault 2007, pp. 123, 147, 364.
55   Foucault 2007, pp. 136 et sqq.
56   Foucault 2007, p. 137.
57   Foucault 2007, p. 138.
58   Foucault 2007, pp. 145 et sq.
59   Foucault 2007, pp. 141 et sq.
60   Foucault 2007, p. 123.

Euripides also applied the title of shepherd 'to military leaders, for example, to captains of ships'.[61] Foucault's association of the pastorate with the Jewish-Christian tradition seems to be inspired by Nietzsche's dichotomy between early Greek thought and the Jewish-Christian 'transvaluation of values'.[62] Furthermore, his assumption of an originally 'oriental' concept of the pastorate is itself what one could describe, following Edward Said, as an 'orientalist' construct that is determined not by the historical materials of the times, but rather by a modern colonialist set of discourses and institutions based on the dichotomy of Occident and Orient.[63] A study of social history could have shown Foucault that stockbreeding (and thereby the figure of the shepherd) was widespread throughout the entire Mediterranean area (and beyond), not only in its 'Eastern' parts.

On a third level the term 'political governmentality' covers a period that starts with the Reformation and Counter-Reformation in the sixteenth century. This period also sees the transition to states having large territories, and in the first half of the seventeenth century coincides with the emergence of 'raison d'Etat'.[64] Foucault is primarily interested in the way the ancient understanding of governing the polis merged with the Christian concept of the shepherd, and how the Christian pastorate became increasingly secularised and reached into everyday life. However, the conceptions of leadership belonging to this type of governmentality – like mercantilism, cameralistics, 'raison d'Etat', 'Polizeiwissenschaft', and the Physiocrats – were still blocked by the predominance of the power of sovereignty, so that 'the art of government could not find its own dimension'.[65]

This concentration on the state was overcome by the 'liberal' art of government only in the middle of the eighteenth century, which in Foucault's account opens up the period of 'modern governmental reason'.[66] It is only in the framework of this fourth meaning that it became 'possible to think, reflect, and calculate the problem of government outside the juridical framework of sovereignty'.[67] What we had learned so far were obviously merely precursors of governmentality; indeed, Foucault proclaims: 'We live in the era of a governmentality discovered in the eighteenth century'.[68] But even this relatively

61   Cf. Engemann 1991, 580.
62   Nietzsche 1999a, Vol. 5, pp. 266 et sqq.
63   Said 2003, pp. 2 et sqq.
64   Foucault 2007, p. 364.
65   Foucault 2007, pp. 102 et sq.
66   Foucault 2008a, pp. 11, 13, 20.
67   Foucault 2007, p. 104.
68   Foucault 2007, p. 109.

narrow usage of the term still covers an enormously complex array which contains multiple formations as varied as liberalism, conservatism, fascism, social democracy, and administrative state-socialism. It remains unclear on what grounds Foucault can put these different varieties in one and the same bag.

So we arrive at four different meanings of 'governmentality', which in Foucault's usage continuously flow into each other: leadership in general as 'a kind of basic condition of human societies';[69] an 'oriental' and then 'Jewish-Christian' pastorate which permeated the culture of the West; political governmentality from the sixteenth century onwards; and liberal governmentality from the eighteenth century onwards. It appears that Foucault made ever new attempts to apply an abstract notion of governmentality to history, without ever arriving at a concrete historical or sociological constellation.

However, not only does the concept's scope oscillate, the level of reality referred to does so as well. Whereas until (and including) Machiavelli the power of sovereignty had the 'territory' and its inhabitants as a target, and, in a 'circular relationship', was its own purpose, the 'government' from La Perrière's *Le Miroir politique* (1555) onwards was related 'to a sort of complex of men and things', 'the intrication of men and things', people involved with wealth, resources, the means of subsistence, etc.[70] However, this certainly cannot be a sustainable definition of a modern, economical type of governmentality. People have always been bound up with 'things', and all domination has had to relate to this connection: for example, to the distribution of natural resources, the conditions of the economic infrastructure, the allocation of the labour-force, and so on. Did Foucault believe in earnest that such an arrangement was a modern invention, whereas the rulers of pre-modern times were only interested in increasing their 'territory' and their power as such? This would indeed be an ideological fairy tale, in which the entire complex of the relations of production, reproduction, and distribution, of the imperial control of raw materials, of the exploitation and over-taxation of the subjugated peoples had vanished. How long could the Roman emperors have entertained the Roman *plebs* with 'bread and circuses' if the provinces had successfully stopped their grain-deliveries for an extended time?

Foucault tried to evade such critical questions by changing the level of argumentation: by the 'art of government' he would not mean 'the way in which governors really governed', but rather 'the reasoned way of governing best and ... reflection on the best possible way of governing'.[71] According to this state-

---

69   Bröckling/Krasmann/Lemke 2000, p. 18.

70   Foucault 2007, pp. 96 et sq.

71   Foucault 2008a, p. 2.

ment, 'governmentality' is not about real practices of leadership and hegemony, but about certain patterns of reflection laid down in guide-books. Such a limitation could indeed be a useful methodological decision. The phenomenological reconstruction of leadership concepts could become an important component of an 'immanent critique' which confronts ideologies with their own 'truth', or in Adorno's words: 'what a society presents itself as being with what it actually is'.[72]

But such a self-limitation contradicts Foucault's definition of governmentality as 'the ensemble formed by institutions, procedures, analyses and reflections, calculations, and tactics that allow the exercise of this very specific, albeit very complex, power that has the population as its target, political economy as its major form of knowledge, and apparatuses of security as its essential technical instrument'.[73] The ensemble of institutions, 'apparatuses of security', practices, and interpretative patterns in a certain historical period would constitute the classical object of an ideology-theoretical research-programme. But the promised research is never realised. Foucault again delivers glossy menus announcing delicious dishes, but the readers never get anything to eat.

This theoretical flimsiness can be studied using the example of liberalism. Foucault claims to analyse liberalism neither as a theory, nor as an ideology, but rather 'as a practice, that is to say, a "way of doing things" directed towards objectives and regulating itself by continuous reflection'.[74] However, this is not what he actually does. Instead of dealing with the real 'practices' of liberalism, he confines himself to the claim that liberalism 'constitutes ... a tool for the criticism of reality', 'a form of critical reflection' on previous or present varieties of governmentality. In particular, liberalism is a critique of excessive government and a concept of governmental self-limitation.[75] In his view, liberalism's capacity of limiting power has to do with the market that operates increasingly as a site of 'veridiction', linking 'a regime of truth to governmental practice'.[76] In an imagined conversation, the *homo oeconomicus* of liberalism talks to the sovereign: 'you must not because you cannot, and you cannot ... because you do not know, and you do not know, because you cannot know'.[77]

---

72   Adorno 1973–86, Vol. 8, p. 347.
73   Foucault 2007, p. 108.
74   Foucault 2008a, p. 318.
75   Foucault 2008a, pp. 16, 28, 320 et sqq.
76   Foucault 2008a, pp. 36 et sq.
77   Foucault 2008a, p. 283.

Foucault assures his audience that he uses the term 'liberal governmental-ity' without 'making a value judgment'.[78] However, the valuation is not to be found in an explicit positive 'judgment', but rather in the way the object of research is construed. According to Michael Behrent, Foucault's liberalism was not one of self-identification, but rather 'an élan implicit in his concepts and arguments'.[79] As Isabelle Garo observes, he applied the discourse of liberalism to liberalism itself.[80] In fact, his narrative never transcends liberalism's ideolo-gical self-image, which portrays itself as a philosophy and politics that stand in opposition to state-regulation. Thereby he obscures the fact that in real his-tory liberalism manifested itself until the late nineteenth century primarily as a 'possessive individualism'[81] aimed at the maintenance of bourgeois property relations, and that it frequently did so with the most violent and disciplinary measures of repressive state apparatuses. Leading liberals not only proclaimed the liberty of the 'individual' against a despotic government, they did so while at the same time declaring slavery to be a 'positive good' that civilization could not possibly renounce. As Domenico Losurdo has shown, the hegemony of lib-eralism coincided with the rise of modern slavery as the most absolute power of humans over humans. 'The paradox ... consists in this: the rise of liberalism and the spread of racial chattel slavery are the product of a twin birth'.[82] Foucault's paradigm, which is often hailed in secondary literature for its superannuation of ideology-critique, does not allow us to grasp the ideological function of lib-eralism in the framework of capitalist and colonialist relations of domination. His account uncritically identifies with the object, thus remaining on the level of an intuitive and empathetic retelling.

If it seemed at first that the late Foucault approached the Gramscian ques-tion of hegemony, it becomes clear now that this was merely a rhetorical ges-ture. Gramsci developed a broad concept of the 'integral state' that combined 'political society' and 'civil society'. This allowed him to analyse the dynamics of hegemony that was 'protected by the armour of coercion' and to focus on the intersections between leadership and domination.[83] Foucault's account makes the overall framework of bourgeois domination and the repressive 'armour' of ideological practices disappear into thin air. The promised investigation of the connection between the techniques of domination and the techniques of

---

78   Foucault 2008a, p. 191.
79   Behrent 2019, p. 27.
80   Garo 2011, p. 155.
81   Macpherson 1962.
82   Losurdo 2011, pp. 35 et sqq.
83   Gramsci 1971, p. 263; Gramsci 1975, Q6, § 88, pp. 763 et sq.; cf. § 155, pp. 810 et sq.

the self gets lost in the immanent reproduction of liberalism's ideological self-understanding.

Thus Foucault's concept of 'governmentality' loses its critical edge on both sides: as it obfuscates capitalist domination, it also severs the aspect of self-conduct and self-techniques from the perspective of collective agency and struggles for social justice, narrowing them down to a neoliberal do-it-yourself ideology.

4   A Sharp Turn against Socialism

When Foucault explained his concept of biopower in the last lecture (17 March 1976) of his course 'Society must be defended', he also tried to demonstrate that socialism is characterised by 'racism from the outset'.[84] It is no surprise that Foucault adduces the example of Stalinist persecutions, which he generalises using the argument that 'biological racism ... is fully operational in the way socialist States (of the Soviet Union type) deal with the mentally ill, criminals, political adversaries, and so on'.[85] The assumption that Stalinist state terrorism can be explained as a continuation of 'biological racism' is of course questionable, and this all the more so when it is indiscriminately extended to the entire bloc of socialist countries. The argument moves within the ideological framework of the totalitarianism theories that became predominant in France in the 1970s.

But I will not discuss here the validity or invalidity of this argument, because whatever the role of 'biological racism' in Stalinism's persecutions might have been, it does not support the preceding assumption that socialism is characterised by racism 'from the outset'. Nor does it support the assumption that 'the most racist forms of socialism were ... Blanquism ..., and then the Commune, and then anarchism' – all of which are forms of a racism that were finally liquidated in Europe by the domination of a reformist social democracy at the end of the nineteenth century.[86] Foucault's assumption is indeed astonishing given the well-documented fact that during the time before World War I it was 'reformist' social democracy in particular that increasingly merged its corporatist class discourses with nationalist and colonialist ideologies.

In order to understand Foucault's reasoning, we must retrace the main argument of his lectures of 1975–6. The course attempts the reconstruction of a

---

84   Foucault 2003c, p. 261.
85   Foucault 2003c, pp. 261 et sq.
86   Foucault 2003c, p. 262.

discourse that conceives of politics as the continuation of war by other means, inverting Clausewitz's statement on war as a 'continuation of political commerce': beneath the state and its peace order there is 'a sort of primitive and permanent war'.[87] Foucault sees this historico-political discourse emerge at the very moment in which, after the end of the civil and religious wars of the sixteenth century, the state gains a monopoly on war, builds up a centralised military apparatus, and eradicates the 'private warfare' of the Middle Ages from the social body.[88] He locates this discourse in the context of popular demands in pre-revolutionary England of the 1630s on the one hand, and on the other hand in a nostalgic 'aristocratic bitterness' towards the end of Louis XIV in France.[89]

Notwithstanding these diverging social locations and perspectives, Foucault subsumes both under the rubric of a 'war discourse' that is to be seen as a 'counterhistory': it challenges the 'Roman' tradition of historiography that was designed to reinvigorate the discourse of power; it breaks the continuity of glory, disrupting the identification of the people with the sovereign; it 'cuts off the king's head', 'inverts the values' of sovereign power, providing an 'explanation from below'; and is closely tied to the idea of revolution.[90] By means of this conceptual arrangement, the political perspective of an embittered and nostalgic aristocracy bemoaning 'the lost age of great ancestors' and invoking 'the rights and privileges of the earliest race'[91] is re-baptised as a 'revolutionary' project 'from below'.

So far we have omitted mentioning that Foucault specifies this supposedly revolutionary 'war discourse' as the discourse of a permanent 'race war', which concerns 'the conquest and subjugation of one race by the other'.[92] Of course this raises the question of the sense in which the term 'race' is being used. Foucault's definitions remain remarkably vague. 'Race' has to do with 'ethnic differences, differences between languages, different degrees of force, vigor, energy, and violence';[93] it is about 'two groups which do not, at least to begin with, have the same language or, in many cases, the same religion'.[94] At one point he specifies that 'the word "race" is not yet pinned to a stable biological meaning', but rather 'designates a certain historico-political divide', whose unity is only the

---

87   Foucault 2003c, pp. 46 et sqq.
88   Foucault 2003c, p. 48.
89   Foucault 2003c, pp. 49 et sq., 56 et sq.
90   Foucault 2003c, pp. 54, 59, 69 et sq., 78.
91   Foucault 2003c, p. 56.
92   Foucault 2003c, p. 60.
93   Ibid.
94   Foucault 2003c, p. 77.

result of 'acts of violence'.[95] Foucault's historical examples include the divide between the Roman conquerors and the conquered Gauls, the chasm between the Norman conquerors and the Saxons in England, or the conquest of Gallo-Roman culture by the Franks. The latter become the imaginary reference point of an aristocratic historiography in France, which Foucault discusses using the example of Henri de Boulainvilliers (1658–1722). According to the perspective of a declining nobility, the 'barbarian' strength of the Francs is derived from the virtues of their warrior aristocracy, whose freedom was 'a freedom of egoism, of greed – a taste for battle, conquest and plunder', to be exercised 'only through domination'.[96] According to this etymology, the term 'franc' is to be derived from Latin 'ferox' (ferocious), i.e. proud, intrepid, haughty, cruel.[97]

Not surprisingly, this is the point where Foucault introduces Nietzsche's notion of the 'great blond ferocity of the Germans', which is obviously a paraphrase of Nietzsche's 'blond Germanic beast' [blonde germanische Bestie] that has lost its dominance over humanity.[98] The suggested etymology of the term 'franc' also coincides ostensibly with Nietzsche's etymological assumptions, for example with the derivation of the Latin word 'bonus' from the warrior. This is meant to prove a connection to the conquering master race, whereas 'malus' supposedly means both 'bad' and 'dark-skinned'.[99] Foucault himself describes the assumption of a permanent race war as 'Nietzsche's hypothesis', opposing it to Wilhelm Reich's 'repression hypothesis'.[100] We are indeed in the midst of a Nietzschean 'grand narrative', which frames the class struggle between aristocracy and a plebeian 'slave revolt' in terms of an antagonism of 'race'. As Domenico Losurdo has shown, the racism of the late Nietzsche and in particular his anti-Semitism are to be analysed in the framework of a 'transversal racialisation' which is directed immediately against the popular classes and the poor (see above Chapter 2.6.3).[101]

Based on this Nietzschean narrative, transposed to the discourses of the sixteenth and seventeenth century, Foucault registers two 'transcriptions' in the early nineteenth century. The first is a biological transcription, articulated with nationalist movements and colonialism, which becomes the discourse of centralised state power. It is a 'state racism', one which claims to 'defend society'

---

95   Ibid.
96   Foucault 2003c, p. 148.
97   Nicolas Freret, quoted in Foucault 2003c, p. 149.
98   Foucault 2003c, 149; cf. Nietzsche, On the *Genealogy of Morality*, Part I, §11; Nietzsche 1999a, Vol. 5, p. 276.
99   Nietzsche, ibid., §5; Nietzsche 1999a, Vol. 5, pp. 263 et sq.
100   Foucault 2003c, p. 16.
101   Cf. Losurdo 2020, pp. 760–63, 782–85, 804–07.

against a hostile race that is infiltrating the social body.[102] The binary of the
former 'race war' is usurped by sovereign power and replaced with that of a
biologically monist society threatened by foreigners and fighting for its 'racial
purity'.[103]

The second transcription is one that redefines the 'race war' in terms of 'class
struggle'.[104] According to this interpretation, the revolutionary project that 'has
constantly undermined Europe since at least the end of the eighteenth century' is 'indissociable' from the 'counterhistory' of races: it has been striving
to 'rekindle' the real race war that once went on at the end of the Middle
Ages.[105] Whenever socialism considers the physical confrontation with the
class enemy, 'racism does raise its head'. This seems to be the reason why Foucault can describe Blanquism, the Commune, and anarchism, none of which
ever assumed a state form, as the 'most racist forms of socialism'.[106]

Foucault's association of 'race war' and 'class struggle' is obviously a dubious
construct. It exploits the etymological ambivalences of the French and English
terms 'race' (Italian 'razza'), which – before their modern racist 'transcription' –
could be used, for example, for tribal affiliations or lineages, for 'zoological'
classifications in the context of animal breeding (in particular horses), and
also for designating the very general meaning of 'species', Latin 'genus' (French
synonyms are 'espèce', 'sorte', 'genre'). This general meaning lived on, so that
even the English version of Eugène Pottier's anthem 'The Internationale' could
include the formulation that the proletarian international 'unites the human
race' (the French original used here the term 'genre humain', the German version changed it to 'erkämpft das Menschenrecht'). Foucault never indicates the
sense in which the historians of the seventeenth and eighteenth century he
refers to used the term.

The groundlessness of Foucault's derivation becomes evident when he tries
to substantiate it with a quote from Marx, who supposedly in 1882, 'toward the
end of his life', wrote in a letter to Engels that 'we found our idea of class struggle
in the work of the French historians who talked about the race struggle'.[107] But
according to the *Marx-Engels Werke* (MEW), no letter sent by Marx to Engels
in 1882 exists, which is why the editors had to add a footnote conjecturing that

102   Foucault 2003c, pp. 60 et sqq.
103   Foucault 2003c, pp. 80 et sqq.
104   Foucault 2003c, p. 60.
105   Foucault 2003c, pp. 79 et sq. Translation corrected: the English translation talks about 'the
      end of the nineteenth century', while the French original correctly indicates the eight-
      eenth century (1997b, p. 69).
106   Foucault 2003c, p. 262.
107   See Foucault 2003c, p. 79.

Foucault might have referred to Marx's letter to Joseph Weydemeyer of 5 March 1852, or to Marx's letter to Engels of 27 July 1854, that is to say, about 30 years before. But this does not help either: in the first letter, Marx points to the historical works of Thierry, Guizot, and John Wade, which should enlighten our democrats of the past 'history of class' – but there is no mentioning of a 'race struggle'.[108] The same is true for the second letter, in which Marx describes Thierry as 'le *père* of the "class struggle" in French historiography'.[109] According to Marx's summary, Thierry's *Histoire de la formation et du progrès du Tiers Etat* argued that the bourgeoisie was able to 'represent' the *Tiers État*, which comprised all estates except the nobility and the clergy. The roots of the bourgeoisie coincide with the emergence of the *Tiers État*. And Marx adds: 'Had Mr. Thierry read our stuff, he would know that the decisive opposition between bourgeoisie and *peuple* does not, of course, crystallize until the former ceases, as *tiers-état*, to oppose the *clergé* and the *noblesse*.'[110]

The 'race war' is obviously a notion that Foucault has taken from Nietzsche's aristocratic 'genealogy' and imposed on the materials of early modernity. It was also Nietzsche who attributed the physical and intellectual features of the 'subjected race' (going back to the *'pre-Aryan* population') to 'modern anarchism, and indeed that predilection to the "Commune", the most primitive form of social structure which is common to all Europe's socialists'.[111]

Up to this point we have dealt with only one component of Foucault's two-pronged critique of socialism's inherent 'racism'. The second component is derived from the concept of biopolitics: the transcription from 'race war' to biological state racism coincides with the transition from sovereign power to 'biopower'. Once the State functions in the biopower mode and assumes control over life through power, 'racism alone can justify the murderous function of the State'.[112] Evidently, the 'murderous' character of the state, its 'right to *take* life or *let* live', relegated by Foucault to a past sovereign power, rebounds with a vengeance. State racism is now 'the precondition that makes killing acceptable'; it 'fragments' the field of the biological that power controls; it 'creates caesuras within the biological continuum addressed by biopower', and introduces a 'break between what must live and what must die'.[113]

---

108   quoted Foucault 2003c, 85 n. 6; cf. Marx and Engels 1957–, Vol. 28, p. 504; Marx and Engels 1975–2005, Vol. 39, p. 61.
109   Marx and Engels 1957-, Vol. 28, p. 381; Marx and Engels 1975–2005, Vol. 39, p. 473.
110   Marx and Engels 1957-, Vol. 28, p. 382; Marx and Engels 1975–2005, Vol. 39, p. 474.
111   Nietzsche, *On the Genealogy of Morality*, I, § 5; Nietzsche 1999a, Vol. 5, pp. 263f.
112   Foucault 2003c, p. 256.
113   Foucault 2003c, pp. 254 et sq.

It remains to demonstrate that socialism, which was already a kind of 'social racism' before the formation of socialist states, also produces a state-racism upon forming a state. The argument is simple: socialism needs to do so because it 'has made no critique of the theme of biopower', and instead has taken it over wholesale.[114] Is Foucault really trying to make the point that socialism has established a 'state racism' simply by introducing universal healthcare, preventive medicine, statistics of the population, cost-free childcare etc.? In any case, Foucault has arranged his concept of 'race war' and racism such that socialism is cornered from two sides: first from its beginnings, then from its post-revolutionary state forms, which are furthermore reduced to one. Socialism in all its varieties is doomed – except when it is superseded by a reformist social democracy at the end of the nineteenth century. And this is actually the time period in which it opens itself up to various ideologies of white supremacy and nationalism.

5   Marx as Stalinism's 'Truth'

It is no surprise that this sharp anti-socialist turn finds its preferred target in Marx. One year after his final lecture in the series *Society must be Defended* (17 March 1976), Foucault published an enthusiastic review of André Glucksmann's book *The Master Thinkers* (1977) in *Le Nouvel Observateur*, March 1977. The review also referred to Glucksmann's earlier book *La cuisinière et le mangeur d'hommes* of 1975, in which the former Maoist broke with his ultra-left past and, inspired by Foucault's *Madness and Civilization*, tried to demonstrate that the Soviet Gulag was the culminating point of Western philosophy, and here in particular of Platonism, classical reason, and Marxism.[115]

Glucksmann's *Master Thinkers* combined this early work by Foucault with his later *Discipline and Punish*, so that, diverging somewhat from Foucault, the disciplinary invention of the 'soul' and the judging 'law' which draws the line between exclusion and inclusion, work simultaneously, not least in penetrating the brains of the revolutionary masses.[116] Glucksmann's narrative of the intellectual preparation of modern mass murder by the 'master thinkers' now focuses on Fichte, Hegel, Marx, and, diverging again from Foucault, Nietzsche. They all 'were not Nazis', but they were linked with Nazism by their 'anti-Semitism', demonstrated, for example in the case of Marx, by the 'furiously

---

114   Foucault 2003c, p. 261.
115   Glucksmann 1975, pp. 109, 112, 173.
116   Glucksmann 1980, pp. 59 et sq.

antisemitic stench of his *On the Jewish Question*'.[117] Of course, Glucksmann omits mentioning that Marx has written this text explicitly against the anti-Semitic argument of the Young Hegelian Bruno Bauer, who claimed that the Jews need to give up their religion in order to become full citizens.[118] Glucksmann comes to the absurd conclusion that it was only with Heidegger 'that a German philosophy appeared that was not antisemitic'.[119] What unites the 'master thinkers' is their orientation towards the power of the state and its 'panoptic apparatus' as the main instrument for transforming the world, thus 'oiling the wheels and tensing the springs of the machinery of extermination'.[120]

Together with Alain Finkielkraut, Bernard-Henri Lévy, and others, Glucksmann belonged to a 'new philosophical vogue' in Paris. 'Suddenly their pictures seemed to be everywhere: on magazines, on television spots, on posters, on t-shirts. Promoted like rock stars, they were immodestly christened, by Lévy himself, "the new philosophers". And in a matter of days, the crux of their "philosophy" ... had been reduced to a jingle: "Marxism is dead." '[121] Gilles Deleuze proclaimed his 'horror' at the new philosophers' recantations and criticised their 'martyrology' as an attitude of 'living on corpses'.[122]

This criticism would apply to Foucault as well. His celebratory review, which leads to the final break with Deleuze and other friends, begins by invoking the 'great rage of facts' against the 'true' discourse and 'thin scenery' of philosophy, political economy, and science. By the former he means the voices of the 'crazies ..., the ill, the women, the children, the prisoners, the tortured, and the dead by the millions', while the latter is characterised as a 'grand theoretical machine that produces dominant rationalities'.[123] Again, Foucault presents himself as an 'insurrectional' intellectual trying to 'desubjugate' local historical knowledge against centralising power-knowledge.[124] But what could once be understood as a strategy of resistance competing with, but also complementary to, a Marxist macro-analysis of the capitalist mode of production, now experiences a decisive shift. What Foucault now attacks as the 'dominant' rationality is, following Glucksmann, 'an entire Left' that explains the Gulag as 'a terrible error' of Stalinism, committed against the intentions of Marx and Lenin. Any attempt

---

117   Glucksmann 1980, p. 94.
118   For a detailed analysis of *Zur Judenfrage*, cf. Haug 1993, pp. 209–216.
119   Glucksmann 1980, p. 94.
120   Glucksmann 1980, p. 118; cf. ibid., pp. 108 et sqq.
121   Miller 1993, p. 295.
122   Quoted after Eribon 1993, pp. 261 et sq.
123   Foucault 2016, pp. 170 et sq.; Foucault 2001b, p. 277.
124   Cf. Foucault 2003c, pp. 7 et sqq.)

at an analytical and political distinction within 'Marxism' is caricatured by the slogan: 'do not listen to the victims; they would only have their torments to relate. Reread the theoreticians; they will tell you the verity of truth'.[125] Against this 'entire Left', Foucault credits Glucksmann with having the 'courage' and 'brilliance' to show 'that there was no "error", that it remained wholly consistent, that Stalinism was the truth – "a little" stripped down, to be sure – of an entire political discourse, that of Marx and perhaps others before him'.[126] His achievement is therefore to '[plaster] onto ideas the death's heads [têtes de mort] that resemble them'.[127]

6   Foucault's Affiliation with Neoliberalism

6.1   *Survey of the Terrain: Ambiguities and Opposite Interpretations*

Foucault's relationship to neoliberalism became an issue widely debated in public, particularly following the publication of the book *Foucault and Neoliberalism*, first in French (2014), then in English (2016).[128] For Daniel Zamora, the late Foucault was 'surprising in his thinly veiled sympathy for, and minimal criticism of, emerging neoliberalism'.[129] Michael Behrent diagnosed a 'deep affinity between Foucault's thought and neoliberalism' and located his 'neoliberal moment' in the 'broad shift of alliances that transformed French intellectual politics in the 1970s' – a shift that found its political expression in August 1976, when President Giscard d'Estaing appointed Raymond Barre, a translator of Friedrich Hayek, as prime minister.[130] Mitchell Dean remarked that Foucault was certainly not 'a card-carrying neoliberal', but that he, 'like many progressive intellectuals of his period ... would look into the liberal and neoliberal repertoire to find ways of renovating social democratic ... politics and escaping its perceived fatal statism'.[131] It is obvious that he was not an admirer of Margret Thatcher or Ronald Reagan, who are not even mentioned in his Lectures on Neoliberalism, nor in his entire *Dits et écrits*, which is itself a symptomatic omission, of course, one that needs to be explained. His context was the formation of a *Second Left*, a minority current in French socialism around Michel Rocard's

125   Foucault 2016, pp. 171 et sq.; Foucault 2001b, p. 278.
126   Foucault 2016, p. 172; Foucault 2001b, p. 278.
127   Foucault 2016, p. 172; Foucault 2001b, p. 279.
128   Zamora 2014, Zamora/Behrent 2016.
129   Zamora 2016b, p. 64.
130   Behrent 2016, pp. 26, 29, 33.
131   Dean 2016, p. 100.

'United Socialist Party' (PSU), the trade union 'French Democratic Confedera-
tion of Labour' (CFDT) and the journal *Faire*, among others. Starting out from
concepts of self-management (autogestion), it defined itself to a large degree by
its opposition to the 'traditional' left's 'social statism', and therefore could open
itself up to neoliberal projects of limiting the state's power.[132] One of the major
intermediaries between the alternative milieu and neoliberal theory was the
economist Henri Lepage, whose popular book *Demain le capitalism* was also
one of the 'main sources' of Foucault's *The Birth of Biopolitics*.[133]

Foucault's affiliation with neoliberalism was also confirmed by some of Foucault's disciples and supporters, who turned neoliberal themselves. The major
witness to this development was François Ewald, who was not only Foucault's
student and wrote his dissertation on the welfare state under his guidance, but
also his assistant from 1976 until Foucault's death in 1984. Ewald was also the
co-editor of his posthumous publications, the *Dits et écrits* and his lectures at
the *Collège de France*. After being a militant Maoist in the early 1970s, Ewald
became a counselor to the French insurance industry, the *Fédération française
des sociétés d'assurance*, as well as an advisor to the primary employers' organisation *Medef*.[134]

In May 2012, Ewald participated in a seminar at the University of Chicago,
where he met the neoliberal economist Gary Becker. He assured Becker that
Foucault fully supported neoliberalism in his lectures on *The Birth of Biopolitics*, and had a positive opinion especially of the works of Becker himself, 'the
most radical of the American neoliberals', as Foucault describes him in that
text.[135] Ewald explained Becker's role as that of a 'liberator for Foucault, a liberator from past models', revealing for him the 'possibility of thinking about
power without discipline ... without coercion, [but] by incitation'. In response
to this, Becker commented on Foucault's work that he 'like[s] most of it and
[doesn't] disagree with much'.[136]

If Ewald is right, the discovery of techniques of the self and the ethical turn
to practices of self-care is due to the encounter with neoliberal concepts of government, and in particular with Becker's concept of 'human capital'. Of course
it can be objected that Foucault must not be held responsible for the interpretation of his work by a companion and successor whom Antonio Negri described

---

132   Behrent 2016, pp. 35 et sqq.
133   Audier 2015, p. 108.
134   Cf. Dean 2016, p. 87.
135   Foucault 2008a, p. 269; cf. Dean 2016, p. 86.
136   Quoted after Dean 2016, pp. 90 et sq. and Newheiser 2016, p. 13.

as a 'rightwing Foucauldian' standing in opposition to the 'true Foucault'.[137] In this vein, David Zeglen questioned an 'unmediated transmission of interpretation from teacher to student, much as Foucault had done when he saw a direct link from Marx to Stalin'.[138]

Several authors argue that the lectures collected as *The Birth of Biopolitics* (1978–9) are to be read as an astonishingly early and clear-sighted critique of neoliberalism. According to David Newheiser, Foucault offers a 'philosophical critique' of neoliberalism that 'traces the contingency of neoliberal biopolitics in order to open a space for concrete acts of resistance'.[139] Andrew Dilts considers the late Foucault's turn to ethics to be a 'sympathetic but ultimately critical response to the emergence of neo-liberal subjectivity, governmentality, and biopower'.[140] Wendy Brown argues that in analysing neoliberalism as a new market-driven political rationality, Foucault's lectures outlined a critique that went beyond the usual perceptions of neoliberalism as an economic policy and demonstrated an 'extraordinary prescience about the contours and importance of a formation that was just then beginning to take shape'.[141] Brown's interpretation is an interesting case in point, because she ultimately leaves open the question of whether Foucault's interest in neoliberalism was 'a reflection of his own attraction to it', or whether his 'seemingly light judgments against neoliberalism' are to be explained by his 'admirable commitment to excavating the novelties that only a genealogical curiosity can discover'.[142] This is not an alternative for Philip Mirowski, who argues that Foucault's prescience is to be explained by the fact that he 'took on board such a large amount of the neoliberal doctrine as a font of deep insight into the nature of governmentality'.[143] And Newheiser, who emphasises Foucault's critique of neoliberalism as biopolitics, seems to be stunned when he observes that 'in contrast to his earlier treatment of biopolitics, Foucault's tone in *The Birth of Biopolitics* is muted'.[144] It seems that the two sides of the controversy cannot evade the problems thrown up by an ambiguous discourse that offers itself to interpretation from opposite perspectives. Zamora explains this ambiguity as Foucault's ability to 'always embody – while distancing himself from – the spirit of his age'.[145]

---

137   Negri in an interview in *Le Monde* (October 3, 2001); quoted after Dean 2016, p. 87.
138   Cf. Zeglen 2017.
139   Newheiser 2016, p. 5.
140   Dilts 2011, p. 132.
141   Brown 2015, pp. 30, 50, 69.
142   Brown 2015, pp. 55, 75, 234 n. 13.
143   Mirowski 2013, p. 97.
144   Newheiser 2016, p. 16.
145   Zamora 2016b, p. 79.

I will approach what Wendy Brown calls Foucault's 'own normative stakes in ... neoliberalism'[146] through a textual analysis that tries to identify both its strengths and the weaknesses. Looking primarily at *The Birth of Biopolitics*, I will submit this approach to a 'symptomatic reading', which, following Althusser, looks at what he detects and what he overlooks, deciphers the not-seen in the seen and as a form of seeing.[147] In order to grasp the different aspects of Foucault's approach to neoliberalism, I will focus first on what he has 'seen' and how his insights could be used for a critical analysis of neoliberalism.

6.2   *Foucault's Contribution to a Critical Analysis of Neoliberalism*
Let us start with an obvious strength: Foucault is indeed one of the few public intellectuals who took neoliberalism seriously and tried to conceptualise it before it came to power through Margret Thatcher's electoral victory in 1979. As Bernhard Walpen has shown, the neoliberal 'Reconquista' during the 1970s, that is to say, the period that witnessed the former minoritarian tendency build up new hegemonic apparatuses, transform existing institutions and parties, and gain traction, was underestimated by both leftist post-68 leaders and Keynesians.[148] With regard to the acute awareness for what is coming, Foucault's lectures could be compared to the work of Stuart Hall, who simultaneously in 1978–9 analysed the dynamics by which neoliberalism, in its British form of 'Thatcherism', merged with right-wing attitudes, and became hegemonic in the conservative party and in large parts of civil society.[149] We will return later to some of the differences between Hall's neo-Gramscian analysis and Foucault's approach.

Another strength of Foucault's approach is an awareness that contradicts the widespread image of neoliberalism as an economic policy oriented towards the withdrawal of the state from the economy. Foucault studies the materials of the Walter Lippmann Colloquium in Paris 1938, an international conference of liberal economists debating the conclusions to be drawn from Lippmann's anti-New Deal book *The Good Society* (1937). This was also the conference where the term 'neo-liberalism' was chosen for the intended new formation. Foucault observes that this new formation defines itself counter to the *laissez-faire* principle of classical liberalism as an 'intervening liberalism', which requires 'an active and extremely vigilant policy'.[150]

146   Brown 2015, p. 55.
147   Cf. Althusser and Balibar 2009, pp. 23 et sqq., 32, 35 et sq.
148   Walpen 2004, pp. 170 et sqq., 193 et sq.
149   Hall 1978.
150   Röpke, quoted after Foucault 2008a, p. 133.

This 'positive' neoliberal interventionism also goes beyond economic policy and can be characterised by the following features: First, by a strong interventionist role for the state. Since the market 'can only appear if it is produced ... by an active governmentality ... government must accompany the market economy from start to finish'; this means that the 'market economy' needs to be uncoupled from the political principle of *laissez faire*.[151] Second, this state interventionism must not be understood as a challenge to the market order or even as its corrective; it does not mean to 'function like a compensatory mechanism for absorbing or nullifying the possible destructive effects of economic freedom on society or the social fabric'.[152] Instead, there is to be an orientation towards a 'privatised social policy', engendered by the assumption that 'it is up to the individual to protect himself against risks through all the reserves he has at his disposal'.[153]

Third, neoliberalism generalises the principles of the market economy and produces its subject as 'an entrepreneur of himself, being for himself his own capital ... his own producer ... the source of his earnings'.[154] German ordoliberalism had already tried to generalise the '"enterprise" form', so that the social fabric is broken down 'not according to the grain of individuals, but according to the grain of enterprises'. Not only must the individual's life 'be lodged ... within the framework of a multiplicity of diverse enterprises', it is also the individual who is to be made 'into a sort of permanent and multiple enterprise'.[155] But whereas the German ordo-liberal model was still tempered by a framework of '"warm" moral and cultural values', liberalism in the US was never just an economic doctrine, but a 'whole way of being and thinking'. US Neoliberalism evidently applies the principles of the market economy to non-economic domains more radically, so that, for example, phenomena like marriage, the care for children, and educational relationships are defined as 'an investment, which can be measured in time'.[156]

Fourth, this generalisation of the 'enterprise form' throughout the social body creates a general consensus buttressed by (and therefore also dependent on) economic growth. Foucault characterises the ordoliberal hegemony in Germany by a 'circuit going constantly from the economic institution to the state ... a permanent genealogy of the state from the economic institution ...

151   Foucault 2008a, pp. 121, 131 et sq.
152   Foucault 2008a, p. 160.
153   Foucault 2008a, p. 145.
154   Foucault 2008a, p. 226.
155   Foucault 2008a, p. 241.
156   Foucault 2008a, pp. 218, 242, 244.

This economic institution ... produces ... a permanent consensus of all those
who may appear as agents within these economic processes, as investors, workers, employers, and trade unions'.[157] He perceives and articulates this interaction between economy and state in terms of a new type of governmentality.
Whereas the classical *homo oeconomicus* was someone 'to be let alone', the
homo oeconomicus designed by Becker is one 'who accepts reality', 'responds
systemically to systematic modifications artificially introduced into the environment', and is therefore 'eminently governable': s/he becomes 'the correlate
of a governmentality which will act on the environment and systematically
modify its variables'.[158]

So far, we can read Foucault's account as a contribution to a critical analysis
of how neoliberalism produces a new hegemony that binds together different
classes and milieus. His observations with regard to the production of a neoliberal *homo oeconomicus* can be compared to Gramsci's analysis of 'Americanism
and Fordism', whose hegemony was 'born in the factory', and was characterised
by the combination of the assembly line, Taylorism, and, in particular in the
Ford factories, high wages that allowed some sections of the workers to participate in mass consumption. Gramsci observed how different agencies, partly
private, partly governmental, organise multiple 'puritan' campaigns against
alcoholism and sexual excesses, thus achieving a 'psycho-physical adaptation
to the new industrial structure'. By means of this 'rationalisation', Fordism created 'with an unheard rapidity and with a sense of purpose never seen in history
a new type of worker and of the human'.[159] Inspired by Gramsci's method of
analysis, W.F. Haug has argued that the hegemonic appeal and perseverance
of neoliberalism are to be explained by its organic connection with the new
mode of production in a 'transnational High-Tech Capitalism'.[160] This mode of
production is characterised (among other things) by an automation of the production process, its deregulation and flexibilisation (often discussed as 'individualisation'), an increase in structural unemployment, and a precarisation
moving from the margins to the centre. Its function of managing the high-tech
mode of production has given neoliberalism several lives and made its resurrection in different political conjunctures possible:[161] after a first conservative
period of neoliberalism in the 1980s (type Reagan and Thatcher), which focused

157 Foucault 2008a, p. 84.
158 Foucault 2008a, pp. 269 et sqq.
159 Gramsci 1971, pp. 285 et sq, 302, 304 et sq. (translation modified); Gramsci 1975, Q 4, § 52,
      pp. 489 et sqq.
160 Haug 2003, p. 41.
161 Haug 2003, pp. 203, 206.

on the dismantling of the Fordist welfare state, a second social-democratic period (type Clinton, Blair, Schröder) was able to integrate entire oppositional groups into the class-compromise of a 'new centre' and thus to generalise neo-liberal hegemony.[162]

This broader context allows us to re-interpret what Foucault describes as a generalisation of the 'enterprise form'. This form is part of neoliberalism's endeavour to create a type of subject, one that is compatible with the new demands of production and reproduction. Obviously, most workers and employees are not being transformed into real 'enterprises'. The formula belongs instead to a complex set of ideological interpellations that call upon people's strivings for self-determination and self-realisation, merging them with the figure of the capitalist 'entrepreneur'. As Frigga Haug has shown with the example of the book *Job Revolution* by Peter Hartz (the former human-resources executive at Volkswagen and adviser to the Social-Democratic chan-cellor Gerhard Schröder), the ideological fusion of self-determined activity and the capitalist 'enterprise-form' is such that it strictly subordinates the invoked creativity and agency to one's 'employability' and 'marketability'. What this comes down to is the 'flexibility' to be brought into action at any time and location, as well as to the quasi-unlimited readiness to work overtime:[163] 'The utopia is brought down to this world and surfaces at the very spot where we are in for it'.[164]

6.3   *Fascinated by Neoliberalism's 'Post-Disciplinary' Governmentality*

Bringing Foucault into dialogue with an ideology-critical analysis of neoliberal hegemony also allows us to perceive what remains 'un-seen' in his account. Similar to his reception of liberalism, which does not consider its actual func-tioning in the context of private property rights, colonialism, and slavery, Fou-cault talks about the neoliberal 'enterprise form' without ever looking at the underlying transformations of the actual enterprises and of the mode of pro-duction in general. It was not least the emerging IT revolution with its tenden-cies toward deregulation and flexibilisation that bumped up against the exist-ing Fordist systems of 'regular' labour contracts, which therefore were criticised for their 'rigidity'. And among other factors it was the increase in unemploy-ment that led to the crisis of the Fordist welfare state, which the elites con-sidered to have become too 'costly'. Confronted with intense class struggles during the 1970s, neoliberalism was not least a political project to restore the

---

162   Candeias 2007, pp. 11 et sqq.
163   Frigga Haug 2003, pp. 610 et sq.
164   Frigga Haug 2003, p. 608.

power of the economic elites.[165] In fact, between 1979 and 2007 the top one percent more than doubled its share of income in the US, whereas that of all other segments of the remaining 99 percent fell.

Instead of locating the emergence of neoliberal hegemony in the contradictions of capitalism leading up to the crisis of Fordism in the 1970s, Foucault adopts the (neo-)liberal terminology of 'the market' and 'market order', which remains fixated on the 'noisy' sphere of circulation and leaves out the 'hidden abode of production'.[166] As we have seen, he also adopts the liberal myth that the 'truth regime' of the market limits the despotism of sovereign power (see above Chapter 5.3). According to Wendy Brown, Foucault speaks 'in an oddly confining liberal idiom', and consequently neglects 'capital as a form of domination' that 'always gives shape to human worlds – relations, arrangements, subject production – in excess of its economic operations and circulations'.[167] Without considering this formative power, 'we will not grasp the intricate dynamics between the political rationality and the economic constraints, and will also not grasp the extent and depth of neoliberalism's power in making this world and unfreedom within it'.[168]

In fact, Foucault has found a theory that allows him to deal with labour, without having to look at the actual sites and conditions in which it takes place. A considerable part of *The Birth of Biopolitics* lectures is dedicated to the explanation of Gary Becker's concept of 'human capital', which performs a miraculous inversion of Marx's theory of labour. Whereas Marx considered capital to be 'dead labour which, vampire-like, lives only by sucking living labour, and lives the more, the more labour it sucks',[169] Becker turned the argument around and conceptualised labour, like all other activities, as a form of 'capital investment'. As Foucault reports, the neoliberal theory of human capital criticises both classical and Marxist approaches for reducing labour to a factor of time or to the commodity of labour-power, and thus to a 'passive' factor of production, submitted to the logic of capital.[170] What Marx analysed as an alienating effect of capitalist relations of production (and of power), is thus imputed to Marx's analysis.[171] Both Becker's concept and Foucault's report erase Marx's analytical distinctions between exchange value and use value, abstract

---

165   Harvey 2005, pp. 16, 19.
166   Marx 1976, p. 279.
167   Brown 2015, pp. 73, 76.
168   Brown 2015, p. 76.
169   Marx 1976, p. 342.
170   Foucault 2008a, pp. 220 et sq.
171   Cf. Garo 2011, p. 173.

labour and concrete labour, thereby obliterating his perspective of an 'association of free people, working with the means of production held in common, and expending their different forms of labor-power in full self-awareness'.[172] Instead, Foucault allows Becker's human capital concept to be disguised as a kind of 'theory of praxis': it claims to rehabilitate the worker as an 'active economic subject' using the means available as an 'economic conduct practiced, implemented, rationalized, and calculated'.[173]

This is where Becker's 'rational choice theory' comes into play: labour is thought of as an activity amongst others that individuals choose over other activities. What Foucault portrays as neoliberalism's 'essential epistemological transformation' consists in a shift from analysing conditions of production or mechanisms of exchange to the study of individuals' 'substitutable choices'.[174] 'Rational conduct', Foucault explains, 'is any conduct which is sensitive to modifications in the variables of the environment and which responds to this in a non-random way'. This leads to the conclusion that economics can be defined 'as the science of the systematic nature of responses to environmental variables'.[175] Since we operate on this model as rational cost-benefit optimisers, all our activities can be analysed as forms of capital investment. 'The neo-liberal analysts look out at the world and ... see heterogeneous human capital, distinct in their specific attributes, abilities, natural endowments, skills. They see entrepreneurs of the self ... responsive agents to the reality of costs and benefits'.[176]

To the extent that Foucault adopts this kind of 'rational choice' concept of human practice, and restricts his analysis to individuals' responses to their respective environment, he jeopardises any possibility for comprehending the structures of power and of domination. His decision to confine himself to the reprogramming of liberal governmentality without considering the development of capitalism, its transformations, its effects on income polarisation and precarisation, etc., is based on the questionable methodological assumption that it is possible to study a change in governmental 'power' patterns without analysing the actual power relations of which they are a part, and by which their change is propelled. As Tilman Reitz observes, this abstraction prevents him from 'establishing a sustainable position towards his object': the neoliberal

---

172   Marx 1976, p. 171.
173   Foucault 2008a, p. 223.
174   Foucault 2008a, p. 222.
175   Foucault 2008a, p. 269.
176   Dilts 2011, p. 138.

theories seem to emerge out of nothing and to find acceptance without any motivation – the reasons for their importance and success remain obscure.[177]

Foucault is fascinated by a new neoliberal 'governmentality', applied not to the subjects directly (like disciplinary power) but rather to their economic and social 'environment'. What is at stake with neoliberalism is 'whether a market economy can in fact serve as the principle, form and model for a state which ... is mistrusted by everyone on both the right and the left ... Can the market really have the power of formalization for both the state and society?'[178] Taking note of a critique of the state shared by both the right and the left, he asks whether the neoliberalisation of the state is providing an adequate response to this criticism. The political stakes are high: if the answer is positive, the state-critical position of the 'second left' could happily merge with neoliberal ideologies.

The question is not answered directly, of course. We have to look elsewhere, namely to where he distances himself from what he calls the 'state-phobia' of the left. By this he means a moral attitude that blames the state for everything evil, assumes its unlimited growth, its seeds of fascism, the inherent violence beneath its social welfare paternalism, thus blurring the differences between social security, the administrative apparatus, and the concentration camps.[179] Of course, what he now questions as an 'inflationary' critique resembles his own former position in Society Must Be Defended, where he argued that the state's biopower necessarily breeds 'state racism', so that, for example, Nazism can be portrayed as a coincidence between a generalised biopower and a generalised sovereign right to kill.[180] It is likely that many students in the audience still remember Foucault's own sweeping critique of the state and are sympathetic to it. Addressing these state-critical attitudes of an anti-authoritarian left, he concludes that what we witness now is not the growth of the state, but rather its reduction: 'all those who share in the great state phobia should know that they are following the direction of the wind and that in fact, for years and years, an effective reduction of the state has been on the way', together with a reduction of a ' "statifying" and "statified" (étatisante et étatisée) governmentality'.[181] What Foucault sees emerging is a neoliberal governmentality characterised by 'an optimization of systems of difference, in which the field is left open to fluctuating processes, in which minority individuals and practices are tolerated ... in which there is an environmental type of intervention instead of the internal

---

177   Reitz 2005, p. 373.
178   Foucault 2008a, p. 117.
179   Foucault 2008a, pp. 186 et sqq.
180   Foucault 2003c, p. 260.
181   Foucault 2008a, pp. 191 et sq.

subjugation of indidviduals'.[182] The message is clear: 'In their critique of state power … leftists were the objective allies of liberals'.[183]

Let us try to dissect Foucault's argument into different layers. Foucault is certainly right when he turns against leftist tendencies to interpret the advent of a neoliberal era in terms of the rise of a new fascism or proto-fascism. In a tumultuous panel discussion of 23 March 1979 at the University of Paris-8 in Vincennes, he complains about a widespread political and moral 'laziness' that obstructs recognition of the new. Instead of a new fascism or totalitarianism that many on the left predict, he argues that neoliberalism offers a 'more sophisticated solution … a sort of disinvestment of the state'.[184] Similarly to his earlier abandonment of a class-reductionist concept of power in 1972 (see above Chapter 3.8), he turns away from an untenable 'gauchist' position, but at the price of a no less simplistic obliteration of class and state power altogether. The assumption of a 'withering away' of the state is of course a neoliberal myth that contradicts even Foucault's own insights into the role of an active, 'intervening' neoliberal state. We can see here the impact of Foucault's main source regarding neoliberalism, namely Henri Lepage's *Demain le capitalism*, which presents neoliberalism as a state-critical project that was compatible with both the radical philosophy of the New Left and the *Nouveau Philosophes*.[185] Apart from the anti-statist perspective, such an alliance requires the common understanding that political liberalism and its human rights discourse are to be based on capitalism and on economic liberalism as its 'scientific foundation'.[186]

Foucault is either not aware of or not interested in the fact that the economic doctrine of neoliberalism was first put into practice in the state-terroristic framework of Chile's military dictatorship under Pinochet. Shortly after the putsch in 1973, the so-called 'Chicago boys' around Milton Friedman and Arnold Harberger submitted their proposals for new economic policies, which were realised in the shocktherapy of 1975 onwards. After around 1978, another neoliberal tendency, the 'Virginia School' or 'Public-Choice-School' around James M. Buchanan and Gordon Tullock, became predominant in Chile – a school which was mainly concerned with the 'marketisation' of the state.[187] But also in the capitalist centres, the neoliberal project was never about a withdrawal of the state in general. Whenever neoliberalism conquered the

---

182   Foucault 2008a, pp. 259 et sq.
183   Behrent 2019, p. 26.
184   Foucault 1979; cf. Behrent 2019, pp. 16–23.
185   Lepage 1978, pp. 55, 422.
186   Lepage 1978, p. 13.
187   Cf. Walpen and Plehwe 2001, pp. 45 et sqq., 56 et sq.

'commanding heights' of state power, it did not reduce 'the state', but only dispensed with the parts of the welfare state that reflected the social-political class-compromise of Fordism. In particular in the USA, the prison system and other predominantly repressive apparatuses skyrocketed. Based on the observation that neoliberalism 'entails the enlargement and exaltation of the penal sector of the bureaucratic field', Loïc Wacquant proposes to go beyond an economic definition, which he considers to be 'thin and incomplete', and to 'elaborate a thicker notion that identifies the institutional machinery and symbolic frames through which neoliberal tenets are being actualized'.[188] As a *transnational political project* aiming to remake the nexus of market, state, and citizenship from above', neoliberalism articulates four institutional logics, namely a) economic reregulation promoting 'the market' as the optimal device for organising the gamut of human activities, b) 'welfare state devolution, retraction, and recomposition', c) the 'cultural trope of individual responsibility', and d) 'an expansive, intrusive, and proactive penal apparatus which penetrates the nether regions of social and physical space'.[189]

In this context, Foucault's assumption of the reduction of a 'statifying' and 'statified' governmentality probably refers to what he perceives as the normative-disciplinary system of the Fordist state. As soon as we try to verify his assumption of a less disciplinary governmentality, we encounter the methodological problem that Foucault confines himself to evaluating the theoretical discourses of neoliberal economists such as Schultz, Buchanan and Becker and fails to consider not only the transformation of (macro- and micropolitical) power relations, but also the political or cultural discourses by which neoliberalism gained hegemony. Tilman Reitz has criticised this as an 'astonishingly narrow methodological framework', whereas Wendy Brown held that it represents an 'un-Foucauldian' archive.[190]

At the same time that Foucault delivered his lectures on neoliberalism, Stuart Hall investigated how neoliberalism in the UK gained hegemony in the political form of a right-wing populism that combined an anti-statist discourse with the principles of 'law and order', the importance of social discipline and authority, and the urgent need for more policing and tougher sentencing.[191] As he specified in a later analysis, it was by means of the contradictory combination of an 'iron regime', racist enemy images, and a populist mobilisation 'from below' that Thatcherism 'effectively penetrated, fractured,

---

188   Wacquant 2009b, pp. 305 et sq.
189   Wacquant 2009b, pp. 306 et sq.
190   Reitz 2005, p. 137; Brown 2015, p. 54.
191   Hall 1979, pp. 15, 17, 19.

and fragmented the territory of the dominated classes'.[192] Since the 1950s and
1960s, numerous intellectuals in the USA worked on the project of a 'fusionism'
between 'libertarians' and conservative 'traditionalists'.[193] Their success manifested itself towards the end of the 1970s, when a neoliberal-neoconservative
bloc made the electoral victory of Ronald Reagan possible.

It is obvious that the neoliberal utopia of a post-disciplinary governmentality received and shared by Foucault does not coincide with neoliberalism's
actual governmental strategies on the ground, in particular not during its
first conservative period. But also in its social-democratic and culturally more
'progressive' stages, neoliberalism developed its own varieties of 'disciplinary
power' through the deregulation of labour relations, 'lean production', the 'just-
in-time' principle, and the privatisation and marketisation of 'non-economic'
domains of society. What Foucault imagined as an open and flexible governmentality was in reality marked by a bifurcation between areas of upper- and
middle-class 'self-regulations' (including more tolerance towards 'minority'
identities and practices), and the disciplinary supervision of the unemployed
and precarised sections of the subaltern classes. According to Wacquant, neoliberalism has produced a 'Janus-faced Leviathan', a *centaur state*, liberal at
the top and paternalistic at the bottom … a comely and caring visage towards
the middle and upper classes, and a fearsome and frowning mug toward the
lower class'.[194] Foucault overlooked the latter and focused on the former: his
expectation of a flexible system of fluctuating differences 'presents neoliberalism as an almost providential alternative to the repressive disciplinary model of
society'.[195] It articulates the point at which the post-68 movements' critique of
disciplinary 'normalisation' could meet and merge with the neoliberal critique
of a bureaucratic and stifling welfare state.

What Foucault sees and at the same time blocks out is a successful 'passive
revolution' (Gramsci), in which neoliberalism has 'converted its enemies unwittingly to its own ideas'.[196] Boltanski and Chiapello describe this co-optation
using the framework of a contentious relationship between two different types
of critique, a 'social critique' anchored in the labour movement and focused
on the struggle against exploitation and social injustice, and an 'artistic cri-

192   Hall 1988, p. 42.
193   Cf. Walpen 2004, pp. 172 et sq., 203 et sq.; Diamond 1995, pp. 29 et sqq. 'Reverence for the
       past and an enduring social order balanced the fusionists' adjoining commitment to indi-
       vidualism' (p. 30).
194   Wacquant 2009b, p. 312.
195   Behrent 2016, p. 52.
196   Zamora 2016b, p. 80.

tique' emerging from intellectual and student milieus targeting hierarchical power, authoritarianism and discipline. The two types were temporarily connected during the 68-movement in France, but parted company afterwards and increasingly turned against each other. The radical 'artistic critique' first took on the 'social critique', dismantled the 'statism' of the PCF and the 'bureaucracy' of the trade unions and foiled the attempts at an alliance between leftists and parts of the Catholic Church. It was then successfully co-opted by a 'new spirit of capitalism'.[197] The post-68 constituents of a new politico-administrative elite 'had become experts in the Foucauldian critique of power, the denunciation of union usurpation, and the rejection of authoritarianism in all its forms, above all that of petits tyrants'.[198]

   We can see in hindsight that neoliberalism's successful absorption of the left, which was facilitated by the latter's incapabability to organically connect 'class politics' with 'new social movements', had a long-term impact on the hegemonic constellation that paved the way for the ascent of right-wing populism: as the leftist intellectuals turned away from workers' concerns for the conditions of their daily lives, whole sectors of the subaltern classes sought out a different type of representative, and, in a 'negative form of self-affirmation', shifted over to the *Front National* (renamed *Rassemblement national*) as 'the only party that seemed to care about them'.[199]

6.4   *The Assault on the Fordist Welfare State*

The implications of Foucault's affiliation with neoliberalism become clearer when we look at the counterpart of his utopia of neoliberal governmentality, namely his critique of the French system of social security. Foucault's critical stance goes back to his earlier 'gauchist' position, according to which the working class was irrevocably integrated in bourgeois society. Consequently the spirit of insurgency was to be found instead at the margins of society, in the 'underclass', among the 'excluded', in the youth gangs of the banlieues, etc.[200] As Daniel Zamora has shown, significant parts of the post-68 movements, and among them Foucault, had given up examining the connections between 'exploitation' and 'exclusion', and increasingly opposed them to each other. As the concept of 'social class' receded, the focus shifted from the struggle against social inequality to that against 'normalizations of behaviors and iden-

197   Boltanski/Chiapello 2007, pp. 36 et sqq., 167 et sqq., 326, 441 et sqq.
198   Boltanski/Chiapello 2007, p. 198.
199   Eribon 2013, pp. 131, 133.
200   Foucault 2001a, Nr. 105, pp. 1170 et sq.

tities imposed on subjects, as well as against Marxism's "social statism" ' – a trajectory which ultimately 'paved the way for the neoliberal assault on the welfare state'.[201]

When Foucault addressed the apparatuses of the 'disciplinary machinery' in an interview in 1978 he referred to the barracks, schools, workshops, and prisons that ensure that no individual escapes supervision and control; significantly, he added the 'mechanisms of assistance and insurance', which not only contribute to economic rationalisation and political stabilisation, but also individualise each person's life, which is 'indispensable to the exercise of power in modern societies'.[202] We can see here a combination of biopower, directed to the 'life' of the population, and disciplinary power, which seeks the normalisation of each individual. A similar intersection is at play when Foucault argues in another interview (1977) that today's relationship between state and population 'operates essentially in the form of a "security pact"': as the state guarantees 'security', it also intervenes whenever the 'weft of daily life [trame de la vie quotidienne]' is perforated by unforeseeable events, which amounts to an 'omnipresent solicitude'.[203] The power of this 'insurance society' [société assurancielle] is more skillful and more subtle than the one in totalitarian states. Consequently, according to Foucault, we must leave behind the old struggles against nationalism, fascism, imperialism and instead start from 'the anxious relationship people have with these mechanisms of security', that is with the 'social security mechanisms, which surveil people day in and day out'.[204]

François Ewald emphasises one aspect of the 'insurance society' when he describes the welfare state as fulfilling the 'dream of "biopower"'. According to him, the welfare state criticises the liberal state for being a 'bad manager of life', and claims to protect not what people make of their lives, but rather 'life' itself, being alive and having basic needs:[205] 'This is the great displacement: value is no longer in freedom, but in the fact of being alive'.[206] Ewald's opposition between 'liberty' and the protection of 'life' associated with 'basic needs' reveals his own neoliberal perspective and points to an underlying ideological struggle about the definition and interpretation of human rights. This question is also at stake when Foucault questions the Fordist social security system.

201   Zamora 2016b, pp. 64, 67, 73.
202   Foucault 2001b, p. 551.
203   Foucault 2001b, p. 385.
204   Foucault 2001b, pp. 386 et sq.
205   Ewald 1986, pp. 374 et sq.
206   Ewald 1986, p. 375.

As a first example of Foucault's critique let us take his comments on the 'negative income tax'. This tax, proposed by Milton Friedman, but also taken up by Giscard d'Estaing and other politicians in France, is a recurring but never fully implemented neoliberal proposal to provide a minimum standard of living for the poor by distributing a cash benefit. The immediate advantage for its neoliberal proponents is that it would render an increase in the minimum wage superfluous and could justify the cancellation of various assistance measures such as food stamps and additional social security programmes. In his report, which veers subtly back and forth 'between analysis and positive evaluations',[207] Foucault points out that the state provides a minimum level of security for the poor in the form of a cash benefit, while at the same time 'giving up the idea that society as a whole owes services like health and education to each of its members'.[208] The tax is not concerned with equality, social justice or 'relative poverty', but only with attenuating 'absolute poverty'; it does not modify this or that cause of poverty, is even not interested in investigating why 'someone falls below the level of the social game', but only functions on the level of its effects.[209] It does not contain a redistributive strategy that tries to change the mechanisms of the economic 'game' (for example, by a progressive tax). Above the threshold of the negative tax, 'everyone will have to be an enterprise for himself or for his family'. The tax is also no longer bound to the Keynesian objective of full employment, but instead provides 'a kind of infra- and supraliminal floating population ... a constant reserve of manpower which can be drawn on if need be'.[210]

A 'floating' surplus population of this kind is not a new invention, of course, but existed already in 'liberal' capitalism of the nineteenth century. Marx analysed it as a necessary component of capitalist accumulation, which – together with 'latent', 'stagnant' and pauperist layers of the industrial 'reserve army' – demonstrates the structural irrationality of the capitalist mode of production.[211] It is obvious why corporate elites have a vital interest in getting rid of the 'rigid' labour regulations of Fordism; this enables them to better exploit the economic and psychological pressure that unemployment and precarity exert on wages and working conditions. This does not prevent Foucault from celebrating the negative tax as a new governmental variety, by which 'the assisted population ... is assisted in a very liberal and much less bureaucratic way than

207   Pestaña 2011, p. 120.
208   Foucault 2008a, pp. 203 et sq.
209   Foucault 2008a, pp. 204 et sq.
210   Foucault 2008a, p. 206.
211   Marx 1976, pp. 794 et sqq.

it is by a system focused on full employment … Ultimately it is up to people to work if they want or not work if they don't'.[212] As neoliberalism's actual social politics – from Clinton's 'workfare' to Schröder's 'Hartz IV laws' – exhibits, Foucault's expectation that disciplinary power would be overcome was an illusion.

Without any critical distance, Foucault quotes a report of 1976 in the *Revue française des affaires sociales*, which complains that social security increases the cost of labour, thus endangering employment and distorting international competition to the detriment of countries with the most expensive social security.[213] What is under attack here is a social security system (called 'La Sécu') that the labor movement has been fighting for since its beginnings. After parts of that system became law during the *Front Populaire* (1936–8), it was finally implemented directly after the Second World War in 1945, during the provisional French government and under the leadership of the communist labour secretary Ambroise Croizat. As usual, it remains an open question as to whether Foucault is just reporting the talking points of the neoliberal assault, or whether they correspond to his own views.

But this ambiguity vanishes when he argues in the panel discussion of 23 March 1979 at the University of Paris-8 in Vincennes that under the conditions of the oil crisis of the 1970s, the state 'can no longer … be a welfare state'.[214] In an interview in 1983 with Robert Bono, the general secretary of the CFDT at the time, he declares the existing system of social guarantees to be no longer viable: first, it has reached the financial limits of the 'rationality of modern societies'; second, it is obsolete because of its 'perverse effects', namely its increasing 'rigidity' and 'growth in dependence'.[215] To be sure, Foucault distances himself from a 'wild liberalism that could lead to individual coverage for those with means and an absence of cover for the rest'. And he proclaims to associate the notion of security with 'more diverse, and more flexible relations with oneself and with one's environment', and proposes an arrangement by which 'the individual would no longer be a "subject" in the sense of subjection [au sens de l'assujettissement]'.[216] However, when he recommends the transformation of 'the field of social institutions into a vast experimental field',[217] he seems to forget that the actual relations of force in this 'experimental field' are increasingly determined by neoliberal hegemony.

---

212   Foucault 2008a, p. 207.
213   Foucault 2008a, pp. 199 et sq.
214   Foucault 1979; cf. Behrent 2019, p. 17.
215   Foucault 1988a, p. 160; Foucault 2001b, p. 1187.
216   Foucault 1988a, pp. 161 et sq., 166, 175; Foucault 2001b, pp. 1187 et sq., 1192, 1200.
217   Foucault 1988a, p. 165; Foucault 2001b, p. 1191.

But there is more at stake than a naïve misconception of the political con-juncture. The decisive point is that he himself deconstructs the notion that adequate healthcare for all is to be recognised as a human right. The imple-mentation of this right was not only an essential demand of the international labour movement, it was also anchored after World War II in the *Universal Declaration of Human Rights* of 1948, which in its in Art. 25,1 asserted the 'right to a standard of living adequate for the health and well-being ... including food, clothing, housing and medical care and necessary social services'. It belongs to the 'collective rights' that were part of the East-West compromise formation in the United Nations. It is no coincidence that this 'postwar' combination of indi-vidual and collective rights was denounced by neoliberal ideologues, among them Friedrich Hayek, as being 'totalitarian in the fullest sense of the word', because it was based on an interpretation of society as a 'deliberately made organization' capable of securing social justice.[218]

Foucault questions the notion of a 'right to health' [droit à la santé] with the remark that good health does not derive from a 'right',[219] which of course down-plays the possibility that rights can be substantiated in a way such that they do help to protect people's life and well-being. The 'argument' is more a gesture meant to refer back to Foucault's critique of the 'law' and the corresponding 'rights' as belonging to an outdated 'sovereign power'. Foucault goes on: if one specifies the 'right to health' as a right to medical care, healthy work conditions, etc., the question arises as to whether a society 'must try to satisfy by collective means individuals' need for health'. As soon as its pracitical realisation is con-sidered, this question cannot be answered positively.[220] What is delegitimised here is even society's modest Keynesian obligation to '*try* to satisfy' (chercher à satisfaire) these basic needs, for example through 'Medicare for all' or other varieties of universal health care.

According to Foucault, a collective right of this kind cannot be realised because of 'the relationship between an infinite demand and a finite system'.[221] In his view, the social-security machinery has reached 'a point in its develop-ment at which we will have to decide what illness, what type of suffering, will no longer receive coverage – a point at which, in certain cases, life itself will be at risk'.[222] At this point, Robert Bono seems to sense the social-Darwinistic and also (late) Nietzschean implication of this triage fantasy. He asks Foucault

---

218   Hayek 1976, p. 104; cf. the evaluation in Rehmann 2013, pp. 275–83.
219   Foucault 1988a, p, 170; Foucault 2001b, pp. 1195 et sq.
220   Foucault 1988a, p, 170; Foucault 2001b, pp. 1195 et sq.
221   Foucault 1988a, p, 173; Foucault 2001b, p. 1198.
222   Foucault 1988a, p. 171; Foucault 2001b, p. 1197.

whether we need to go back to 'a certain way of eliminating the most biologically weak individuals'. Foucault responds with the sweeping assumption that
'such choices are being made all the time', following a certain rationality, and
that he himself has 'no solution to offer'.[223] It is obvious that Foucault is dodging
the question. He cannot deny such horrible consequences, and yet is not able
or willing to rethink his assault on collective human rights and social guarantees. This is obviously a low point for an intellectual who, by his early books
Birth of the Clinic and *Madness and Civilization*, obtained his fame for exploring the construction of 'illness' and was considered to be a radical champion
for the populations marginalised as 'sick' and 'pathological'.

6.5   *Foucault's Self-Techniques as Part of a Neoliberal Transvaluation*
With the electoral victories of Margaret Thatcher in the UK in 1979 and of
Ronald Reagan in the USA in 1980, neoliberalism started its conquest of the
'commanding heights' in the capitalist centres. In the mid-1980s, the Thatcher
government crushed the miners' strike led by the National Union of Minework-
ers, breaking the backbone of the labour movement; the Reagan administration
achieved a similar goal by suppressing the strike of the air traffic controllers'
union (PATCO). Neoliberal governments issued dramatic tax cuts for the rich
and pushed through an austerity regime that led to an extraordinary wealth
polarisation, real wage stagnation, increased precarity and an escalation of
poverty rates.

   Foucault did not bother to make his vision of a tolerant post-disciplinary governmentality congruent with the workings of 'really existing Neoliberalism'. He
moved on and simultaneously went back in history. His research, which finally
materialised (among other places) in the second, third and fourth volume of
his *History of Sexuality*, focused on the genealogy of the techniques of the self.
In his second volume he investigated the classical Greek culture of the fourth
century B.C.E. and focused on discourses around *aphrodisiac* and 'practices
of the self' constituting an 'aesthetics of existence'.[224] His third volume, *The
Care of the Self*, dealt with the Hellenistic-Roman ethics of the first two centuries C.E., in which he observed a more pugnacious relationship to one's desires
and pleasures and diagnosed a generalisation of self-care practices towards
a self-reflexive 'cultivation of the self'.[225] Expanding and complementing his
earlier studies of confession and the 'pastorate', his fourth volume, *Les aveux de
la chair*, unfinished and published posthumously in 2018 (against his declared

223   Foucault 1988a, p. 172; Foucault 2001b, p. 1197.
224   Foucault 1990, pp. 12 et sq, 35 et sqq., 89 et sqq.
225   Foucault 1986, pp. 39 et sqq., 81 et sqq., 122 et sqq.

will), investigated the discourses of the Christian 'Church Fathers' who were obsessed by the 'experiences of the flesh', that is of the 'body consumed by concupiscence', and construed a subject of desire whose hidden truth needs to be scrutinised, deciphered and talked about.[226]

I will not follow Foucault into his enormous research on the genealogy of self-care discourses and the corresponding ethics. The empirical strengths and potential weaknesses of these late works cannot be discussed here. But it should be noted that the theoretical arrangement is still inspired by his Nietzscheanism, which is not to be reduced to his former 'war hypothesis', as Thomas Lemke assumes (see above Chapter 3.2),[227] but manifests itself now in a different way. Foucault's trajectory from a Greek-Roman ethics centred on techniques of the self to the 'pastoral' morality of Christianity, which was then developed further by modern power-knowledge combinations that engendered the 'normalisation' of Western society, both moves within and fine-tunes Nietzsche's grand narrative stretching from an ancient ur-aristocratic 'pathos of distance' to its 'transvaluation' by the Judeo-Christian 'slave-revolt in morals', and from there to the ideologies of modern democracy (including its socialist and anarchistic derivates). The parallelism already applies to Foucault's opposition between an ethics as an 'aesthetics of existence' and a morality of duties, which echoes Nietzsche's endeavour to overcome universal moral concepts (be they Christian or Kantian) by an ethics conceived of as an art of living, whereby one is capable of ' "giving style" to one's character'.[228] Both Nietzsche and Foucault start their moral genealogy from the conduct of life of a male and aristocratic elite of an ancient slaveholder society. Foucault is well aware that the Greek ethics he interpreted as an ensemble of self-care practices was confined to a 'very small number of individuals' and belonged 'to a virile society, to dissymmetry, exclusion of the other, obsession with penetration'. However, what interests him in this regard is not the ethical impact of the exclusionary elitism or the intersection of class and patriarchal domination, but rather the fact that it did not set up the demand 'that all obey the same behavior pattern', but was based on 'individual choice', driven by the will to live a beautiful life.[229] Similarly to Nietzsche, the loss of an uninhibited relationship to the Aphrodisia, and the ensuing moralisation and pathologisation, are connected to a certain levelling down of the relations of domination, which now (during Roman Hellenism) 'had to be associated with certain forms of recipro-

---

226 Foucault 2018, pp. 50 et sq., 235, 245; cf. Elden 2018 and Lemke 2019, pp. 300 et sqq.
227 Lemke 2019, pp. 101 et sqq.
228 *Gay Science*, Aph. 290; Nietzsche 1999a, Vol. 3, p. 530; cf. Schmid 1991, pp. 187–99.
229 Foucault 1988b, p. 245; Foucault 2001b, Nr. 354, pp. 1517 et sq.; Foucault 1983, pp. 230, 233.

city and equality' and are mediated by a more independent position of the
woman, a more important role of the 'law of the heart' and an encompassing
'reason'.[230] What in Nietzsche's account is a critique not only of Christianity
and philosophical idealism, but also of democratic and humanistic concepts
that contained the plebeian perspectives of the 'little people' (even if only in
a subaltern position) and therefore belittled and humiliated what is (for Nietzsche) valuable in humanity, is transformed by Foucault into the more subtle
critique of an 'anthropological era', which by its humanistic power-truth nexus
produces the modern subject as a 'confessing animal' and submits modern society to a (disciplinary and biopolitical) normalisation.

It is not surprising that Foucault's new emphasis on techniques of the self
was perceived as an 'in-group-privatism', privileged aestheticism, or the celebration of an individualistic masculinist morality.[231] Arguing from the perspective of a 'social anarchism', Murray Bookchin questioned Foucault's 'lifestyle
anarchism' which, by replacing political engagement with 'personal insurrection', denied the need for 'establishing distinctly empowered self-managing
institutions against the very real power of capitalist and hierarchical institutions'.[232] Looking at Foucault's theoretical arrangement, we are confronted
with the paradox that the opening up of Foucault's concept of power towards
techniques of the self, which contains valuable potentials for a differentiated
power analysis, coincides with his being fascinated by a neoliberal 'governmentality' that he expected to allow for more self-determination. The intersection of his Nietzschean grand narrative and his affiliation with neoliberal
theory helps explain why Foucault does not complement his earlier power
concepts 'from above' with a Spinozian concept of power as a cooperative
capacity to act (*potentia agendi*), and instead subjects the agency he has discovered to the individualistic forms of self-centred techniques (see above,
Chapter 5.2).

Let us look at some of the debates in the scholarly literature. Echoing François Ewald, Andrew Dilts argues that Foucault's turn to practices of the self is
'indebted to the radical form of neo-liberal subjectivity expressed in the theory of human capital', and that particularly Becker's elaboration of it allowed
him to think about the role that subjects play in their own formation.[233] But
he interprets this shift as a critique of neoliberalism in the sense of an 'internal
response' that uses the space opened up by neoliberal subjectivity, and at the

---

230   Foucault 1986, pp. 75 ff., 91 ff., 95.
231   Cf. Kammler 1986, pp. 203 et sq.; Rochlitz 1989, p. 297; Schlesier 1984, pp. 819 et sq., pp. 823.
232   Bookchin 1995.
233   Dilts 2011, pp. 132, 145.

same time goes beyond it by linking freedom to ethics.[234] But why would the 'linkage of freedom to ethics' in itself constitute a critique of neoliberalism? The underlying assumption that neoliberals do not understand 'that they are part of an ethical project',[235] is unconvincing: every new social and political formation needs to develop its moral justifications, and there is no reason to believe that neoliberals are unaware of this. David Newheiser argues that Foucault considered neoliberal governmentality to be still a variety of 'biopolitics', whereby the state manages human behaviour by modifying its economic and social 'environment', so that 'a society without subjection remains on the horizon, as yet unrealized'.[236] But his conclusion that this proves Foucault's critical distance to neoliberalism does not account for his own observation that the meaning of 'biopolitics' has in the meantime shifted considerably: as soon as Foucault addresses the specific neoliberal variety of 'biopolitics', all his former accusations of it being linked to genocide, to state racism, concentration camps and Gulags[237] have miraculously vanished. And if we follow Newheiser's assessment that Foucault confronts neoliberalism with a utopian horizon of a not-yet realised 'society without subjection' – an interpretation which, however, contradicts Foucault's persistent rejection of 'utopias' – this 'not-yet' could also be an integral part of the utopian 'excess' ('Überschuss' in the sense of Ernst Bloch) of neoliberal ideologies. Foucault himself reports that (neo-)liberalism in the US 'is a sort of utopian focus which is always being revived', and he complements this with an assessment attributed to Hayek that neoliberalism 'needs utopia', and should therefore not leave the production of utopias to the socialists.[238] According to Trent Hamann, Foucault's work on self-care and techniques of the self 'lends itself quite nicely to neoliberalism's aim of producing free and autonomous individuals concerned with cultivating themselves', and thus provides a 'technical support manual for the neoliberal agenda of recoding society and its subjects'.[239]

'Technical support manual' is certainly not a sufficient description of what is at stake. Foucault's reconstruction of ethics in terms of individual self-techniques supplies neoliberalism with both an ethical foundation and a utopian horizon. What fascinates Foucault in Greco-Roman ethics is that it repres-

234 Dilts 2011, pp. 143 et sq.
235 Dilts 2011, p. 145.
236 Newheiser 2016, pp. 11 et sq.
237 For example, Foucault 1978, p. 137; Foucault 2003c, pp. 254 et sqq.
238 Foucault 2008a, pp. 218 et sq. According to the editors (in ibid., p. 234 n. 11), this is a 'fairly free reformulation' of the postscript of Hayek's *The Constitution of Liberty*, but there is nothing to be found in the indicated pages (Hayek 1960, pp. 398 et sq.).
239 Hamann 2009, p. 48.

ented an 'autonomous culture of the self', by which he means that its ethical practices were 'independent of pedagogical, religious, social institutions'.[240] It is clear for him that we cannot 'return to this Greco-Roman ethic', but he finds it necessary to explore it in order to 'build a new ethic ... without any reference to religion, law and science'.[241]

Such a 'new ethic' seems possible in a time of hegemonic crisis, during which the old, 'statist' and to a certain extent also 'egalitarian' post-war order of French Fordism begins to disintegrate. The humanist values and ideals that in Foucault's opinion covered up the silent workings of modern power are finally questioned by the 'anthropological erasure' (gommage anthropologique)[242] brought about by neoliberalism's concept of a *homo economicus*, who reacts 'rationally' and thus 'beyond good and evil' to the incentives of the economic environment. When Nietzsche, in the last sentence of the *Antichrist*, demands the 'transvaluation of all values' that undoes and reverts the fateful Judeo-Christian 'transvaluation' of the original aristocratic valuation,[243] Foucault has good reasons to locate its opportunity in a historical constellation in which, as he observes in 1978, the 'three great references of our ethics to religion, law and science are ... worn out'.[244]

---

240   Foucault 2015, p. 140; cf. Zamora 2019, p. 61.
241   Foucault 2015, p. 143; cf. Zamora 2019, p. 62.
242   Foucault 2008a, p. 258; Foucault 2004, p. 264.
243   Nietzsche 1999a, Vol. 6, p. 253; cf. Nietzsche 1999a, Vol. 5, pp. 266 et sqq.
244   Foucault 2015, p. 143; cf. Zamora 2019, p. 62.

CHAPTER 6

Governmentality Studies, or the Reproduction of Neoliberal Ideology

Turning to one of Foucault's major 'schools' which emerged after his death, I am going to discuss 'governmentality studies' and its interpretation of neoliberalism, primarily using examples from the works of Ulrich Bröckling and Sven Opitz.[1] To a large extent their readers learn what they can know anyway from the statements of entrepreneurs, from management-literature, government-proclamations, and the mainstream press: that we are all called upon to take initiative in our jobs, that the service to the customer is all that counts, that each of us needs to be our own entrepreneur – personally responsible, creative and flexible, etc. In between, the authors insert some Foucauldian terms such as the 'pastoral' model of leadership, the 'hermeneutics of desire', the indefatigable will to knowledge, etc., that is to say gestures which serve to signify some sort of theoretical 'distance' to the respective materials. But this is a simulation. The interpretation the 'governmentality studies' approach offers comes down to the assumption that neoliberal 'governmentality' should be characterised by the mobilisation of capacities of self-conduct. This does not do much more than translate the overall rhetoric of activation in the management literature into a theoretical discourse. There is hardly any indication of the real place, relevance, and function of these highly ideological texts within the actual culture of enterprises, or in the general framework of neoliberal domination and its leadership-methods. Thus the approach shares the 'destiny of a shadow-boxer who never gets hold of his opponent'.[2]

Some examples might illustrate how 'governmentality studies' fails to keep a critical distance from the advertising-language of the neoliberal management-literature and the guide-books they claim to investigate. So-called 'total quality management', which endeavours to apply quality-control to all activities of the enterprise and to prioritise the orientation towards the consumer above everything else, is characterised by Bröckling as follows: quality is now determined by the 'principle of prophylaxis'; it obtains a 'proactive' character and a 'preventive orientation'. The idea behind these glittering words is basically that

---

1 Bröckling 2000 and 2002; Opitz 2004 and 2007.
2 Reitz and Draheim 2007, p. 119.

mistakes of production or service are to be prevented beforehand instead of being corrected afterwards.[3] However, such a concern is, at least on this level of generality, in no sense a new achievement – it could apply to the assembly-line as well.

Quality is 'no goal', but rather a 'process that never ends' – not a result, but an 'action parameter', reports Bröckling.[4] But this is obviously a nonsensical assumption: quality is of course still a 'goal' and a 'result' as well, or else the clients would immediately return the product or refuse to pay for an unsatis-factory service. Since Bröckling believes he has left ideology-critique far behind, he is not interested in (or capable of) revealing the abuse of language by an advertisement-discourse which tries to sell its 'products' in the brightest col-ours as the newest and most revolutionary development. The more social the-ory gives in to such advertisement language, the more unprepared it becomes for the task of identifying what is really new.

Bröckling asserts that the requirement of focusing entirely on the client has replaced the 'factory rules of the disciplinary era', which still insisted on punctu-ality, diligence, and order.[5] This coincides with Opitz's assumption that neolib-eral leadership-technologies are 'post-disciplinary'.[6] But such a juxtaposition does not hold water. What happens when a worker or employee does not arrive on time, for example when meeting a client? More 'flexibility', or more flexible working hours, do not at all imply that the products of labour do not need to be delivered at a pre-given (or negotiated) time. This can also be gleaned from neo-liberal discourse itself: since *lean production* is (among other things) about the reduction of stock levels and storage-time, its *just in time* principle' proclaims punctual delivery as an absolute requirement – otherwise the subcontractor might immediately lose its contract. Instead of declaring the era of discipline to be over and to have been replaced by the era of client-orientation and self-conduct, it would be more productive to look for specific forms of disciplinary demands under the conditions of computerised labour in high-tech capitalism. It is symptomatic that some of the more substantial investigations of neoliberal management go back again to Foucault's earlier concept of disciplinary power.[7]

When Bröckling reports that during the Taylorist era subjectivity was noth-ing but a 'factor of disturbance' that needs to be controlled, this is another

---

3 Bröckling 2000, pp. 136–7.
4 Bröckling 2000, p. 137.
5 Bröckling 2000, p. 137.
6 Opitz 2007, p. 102.
7 Cf. Petersen 2004.

misleading juxtaposition.[8] It underestimates how Fordism, through its puritan campaigns, its education of hygiene and morality as well as through its compensating family-ideologies, engendered a highly intense formation of subjectivities. According to Gramsci, Fordism can be described as 'the biggest collective effort to date to create, with unprecedented speed, and with a consciousness of purpose unmatched in history, a new type of worker and of man'.[9] What should be investigated is how, in the transition to a high-tech mode of production and at the critical juncture of labour-conditions, education, mass-culture and ideological socialisation, subjectivities are generated in a new way.

Bröckling informs us of *kaizen*, a Japanese term for 'improvement', or 'change for the better', which signifies a critical search for amelioration in which the employees engage in a common diagnosis of mistakes and shortcomings – without moralising or looking for 'culprits'. 'In order to investigate and to overcome mistakes, these need to be laid open without any fear of sanctions'.[10] It is indeed an interesting phenomenon that neoliberal management literature, in its efforts to enhance labour productivity, is compelled to take up elements that could be part of a 'horizontal' communication. We encounter a similar phenomenon in the internet, which, being a network, is 'horizontally' designed and at the same time exposed to verticalisation by corporations (and, of course, to systematic spying); it is 'anarchic and nevertheless reproduces relations of domination'.[11] Unfortunately, Bröckling does not investigate the contradictions that emerge whenever such 'horizontal' interpellations collide with the hierarchical realities of capitalist enterprises. How could an anxiety-free discussion of mistakes be possible in the context of mass unemployment and job insecurity, in which every revelation of errors can become a personal survival risk? Engaging in a 'communication free of domination', to take up Habermas' famous term,[12] would in principle require sustainable relations of economic democracy. Under capitalist conditions, it can only be realised in a restricted and partial manner, and is only realistic amongst privileged sections of the labour-process, in which the demand for qualified workers is high and jobs are secure.

Bröckling describes the so-called '360-degree-evaluation', by which every employee is exposed to the anonymous judgment of all the others, as a 'democratic panopticism', a 'non-hierarchical model of reciprocal visibility, in which

---

8   Bröckling 2004, p. 142. Cf. the critique of Moldaschl's similar argument by Ines Langemeyer
      (Langemeyer 2004, pp. 66 et sqq.).
9   Gramsci 1971, p. 302; Gramsci 1975, Q 4, § 52, p. 489.
10   Bröckling 2004, p. 144.
11   W.F. Haug 2003, p. 67.
12   Habermas 1970, p. 93.

everyone is both the observer of all the others and observed by all the others'.[13] However, this description is naïve and misleading because it severs the form of evaluation from the surrounding asymmetrical power-relations of the enterprise. A critical ideology-theoretical analysis would instead be interested, first, in the way the results of such an evaluation can be utilised for promotions, transfers, or dismissals; and second, in how the mere possibility of such a utilisation reacts back on relationships among the workforce and enhances attitudes that mobilise the employees against each other and against their own cooperative interests. According to Petersen, in his experience the 360-degree-evaluation had the effect that 'the interactions with the colleagues were superimposed by ... tactical considerations and prevented the development of relations of friendship'.[14] The assumption of a 'flattening of the panoptic asymmetry'[15] dissimulates the development of a vertical panopticism which, based on electronic-surveillance and network-technologies, exceeds by far what Foucault analysed in *Discipline and Punish*. According to the *American Management Association*, about 75 percent of employees in the private sector are subjected to electronic-surveillance monitoring, which for Stephen Gill, who reports this, is one of the characteristics that justify speaking of a 'disciplinary neoliberalism'.[16]

In their eagerness to renounce ideology-critique and to focus instead on a 'positive' account of leadership techniques, governmentality studies thinkers establish an intuitive and empathetic relationship to the management programmes they claim to analyse. Since they do not investigate their ideological functions and functioning in the framework of neoliberal high-tech capitalism, they have no methodical instrument with which to distinguish between real new patterns of hegemonic leadership, on the one hand, and contrived fantasies and empty rhetoric on the other. Above all, they reproduce the view of a management literature which looks at employees from the perspective of their managerial leaders and dissimulates the domination and alienation engendered by neoliberal capitalism behind the smokescreen of motivational incentives and appeals to teamwork.

Opitz comes to the conclusion that neoliberal leadership techniques aim to enhance capacities for self-governance and favour an 'extremely loose coupling' of power relations, which 'under no circumstances may turn into a relation

---

13   Bröckling 2004, p. 152.
14   Peterson 2004, p. 141.
15   Opitz 2007, p. 141.
16   Cf. Bakker and Gill 2003, p. 192.

of domination'.[17] According to his 'positive' interpretation, neoliberal leaders are even supposed to withdraw in a 'post-heroic' way in order to open up a space where the employees 'can constitute a subjective desire'.[18] Such evaluations are deeply embedded in neoliberal ideology. A critical ideology-theory would look instead at the overall arrangement of the social order: the neoliberal interpellations aiming at the mobilisation of capacities for 'self-conduct' operate within specific relations of domination, are superimposed and limited by them, and can only be grasped in their functioning within this comprehensive framework.

The alleged homogeneous efficacy of the neoliberal discourse of self-conduct results from a twofold methodical abstraction. First, the 'governmentality studies' approach overlooks the fact that neoliberal class divides also translate into different strategies of subjection: on the one hand there is 'positive' motivation, the social integration of different milieus, manifold offers on the therapy market, while on the other hand we see the build up of a huge prison system, surveillance and police-control. The former is directed primarily towards the middle classes and sometimes some 'qualified' sections of the working class, the latter mainly towards the underemployed, the poor and the 'dangerous classes' (the concrete delimitations might vary considerably). Second, 'governmentality studies' does not take into account that even similar neoliberal interpellations may have different and even opposite effects in different 'milieus': the appeals to creativity and initiative might play a supportive and constructive role in the formation of identities if they correlate to labour conditions that actually require and bolster a certain (relative) autonomy and freedom; they tend to destroy agency and subjectivities if there are no, or very restricted alternative possibilities to act. Neoliberal interpellations of 'empowerment' then have the effect of confirming the individual's lack of capabilities and 'worthlessness'. What Bourdieu analysed as the 'destiny-effect' among contingent labourers and marginalised youngsters[19] can be seen as the dark flipside of the neoliberal interpellations of self-mobilisation and creativity. A complementary ideological effect could be described as the illusory 'opiate' of the excluded and marginalised: as Loïc Wacquant shows in his study of a Chicago ghetto, the interviewees gave the same completely unrealistic, but honestly believed, statement that they would enroll in a college in the near future.[20]

---

17   Opitz 2004, 141.
18   Opitz 2007, 103.
19   Bourdieu et al. (eds.) 1999, p. 63.
20   Wacquant 1999, p. 148 and n. 9.

It is not just techniques of domination that drop out of the view of 'governmentality studies'. It does not look any better on the side of self-conduct: since the interpretation is restricted to the programmatic interpellations of management literature without investigating their encounter with real subjects, the distinction between techniques of self-conduct and those of domination becomes obsolete.[21] This is also due to the theoretical decision to adopt a subject theory, which, often via Judith Butler, equates the emergence of subjects and their subjection, of *subjectivation* and *subjection/assujetissment*.[22] The conduct of individuals and their ideological integration into the *dispositif* of neoliberalism cannot be analytically distinguished using this equation. By removing the contradictions of socialisation under the antagonistic conditions of neoliberal capitalism, governmentality studies can no longer identify where and how neoliberalism takes up and hijacks emancipatory elements of self-socialisation and self-conduct, and in what way it integrates them in a modernised system of bourgeois hegemony.

The renunciation of analytical distinctions not only overlooks the contradictory dialectics of neoliberal socialisation, it also impedes the development of a sustainable concept of resistance. For Opitz, resistance is only conceivable as a 'border attitude' (*Grenzhaltung*), an 'operation at the margins' (*Randgang*), or a 'line of escape' (*Fluchtlinie*), which does no more than complement the *techne* of government.[23] 'Resistance' is thus restricted to small displacements within the framework of domination and its hegemonic ideologies. Any attempt to formulate a 'global alternative to the existing conditions' is denounced as an illusory fallacy because it would mean becoming entrapped in a utopian concept of subject-liberation already criticised by Foucault.[24] This corresponds to a notion of critique that needs to become as flexible as its objects, and therefore has to renounce any 'standpoint'.[25]

'Governmentality studies' thus provides the neoliberal dispersion und fragmentation of social movements with a theoretical justification. Instead of looking for strategies to overcome the movements' weaknesses, it confirms and naturalises them. What this theoretical framework makes systematically inconceivable is the possibility of finding the coalescing points of social movements, of identifying the opportunities to move people's common sense to the left, and of building a counter-hegemony from below, which is able to reclaim and

---

21   Cf. the critique of Cathren Müller 2003, pp. 101–2.
22   Cf. Bröckling 2002; Opitz 2004, p. 103.
23   Opitz 2004, pp. 84, 164–5.
24   Opitz 2004, p. 84.
25   Bröckling, Krasman and Lemke, 2000, p. 13.

reappropriate the elements of self-conduct that were captured and alienated by neoliberalism.[26]

The Foucauldian account of governmentality techniques needs to be re-interpreted on the basis of a subject-theory that takes seriously the agency of the individuals and their attempts at self-socialisation and self-conduct. As Ines Langemeyer has shown, the development of capacities to act is not to be equated beforehand with subjection.[27] To insist on the analytical distinction between the two does not mean falling back on an 'essentialist' approach which invokes the ahistorical notion of a benign and joyful 'essence' slumbering within humans, just waiting to emerge in a society without classes and state-domination. Over and again, alternative and emancipatory movements are confronted with the task of distinguishing between aspects of alienated socialisation and cooperative self-determination – not once and for all, not set in stone, but ever anew in any given concrete conjuncture. Only with the help of such recurring and ever-new distinctions will it be possible to break the appeal of neoliberal ideologies and to build a counter-hegemony.

26   For a neo-Gramscian analysis of the Bernie Sanders campaign of 2016, see Rehmann 2016b.
27   Cf. Langemeyer 2004, p. 73.

Bibliography

Abel, Günter 1998 [1984], *Nietzsche: Die Dynamik der Willen zur Macht und die ewige Wiederkehr*, 2nd ed., Berlin: de Gruyter.

Adorno, Theodor 1973 [1966], *Negative Dialectics*, translated by E.B. Ashton, New York: Seabury Press.

Adorno, Theodor 1973–86, *Gesammelte Schriften*, 20 volumes, edited by Rolf Tiedemann, Frankfurt/M: Suhrkamp.

Adorno, Theodor 1974 [1951], *Minima Moralia. Reflections from Damaged Life*, translated by E.F.N. Jephcott, London: Verso.

Adorno, Theodor 2003 [1964], *The Jargon of Authenticity*, translated by K. Tarnowski and F. Will, London: Routledge.

Agamben, Giorgio 1998, *Homo Sacer: Sovereign Power and Bare Life*, translated by D. Heller-Roazen, Stanford, Calif.: Stanford University Press.

Ahlsdorf, Michael 1997, *Nietzsches Juden. Ein Philosoph formt sich ein Bild*, Aachen: Shaker Verlag.

Alexander, Michelle 2012, *The New Jim Crow: Mass Incarceration in the Age of Colorblindness*, 2nd ed., New York: New Press

Allison, David B. (ed.) 1995 [1977], *The New Nietzsche. Contemporary Styles of Interpretation*, Cambridge, Mass: MIT Press.

Althusser, Louis 1966, *Pour Marx*, Paris: Maspero.

Althusser, Louis 1974, *Élements d'autocritique*, Paris: Hachette.

Althusser 1976 [1974], *Essays in Self-Criticism*, translated by Grahame Lock, London: New Left Books.

Althusser, Louis 1995 [1970], 'Idéologie et appareils idéologiques d'Etat', in *Sur la reproduction*, introduction de Jacques Bidet, Paris: Presses Universitaires de France: 269–314.

Althusser, Louis 1996a [1965], *For Marx*, translated by Ben Brewster, London, New York: Verso.

Althusser, Louis 1996b [1976], *Freud and Lacan*, translated by Jeffrey Mehlman, New York: Columbia University Press.

Althusser, Louis 2014 [1970], *Ideology and Ideological State Apparatuses*, translated by G.M. Goshgarian, London, New York: Verso.

Althusser, Louis and Étienne Balibar 2009 [1968], *Reading Capital*, translated by Ben Brewster, London: Verso.

Anders, Günther 1982, *Ketzereien*, München: Beck.

Anders, Günther 2001, *Über Heidegger*, edited by Gerhard Oberschlick in association with Werner Reimann, Munich: Beck.

Andresen, Sünne 2001, *Der Preis der Anerkennung. Frauenforscherinnen im Konkurrenzfeld Hochschule*, Münster: Westfälisches Dampfboot.

Ansell Pearson, Keith 1999, *Germinal Life: The Difference and Repetition of Deleuze*, London, New York: Routledge.

Appel, Fredrick 1999, *Nietzsche contra Democracy*, Ithaca, London: Cornell University Press.

Arac, Jonthan (ed.) 1988, *After Foucault: Humanistic Knowledge, Postmodern Challenges*, New Brunswick: Rutgers University Press.

Aronowitz, Stanley and Peter Bratsis (eds.) 2002, *State Theory Reconsidered*, Minnesota: University of Minnesota Press.

Aschheim, Steven E. 1992, *The Nietzsche Legacy in Germany – 1890–1990*, Berkeley, Los Angeles: University of California Press.

Ashenden, Samantha and David Owen (eds.) 1999, *Foucault contra Habermas: Recasting the Dialogue between Genealogy and Critical Theory*, London: SAGE.

Audier, Serge 2015, *Penser le 'néoliberalism'. Le moment néoliberal et la crise du socialisme*, Lormont: Le Bord de l' Eau.

Baecker, Dirk 1996, 'Was leistet die Negation?', in *Gilles Deleuze- Fluchtlinien der Philosophie*, edited by Friedrich Balke and Joseph Vogel, Munich: Fink.

Bakker, Isabella and Stephen Gill 2003, *Power and Resistance in the New World Order*, London: Palgrave Macmillan.

Balibar, Étienne 1991 [1989], 'Foucault und Marx. Der Einsatz des Nominalismus', in *Spiele der Wuhrheit. Michel Foucaults Denken*, edited by Francois Ewald and Bernhard Waldenfels, Frankfurt/Main: Suhrkamp.

Balibar, Étienne 1997a [1985], 'Jus-Pactum-Lex: On the Constitution of the Subject in the Theologico-Political Treatise', in *The New Spinoza*, Warren Montag and Ted Stolze (eds.), Minneapolis, MN: University of Minnesota Press.

Balibar, Étienne 1997b, *Spinoza: From Individuality to Transindividuality*, Delft: Eburon.

Balibar, Étienne 1998, *Spinoza and Politics*, translated by Peter Snowdon, London, New York: Verso.

Balke, Friedrich and Joseph Vogel (eds.) 1996, *Gilles Deleuze- Fluchtlinien der Philosophie*, Munich: Fink.

Barrett, Michèle 1991, *The Politics of Truth. From Marx to Foucault*, Cambridge: Polity.

Barth, Karl 1926, 'Ludwig Feuerbach. Fragment aus einer Vorlesung über "Geschichte der protestantischen Theologie seit Schleiermacher" im Sommersemester 1926 in Münster', in: Thies, Erich (ed.) 1976: *Ludwig Feuerbach*, Darmstadt, 1–32.

Barth, Karl 1960 [1948], *Church Dogmatics*, Vol III/2; ed. G.W. Bromiley and T.F. Torrance, translated by G.T. Thompson and Harold Knight, Edinburgh: T&T Clark.

Barth, Karl 1968 [1922], *Epistle to the Romans*, translated by Edwyn C. Hoskyns, London: Oxford Univ. Press.

Baudrillard, Jean 2010 [1981], *Simulacra and Simulation*, translated by Sheila F. Glaser, Ann Arbor: University of Michigan Press.

Beaumont, Gustave de, and Alexis de Tocqueville 1836a (1833), *Du systeme pénitentiaire aux États-Unis et de son application en France*, Volume 1, Paris: C. Gosselin.

Beaumont, Gustave de, and Alexis de Tocqueville 1836b (1833), *Du systeme pénitentiaire aux États-Unis et de son application en France*, Volume 2, Paris: C. Gosselin.

Beck, Ulrich 1997, *The Reinvention of Politics: Rethinking Modernity in the Global Social Order*, translated by Mark Ritter, Cambridge: Polity Press.

Beck, Ulrich, Anthony Giddens and Scott Lash 2007 [1994], *Reflexive Modernization*, Cambridge: Polity Press.

Becker, Gary S., François Ewald and Bernard E. Harcourt 2012, *American Neoliberalism and Michel Foucault's 1979 Birth of Biopolitics Lectures*. Working Paper No. 614, Coase-Sandor Institute for Law and Economics.

Behrent, Michael 2016, 'Liberalism without Humanism: Michel Foucault and the Free-Market-Creed, 1976–1979', in Zamora and Behrent (eds.) 2016, 24–62.

Behrent, Michael 2019, 'A Liberal Despite Himself: Reflections on a Debate, Reappraisal of a Question', in Sawyer, Steinmetz-Jenkins (eds.) 2019, 1–31.

Benjamin, Walter 1920/22, *Theologisch-politisches Fragment*, in *Gesammelte Schriften*, edited by Rolf Tiedemann and Hermann Schwepenhäuser, Vol. II.1, Frankfurt/M: Suhrkamp.

Benjamin, Walter 1921, *Kapitalismus als Religion*, in *Gesammelte Schriften*, edited by Rolf Tiedemann and Hermann Schwepenhäuser, Vol. VII.2, Frankfurt/Main: Suhrkamp.

Benjamin, Walter 1928, *Ursprung des deutschen Trauerspiels*, in *Gesammelte Schriften*, edited by Rolf Tiedemann and Hermann Schwepenhäuser, Vol. I./1, Frankfurt/: Suhrkamp.

Benjamin, Walter 1999 [1927–1940], *The Arcades Project*, translated by Howard Eiland and Kevin McLaughlin, Cambridge, Massachusetts: Belknap Press of Harvard University Press.

Benjamin, Walter 2003 [1928], *The Origin of German Tragic Drama*, translated by John Osborne, London: Verso.

Benjamin, Walter 2004 [1921], 'Capitalism as Religion', fragment 74, translated by Chad Kautzer, in *The Frankfurt School on Religion*, edited by E. Mendieta, New York and London: Routledge.

Bentham, Jeremy 1787, 'Panopticon, or The Inspection-House: Letters', *The Works of Jeremy Bentham*, edited by J. Bowring, Wedingburgh 1838–1843, Vol. IV, 39–66.

Bentham, Jeremy 1791: 'Panopticon: Postscript', in *The Works of Jeremy Bentham*, edited by J. Bowring, Wedingburgh 1838–1843, Vol. IV, 67–172.

Bentham, Jeremy 1797, 'Outline of a Work entitled Pauper Management Improved', in *The Works of Jeremy Bentham*, edited by J. Bowring, Wedingburgh 1838–1843, Vol. VIII, 369–439.

Bergson, Henri 1966 [1907], *L'évolution créatrice*, Paris: Presses universitaires de France.

Bergson, Henri 1998 [1907], *Creative Evolution*, translated by Arthur Mitchell, Mineola, New York: Dover Publications.

Binswanger, Ludwig and Michel Foucault 1986 [1954], 'Dream and Existence', in *Review of Existential Psychology and Psychiatry* Vol. XIX, no. 1 1984–5, translated by Forrest Williams and Jacob Needleman, Seattle, Washington: K. Hoeller, et al.

Bloch, Ernst 1950, 'Über Fiktion und Hypothese', in *Philosophische Aufsätze zur objektiven Phantasie, Gesamtausgabe*, Vol. 10, Frankfurt/M: Suhrkamp.

Bloch, Ernst 1986 [1959], *The Principle of Hope*, translated by Neville Plaice, Steven Plaice, Paul Knight, Cambridge, MA: MIT Press.

Bloch, Ernst 1991 [1935], *Heritage of our Times*, translated by Neville and Stephen Plaice, Berkeley and Los Angeles: Polity Press.

Bloch, Ernst 2009, *Atheism in Christianity*, translated by J.T. Swann, London: Verso.

Bogue, Ronald 1989, *Deleuze and Guattari*, London and New York: Routledge.

Böhm, Christopher 1993, 'Egalitarian Behavior and Reserve Dominance Hierarchy', in *Current Anthropology*, Vol. 34, No. 3, 227–54, Chicago: University of Chicago Press.

Boltanski, Luc and Eve Chiapello 2007, *The New Spirit of Capitalism*, translated by Gregory Elliot, London, New York: Verso.

Bookchin, Murray 1995, *Social Anarchism or Lifestyle Anarchism: An Unbridgeable Chasm*, Stirling: AK Press.

Bourdieu, Pierre 1982, *Ce que parler veut dire. L'économie des échanges linguistiques*, Paris: Fayard.

Bourdieu, Pierre 1990: *The Logic of Practice*, translated by Richard Nice, Stanford: Stanford University Press.

Bourdieu, Pierre 2000: *Pascalian Meditations*, translated by Richard Nice, Cambridge: Polity Press.

Bourdieu, Pierre 2010 [1979], *Distinction*, translated by Richard Nice, London: Routledge.

Bourdieu, Pierre and Jean Claude Passeron 1977, *Reproduction in Education, Society, and Culture*, translated by Loïc Wacquant, London: Sage.

Bourdieu, Pierre et al. (eds.) 1999 [1993], *The Weight of the World. Social Suffering in Contemporary Society*, translated by Priscilla Parkhurst Ferguson et al., Stanford: Stanford University Press.

Boyer, Alain 1997 'Hierarchy and Truth', in *Why We Are Not Nietzscheans*, edited by Luc Ferry and Alain Renaut, translated by Robert de Loaiza, Chicago: University of Chicago Press.

Boyne, Roy und Ali Rattansi (eds.) 1990, *Postmodernism and Society*, London: Macmillan.

Brecht, Bertolt 1967, *Gesammelte Werke*, 20 Vols., Frankfurt/Main: Suhrkamp.

Brecht, Bertolt 2016, *Meti Book of Interventions in the Flow of Things*, translated by Antony Tatlow, London and New York: Bloomsbury.

Breuer, Stefan 1978, 'Die Evolution der Disziplin. Zum Verhältnis von Rationalität und Herrschaft in Max Weber's Theorie der vorrationalen Welt', in *Kölner Zeitschrift für Soziologie und Sozialpsychologie*, vol. 30: 409–37.

Breuer, Stefan 1983, 'Die Formierung der Disziplinargesellschaft: Michel Foucault und die Probleme einer Theorie der Sozialdisziplinierung', in *Sozialwissenschaftliche Informationen für Unterricht und Studium*, no. 4: 257–64.

Breuer, Stefan 1986: 'Sozialdisziplinierung. Probleme und Problemverlagerungen eines Konzepts bei Max Weber, Gerhard Oestreich und Michel Foucault', in *Soziale Sicherheit und soziale Disziplinierung. Beiträge zu einer historischen Theorie der Sozialpolitik*, edited by Christoph Sachße and Florian Tennstedt, Frankfurt/Main: Suhrkamp.

Breuer, Stefan 1987: 'Foucaults Theorie der Disziplinargesellschaft. Eine Zwischenbilanz', in *Leviathan*, No. 3: 319–37.

Brieler, Ulrich 1998, Die *Unerbittlichkeit der Historizität. Foucault als Historiker*, Köln: Böhlau.

Brobjer, Thomas 2004: 'Nietzsche's knowledge of Spinoza', *Spinoza in Nordic countries: Spinoza im Norden*, edited by V. Oittinen, Helsinki: University of Helsinki: 203–216.

Bröckling, Ulrich 2000, 'Totale Mobilmachung. Menschenführung im Qualitats- und Selbstmanagement', in Bröckling, Krasmann and Lemke (eds.) 2000.

Bröckling, Ulrich 2002, 'Jeder könnte, aber nicht alle können. Konturen des unternehmerischen Selbst', in *Mittelweg 36*, 11, 4: 6–26 available at: www.eurozine.com/article/2002-10-02-broeckling-de.html.

Bröckling, Ulrich, Susanne Krasmann and Thomas Lemke (eds.) 2000, *Gouvernementalität der Gegenwart. Studien zur Ökonomisierung des Sozialen*, Frankfurt am Main: Suhrkamp.

Brown, Wendy 2015, *Undoing the Demos. Neoliberalism's Stealth Revolution*, New York: Zone Books.

Buci-Glucksmann 1979, 'State, transition and passive revolution', *Gramsci and Marxist Theory*, edited by Chantal Mouffe, London: Routledge and Kegan Paul.

Butler, Judith 1993, *Bodies that Matter*, New York: Routledge.

Butler, Judith 1997, *The Psychic Life of Power*, Stanford: Stanford University Press.

Cancik, Hubert 1995: *Nietzsches Antike. Vorlesung*, Stuttgart: Metzler.

Cancik-Lindemaier, Hildgard and Hubert Cancik 1999, *Philolog und Kultfigur. Friedrich Nietzsche und seine Antike in Deutschland*, Stuttgart: Metzler.

Candeias, Mario 2007, 'Konjunkturen des Neoliberalismus', in Kaindl (ed.) 2007.

Chlada, Marvin (ed.) 2000, *Das Universum des Gilles Deleuze*, Aschaffenburg: Alibri.

Clastres, Pierre 1989 [1976], *Society Against the State – Esssays in Political Anthropology*, translated by Robert Hurley and Abe Stein, New York: Zone Books.

Colletti, Lucio 1975, 'Marxism and the Dialectic', *New Left Review*, I/93: 3–29.

Cook, Deborah, 1990, 'Nietzsche and Foucault on "Ursprung and Geneology"', in *Clio*, vol. 19., no. 4, 299–309.

Cooper, Melinda 2008, *Life as Surplus: Biotechnology and Capitalism in the Neoliberal Era*, Seattle: University of Washington Press.

Croce 1969 [1907], *What is Living and What is Dead in the Philosophy of Hegel*, translated from the Italian by Douglas Ainslie, New York: Russell and Russell.

Cronin, Joseph 2001, *Foucault's Antihumanist Historiography*, Lewiston, N.Y.: E. Mellen Press.

Cusset, François 2003, *French Theory. Foucault, Derrida, Deleuze & Cie et les mutations de la vie intellectuelle aux États-Unis*, Paris: La Découverte.

Davis, Angela 1998, *Racialized Punishment and Prison Abolition*, in James, Joy (ed.) 1998.

Dean, Mitchell 1999, *Governmentality. Power and Rule in Modern Society*, London: Sage Publications

Dean, Mitchell 2016, 'Foucault, Ewald, Neoliberalism, and the Left', in Zamora and Behrent (eds.) 2016: 85–113.

Deleuze, Gilles 1953, *Empirisme et subjectivité. Essai sur la nature humaine selon Hume*, Paris: Presses Universitaires de France.

Deleuze, Gilles 1956a, 'Bergson: 1859–1941' in *Les philosophes célèbres*, edited by M. Merleau-Ponty, Paris: Mazenod.

Deleuze, Gilles 1956b, 'La conception de la différence chez Bergson', in *Les Études Bergsoniennes*, no. 4, Paris: A. Michel.

Deleuze, Gilles 1962, *Nietzsche et la philosophie*, Paris: Presses Universitaires de France.

Deleuze, Gilles 1968a [1966], *Le Bergsonisme*, Paris: Presses Universitaires de France.

Deleuze, Gilles 1968b, *Différence et répétition*, Paris: Presses Universitaires de France.

Deleuze, Gilles 1968c, *Spinoza et le problème de l'expression*, Paris: Les Éditions de Minuit.

Deleuze, Gilles 1970, *Spinoza*, Paris: Presses Universitaires de France.

Deleuze, Gilles 1981, *Spinoza: Philosophie pratique*, Paris: Les Éditions de Minuit.

Deleuze, Gilles 1986, *Foucault*, Paris: Les Éditions de Minuit.

Deleuze, Gilles 1988 [1981], *Spinoza: Practical Philosophy*, translated by Robert Hurley, San Francisco, CA: City Lights Books.

Deleuze, Gilles 1991a [1953], *Empiricism and Subjectivity*, translated by C.V. Boundas 1991, New York: Columbia University Press.

Deleuze, Gilles 1991b [1966], *Bergsonism*, translated by Hugh Tomlinson and Barbara Habberjam, Cambridge, Mass.: MIT Press.

Deleuze, Gilles 1994 [1968], *Difference and Repetition*, translated by Paul Patton, London: Athlone Press.

Deleuze, Gilles 1995 [1973], 'Nomad Thought', in *The New Nietzsche. Contemporary Styles of Interpretation*, edited by David B. Allison, Cambridge, MA: MIT Press.

Deleuze, Gilles 2000 [1986], *Foucault*, translated by Seán Hand, Minnesota: University of Minnesota Press

Deleuze, Gilles 2013 [1962], *Nietzsche and Philosophy*, translated by H. Tomlinson, London: Bloomsbury.

Deleuze, Gilles and Félix Guattari 1972, *L'Anti-Oedipe, capitalism et schizophrénie*, Vol. I, nouvelle édition augmentée, Paris: Les Éditions de Minuit.

Deleuze, Gilles and Félix Guattari 1980, *Milles Plateaux, capitalism et schizophrénie*, Vol. II, Paris: Les Éditions de Minuit.

Deleuze, Gilles and Félix Guattari 1987 [1980], *A Thousand Plateaus*, translated by Brian Massumi, Minnesota: University of Minnesota Press.

Deleuze, Gilles and Félix Guattari 2009 [1972], *Anti-Oedipus: Capitalism and Schizophrenia*, translated by Robert Hurley, Mark Seem and Helen R. Lane, London: Penguin Books.

Derrida, Jacques 1972, *Marges de la philosophie*, Paris: Les Editions de Minuit.

Derrida, Jacques 1985, 'Otobiographies. The Teaching of Nietzsche and the Politics of the Proper Name' in *The Ear of the Other. Otobiography, Transference, Translation*, translated by Avital Ronell, edited by Christie V. McDonald, New York: Schocken Books.

Derrida, Jacques 1986 [1972], *Margins of Philosophy*, translated by Alan Bass, Chicago: University of Chicago Press.

Descombes, Vincent 1980 [1979], *Modern French Philosophy*, translated by L. Scott-Fox and J.M. Harding, Cambridge: Cambridge University Press.

Diamond, Sara 1995, *Roads to Dominion. Right-Wing Movements and Political Power in the United States*, New York.

Dilts, Andrew 2011, 'From "Entrepreneur of the Self" to "Care of the Self": Neo-liberal Governmentality and Foucault's Ethics', in *Foucault Studies*, 12: 130–146.

Dölling, Irene and Beate Krais (eds.)1997, *Ein alltägliches Spiel. Geschlechterkonstruktion in der sozialen Praxis*, Frankfurt/Main: Suhrkamp.

Donnellan, Brendan 1982, *Nietzsche and the French Moralists*, Bonn: Bouvier.

Dreyfus, Hubert L. and Paul Rabinow 1983, *Michel Foucault. Beyond Structuralism and Hermeneutics*, Chicago: Chicago University Press.

Dreyfus, Hubert L. and Paul Rabinow 1986, 'What is Maturity? Habermas and Foucault on "What is Enlightenment?"', in Hoy (ed.), 1986.

Dühring, Eugen 1865, *Der Werth des Lebens. Eine philosophische Betrachtung*, Breslau.

Dülmen, Richard van, 1990 [1985], *Theatre of Horror. Crime and Punishment in Early Modern Germany*, Cambridge: Cambridge University Press.

Eagleton, Terry 1990, *The Ideology of the Aesthetic*, Oxford: Blackwell.

Eagleton, Terry 1996, *The Illusions of Postmodernism*, Oxford: Blackwell.

Eco, Umberto 1989 [1984], *Reflections on The Name of the Rose*, translated from the Italian by William Weaver, London: Secker and Warburg.

Elden, Stuart 2018, 'Review: Foucault's Confessions of the Flesh', in *Theory, Culture & Society*, March 20, 2018, available at: https://www.theoryculturesociety.org/blog/review-michel-foucault-confessions-of-the-flesh

Engels, Friedrich 1878, 'Dialectics of Nature. Outline of the General Plan', in Marx and Engels 1975–2005, Vol. 25.

Engels, Friedrich 1894–5, *On the History of Early Christianity*, in Marx an Engels 1975–2005, Vol. 27.

Engels, Friedrich 1886, 'Ludwig Feuerbach and the End of Classical German Philosophy', in Marx and Engels 1975–2005, Vol. 26.

Engels, Friedrich 1892, *The Origin of the Family, Private Property and State*, in Marx and Engels 1975–2005, Vol. 26.

Engemann, Josef 1991, 'Hirt' [shepherd], in *Reallexikon für Antike und Christentum*, edited by Dassmann, Ernst et al. 1950–, Volume 15, Stuttgart: Anton Hiersemann Verlag.

Erdmann, Eva, Rainer Forst and Axel Honneth (eds.) 1990, *Ethos der Modeme. Foucaults Kritik der Aufklärung*, Frankfurt/Main, New York: Campus.

Eribon, Didier 1993 [1989], *Michel Foucault*, translated by Betsy Wing, Cambridge, MA: Harvard University Press.

Eribon, Didier 1994, *Michel Foucault et ses contemporains*, Paris: Fayard.

Eribon, Didier 2013, *Returning to Reims*. Los Angeles: Semiotext(e).

Ermarth, Elizabeth D. 1998, 'Postmodernism', in *Routledge Encyclopedia of Philosophy*, edited by Edward Craig, Vol. 7, 587–90, London, New York: Routledge.

Ewald, François 1986, *L'Etat Providence*, Paris: Bernard Grasset.

Ewald, François and Bernhard Waldenfels (eds.) 1991, *Spiele der Wahrheit. Michel Foucaults Denken*, Frankfurt/Main: Suhrkamp.

Fahrenbach, Helmut 2017, *Ernst Blochs Philosophie der Hoffnung und Utopie. Im Kontext und Diskurs*, Thalheimer: Mössingen.

Farias, Victor, 1989 [1987], *Heidegger und der Nationalsozialismus*, Frankfurt/Main: Suhrkamp.

Ferry, Luc and Alain Renaut 1985, *La pensée 68. Essai sur l'anti-humanisme contemporain*, Paris: Gallimard.

Ferry, Luc and Alain Renaut 1990 [1985], *French Philosophy of the Sixties: an Essay on Anti-humanism*, translated by Mary H.S. Cattani, Amherst, MA: University of Massachusetts Press.

Ferry, Luc and Alain Renaut (eds.) 1997 [1991], *Why We Are Not Nietzscheans*, translated by Robert de Loaiza, Chicago: University of Chicago Press.

Feuerbach, Ludwig 1966 [1843] *Principles of the Philosophy of the Future*, translated by Manfred H. Vogel, Indianapolis, New York: Bobbs-Merrill Company, Inc.

Feuerbach, Ludwig 1967 [1843]: *Grundsätze einer Philosophie der Zukunft*, Kritische Ausgabe mit Einleitung und Anmerkungen von Gerhard Schmidt, Frankfurt/Main.

Fine, Bob, Richard Kinsey, John Lea, Sol Picciotto, Jock Young (eds.) 1979: *Capitalism and the Rule of Law. From Deviancy Theory to Marxism*, London: Hutchinson.

Fink-Eitel, Hinrich, 1980, 'Michel Foucaults Analytik der Macht' in F.A. Kittler (ed.) 1980.

Fink-Eitel, Hinrich 1990, 'Zwischen Nietzsche und Heidegger. Michel Foucaults, Sexualität und Wahrheit, im Spiegel neuerer Sekundärliteratur', in *Philosophisches Jahrbuch*, Vol. 97: 367–90.

Fischer, Kuno 1880, *Geschichte der neuern Philosophie*, 3. edition, Vol. 1, Part 11: Fortbildung der Lehre Descartes. Spinoza, München.

Forman, J. 2012. Racial Critiques of Mass Incarceration: Beyond the New Jim Crow. *New York University Law Review* 21 (April): 101–46.

Forst, Rainer 1990, 'Endlichkeit Freiheit Individualität. Die Sorge um das Selbst bei Heidegger und Foucault', in Erdmann, Forst and Honneth (eds.) 1990.

Foster, John Bellamy, Brett Clark and Richard York 2010, *The Ecological Rift. Capitalism's War on the Earth*, New York: Monthly Review Press.

Foucault, Michel 1961, *Folie et déraison. Histoire de la folie à l'âge classique*, Paris: Plon.

Foucault, Michel 1963, *Naissance de la clinique*, Paris: Presses Universitaires de France.

Foucault, Michel 1965, *Madness and Civilization*, translated by Richard Howard, New York: Pantheon.

Foucault, Michel 1966, *Les mots et les choses. Une archéologie des sciences humaines*, Paris: Gallimard.

Foucault, Michel 1969, *L'archéologie du savoir*, Paris: Gallimard.

Foucault, Michel 1970, 'Theatrum Philosophicum' in *Essential Works of Foucault, volume 2: Aesthetics, Method and Epistemology*, edited by James Faubion, London: Penguin Books.

Foucault, Michel 1971, *L'ordre du discours, Leçon inaugurale au Collège de France prononcée le 2 décembre 1970*, Paris: Gallimard.

Foucault, Michel 1975, *Surveiller et punir. Naissance de la prison*, Paris: Gallimard.

Foucault, Michel 1976a, *Histoire de la sexualité 1. La Volonté de savoir*, Paris: Gallimard.

Foucault, Michel 1976b, *Mikrophysik der Macht. Über Strafjustiz, Psychiatrie und Medizin*, Berlin: Merve Verlag.

Foucault, Michel 1977, *Language, Counter-Memory, Practice. Selected Essays and Interviews*, edited with an introduction by Donald F. Bouchard, translated from the French by Donald F. Bouchard and Sherry Simon, Ithaca, New York: Cornell University Press.

Foucault, Michel 1978, *The History of Sexuality, Volume 1: An Introduction*. translated from the French by Robert Hurley, New York: Random House.

Foucault, Michel 1979, 'Le nouvel ordre intérieur', panel discussion at the University of Paris-8 in Vincennes, on March 3, 1979, available as video at: http://www.archives-video.univ-paris8.fr/video.php?recordID=111.

Foucault, Michel 1980, *Power/Knowledge: Selected Writings & Other Writings 1972–1977*, translated by Colin Gordon (ed.), New York: Pantheon.

Foucault, Michel 1981, 'The Order of Discourse. Inaugural Lecture at the Collège de France, given 2 December 1970', in *Untying the Text: A Post-Structuralist Reader*, edited and introduced by Robert Young, translated by Ian McLeod, Boston: Routledge & Kegan Paul Ltd.: 51–77.

Foucault, Michel 1983, *On the Genealogy of Ethics: An Overview of Work in Progress*, in Dreyfus and Rabinow 1983: 229–52.

Foucault, Michel 1984a, *Histoire de la sexualité II. L'usage des plaisirs*, Paris: Gallimard.

Foucault, Michel 1984b, *Histoire de la sexualité III. Le souci de soi*, Paris: Gallimard.

Foucault, Michel 1986, *The Care of the Self. Volume 3 of The History of Sexuality*, translated by Robert Hurley, New York: Pantheon Books.

Foucault, Michel 1988a, 'Social Security', in *Michel Foucault, Politics, Philosophy. Interviews and other Writings 1977–1984*, edited by Kritzman, Lawrence D. 1988, Routledge: New York and London: 159–77.

Foucault, Michel 1988b, *Politics, Philosophy, Culture. Interviews and other writings 1977–1984*, translated by Alan Sheridan and others, New York and London: Routledge.

Foucault, Michel 1990, *The Use of Pleasure. Volume 2 of The History of Sexuality*, translated by Robert Hurley, Vintage Books: New York.

Foucault, Michel 1994, *The Order of Things*, New York: Random House

Foucault, Michel 1995, *Discipline and Punish – The Birth of the Prison*, translated from the French byAlan Sheridan, New York, Random House/Vintage.

Foucault 1996, *Foucault Live: Collected Interviews*, translated by Lysa Hochroth and J. Johnston, New York: Semiotext(e).

Foucault, Michel 1997a, *Ethics, Subjectivity and Truth*, Vol. 1 of *The Essential Works of Michel Foucault*, edited by Paul Rabinow, translated by Robert Hurley and others, New York: The New Press.

Foucault, Michel 1997b, 'Il faut défendreer la société'. Cours au Collège de France (1975–1976), Paris: Gallimard/Seuil.

Foucault, Michel 1998a, *Aesthetics, Method, and Epistemology*, Vol. 2 of *The Essential Works of Michel Foucault*, edited by James D. Faubion, translated by Robert Hurley and others, New York: The New Press/Penguin.

Foucault 1998b [1963], 'Distance, Aspect, Origin' translated by Patrick ffrench in *The Tel Quel Reader*, edited by Patrick ffrench and Roland-Francois Lack, London and New York: Routledge.

Foucault, Michel 2000, *Power*, Vol. 3 of *The Essential Works of Michel Foucault*, edited by James D. Faubion, translated by Robert Hurley and others, New York: The New Press/Penguin.

Foucault, Michel 2001a, *Dits et écrits I, 1954–1975*, Paris: Gaillimard.

Foucault, Michel 2001b, *Dits et écrits II, 1976–1988*, Paris: Gallimard.

Foucault, Michel, 2003a, *TheBirth of the Clinic*, translated by A.M. Sheridan, London: Routeledge.

Foucault, Michel 2003b, *The Essential Foucault – Selections from The Essential Works of Foucault 1954–1984*, edited by Paul Rabinow and Nikolas Rose. New York and London: The New Press.

Foucault, Michel 2003c [1975–1976], *Society Must be Defended*, translated by David Macey, New York: Picador.

Foucault, Michel 2004, *Naissance de la biopolitique: Cours au Collège de France, 1978–1979*, Paris: Editions du Seuil/Gallimard.

Foucault, Michel 2007: *Security, Territory, Population. Lectures at the College de France 1977–1978*, Palgrave Macmillan: New York.

Foucault, Michel, 2008a, *The Birth of Biopolitics. Lectures at the College de France, 1978–1979*, translated by Graham Burchell, New York: Palgrave Macmillan.

Foucault, Michel 2008b, *Introduction to Kant's Anthropology*, edited, with an afterword and critical notes, by Roberto Nigro, translated by Roberto Nigro and Kate Briggs, Los Angeles, CA: Semiotext(e).

Foucault, Michel 2010a [1973], *The Archaeology of Knowledge*, translated by A.M. Sheridan Smith, London, New York: Random House/Vintage.

Foucault, Michel, 2010b, *The Government of Self and Others. Lectures at the College de France, 1982–1983*, translated by Graham Burchell, New York: Palgrave Macmillan.

Foucault, Michel 2015, *Qu'est-ce que la critique?*, edited by Henri-Paul Fruchaud, Daniele Lorenzini and Arnold Davidson, Paris: Vrin.

Foucault, Michel 2016, 'The Great Rage of Facts', in Zamora and Behrent (eds.) 2016.

Foucault, Michel 2018, *Les aveux de la chair*. Volume 4 de *L'Histoire de la Sexualité*, Paris: Gallimard.

Foucault and Binswanger 1986 (1954), 'Introduction' to *Dream and Existence* in *Review of Existential Psychiatry*, vol. XIX, No. 1, translated by Forrest Williams and Jacob Needleman, edited by Keith Hoeller.

Foucault, Michel and Noam Chomsky 1974, 'Human Nature: Justice versus Power' in *Reflexive Water*, eds. A.J. Ayer, Arne Naess, Sir Karl Popper, Sir John Eccles, Noam Chomsky, et al., London: Souvenir Press.

Frank, Manfred, 1989, *What is Neostructuralism?*, translated by S. Wilke and R. Gray, Minneapolis: Univ. of Minnesota Press.

Franz, Michael 1995, 'Bild' in Haug et al. (eds.), 1994-, 2: 225–39.

Fraser, Nancy 1989: *Unruly Practices. Power, Discourse, and Gender in Contemporary Social Theory*, University of Minnesota Press: Minneapolis.

Freud, Sigmund 1953–74, *The Standard Edition of the Complete Psychological Works of Sigmund Freud*, translated by James Strachey, London: The Hoghart Press and the Institute of Psycho-Analysis.

Freud, Sigmund 1963 [1915], 'Instincts and Their Vicissitudes', in *General Psychological Theory*, edited by Philip Rieff, translated by Cecil Baines, New York: Collier Books.

Freud, Sigmund 1969–1975 in *Studienausgabe*, edited by A. Mitscherlich, A. Richards and J. Strachey, Frankfurt/Main: S. Fischer Verlag.

Frim, Landon and Harrison Fluss 2018, 'Substance Abuse: Spinoza contra Deleuze', in *Epoché: A Journal for the History of Philosophy*, 23, 1: 191–217.

Garo, Isabelle 2011, *Foucault, Deleuze, Althusser & Marx. La Politique dans la Philosophie*, Paris: Editions Demopolis.

Gebauer, Gunter and Christoph Wulf (ed.) 1993, *Praxis und Ästhetik. Neue Perspektiven im Denken Pierre Bourdieus*, Frankfurt/Main: Suhrkamp.

Geiss, Karl-Heinz 1993, *Foucault-Nietzsche-Foucault. Die Wahlverwandtschaft*, Pfaffenweiler: Centaurus.

Genel, Katia 2006, 'The Question of Biopower: Foucault and Agamben', in *Rethinking Marxism*, 18, 1: 43–62, avaible at: https://www.tandfonline.com/doi/full/10.1080/08935690500410635.

Glucksmann, André 1975, *La cuisinière et le mangeur d'hommes. Essai sur les rapports entre l'État, le marxisme et les camps de concentration*, Paris: Éditions du Seuil.

Glucksmann, André 1980 [1977], *The Master Thinkers*, translated by Brian Pearce, New York: Harper & Row, Publishers.

Goldmann, Lucien 1977: *Lukács and Heidegger. Towards a New Philosophy*, translated by William Q. Boelhower, London: Routledge & Kegan Paul.

Goldschmidt, Werner 2004: 'Herrschaft', in Haug et al. (eds.), 1994-, 6/2: 82–127.

Goffman, Erving 1961, *Asylums. Essays on the Social Situation of Mental Patients and Other Inmates*, NewYork: Anchor Books.

Gramsci, Antonio 1971, *Selections from the Prison Notebooks*, edited and translated by Quintin Hoare and Geoffrey Nowell Smith, New York: International Publishers.

Gramsci, Antonio 1975, *Quaderni del carcere*, four volumes, critical edition by the Gramsci Institute, edited by Valerio Gerratana, Turin: Einaudi.

Gramsci, Antonio 1992, *Prison Notebooks*, Vol. I, edited by Joseph Buttigieg, translated by Joseph Buttigieg and Antonio Callari, New York: Columbia University Press.

Gramsci, Antonio 1995, *Further Selections from the Prison Notebooks*, edited and translated by Derek Boothman, London: Lawrence and Wishart.

Gramsci, Antonio 2007, *Prison Notebooks*, Vol. III, edited and translated by Joseph Buttigieg, New York: Columbia University Press.

Grosse Wiesmann, Hannah 2013, 'Spinoza's conatus and Nietzsche's will to power: Self-preservation vs. increase of power?' Backdoor Broadcasting Company, available at (accessed 28 November 2016): http://backdoorbroadcasting.net/2013/05/hannah-grosse-wiesmann-spinozas-conatus-and-nietzsches-will-to-powerself-preservation-vs-increase-of-power.

Habermas, Jügen 1970 [1968], *Toward a Rational Society. Student Protest, Science, and Politics*, translated by Jeremy J. Shapiro, Boston: Beacon Press.

Habermas, Jürgen 1987, 'Modernity, an Incomplete Project', in *Interpretive social science: a second look*, edited by Paul Rabinow and William Sullivan, Berkeley, Calif.: University of California Press.

Habermas, Jürgen, 1990 [1987], *The Philosophical Discourse of Modernity*, translated by F.G. Lawrence, Cambridge, Mass.: MIT Press.

Hall, Stuart 1979, 'The Great Moving Right Show', in *Marxism Today*, January 1979: 14–20.

Hall, Stuart 1988, 'The Toad in the Garden. Thatcherism among the Theorists', in *Marxism and the Interpretation of Culture*, edited by Nelson, Cary and Lawrence Grossberg 1988, Urbana: University of Illinois Press.

Hamann, Trent 2009, 'Neoliberalism, Governmentality, and Ethics', in *Foucault Studies*, 6: 37–59.

Harcourt, Bernard E. 2021, 'Five Modalities of Michel Foucault's Use of Nietzsche's Writings (1959–73): Critical, Epistemological, Linguistic, Alethurgic and Political', in: *Theory, Culture & Society* 2021: 1–22.

Hardt, Michael 1993, *Gilles Deleuze: An Apprenticeship in Philosophy*. Minneapolis, MN: University of Minnesota Press.

Hardt, Michael and Antonio Negri, 2000: *Empire*, Cambridge, MA: Harvard University Press.

Hardt, Michael and Antonio Negri 2004, *Multitude. War and Democracy in the Age of Empire*, New York: Penguin Press.

Hardt, Michael and Antonio Negri 2009, *Commonwealth*, Cambridge, Massachusetts: The Belknap Press of Harvard University Press.

Harvey, David, 1990, *The Condition of Postmodernity*, Cambridge (USA), Oxford (UK): Blackwell.

Harvey, David 2005, *A Brief History of Neoliberalism*, Oxford: Oxford University Press.

Haude, Rüdiger and Thomas Wagner 1998, 'Herrschaft oder Macht. Begriffsstrategien um herrschaftsfreie Gesellschaften', in *DasArgument* 225:371–83.

Haug, Frigga 1995, 'Disziplin', in Haug et al. (eds.), 1994–, 2: 788–801.

Haug, Frigga 2002, 'Towards a Theory of Gender Relations', in *Socialism and Democracy*, Vol. 16, No. 1: 33–46.

Haug, Frigga 2003, ' "Schaffen wir einen neuen Menschentyp". Von Henry Ford zu Peter Hartz', *Das Argument*, 252: 606–17.

Haug, Frigga 2005, 'Gender Relations' in *Historical Materialism*, 13.2: 279–302.

Haug, Wolfgang Fritz 1984, 'Aufklärung', Haug et al. (eds.), 1994–, 1: 719–30.

Haug, Wolfgang Fritz 1986, *Die Faschisierung des bürgerlichen Subjekts. Die Ideologie der gesunden Normalität und die Ausrottungspolitiken im deutschen Faschismus. Materialanalysen*, Berlin: Argument-Verlag.

Haug, Wolfgang Fritz 1987: *Commodity Aesthetics, Ideology &Culture*, New York and Bagnolet (France): International General.

Haug, Wolfgang Fritz 1993, *Elemente einer Theorie des Ideologischen*, Hamburg, Berlin: Argument Verlag.

Haug, Wolfgang Fritz 1994, 'Abbild', in Haug et al. (eds.), 1994-, 1: 7–21.

Haug, Wolfgang Fritz 1995, 'Dialektik', in Haug et al. (eds.), 1994–, 2: 657–93.

Haug, Wolfgang Fritz 1997, 'Ewigkeit', in Haug et al. (eds.), 1994–, 3: 1079–1091.

Haug, Wolfgang Fritz 1999a 'Feuerbach-Thesen', in Haug et al. (eds.), 1994–, 4: 402–20.

Haug, Wolfgang Fritz 1999b, 'Fiktionalismus', in Haug et al. (eds.), 1994–, 4: 449–63.

Haug, Wolfgang Fritz 2001a, *Dreizehn Versuche, marxistisches Denken zu erneuern*, Berlin: Karl Dietz.

Haug, Wolfgang Fritz 2001b, 'Genesis', in Haug et al. (eds.), 1994-, 5: 261–74.

Haug, Wolfgang Fritz 2001c, 'Grenzen der Dialektik', Haug et al. (eds.), 1994–, 5: 957–62.

Haug, Wolfgang Fritz 2003, *High-Tech-Kapitalismus. Analysen zu Produktionsweise, Arbeit, Sexualität, Krieg und Hegemonie*, Hamburg: Argument Verlag.

Haug, Wolfgang Fritz 2006, *Einführung in marxistisches Philosophieren. Die Abschieds-vorlesung*, Hamburg: Argument Verlag.

Haug, Wolfgang Fritz, Frigga Haug, Peter Jehle, and Wolfgang Küttler (eds.) 1994–, *Historisch-Kritisches Wörterbuch des Marxismus (HKWM)*, Hamburg: Argument-Verlag.

Hayek, Friedrich A. 1960, *The Constitution of Liberty*, Chicago: The University of Chicago Press.

Hayek, Friedrich A. 1976, *Law, Legislation, and Liberty*, Volume 2, *The Mirage of Social Justice*, Chicago: The University of Chicago Press.

Hegel, Georg Wilhelm Friedrich 1977 [1807], *Phenomenology of Spirit*, translated by A.V. Miller, Oxford: Calerendon Press.

Hegel, Georg Wilhelm Friedrich, 1986a [1807]: *Phänomenologie des Geistes* in *Werke in zwanzig Bänden*, Vol. III, Frankfurt/Main: Suhrkamp.

Hegel, Georg Wilhelm Friedrich 1986b [1812–16], *Wissenschaft der Logik II* in *Werke in zwanzig Bänden*, Vol. VI, Frankfurt/Main: Suhrkamp.

Hegel, Georg Wilhelm Friedrich 2010, *The Science of Logic*, translated by George Di Giovanni, Cambridge UK: Cambridge University Press.

Heidegger, Martin 1977 [1947], 'Letter on Humanism' in *Martin Heidegger Basic Writings*, edited by David Farrell Krell, New York, London: Harper and Row.

Heidegger, Martin 1988, *Being and Time*, translated by John Macquarrie and Edward Robinson, Oxford: Basil Blackwell.

Heidegger, Martin 1991a, *Nietzsche–I. The Will to Power as Art* and *II. The Eternal Recurrence of the Same*, translated by David F. Krell, New York: Harper Collins.

Heidegger, Martin 1991b, *Nietzsche–III. The Will to Power as Knowledge and as Metaphysics* and *IV. Nihilism*, edited by David F. Krell, New York: Harper Collins.

Heidegger, Martin 1997 [1929], *Kant and the Problem of Metaphysics*, translated by Richard Taft, Bloomington and Indianapolis: Indiana University Press.

Heidegger 1998 [1942/43], *Parmenides*, translated by André Schuwer and Richard Rojcewicz, Indianapolis: Indiana University Press.

Heidegger, Martin 1999 [1929], 'The Essence of Being' in *Pathmarks*, translated by William McNiell, Cambridge: Cambridge University Press.

Heidegger, Martin 2002 [1938], 'The Age of the World Picture', in *Off the Beaten Track*, translated by Julian Young and Kenneth Haynes, New York and Cambridge, U.K.: Cambridge University Press.

Henrich, Dieter 1976, 'Hegels Grundoperation. Eine Einleitung in die "Wissenschaft der Logik"', in *Der Idealismus und seine Gegenwart*, Festschrift für Werner Marx, edited by Ute Guzzoni, Bernhard Lang, and Ludwig Siep, Hamburg: Felix Meiner.

Hesiod 1998, *Works and Days*, translated by Richard Lattimore, Ann Arbor Michigan: University of Michigan Press.

Hill, R. Kevin 1998, 'Genealogy' in *Routledge Encyclopedia of Philosophy*, Vol. IV: 1–5, London and New York: Routledge.

Himmelfarb, Gertrude 1968, 'The Haunted House of Jeremy Bentham', in Himmelfarb 1968, *Victorian Minds*: 32–81, New York: Harper and Row.

Hobbes, Thomas 1961/62 [1839–1845], *The English Works*, edited by Molesworth, 11vols., reprinted Aalen, Germany: Scientia-Verlag.

Holub, Robert C. 2016, *Nietzsche's Jewish Problem. Between Anti-Semitism and Anti-Judaism*, Princeton and Oxford: Princeton University Press.

Holzkamp, Klaus 1985, *Grundlegung der Psychologie*, Frankfurt/New York: Campus Verlag.

Holzkamp, Klaus 1995, 'Alltägliche Lebensführung als subjektwissenschaftliches Grundkonzept', in *Das Argument*, 212: 817–46.

Holzkamp, Klaus 2013, *Psychology from the Standpoint of the Subject. Selected Writings of Klaus Holzkamp*, edited by Ernst Schraube and Ute Osterkamp, translated by Andrew Boreham and Ute Osterkamp, Basingstoke: Palgrave Macmillan.

Honneth, Axel 1985, *Kritik der Macht. Reflexionsstufen einer kritischen Gesellschaftstheorie*, Frankfurt/M: Suhrkamp.

Honneth, Axel 1991 [1985], *The Critique of Power*, translated by Kenneth Baynes, Cambridge USA: MIT Press.

Honneth, Axel 1990, 'Einleitung. Zur philosophisch-soziologischen Diskussion um Michel Foucault', in Erdmann, Forst and Honneth (eds.) 1990.

Horkheimer, Max 1974 [1934], 'Dämmerung. Notizen in Deutschland', *Notizen 1950 bis 1969 und Dämmerung. Notizen in Deutschland*, edited by Werner Brede, Frankfurt/Main: S. Fischer.

Horkheimer, Max 1978, *Dawn & Decline: Notes 1926–1931 & 1950–1969*, translated by Michael Shaw, New York: Seabury Press.

Horkheimer, Max 1988 [1934] 'Zu Bergsons Metaphysik der Zeit', in *Gesammelte Schriften*, edited by Alfred Schmidt, Vol. III, Frankfurt/Main: S. Fischer.

Horkheimer, Max 1989, *Nachgelassene Schriften: 1949–1972* in *GesammelteSchriften*, Vol. 13, edited by A. Schmidt and G. Schmid-Noerr, Frankfurt/Main: S. Fischer.

Horkheimer, Max 2005 [1934], *On Bergson's Metaphysics of Time*, translated by Peter Thomas, revised by Stewart Martin, 1968 in *Radical Philosophy. A Journal of Socialist and Feminist Philosophy*, 131 May/June: 9–19.

Hoy, David Couzens (ed.) 1986, *Foucault. A Critical Reader*, Oxford UK & Cambridge USA: Basil Blackwell.

Hume, David 1978 [1739], *A Treatise of Human Nature*, edited by L.A. Selby-Bigge, 2nd edition, Oxford: Oxford University Press.

Huyssen, Andreas 1993, 'Postmoderne – eine amerikanische Internationale?', in Huyssen and Scherpe (eds.) 1993: 13–44.

Huyssen, A. and Klaus Scherpe (eds.) 1993 [1986], *Postmoderne. Zeichen eines kulturellen Wandels*, Reinbek: Rowohlt Taschenbuch Verlag.

Ignatieff, Michael 1978, *A Just Measure of Pain. The Penitentiary in the Industrial Revolution 1750–1850*, London: Pantheon Books.

Ives, Peter 2001, 'Grammatik', in Haug et al. (eds.), 1994–, 5: 935–944.

Jacolliot, Louis 1876, *Les législateurs religieux. Manu-Moise-Mahomet*, Paris: Hachette BNF.

James, Joy 1996, *Resisting State Violence. Radicalism, Gender, and Race in U.S. Culture*, Minneapolis: University of Minnesota Press.

James, Joy 1998 (ed.), *The Angela Y. Davis Reader*, Maldeen, Oxford: Blackwell Publishers.

Jameson, Frederic 1984, 'Postmodernism, or the Cultural Logic of Late Capitalism', *New Left Review*, I/146: 53–92.

Jameson, Frederic 1991, *Postmodernism, or, The Cultural Logic of Late Capitalism*, Durham.

Janz, Curt Paul 1978/79, *Friedrich Nietzsche Biographie in drei Bänden*, München: Hanser.

Jaspers, Karl 1950 (1935), *Nietzsche. Einführung in das Verständnis seines Philosophierens*, Berlin.

Jaspers, Karl 1997, *Nietzsche. An Introduction to the Understanding of his Philosophical Activity*, translated by C.F. Wallraff and F.J. Schmitz, Baltimore and London: Johns Hopkins University Press.

Jehle, Peter 2004, 'Irrationalismus', in Haug et al. (eds.), 1994–, 6/2: 1531–1542.

Jessop, Bob 1990, *State Theory. Putting the Capitalist State in its Place*, Cambridge: Polity Press.

Jütte, Robert 1986: 'Disziplinierungsmechanismen in der städtischen Armenfürsorge der Frühneuzeit', in *Soziale Sicherheit und soziale Disziplinierung. Beiträge zu einer historischen Theorie der Sozialpolitik*, edited by Christoph Sachße and Florian Tennstedt, Frankfurt/Main: Suhrkamp.

Kahl, Brigitte 2010, *Galatians Re-Imagined: Reading with the Eyes of the Vanquished. Paul in Critical Contexts*, Minneapolis: August Fortress Press.

Kaindl, Christina (ed.) 2007, *Subjekte im Neoliberalismus*, Marburg: BdWi-Verlag.

Kalyvas, Andreas 2002, 'The Stateless Theory: Poulantzas's Challenge to Postmodernism', in Aronowitz and Bratsis (eds.), 2002.

Kammler, Clemens 1986: *Michel Foucault. Eine kritische Analyse seines Werks*, Bonn: Bouvier.

Kant, Immanuel 1968a [1763], *Versuch, die negative Größen in die Weltweisheit einzu-führen*, in *Werkausgabe*, edited by Wilhelm Weischedel, Volume 2, Frankfurt/Main: Suhrkamp.

Kant, Immanuel 1968b [1790], *Kritik der Urteilskraft*, in *Werkausgabe*, edited by Wilhelm Weischedel, Volume 10, Frankfurt/Main: Suhrkamp.

Kant, Immanuel 1968c [1800], *Logik*, in *Werkausgabe*, edited by Wilhelm Weischedel, Volume 6, Frankfurt/Main: Suhrkamp.

Kant, Immanuel 1974 [1781=A; 1789=B], *Kritik der reinen Vernunft*, in *Werkausgabe*, edited by Wilhelm Weischedel, Volume 3/4, Frankfurt/Main: Suhrkamp.

Kant, Immanuel 1980 [1798=A; 1800=B], *Anthropologie in pragmatischer Absicht*, edited by Karl Vorländer, Hamburg: Felix Meiner.

Kant, Immanuel 1984 [1787], *Critique of Pure Reason*, translated by J.M.D. Meiklejohn, London: Everyman.

Kant, Immanuel 1992a (1763), *Theoretical Philosophy 1755–1770*, translated by David Walford and Ralf Meerbote, New York: Cambridge University Press.

Kant, Immanuel 1992b, *Lectures on Logic*, translated by J.M. Young, Cambridge: Cambridge University Press.

Kant, Immanuel 2002 [1790], *Critique of the Power of Judgement*, translated by Paul Guyer, New York: Cambridge University Press.

Kant, Immanuel 2006, *Anthropology from a Pragmatic Point of View*, translated by Robert B. Louden, Cambridge, UK: Cambridge University Press.

Kaufmann, Walter 1974 [1950], *Nietzsche. Philosopher, Psychologist, Antichrist*, Princeton.

Kittler, Friedrich A. (ed.) 1980, *Die Austreibung des Geistes aus den Geisteswissen-schaften. Programme des Poststrukturalismus*, Paderborn, München, Wien, Zürich: Schöningh.

Klee, Ernst 1983, '"Euthanasie" im NS-Staat. Die Vernichtung lebensunwerten Lebens', Frankfurt: S. Fischer.

Klossowski, Pierre 1969: *Nietzsche et le cercle vicieux*, Paris: Mercure de France.

Klossowski, Pierre 2009 [1969], *Nietzsche and the Vicious Circle*, translated by Dan Smith, London: Continuum.

Knebel, Sven K. 2001, 'Artikel Unterschied', in Ritter, Joachim, Karlfried Gründer and Gottfried Gabriel (eds.) 1971–2007, Vol. 11: 310–13.

Krais, Beate 1993, 'Geschlechterverhältnis und symbolische Gewalt', in Gebauer and Wulf (eds.) 1993.

Laclau, Ernesto and Chantal Mouffe 1985, *Hegemony and Socialist Strategy*, London: Verso.

Landa, Ishay 2005, 'Aroma and Shadow: Marx vs. Nietzsche on Religion', in: *Nature, Society, and Thought*, vol. 18, no. 4 (2005): 461–499.

Landa Ishay 2007, *The Overman in the Marketplace: Nietzschean Heroism in Popular Culture*, Lanham, MD: Lexington Books.

Landa, Ishay 2018, *Fascism and the Masses. The Revolt against the Last Humans, 1848–1945*, New York, London: Routledge.

Lange, Friedrich Albert, 1873/1875 (1866), *Geschichte des Materialismus und Kritik seiner Bedeutung in der Gegenwart*, 2 vols., Iserlohn: J. Baedeker.

Lange, Friedrich Albert 2000 [1892], *The History of Materialism, and Criticism of its Present Importance*, London: Routledge.

Lange, Thomas 1989, *Die Ordnung des Begehrens. Nietzscheanische Aspekte im philosophischen Werk von Gilles Deleuze*, Bielefeld: Aisthesis Verlag.

Langemeyer, Ines 2004, 'Subjektivität und kollektive Erfahrung. Subjektivierung als Machtinstrument im Produktionsprozess', in *Widerspruch. Beiträge zu sozialistischer Politik*, 46: 65–78.

Larrain, Jorge 1994, *Ideology and Cultural Identity. Modernity and the Third World Presence*, Cambridge: Polity Press.

Lecourt, Dominique 1972, *Pour une critique de l'épistémologie (Bachelard, Canguilhem, Foucault)*, Paris: Maspero.

Lecourt, Dominique 1975, *Marxism and Epistemology*, translated by Ben Brewster, London: NLB.

Lemke, Thomas 2011, *Biopolitics. An Advanced Introduction*, translated by Eric Frederick Trump, London, New York: New York University Press.

Lemke, Thomas 2019, *Foucault's Analysis of Modern Governmentality. A Critique of Political Reason*, translated by Erik Butler, London, New York: Verso.

Léonard, Jacques 1977, 'L' Historien et le philosophe. Apropos de "Surveiller et punir. Naissance de la prison"', in *Annales Historiques de la Révolution Française*, No. 228, Juillet–Septembre: 163–181.

Lepage, Henri 1978, *Demain le capitalism*, Paris: Hachette.

Lettow, Susanne 2001, 'Geworfenheit', in Haug et al. (eds.), 1994–, 5: 775–81.

Lettow, Susanne 2018, 'Biocapitalism', in *Krisis. Journal for contemporary philosophy*, 2: Marx from the Margins: A Collective Project, from A to Z.

Loick, Daniel 2000, 'Eine eigene Geschichte aus reiner Gegenwart sammelt und stapelt sich von sich selbst herum um mich. Zur Kritik an Gilles Deleuzes Mord am Subjekt', in Chlada (ed.) 2000.

Losurdo, Domenico 2001 [1991], *Heidegger and the Ideology of War. Community, Death, and the West*, Amherst: Humanity Books.

Losurdo, Domenico 2002, *Nietzsche, il ribelle aristocratico. Biografia intellettuale e bilancio critico*, Torino: Bollati Boringhieri.

Losurdo, Domenico 2009 [2002], *Nietzsche der aristokratische Rebell. Intellektuelle Biographie und kritische Bilanz*, 2 volumes, translated by Erdmute Brielmayer, edited and with an introduction by Jan Rehmann, Hamburg: Argument.

Losurdo, Domenico 2011, *Liberalism. A Counter-History*, translated by Gregory Elliot, London, New York: Verso.

Losurdo, Domenico 2020 [2002], *Nietzsche, the Aristocratic Rebel. Intellectual Biography and Critical Balance-Sheet*, translated by Gregor Benton, with an introduction by Harrison Fluss, Leiden, Boston: Brill.

Lukács, Georg 1934, 'Nietzsche als Vorläufer der faschistischen Ästhetik', in: *Georg Lukács Werke*, Volume 10: 307–39.

Lukács, Georg 1955, *Die Zerstörung der Vernunft. Der Weg des Irrationalismus von Schelling zu Hitler*, Berlin/DDR: Aufbau-Verlag.

Lyotard, Jean Francois 1979, *La condition postmoderne*, Paris: Les Éditions de Minuit.

Lyotard, Jean Francois 1984 [1979], *The Postmodern Condition: A Report on Knowledge*, translated by Geoffrey Bennington and Brian Massumi, Minneapolis: University of Minnesota Press.

Macpherson, Crawford Borough 1962, *The Political Theory of Possessive Individualism. Hobbes to Locke*, Oxford: Clarendon Press.

Maiers, Wolfgang 1999, 'funktional-historische Analyse', in Haug et al. (eds.), 1994-, 4: 1133–1140.

Mann, Michael 1986, *The Sources of Social Power. Volume 1: A History of Power from the Beginning to A.D. 1760*, Cambridge [a.o.]: Cambridge University Press.

Marcuse, Herbert 1928, 'Beiträge zu einer Phänomenologie des historischen Materialismus', in Marcuse and Schmidt: 41–84.

Marcuse, Herbert and Alfred Schmidt 1973, *Existentialistische Marx-Interpretation*, Frankfurt/Main: Europäische Verlagsanstalt.

Markard, Morus 2001, 'Handlungsfähigkeit II', in Haug et al. (eds.), 1994–, 5: 1174–1181.

Marx, Karl 1843, 'A Contribution to the Critique of Hegel's Philosophy of Law. Introduction', in Marx and Engels 1975–2005, Vol. 3.

Marx, Karl 1844a, *The Economic and Philosophic Manuscripts of 1844*, in Marx and Engels 1975–2005, Vol. 3.

Marx, Karl 1844b, *On the Jewish Question*, in Marx and Engels 1975–2005, Vol. 3.

Marx, Karl 1845, 'These on Feuerbach', in Marx and Engels 1975–2005, Vol. 5.

Marx, Karl 1857a, 'Introduction to the *Outlines of the Critique of Political Economy*', in Marx and Engels 1975–2005, Vol. 28.

Marx, Karl 1857b, *Outlines of the Critique of Political Economy*, in Marx and Engels 1975–2005, Vol. 28.

Marx, Karl 1862, *Theories of Surplus Value*, in Marx and Engels 1975–2005, Vol. 31.

Marx, Karl 1867, *Capital*. Volume I, in Marx and Engels 1975–2005, Vol. 35.

Marx, Karl 1868, 'Marx to Kugelmann. 11 July 1868', in Marx and Engels 1975–2005, Vol. 43.

Marx, Karl 1875, *Critique of the Gotha Programme*, in Marx and Engels 1975–2005, Vol. 24.

Marx, Karl 1953, *Grundrisse der Kritik der politischen Ökonomie (Rohentwurf)*, 1857–58, first published 1939/41, Berlin/DDR: Dietz Verlag.

Marx, Karl 1976, *Capital. A Critique of Political Economy*, Vol. I, translated by Ben Fowkes, London: Penguin Books.

Marx, Karl and Friedrich Engels 1845a, *The Holy Family*, in Marx and Engels 1975–2005, Vol. 4.

Marx, Karl and Friedrich Engels 1845b, *The German Ideology*, in Marx and Engels 1975–2005, Vol. 5.

Marx, Karl and Friedrich Engels 1957–, *Marx-Engels-Werke* (*MEW*), 42 Vols., edited by the Institute of Marxism-Leninism beim ZK der SED, Berlin: Dietz Verlag.

Marx, Karl and Friedrich Engels 1975–2005, *Marx Engels Collected Works* (*MECW*), London: Lawrence & Wishart.

Marx, Karl and Friedrich Engels 1975–, *Marx-Engels-Gesamtausgabe* (*MEGA*), Berlin: Akademie-Verlag.

Matheron, Alexandre 1969, *Individu et communauté chez Spinoza*, Paris: Les Éditions de Minuit.

Matheron, Alexandre 1997 (1985): 'The Theoretical Function of Democracy in Spinoza and Hobbes', in Montag and Stolze (eds.) 1997.

Mauss, Marcel 1966 [1950], *The Gift: Forms and Functions of Exchange in Archaic Societies*, translated by Ian Cunnison, Liverpool, UK: Cohen & West Ltd.

Mbembe, Achilles 2003, 'Necropolitics', in *Public Culture*, Duke University Press, 15(1): 11–40.

McNally, David 2001, *Bodies of Meaning. Studies in Language, Labor, and Liberation*, New York: State University of New York Press.

McNally, David 2011, *Monsters of the Market. Zombies, Vampires and Global Capitalism*, Chicago, Il.: Haymarket Books.

Meier, S. 1989, 'Postmoderne', in Ritter, Joachim, Karlfried Gründer and Gottfried Gabriel (eds.) 1971–2007, Vol. 7: 1141–1145.

Meillassoux, Claude 1981, *Maidens, Meal and Money. Capitalism and the Domestic Community*, edited by Jack Goody and Geoffrey Hawthorn, Cambridge: Cambridge University Press.

Melossi, Dario 1979, 'Institutions of Social Control and Capitalist Organization of Work', in Fine et al. (eds.), 1979: 90–9.

Melossi, Dario 1980, 'GeorgRusche: A Biographical Essay', in *Crime and Social Justice*, 14: 51–63.

Melossi, Dario 2008, 'Introduction to the Transaction Edition', in Rusche and Kirchheimer 2009: ix–xlii.

Melossi, Dario and Massimo Pavarini 1981 [1977], *The Prison and the Factory. Origins of the Penitentiary System*, London and Basingstoke: Macmillan.

Miller, James 1993, *The Passion of Michel Foucault*, Cambridge (USA): Harvard University Press.

Mirowski, Philip 2013, *Never Let a Serious Crisis Go to Waste: How Neoliberalism Survived the Financial Meltdown*. London: Verso.

Montag, Warren 1995, '"The Soul is the Prison of the Body": Althusser and Foucault, 1970–1975', in *Yale French Studies. Depositions: Althusser, Balibar, Macherey, and the Labour of Reading*, No. 88: 53–77.

Montag, Warren and Ted Stolze (eds.) 1997, *The New Spinoza*, Minneapolis, London: University of Minnesota Press.

Moore, Barrington, Jr. 1978, *Injustice: The Social Basis for Obedience and Revolt*, White Plains: M.E. Sharpe.

Moore, Jason W. 2015, *Capitalism in the Web of Life. Ecology and the Accumulation of Capital*, London, New York: Verso.

Muck, Otto 1972, 'Differenz', in Ritter, Joachim, Karlfried Gründer and Gottfried Gabriel (eds.) 1971–2007, Vol. 2: 235–6.

Müller, Cathreen 2003, 'Neoliberalismus als Selbstführung. Anmerkungen zu den "Governmentality Studies"', *Das Argument*, 249: 98–106.

Müller, Heiner and Robert Weimann 1991 [1989], 'Gleichzeitigkeit und Repräsentation. Ein Gespräch', in Weimann and Gumbrecht (eds.), 1991.

Müller-Lauter, Wolfgang 1992, 'Nietzsche's Teaching of the Will to Power', *The Journal of Nietzsche Studies*, No. 4: 37–101.

Müller-Lauter, Wolfgang 1999: *Über Werden und Wille zur Macht*. Nietzsche-Interpretationen I, Berlin, New York: de Gruyter.

Münker, Stefan and Alexander Roesler 2012, *Poststrukturalismus*, Stuttgart, Weimar: J.B. Metzler.

Negri, Antonio 1991, *The Savage Anomaly: The Power of Spinoza's Metaphysics and Politics*, translated by Michael Hardt, Minneapolis, MN: University of Minnesota Press.

Negri, Antonio 2013, *Spinoza for Our Time. Politics and Postmodernity*, translated by William McCuaig, New York: Columbia University Press.

Neusüss, Christel 1985, *Die Kopfgeburten der Arbeiterbewegung oder die Genossin Luxemburg bringt alles durcheinander*, Hamburg, Zürich: Rasch und Röhring.

Newheiser, David 2016, 'Foucault, Gary Becker and the Critique of Neoliberalism', in *Theory, Culture & Society*, 2016, 33(5): 3–21.

Nietzsche, Friedrich 1933–1942, *Historisch-Kritische Gesamtausgabe der Werke und Briefe Nietzsches*, edited by the Nietzsche-Archiv, 9 volumes, Munich: Beck

Nietzsche, Friedrich 1968a [1889], *Twilight of the Idols*, translated by R.J. Hollingdale, London: Penguin.

Nietzsche, Friedrich 1968b [1889], *The Antichrist*, translated by R.J. Hollingdale, London: Penguin.

Nietzsche, Friedrich 1975–, *Briefwechsel. Kritische Gesamtausgabe*, edited by Giorgio Colli and Mazino Montinari, Berlin, New York: de Gruyter.

Nietzsche, Friedrich 1982 [1888], *The Portable Nietzsche*, translated by Walter Kaufmann, United States: Viking Penguin.

Nietzsche, Friedrich 1986, *Sämtliche Briefe. Kritische Studienausgabe*, edited by Giorgio Colli and Mazino Montinari, Berlin/New York.

Nietzsche, Friedrich 1989 [1888], *Ecce Homo*, translated by Walter Kaufmann, New York: Random House/Vintage Books.

Nietzsche, Friedrich 1994 [1878], *Human, All Too Human*, translated by M Faber and S. Lehmann, London: Penguin.

Nietzsche, Friedrich 1997 [1886], *Beyond Good and Evil*, translated by Helen Zimmern, New York: Dover Publications.

Nietzsche, Friedrich 1999a, *Kritische Studienausgabe*, edited by Giorgio Colli and Mazino Montinari, Munich: de Gruyter.

Nietzsche, Friedrich 1999b [1872–1874], *Unpublished Writings from the period of Unfashionable Observations*, translated by Richard T. Gray, Stanford, CA: Stanford University Press.

Nietzsche, Friedrich 2000, *Basic Writings*, translated by Walter Kaufmann, New York: Modern Library.

Nietzsche, Friedrich 2003a [1873–1876], *Unfashionable Observations*, translated by Richard T. Gray, Stanford, CA: Stanford Univ. Press.

Nietzsche, Friedrich 2003b [1887], *Writings from the Late Notebooks*, edited by Rüdiger Bittner, translated by Kate Sturge, Cambridge UK: Cambridge University Press.

Nietzsche, Friedrich 2005, *The Anti-Christ, Ecce Homo, Twilight of the Idols, and Other Writings*, translated by Judith Norman, Cambridge, UK: Cambridge University Press.

Nietzsche, Friedrich 2006 [1883–85], *Thus Spoke Zarathustra*, edited by Adrian Del Caro and Robert B. Pippin, translated by Adrian Del Caro, Cambridge: Cambridge University Press.

Nietzsche, Friedrich 2007 [1872], *The Birth of Tragedy and Other Writings*, translated by R. Speirs, edited by Raymond Geuss, New York: Cambridge University Press.

Nietzsche, Friedrich 2011 [1881], *Dawn – Thoughts on the Presumptions of Morality*, translated by Brittain Smith, Stanford: Stanford University Press.

Nietzsche, Friedrich 2013a [1887], *On the Genealogy of Morals*, translated by M.R. Scarpitti, London: Penguin.

Nietzsche, Friedrich 2013b, *Human All too Human II*, translated by Gary Handwerk, Stanford, CA: Stanford University Press.

Nietzsche, Friedrich 2017a [1871/72], *Nietzsche on the Genealogy of Morality and Other Writings*, translated by Carol Diethe, Cambridge UK: Cambridge University Press.

Nietzsche, Friedrich 2017b [1882], *The Gay Science*, translated by Thomas Common, Whithorn: Anodos Books.

Oestreich, Gerhard 1969, *Geist und Gestalt des frühmodernen Staates. Ausgewählte Aufsätze*, Berlin: Duncker und Humbolt.

Oittinen, Vesa 1994, *Spinozistische Dialektik: Die Spinoza-Lektüre des französischen Strukturalismus und Poststrukturalismus*, Frankfurt: Peter Lang.

Opitz, Sven 2004, *Gouvernementalität im Postfordismus. Macht, Wissen und Techniken des Selbst im Feld unternehmerischer Rationalität*, Hamburg: Argument-Verlag.

Opitz, Sven 2007, 'Gouvernementalitat im Postfordismus. Zur Erkundung unternehmerischer Steuerungsregime der Gegenwart', in Kaindl, Christina (ed.) 2007.

Orsucci, Andrea 1997, *Orient-Okzident. Nietzsches Versuch einer Loslösung vom europäischen Weltbild*, Berlin, New York.

Osborne, Peter 1995, *The Politics of Time*, London: Verso.

Ottmann, Henning 1999 [1987], *Philosophie und Politik bei Nietzsche*, 2nd edition, Berlin, New York: de Gruyter.

Pannwitz, Rudolf 1917, *Die Krisis der europäischen Kultur*, in *Werke, Volume 2*, Nürnberg: Verlag Hans Carl.

Parenti, Christian 1999, *Lockdown America. Police and Prisons in the Age of Crisis*, London, New York: Verso.

Pascal, Blaise 1954, *Oeuvres complètes*. Texte établi, présenté et annoté par Jacques Chevalier, Paris: Éditions Gallimard.

Pêcheux, Michel 1975, *Les vérités de la palice*, Paris: François Maspero.

Pêcheux, Michel 1982 [1975], *Language, Semantics, Ideology: Stating the Obvious*, translated by H. Nagpal, London: Macmillan.

Pêcheux, Michel 1990, *L'inquiétude du Discours. Textes de Michel Pêcheux*, selected and presentedby Denise Maldidier, Paris: Éditions des Cendres.

Pêcheux, Michel 2014 [1984], 'Dare to Think and Dare to Rebel! Ideology, Marxism, Resistance, Class Struggle', translated by Ted Stolze, *Décalages*: vol. 1, no. 4: 1–27, available at: https://scholar.oxy.edu/bitstream/handle/20.500.12711/12918/Dare to Think a nd Dare to Rebel.pdf?sequence=1&isAllowed=y.

Perlitt, Lothar 1965, *Vatke und Wellhausen. Geschichtsphilosophische Voraussetzungen und historiographische Motive für die Darstellung der Religion und Geschichte Israels durch Wilhelm Vatke und Julius Wellhausen*, Berlin.

Perrot, Michelle 1980 (ed.), *L'Impossible Prison. Recherches sur le Système Pénitentiaire au XIXe Siècle. Débat avec Michel Foucault*, Paris: Éditions du Seuil.

Perrot, Michelle 2001, *Les Ombres de l'Histoire. Crime et Châtiment au XIXe Siècle*, Paris: Éditions du Seuil.

Pestaña, J.L. Moreno 2011, *Foucault, la gauche et la politique*, Paris: Textuel.

Petersen, Olaf 2004, 'Ausfaltung und Verfeinerung der Disziplinarmacht im Management – Erfahrungsbericht aus einer internationalen Unternehmensberatung', in *Forum Kritische Psychologie*, 47: 120–44.

Petit, Jacques-Guy 1990, *Ces Peines Obscures. La Prison Pénale en France (1780–1875)*, Paris: Fayard.

Petit, Jacques-Guy et al. (eds.) 1984, *La Prison, le Bagne et l'Histoire*, Genève: Médecine et Hygiéne.

Petit, Jacques-Guy et al. (eds.), 1991: *Histoire des Galères, Bagnes et Prisons. XIIIe–XXe siècles. Introduction à l'histoire pénale de la France*, Toulouse: Privat.

Peukert, Detlev J.K. 1986, *Grenzen der Sozialdisziplinierung. Aufstieg der Krise der deutschen Jugendfürsorge von 1878 bis 1932*, Köln: Bund Verlag.

Peukert, Detlev J.K. 1991, 'Die Unordnung der Dinge. Michel Foucault und die deutsche Geschichtswissenschaft', in *Spiele der Wahrheit. Michel Foucaults Denken*, edited by François Ewald and Bernhard Waldenfels, Frankfurt/Main: Suhrkamp.

Pfeiffer, Ernst (ed.) 1970, *Friedrich Nietzsche, Paul Rée, Lou von Salomé. Die Dokumente ihrer Begegnung*, Frankfurt/Main: Insel Verlag.

Pizer, John 1990, 'The Use and Abuse of, "Ursprung": On Foucault's Reading of Nietzsche', in *Nietzsche-Studien. Internationales Jahrbuch für die Nietzsche-Forschung*, Volume 19: 462–78.

Plato, *Respublica/Politeia*

Plato, *Sophista*

Pocai, Romano 2001, 'Die Weltlichkeit der Welt und ihre abgedrängte Faktizität', in Rentsch (ed.) 2001.

Polanyi, Karl, 1975 [1944], *The Great Transformation*, New York: Octagon Books.

Poster, Mark 1984, *Foucault, Marxism and History. Mode of Production versus Mode of Information*, Cambridge: Polity Press.

Poulantzas, Nicos 1968, *Pouvoir politique et classes sociales*, Vol. 1, Paris: Maspero.

Poulantzas, Nicos 1978a, *L'État, le Pouvoir, le Socialisme*, Paris: Presses Universitaires de France.

Poulantzas, Nicos 1978b [1968], *Political Power and Social Classes*, translated by and edited by Timothy O'Hagan, London: Verso Editions.

Poulantzas, Nicos 2014 [1978], *State, Power, Socialism*, translated by Patrick Camiller, London, Brooklyn: Verso.

Prado, Carlos G. 2000 [1995], *Starting with Foucault. An Introduction to Genealogy*, Boulder, Colorado: Westview Press.

Probst, P. 1972, 'Differenz, ontologische', in Ritter, Joachim, Karlfried Gründer and Gottfried Gabriel (eds.) 1971–2007, Vol. 2: 236–7.

Projekt Ideologietheorie (PIT) 1979, *Theorien über Ideologie*, Hamburg, Berlin/West: Argument Verlag.

Projekt Ideologietheorie 2007 (1980), *Faschismus und Ideologie*, newly edited by Klaus Weber, Hamburg: Argument Verlag.

Rancière, Jacques 2011 [1974], *Althusser's Lesson*, translated by Emiliano Battista, London, New York: Continuum.

Ransom, John S. 1997, *Foucault's Discipline. The Politics of Subjectivity*, Durham, N.C.: Duke University Press.

Rausch, Karin 1975, 'Georg Rusche/Otto Kirchheimer, Sozialstruktur und Strafvollzug', in *Kritische Justiz*, vol. 8, no. 2: 215–18.

Rée, Paul 1875, *Psychologische Beobachtungen*, Berlin: Carl Duncker.

Rée, Paul 1877, *Ursprung der moralischen Empfindungen*, Chemnitz: Ernst Schmeitzner.

Rée, Paul 2003 [1875], *Basic Writings*, translated and edited by Robin Small, Urbana: University of Illinois Press.

Reed, Adolph 2013, 'Marx, Race, and Neoliberalism', in *New Labor Forum* 22 (1): 49–57.

Reeling Brower, Rinse 2001, 'Handlungsfähigkeit I', in Haug et al. (eds.), 1994–, 5: 1169–1174.

Rehmann, Jan 2001, 'Glauben' [Belief/Faith], in: Haug et al. (eds.), 1994–, 5:787–808.

Rehmann, Jan 2004a, *Postmoderner Links-Nietzscheanismus. Deleuze & Foucault. Eine Dekonstruktion, Hamburg: Argument.*

Rehmann, Jan 2004b, 'Nietzsches Umarbeitung des kulturprotestantischen Antijudaismus – Das Beispiel Wellhausen', in *Das Argument 255*, March/April 2004: 278–91.

Rehmann, Jan 2005a, 'Ist die Postmoderne anti-amerikanisch? Zur Enteignung und Umwertung linker Kritik in Richard Wolins *The Seduction of Reason*', in *Das Argument*, 259: 22–32.

Rehmann, Jan 2005b, 'Nietzsche, Paul, and the Subversion of Empire', in *Union Seminary Quarterly Review (USQR)*: 147–61.

Rehmann, Jan 2007, 'Review of Domenico Losurdo's *Nietzsche: il ribelle aristocratico. Biografia intellettuale e bilancio critico*', in *Historical Materialism*, 15.2: 173–93.

Rehmann, Jan 2009, *I Nietzschani di Sinistra. Deleuze, Foucault e il postmodernismo: una deconstruzione*, translated and edited by Stefano G. Azzarà, Rome: Odradek.

Rehmann, Jan 2012, 'Antizipation', in Beat Dietschy, Doris Zeilinger, Rainer Zimmermann (eds.), *Bloch-Wörterbuch. Leitbegriffe der Philosophie Ernst Blochs*. Berlin-Boston: De Gruyter.

Rehmann, Jan 2013, *Theories of Ideology. The Powers of Alienation and Subjection*, Leiden: Brill [paperback 2014 in Haymarket Books].

Rehmann, Jan 2014, 'Spinoza und Nietzsche. Wider die Verwechslung von Handlungsmacht und Herrschaftsmacht', in *Das Argument* 307, no. 2: 213–25.

Rehmann, Jan 2015a, *Max Weber. Modernisation as Passive Revolution. A Gramscian Analysis*, Leiden: Brill [paperback 2015 in Haymarket Books].

Rehmann, Jan 2015b, 'Hypercarceration: A Neoliberal Response to "Surplus Population"', in *Rethinking Marxism*, Vol. 27, No. 2: 302–10.

Rehmann, Jan 2016a, 'The Unfulfilled Promises of the Late Foucault and Foucauldian "Governmentality Studies"', in Daniel Zamora and Michael C. Behrent (eds.) 2016.

Rehmann, Jan 2016b, 'Bernie Sanders and the Hegemonic Crisis of Neoliberal Capitalism: What Next?' In *Socialism and Democracy*, 30, 3:1–11.

Rehmann, Jan 2018, 'Marxism's Double Task: Deconstructing and Reconstructing Postmodernism', in *Marxism without Guarantees: Economics, Knowledge, and Class*, edited by Burczak, Theodore, Robert Garnett and Richard McIntyre, London, New York: Routledge.

Rehmann, Jan 2019a, '"Multitude", "Mosaik-Linke" und die Aufgabe politischer Bündelung', *Das Argument*, 331: 81–91.

Rehmann, Jan 2019b, 'Power ≠ Power: Against the Mix-Up of Nietzsche and Spinoza', in *Critical Sociology* 2019, Vol. 45 (2): 239–52.

Reibnitz, Barbara von 1992, *Ein Kommentar zu Friedrich Nietzsche, 'Die Geburt der Tragödie aus dem Geiste der Musik'* (Kap. 1–12), Weimar: Metzler.

Reitter, Karl 2011, *Prozesse der Befreiung: Marx, Spinoza und die Bedingungen eines freien Gemeinwesens*. Münster: Westfälisches Dampfboot.

Reitz, Tilman 1997, 'Lorianismus, Kulturindustrie und Postmoderne. Dimensionen eines gramscianischen Nebenbegriffs', in *Das Argument* 219, Vol. 39, No. 2: 203–214.

Reitz, Tilman 2001, 'Gegensatz', in Haug et al. (eds.), 1994–, 5: 14–35.

Reitz, Tilman 2003, 'Die Sorge um sich und niemand anderen. Foucault als Vordenker neoliberaler Vergesellschaftung', in *Das Argument* 249, Vol. 45, No. 1: 82–97.

Reitz, Tilman 2005, 'Neoliberalismus in Staat und Geist', *Das Argument*, 261: 371–5.

Reitz, Tilman and Susanne Draheim 2007, 'Schattenboxen im Neoliberalismus. Kritik und Perspektiven der deutschen Foucault-Rezeption', in Kaindl (ed.) 2007.

Renan, Ernest 1863: *La vie de Jésus*, Paris: Michel Lévy Frères.

Renan, Ernst 1898 [1863], *Renan's Life of Jesus*, translated by William G. Hutchison, London: Walter Scott Publishing.

Rentsch, Thomas (ed.) 2001, *Martin Heidegger. Sein und Zeit*, Berlin: Akademie Verlag.

Resch, Robert Paul 1989, 'Modernism, Postmodernism, and Social Theory: A Comparison of Althusser and Foucault', in *Poetics Today* 10.3: 511–49.

Ritter, Joachim, Karlfried Gründer and Gottfried Gabriel (eds.) 1971–2007, *Historisches Wörterbuch der Philosophie*, Basel: Schwabe Verlag.

Rochlitz, Rainer 1989, 'Esthétique de l'existence', in *Michel Foucault, philosophe*, Rencontre Internationale, Paris 9, 10, 11 janvier 1988, Paris 1989: 288–300.

Rogozinski, Jacob 1996, 'Ohnmachten (zwischen Nietzsche und Kant)', in Balke and Vogel (eds.), 1996.

Roth, Jürgen 2000, 'Philosophie als Kabarett', in Chlada (ed.), 2000.

Röttgers, Kurt 1980 'Macht I', in Ritter, Joachim, Karlfried Gründer and Gottfried Gabriel (eds.) 1971–2007, Vol. 5: 585–604.

Rusche, Georg, 1930, 'Zuchthausrevolten oder Sozialpolitik. Zu den Vorgängen in Amerika', in *Frankfurter Zeitung* of 1.6.1930, Nr. 403, quoted in Rusche/Kirchheimer 1981: 291–7.

Rusche, Georg 1933, 'Arbeitsmarkt und Strafvollzug. Gedanken zur Soziologie der Strafjustiz' in *Zeitschrift für Sozialforschung*, vol. 2, 1933, 63–78, quoted in Rusche/ Kirchheimer 1981: 298–313.

Rusche, Georg and Otto Kirchheimer 1981 [1939], *Sozialstruktur und Strafvollzug*, 2nd edition, extended by an appendix with two essays by Georg Rusche and an epilogue by Heinz Steinert, Frankfurt/Main, Köln: Europaische Verlagsanstalt.

Rusche, Georg and Otto Kirchheimer 2009 [1939], *Punishment and Social Structure*, New Brunswick: Transaction Publishers.

Rutherford, Donald 2013, 'Perfectionism in Spinoza and Nietzsche', Backdoor Broadcasting Company, available at (accessed 28 November 2016): http://backdoorbroadcasting.net/2013/05/donald-rutherford-perfectionism-in-spinoza-and-nietzsche/.

Saar, Martin 2013, *Die Immanenz der Macht: Politische Theorie nach Spinoza*, Frankfurt: Suhrkamp.

Sachße, Christoph and Florian Tennstedt (eds.) 1986, *Soziale Sicherheit und soziale Disziplinierung. Beiträge zu einer historischen Theorie der Sozialpolitik*, Frankfurt/Main: Suhrkamp.

Said, Edward 1985 [1975], *Beginnings: Intention and Method*, New York: Columbia University Press.

Said, Edward 1988, 'Michel Foucault, 1926–1984', in Arac (ed.) 1988.

Said, Edward W. 2003 (1978), *Orientalism*, 25th Anniversary Edition, New York: Vintage Books.

Salaquarda, Jörg 1978, 'Nietzsche und Lange', in Müller-Lauter, Wolfgang and Jörg Salaquarda (ed.) 1978, *Aneignung und Umwandlung. Friedrich Nietzsche und das 19. Jahrhundert*, Nietzsche-Studien. Internationales Jahrbuch für die Nietzsche-Forschung, vol. 7, 1978: 236–53.

Sartre, Jean-Paul 1966, 'Jean-Paul Sartre répond', in *L'Arc*, Nr. 30: *Sartre aujourd'hui*, 1966: 87–96.

Sartre, Jean-Paul 2007 [1958], *Existentialism is a Humanism*, translated by Carol Macomber, New Haven and London: Yale University Press.

Sawyer, Stephen W. and Daniel Steinmetz-Jenkins (eds.) 2019, *Foucault, Neoliberalism, and Beyond*, London, New York: Rowman & Littlefield.

Schaub, Mirjam 2001, 'Genealogie', in Haug et al. (eds.), 1994–, 5: 319–230.

Schlesier, Renate 1984, 'Humaniora. Eine Kolumne', in *Merkur*, Vol. 38, Nr. 7, Oktober 1984: 817–23.

Schmid, Wilhelm 1991, *Auf der Suche nach einer neuen Lebenskunst. Die Frage nach dem Grund und die Neubegründung der Ethik bei Foucault*, Frankfurt/Main: Suhrkamp.

Schmidgen, Henning 1997, *Das Unbewusste der Maschinen. Konzeptionen des Psychischen bei Guattari, Deleuze und Lacan*, München: Fink.

Schopenhauer, Arthur 1969 [1844], *The World as Will and Representation. In Two Volumes*, Volume I, translated by E.F.J. Payne, New York: Dover Publications.

Schrift, Alan D. 1995, 'Putting Nietzsche to Work: Deleuze', in Sedgwick (ed.) 1995.

Schumann, Karl F. 1981, 'Produktionsverhältnisse und staatliche Strafen. Zur aktuellen Diskussion über Rusche und Kirchheimer', in *Kritische Justiz*, Vol. 14. Jg. 1981: 64–77.

Schweitzer, Albert 1984 [1906], *Geschichte der Leben-Jesu-Forschung*, Tübingen.

Schweitzer, Albert 1998 [1911], *The Mysticism of Paul the Apostle*, Baltimore: The John Hopkins University Press.

Schweppenhäuser, Gerhard 1988, *Nietzsches Überwindung der Moral. Zur Dialektik der*

Moralkritik in 'Jenseits von Gut und Böse' und in der 'Genealogie der Moral', Würzburg: Königshausen & Neumann.

Schwingel, Markus 1993, *Analytik der Kämpfe. Macht und Herrschaft in der Soziologie Bourdieus*, Hamburg: Argument.

Sedgwick, Peter R. (ed.) 1995, *Nietzsche: A Critical Reader*, Oxford (UK), Cambridge (USA): Blackwell.

Semple, Janet 1993, *Bentham's Prison. A Study of the Panopticon Penitentiary*, Oxford: Clarendon Press.

Sève, Lucien 1972, *Marxismus und Theorie der Persönlichkeit*, Frankfurt/M: Verlag Marxistische Blätter.

Sharpe, Matthew 2021, 'Golden calf: Deleuze's Nietzsche in the time of Trump', in: *Thesis Eleven*, 2021: 1–18.

Shelden, Randall, G. 2001, *Controlling the Dangerous Classes. A Critical Introduction to the History of Criminal Justice*, Boston: Allyn and Bacon.

Sigrist, Christian 1994. *Regulierte Anarchie. Untersuchungen zum Fehlen und zur Entstehung politischer Herrschaft in segmentären Gesellschaften Afrikas*, Hamburg: Europäische Verlagsanstalt.

Smart, Barry 1986, 'The Politics of Truth and theProblem of Hegemony', in Hoy (ed.), 1986.

Sommer, Andreas Urs 2000, *Friedrich Nietzsches 'Der Antichrist'. Ein philosophisch-historischer Kommentar*, Basel: Schwabe.

Sommer, Andreas Urs 2012: 'Nietzsche's readings on Spinoza: A contextualist study, particularly on the reception of Kuno Fischer', in *Journal of Nietzsche Studies* 43(2): 156–84.

Sorel, Georges, 2018 [1908], *Reflections on Violence*, translated by T.E. Hulme, London: Routledge.

Spierenburg, Pieter 1984, *The Spectacle of Suffering. Executions and the Evolution of Repression: from a Preindustrial Metropolis to the European Experience*, Cambridge: Cambridge University Press.

Spinoza, Benedictus de 2016 [1670], *Theological-Political Treatise*, translated by M. Silverthorne and Jonathan Israel, United Kingdom: Cambridge University Press.

Spinoza, Benedictus de 1996, *Ethics*, translated by Edwin Curley, London: Penguin Books.

Stack, George J., 1983, *Lange and Nietzsche*, Berlin, New York: de Gruyter.

Stegmaier, Werner 1994, *Nietzsches 'Genealogie der Moral'*, Darmstadt: Wissenschaftliches Buchgesellschaft.

Steinert, Heinz 1978, 'Ist es denn aber auch wahr, Herr F.? "Überwachen und Strafen" unter der Fiktion gelesen, es handle sich dabei um eine sozialgeschichtliche Darstellung', in *Kriminalsoziologische Bibliografie* 1978, Vol. 5, No. 19–20, 'Michel Foucault und das Gefängnis': 30–45.

Steinert, Heinz 1981, 'Nachwort. Dringliche Aufforderung, an der Studie von Rusche und Kirchheimer weiterzuarbeiten', in Rusche/Kirchheimer 1981, pp. 314–36.

Steinert, Heinz and Hubert Treiber 1978, 'Versuch, die These von der strafrechtlichen Ausrottungspolitik im Spätmittelalter "auszurotten". Eine Kritik an Rusche/Kirchheimer und dem Ökonomismus in der Theorie der Strafrechtsentwicklung', in *Kriminologisches Journal*, vol. 10, 1978: 81–106.

Stekl, Hannes 1986, ' "Labore et fame", – Sozialdisziplinierung in Zucht- und Arbeitshäusern des 17. und 18. Jahrhunderts', in *Soziale Sicherheit und soziale Disziplinierung. Beiträge zu einer historischen Theorie der Sozialpolitik*, edited by Christoph Sachße and Florian Tennstedt, Frankfurt/Main: Suhrkamp.

Sullivan, Larry E. 1990, *The Prison Reform Movement. Forlorn Hope*, Boston: Twayne Publishers.

Swartz, David 1997, *Culture & Power. The Sociology of Pierre Bourdieu*, Chicago: University of Chicago Press.

Taubes, Jacob 1995, *Die politische Theologie des Paulus*, München: Wilhelm Fink.

Taylor, M.L. 2001, *The Executed God: The Way of the Cross in Lockdown America*, Minneapolis: Fortress.

Terpstra, Marin 1990: *De wending naar de politiek. Een studie over de begrippen 'potentia' en 'potestas' bij Spinoza*, Nijmegen.

Theweleit, Klaus, 1987 [1977], *Male Fantasies*, Volume 1, translated by Stephen Conway in collaboration with Erica Carter and Chris Turner, Minneapolis: University of Minnesota Press.

Thompson, Edward P. 1971, 'The Moral Economy of the English Crowd in the Eighteenth Century', in *Past and Present*, No. 50: 76–136.

Thompson, Edward P. 1995 [1978], *The Poverty of Theory: or an Orrery of Errors*, London: Merlin Press.

Toscano, Alberto 2007, 'Always Already Only Now: Negri and the Biopolitical', in *The Philosophy of Antonio Negri, Vol. 2: Revolution in Theory*, edited by Murphy, Timothy S. and Abdul-Karim, London: Pluto Press.

Treiber, Hubert 1999, 'Nachträge zu Paul Rée'. *Nietzsche-Studien: Internationales Jahrbuch für die Nietzscheforschung* 27: 515–16.

Treiber, Hubert and Heinz Steinert 1980, *Die Fabrikation des zuverlässigen Menschen. Über die 'Wahlverwandtschaft' von Kloster- und Fabriksystem*, München: Moos.

Tugendhat, Ernst 1997 [1993], *Vorlesungen über Ethik*, Frankfurt/Main: Suhrkamp.

Varela, Nicolás Gonzáles 2010, *Nietzsche contra la Democracia. El pensiamento político de Friedrich Nietzsche 1862–1872*, Ensayo: Montesinos.

Vattimo Gianni 1994 [1985], *The End of Modernity*, translated from Italian by J.R. Snyder, Oxford UK: Polity Press.

Veerkamp, Ton 2001, 'Gott', in Haug et al. (eds.), 1994–, 5: 917–31.

Wacquant, Loïc 1999 [1993], 'Inside "The Zone". The Social Art of the Hustler in the American Ghetto', in Bourdieu et al. (eds.) 1999.

Wacquant, Loïc 2009a: *Prisons of Poverty*. 2nd edition, Minneapolis: University of Minnesota Press.

Wacquant, Loïc 2009b. *Punishing the poor: The neoliberal government of social insecurity*. Durham, N.C.: Duke University Press.

Wacquant, Loïc 2016: 'Bourdieu, Foucault and the Penal State in the Neoliberal Era', in *Foucault and Neoliberalism*, edited by Daniel Zamora and Michael C. Behrent, Cambridge/Malden: Polity Press.

Waite, Geoff 1996, *Nietzsche's Corps/e. Aesthetics, Politics, Prophecy, or, The Spectacular Technoculture of Everyday Life*, Durham, London: Duke University Press.

Walpen, Bernhard 2004, *Die offenen Feinde und ihre Gesellschaft. Eine hegemonie-theoretische Studie zur Mont Pèlerin Society*, Hamburg: VSA Verlag.

Walpen, Bernhard and Dieter Plehwe 2001, '"Wahrheitsgetreue Berichte über Chile", Die Mont Pèlerin Society und die Diktatur Pinochet', *1999. Zeitschrift für Sozialgeschichte des 20. und 21. Jahrhunderts*, 16, 2: 42–70.

Weber, Max 1946, *From Max Weber: Essays in Sociology*, translated and edited and with an introduction by H.H. Gerth and C. Wright Mills, New York: Oxford University Press.

Weber, Max 1978 [1921], *Economy and Society: An Outline of Interpretative Sociology*, edited by Guenther Roth and Claus Wittich, Berkeley: University of California Press.

Weber, Max 1980 [1921], *Wirtschaft und Gesellschaft. Grundriss der verstehenden Soziologie*. 5. revised edition, edited by Johannes Winckelmann, Tübingen: Mohr Siebeck.

Weimann, Robert and Hans Ulrich Gumbrecht (ed.) 1991, *Postmoderne – globale Differenz*, Frankfurt/Main: Suhrkamp.

Wellhausen, Julius 1883 (1878), *Prolegomena zur Geschichte Israels*, quoted from the 6th edition (reprint) of 1927, Berlin, Leipzig.

Wellhausen, Julius 1884, 'Abriss der Geschichte Israels und Judas', in id., 1884: *Skizzen und Vorarbeiten. Erstes Heft*, Berlin.

Wellhausen, Julius 1891, *Sketch of the History of Israel and Judah*, reprint of the 1881 Third Edition, London: Leopold Classic Library.

Wellhausen, Julius 1957 (1878), *Prolegomena to the History of Ancient Israel*, translated by Black and Menzies, New York: Meridian Books.

Wellhausen, Julius 1958 (1894), *Israelitische und jüdische Geschichte*, Ninth Edition, Berlin.

Welsch, Wolfgang 1991, *Unsere postmoderne Moderne*, Weinheim: VCH, Acta Humaniora.

West, Cornel 1999 [1987], 'The Political Intellectual', in *The Cornel West Reader*, New York: Basic Civitas Books.

Wittgenstein, Ludwig 1963 [1945], *Philosophical Investigations*, translated by G.E.M. Anscombe, Oxford: Basil Blackwood.

Wolin, Richard 2004, *The Seduction of Unreason. The Intellectual Romance with Fascism from Nietzsche to Postmodernism*, Princeton: Princeton University Press.

Wurzer, William S. 1975, *Nietzsche und Spinoza*, Meisenheim am Glan: A. Hain.

Zamora, Daniel (ed.) 2014, *Critiquer Foucault: les années 1980 et la tentation néolibérale*, Brussels: Aden.

Zamora, Daniel 2016a, 'Introduction: Foucault, the Left, and the 1980s', in *Foucault and Neoliberalism*, edited by Daniel Zamora and Michael C. Behrent, Cambridge/ Malden: Polity Press.

Zamora, Daniel 2016b, 'Foucault, the Excluded, and the Neoliberal Erosion of the State', in Zamora and Behrent (eds.) 2016: 63–84.

Zamora, Daniel 2019, 'Finding a "Left Governmentality": Foucault's Last Decade', in Sawyer, Steinmetz-Jenkins (eds.) 2019: 53–72.

Zamora, Daniel and Michael C. Behrent (eds.) 2016, *Foucault and Neoliberalism*, Cambridge/Malden: Polity Press.

Zander, Hartwig 1980, 'Georg Rusche, marché du travail et régime des peines: introduction à la genèse de l' oeuvre de Georg Rusche', in *Déviance et Société*, September 1980, Vol. IV, No. 3: 199–213.

Zapata Galinda, Martha, 1995, *Triumph des Willens zur Macht. Zur Nietzsche-Rezeption im NS-Staat*, Hamburg: Argument.

Zaret, David, 1989, 'Religion and the Rise of liberal-democratic Ideology in 17th Century England', in *American Sociological Review*, Vol. 54, April 1989, No. 2: 163–79.

Zeglen, David 2017: Review of *Foucault and Neoliberalism*, edited by Daniel Zamora and Michael C. Behrent (Polity), in *Lateral. Journal of the Cultural Studies Association*, 6.2, Winter 2017, available at: https://csalateral.org/reviews/foucault-and-neoliberalism -zamora-behrent-zeglen/.

Zima, Peter V. 2012 [1997], *Modern/Postmodern: Society, Philosophy, Literature*, translated by Francke 2001, London: Continuum.

Name Index

Subject Index

Printed in the USA
CPSIA information can be obtained
at www.ICGtesting.com
LVHW011237150324
774517LV00048B/2360